T0345201

Cyberpredators and Their Prey

Cyberpredators and Their Prey

Lauren R. Shapiro

CRC Press
Taylor & Francis Group
Boca Raton London New York

CRC Press is an imprint of the
Taylor & Francis Group, an **informa** business

First edition published 2023
by CRC Press
6000 Broken Sound Parkway NW, Suite 300, Boca Raton, FL 33487-2742

and by CRC Press
4 Park Square, Milton Park, Abingdon, Oxon, OX14 4RN

CRC Press is an imprint of Taylor & Francis Group, LLC

© 2023 Lauren R. Shapiro

Library of Congress Cataloging-in-Publication Data
Names: Shapiro, Lauren R., author.
Title: Cyberpredators and their prey / Lauren R. Shapiro.
Identifiers: LCCN 2021061739 (print) | LCCN 2021061740 (ebook) | ISBN
   9780367551711 (hardback) | ISBN 9780367551698 (paperback) | ISBN
   9781003092292 (ebook)
Subjects: LCSH: Computer crimes. | Computer crimes—Prevention. |
   Internet—Security measures. | Internet—Psychological aspects. | Social
   media—Moral and ethical aspects.
Classification: LCC HV6773 .S533 2022 (print) | LCC HV6773 (ebook) | DDC
   364.16/8—dc23/eng/20220228
LC record available at https://lccn.loc.gov/2021061739
LC ebook record available at https://lccn.loc.gov/2021061740

ISBN: 978-0-367-55171-1 (hbk)
ISBN: 978-0-367-55169-8 (pbk)
ISBN: 978-1-003-09229-2 (ebk)

DOI: 10.4324/9781003092292

Typeset in Palatino
by codeMantra

To the Female First Cousins Club ~ Caren A. Shapiro, Ilene B. (Shapiro) Kramer, Robin E. Klein, Bridget Klein, Rhonda (Leipzig) Cook, Deborah (Leipzig) Ritornaro, and honorary members Joan Harris and Hope Blum.

~

Thank you for the many stress-relieving outings over the years that enriched my life by providing hours of laughter, amusement, nostalgia, and entertainment. We are the main attraction!

CONTENTS

PREFACE

The idea for writing this book arose after teaching a course on cyber-predators for my department's cybercrime minor. The literature available provided an inconsistent picture of cybercriminals, victims, laws, and solutions. Consequently, I intended this book to provide practical information to readers. First, it describes different types of interpersonal cybercriminals, including their motives and methods. Second, it discusses typical targets of each cybercriminal and explain explains the effects these crimes have on victims and society. Third, it examines the relevance of current laws in prosecuting cyberpredators and opens the discussion for determining whether what is in place legally is adequate. Fourth, it recommends cybersecurity strategies and education in preventing and mitigating victimization. Most importantly, the issue of whether internet and social media platforms are taking responsibility for their role in cybercrime is raised. The advantage of this book is that it uses a multidisciplinary perspective—combining psychology, criminal justice, law, and security—to understand the interpersonal cybercriminal and the victim. It also explores the online forums in which these crimes occur and the unique challenges that the regulation, investigation, and prosecution of these interpersonal cybercrimes pose to criminal justice and private security agents worldwide.

The chapters in the first half of the book cover non-sexually based interpersonal cybercrimes: online romance scams, online swatting, internet trolling, cyberstalking, and cyberbullying/harassment. The chapters in the second half of the book focus on sexually based cybercrimes: minor online sexting, online sexual trafficking, child sexual abuse material offenses, cyber sextortion, and image-based sexual abuse. Except for the introduction and education chapters, the remaining chapters all begin with a definition of the cybercrime and discussion of relevant issues involved, followed by cyberpredator, motives and methods, typical victim, laws, individual and societal consequences, and cybersecurity solutions. There is some overlap in the concepts examined, mainly because there are not separate laws for prosecuting each cyberpredator examined; instead, prosecution relies on matching the acts of the crime with the laws criminalizing them. The book is intended to be useful to current/future security managers, security operators, emergency management professionals, intelligence agents, private investigators, lawyers, compliance officers, social service workers, mental health therapists, and many other professionals who deal with interpersonal cybercrime through the lens of social science.

ACKNOWLEDGMENTS

Several people provided support to me on this book and I owe them my gratitude. Several people critically reviewed chapters and gave me feed-back, including Jonathan Blackford, Lisa Mattaway, Marie-Helen Maras, Susan Pickman, Christine Raino, and Adam Wandt. I am indebted to my graduate assistant, Stacy Quashie, whose work was supported by a Faculty Scholarship grant from the Office for the Advancement of Research at John Jay College. I would also like to thank my family and friends who provided love, support, and encouragement along the way.

AUTHOR

Dr. Lauren R. Shapiro is an Associate Professor at the John Jay College of Criminal Justice at the City University of New York. She has degrees in Psychology (B.A., M.S., Ph.D.) and Criminal Justice (M.S. specializing in Law Enforcement); postdoctoral research (Fellow in the Carolina Consortium on Human Development at UNC/CH; Associate and Project Coordinator at Rutgers University); and legal and police work experience (Extern with the Honorable Ralph Erickson in the U.S. District Court of North Dakota; Intern with the Fargo North Dakota Police Department). Dr. Shapiro focuses on physical security, cybersecurity, and private investigation. She co-authored *Multidisciplinary Investigation of Child Maltreatment* (Jones & Bartlett Learning, 2016) and co-edited *Encyclopedia of Security and Emergency Management* (Springer, 2021) with Dr. Marie-Helen Maras.

1

Introduction: The Internet as a Criminal Enabler

The online environment has emerged as a continuous source of inter-personal criminal activity beyond physical boundaries—one that is used to abuse, attack, bully, exploit, extort, harm, humiliate, harass,

DOI: 10.4324/9781003092292-1

offend, rob, and threaten victims of all ages. Cyberpredators employ the internet and online services (i.e., social network platforms, online groups and organizations, smart phone apps, discussion forums/bulletin board systems, websites, internet relay chat channels) to locate targets and commit their crimes. By using a variety of virtual platforms, cyberpredators have complete control over their prey, are able to victimize them almost continuously, and can even get others to help in harming them too. The cloak of anonymity provided online promotes a cycle of abuse, particularly when enacted by individuals as part of a group attack. Thus, even those who in real life never would have acted abusively toward others may do so to be "included" in the group and avoid being the next target or to seek revenge for wrongs committed against them. Public and private security sectors are at the forefront of identifying, investigating, and combating cyberpredators, but it is clear from the sheer number of victims reported through various law enforcement agencies (e.g., Internet Crime Complaint Center) and self-reported research studies that it is an ongoing battle.

Adolescents and young adults are particularly susceptible to cyberpredators mainly because they are the most active online, but anyone can be targeted. For those under age 30, vulnerability is a by-product of their limited cognitive capabilities and experiences with the world, lack of confidence in their abilities, and/or high need for approval from others. For example, people who geotag their photos or post their current location on social media are easy targets for cyberstalkers, whereas those who post blogs/vlogs are targets for internet trolls and cyberbullies/harassers. Young people, despite being able to navigate away from predators in real life, may be fooled online because there are no available social cues to guide them. As a result, sexual cyberpredators are able to use the internet to stalk, lure, and victimize their targets over a period of time, grooming them until the victims are ready to meet, at which point, they mistakenly believe it is too late to say 'no.' Additionally, many people do not understand or are not tech savvy enough to understand the motives and methods of cyberpredators to protect themselves or advise others how to be safe. In particular, parents and school officials often do not know enough about how cyberpredators operate or even the fads of youth culture, preventing them from effectively protecting children whose actions (e.g., exchange sexually explicit images with strangers) increase their victimization risks for child sexual abuse, sex trafficking, sextortion, and image-based sexual abuse. Another issue is that criminal laws, investigations, and prosecutions have not been able to catch up with the rapid growth of technology, creating a multitude of problems for society as a result. For example, the cyber-criminals who manufacture, possess, and distribute child sexual abuse material are able to continue offending because their victims and the host websites used for storage and retrieval are in different jurisdictions, making the investigation and prosecution of these crimes (or even locating the victim) difficult (Shapiro, 2020).

INTERPERSONAL CYBERCRIME VS. TRADITIONAL CRIME

The focus of this book is on the interpersonal attacks by cybercriminals who commit various crimes against *individuals* (e.g., stalking, fraud, harassment), *property* (e.g., malware, trespassing, intellectual property theft), or *society* (e.g., prostitution, child sexual abuse material). In some ways, cybercrimes are a type of offending similar to their offline counterparts, but in other ways they are new forms of offending. Similarities between the cyber and traditional crimes include the motives for committing them (e.g., revenge, financial, status/notoriety, political, ideological), whereas the methods for the former often require some level of technological skills and ability to navigate the internet in order to achieve the same nefarious ends as the latter. Moreover, the same laws are often used to criminalize offenses, regardless if they are traditional or cybercrimes (Rouse, 2019). Traditional crimes and cybercrimes mainly differ in their use of computers (U.S. Department of Justice, 1996)—as **the target** for gaining access to information (e.g., by hacking or social engineering), **tool or weapon** for launching attacks (e.g., blackmail, stalk, harass, defraud), or **repository** of illegal information/material (e.g., child sexual abuse material, electronic records for sex trafficking). Other Western countries (e.g., the UK, Canada, Australia) besides the US use the tripartite classification of computer crimes, computer-facilitated crimes, and computer-supported crimes (Clough, 2010). Cybercrimes also differ from traditional crimes in other ways, including that the former, by occurring in cyberspace, are international, render more severe consequences for victims, and evolve faster than the latter (Payne et al., 2019).

Concepts and Organization of the Book

Digital technologies provide users with the ability to share content and interact in a virtual space. Although users are excited by these opportunities, the theme of this book is focused on the darker side—that is, harmful and abusive interpersonal interactions online, also called *technology-facilitated abuse* (Witwer et al., 2020). An online interaction is considered to be technology-facilitated abuse when it affects the user's privacy and/or causes the person immediate and/or long-term harm (Witwer et al., 2020). Cyberpredators not only injure their targeted prey, but they also victimize our society. The rate of growth in digital technologies is faster than the public's ability to train users how to prevent and mitigate victimization; quantify the prevalence of harm through specific online activity that would justify new or modified legislation to criminalize it; and subsequently investigate, prosecute, and punish cyberpredators (Shapiro, 2021; Witwer et al., 2020). This book can inform citizens, researchers, service providers, educators, criminal justice and private security personnel, and the legislature about interpersonal cybercrimes; aid understanding of the needs of victims and their communities; and facilitate development of appropriate laws, protection, and services to meet those needs.

Five important concepts are relevant to the readers' understanding of interpersonal cyberpredators who are discussed in this book. First, cyberpredators impose one or more types of abuse—financial, emotional, verbal, psychological, physical, sexual—on their victims (Kirby, 2020; Shapiro & Maras, 2016). Second, four qualities of the online environment—toxic disinhibition, de-individuation, anonymity, and inculpability—are conducive to the unfettered occurrence of cybercrime. Third, many cyberpredators rely on social engineering as a tool to gain access and keep control over their targets. Fourth, the relationship between cyberpredators and their prey often is that of current or previous intimate partners; consequently, intimate partner violence (IPV) enacted online is a notable element of their crimes. Fifth, sexual cyberpredators can be dichotomized as those who sexually abuse and exploit only online and those who use cyberspace as a stepping stone to entice victims for the purpose of sexually abusing and exploiting them in the physical world. Each of these concepts is explained in subsequent sections.

TYPES OF ABUSE

Cybercriminals impose one or more types of abuse on their targets, as shown in Table 1.1. Maltreatment may be their goal and/or merely the consequences of their actions. **Financial abuse** entails curtailing the victim's current and future ability to decide how to use his/her personal or family assets (e.g., savings, credit cards, loans). Common techniques include *taking out loans/mortgages* and/or *making credit card purchases* without

4

Table 1.1 Cyberpredator and Corresponding Types of Abuse Imposed

Cyberpredator	Financial	Emotional	Verbal	Psychological	Physical	Sexual
Online romance scammer	×		×	×		
Online swatter		×	×		×	
Internet troll		×	×			
Cyberstalker		×	×	×	×	
Cyberbully/ harasser		×	×	×	×	
Minor online sextor		×	×			×
Online sexual trafficker	×	×	×	×	×	×
CSAM offender				×	×	×
Cyber sextortionist	×	×	×	×	×	×
Image-based sexual abuser		×	×	×	×	×

prior discussion or approval of the victim; *preventing victim's access* to or *completely emptying* his/her savings account, checking account, or both; *borrowing money and not repaying* it; *failing to pay bills* in the victim's name; and *coercing the victim into making "loans"* to the perpetrator. **Physical abuse** involves the intentional act to cause victim injury or trauma that endangers the victim's health and/or life, including self-imposed harm. Common techniques include the weaponized use of *hands* (e.g., slapping, hair-pulling, choking, punching, shaking), *feet* (kicking), and *objects* (e.g., stabbing, shooting, burning, smashing) to impose harm offline. This type of abuse is also associated with other offline criminal acts, such as bullying, stalking, kidnapping, false arrest and/or false imprisonment, intimate partner violence (IPV), and neglect (e.g., starving, preventing medical intervention). **Sexual abuse** involves the use of force, threats, or coercion of victims for the purpose of unwanted sexual activity, including self-imposed. Types of sexual abuse include *assault* (e.g., attempted rape, unwanted fondling/sexual touching, forcible object penetration, drug-facilitated, forcing someone to engage in self-penetration); *forcible sodomy* (i.e., non-consensual anal or oral sex); *bestiality* (i.e., sexual intercourse with animals); *incest* (i.e., sexual intercourse with closely related family members who they would not be permitted legally to marry); *sadism* (i.e., inflicting physical or psychological pain to achieve sexual excitement); *sexual contact with minors* (e.g., forcing minors to engage in sex acts on offender or others, including those recorded, photographed, or performed live online; exposing genitals to minors); and *rape* (non-consensual sexual intercourse).

Three additional types—psychological, verbal, and emotional—are sometimes used interchangeably by the public, but are actually distinct from each other. **Psychological abuse** involves controlling the victim's mind by distorting his/her sense of reality to make the person believe that s/he is mentally unbalanced. Common techniques include *gaslighting* (i.e., convincing the victim that what s/he experienced did not actually happen) and *passive aggressive mind games*—such as *scapegoating* (i.e., blame victim for the abuser's bad behavior); *pretending confusion* (i.e., the victim is not making sense or the abuser cannot hear or understand him/her); or *isolation* (i.e., abuser limits victim's contact with others to ensure no one figures out what s/he is doing)—to undermine the victim's confidence and facilitate his/her compliance. **Verbal abuse** involves the use of either disparaging or patronizing aggressive language to belittle and control the victim or the suppression of communication and cooperation (aka stonewalling) to frustrate, punish, and dehumanize the victim. Common techniques include *countering* (i.e., habitual use of starting arguments to keep victim on the defensive); *discounting* (i.e., regularly denying the victim's feelings, indicating the victim is being oversensitive, immature, or humorless); *trivializing* (i.e., reducing the importance of victim's concerns); and *love-withdrawal* (i.e., concealing thoughts, information, and love to disorient the victim). **Emotional abuse** involves the use of hurtful, emotional tactics (e.g., intimidation, shaming) to mistreat the victim and make him/her feel incompetent. Common techniques include *criticism and manipulation* (i.e., abuser consistently reproaches victim and makes him/her believe the criticism is deserved); *humiliation* (i.e., abuser shames and embarrasses victim publicly); *social isolation* (i.e., abuser controls victim's social life, especially the people with whom s/he can interact; preventing victims from interacting with loved ones; ruining the victim's reputation); and *micromanaging every aspect of the victim's life* (i.e., abuser uses financial and social manipulation to coerce victim's compliance; reads texts). Emotional abusers will also use other types of abusers' techniques to control victims, such as withholding funds like financial abusers; playing mind games like psychological abusers; and using love-withdrawal, aggressive language, and trivializing like verbal abusers.

QUALITIES OF THE ONLINE ENVIRONMENT

The online environment fosters cybercriminal activity because of its specific qualities that fail to implement the same types of social controls available when people interact in the real world. The first quality, **toxic disinhibition**, refers to the limited or total absence of concern expressed when the cyberpredator inflicts harm on someone. This phenomenon occurs because there is no tangible feedback provided to cyberpredators indicating how their negative behaviors (e.g., rudeness, criticism, threats, hate) affect the victim (e.g., emotional distress that triggers empathy and remorse). For example, in the physical world, the target cries or shows anger in response to victimization. The second quality, **de-individuation**, refers to the phenomenon in which cyberpredators and bystanders—when they are part of a group rather than personally identified—assume a cyber mob mentality. Consequently, offenders are encouraged to engage in more deviant and impulsive acts against the victim than they typically would in offline situations. The third quality, **anonymity**, operates by allowing cyberpredators and bystanders to hide from any deserved consequences, particularly society's reproach of their online bad behavior toward the victim. In the physical world, one or more people would tell the cyberpredator to stop as part of the social agreement on civil behavior or even seek an authority figure to rescue the victim and impose consequences on the criminal. The fourth quality, **inculpability**, refers to the failure of cyberpredators and bystanders to accept responsibility for the roles they played in causing harm to the victim. While in a group, there is "diffusion of responsibility" for bad behaviors, including inaction by bystanders who witness harm to victims but fail to stop or report it (Suler, 2004; Willard, 2007).

SOCIAL ENGINEERING TECHNIQUES

Many of the cyberpredators are interested in obtaining personal identifiable information (PII) about their targets (e.g., login credentials, credit card numbers), either to enhance their pursuit of targets or for the purpose of doxing them (i.e., online distribution or publication of the information). This task is not hard given that many people voluntarily provide personal information in public forums, especially social media sites (e.g., Facebook, Instagram). By employing a search engine, such as Yahoo and Google, anyone can find various data—such as a person's current and past addresses, phone number, age and/or birthdate, family members, school affiliations, past and current occupation, images, and court cases (see Chapter 3 to learn about data brokers). It is also possible to accomplish this objective through social engineering techniques, such as phishing, that manipulate people psychologically into compliance by taking advantage of their cognitive biases and flaws in logic[1] (Bullée et al., 2017; Bullée & Junger, 2020; Button et al., 2015; Hewitt, 2021; Lee & Paek, 2020).

Phishing involves sending out fraudulent (spoofed) spam that appears to be from a known/familiar entity and uses three or four known triggers: (1) inducing a sense of urgency to create fear and elicit a response; (2) presenting as an authority; (3) establishing trust via deceptive relationships (e.g., addressing them by name or using partially factual information); and/or (4) promising rewards or fulfilling needs (Ferreira et al., 2015; Stojnic et al., 2021). Most people comply with the authority's request (e.g., open attached file) because society conditions them to do so and believing what is said or done is consistent with how they normally interact socially (Ferreira et al., 2015). The types of phishing attacks by how they are implemented—email, website, and telecommunication—appears in Table 1.2. Targets who download attachments or click on fake links (aka bait) will typically infect their computers with viruses, worms, or trojans which then launch attacks to gain access to PII and files. Table 1.3 provides malware classifications and attack techniques most relevant in social engineering (Fruhlinger, 2019; Moes, 2021).

CYBER INTIMATE PARTNER VIOLENCE

The internet provides intimate partner abusers with almost nonstop access to harm their victims, regardless of whether the relationship currently is or ever was real (e.g., image-based sexual abuse) or was only perceived to be real by the victim (e.g., online romance scam, online sex trafficking). For example, IPV perpetrators use technology to monitor and stalk victims' location and online actions and even issue threats (Clevenger & Gilliam, 2020). Previous or current intimate partners may perpetrate online romance scams, cyber stalking, cyberbullying and harassment, online minor sexting, online sexual trafficking, cyber sextortion, and/or

---

[1] Cognitive bias is a systematic error that occurs when people attempt to simplify the process and interpretation of their complex world. For example, confirmation bias filters out ideas that contradict preexisting beliefs so people seek only information that confirms what they already believe.

8

Table 1.2 Types of Phishing Attacks

1. Email-based

a. *Deception phishing* uses emails to get recipients to provide PII through downloading attachments or clicking on HTTPs fake links disguised as secure ones;

b. *Clone phishing* refers to targeted emails seemingly sent by organizations that a recipient just researched;

c. *Spear-phishing* is similar to deception phishing, except that it targets a specific set of individuals; and

d. *Social phishing* involves getting the trust of an individual to gain unauthorized access to their contacts and/or account in order to send spam to everyone on the list.

2. Website-based

a. *Angler phishing* uses notifications or direct messaging features in social media;

b. *Pop-up phishing* refers to malicious code (malware) that appears in small notification boxes (aka pop-ups) on websites to attract attention and action from recipient;

c. *Pharming* refers to a fake site created to redirect traffic away from real website;

d. *Whaling* refers to the use of social media or corporate website to find name of organization's CEO or senior leadership members to impersonate them using a similar email address and requesting employees to make a money transfer or review a document;

e. *Water-holing* is an advanced level attack that not only infects a website with malware, but also its visitors; and

f. *Catfishing* involves the perpetrator assuming a fake identity in order to lure the recipient into a trusting relationship.

3. Telecommunication-based

a. *Evil twin phishing* refers to fake Wi-Fi hotspots used to intercept PII during transfer (often with man-in-the-middle or eavesdropping attacks)[a];

b. *Smishing* uses short message service to entice recipients to respond; and

c. *Vishing* (i.e., voice phishing) uses a phone to obtain PII by asking recipients to respond to a series of questions, typically part of an organized script.

[a] Man-in-the-middle (MITM) attacks occur when a perpetrator either is in close physical proximity to the target to intercept the information or malicious software/malware acts at the MITM (or browser). The traditional MITM attack has two phases—interception and decryption of data (Norton, 2021).

image-based sexual abuse (Zweig et al., 2013). Clevenger and Gilliam (2020) reported that cyber intimate partner violence occurs across sex, age, social class, and sexual orientation (e.g., heterosexual, homosexual, transgender),

Table 1.3 Malware Classes and Attack Techniques

Class of Malware	Definition	Transfer/Spread
Virus	Computer code that modifies (infects) code in legitimate host files, programs, or pointers; enacts malicious act and spreads itself among computers.	Email attachments; network attachments; and file-sharing.
Worm	Stand-alone malicious software that self-replicates; causes delays and system overloads.	Internet websites; email attachments and links; instant message links; file-sharing and peer-to-peer file transfers; and internet relay chat links and attachments.
Trojan	Malicious code embedded inside seemingly legitimate programs, delivered through email or by accessing infected websites; cannot be prevented by patch or firewall.	Download program or email attachment.
Attack techniques	**Definition**	**Example**
Spyware	Operates by gathering data covertly from target and sends it to a third-party actor.	*Keylogger* records keystrokes to capture login credentials.
Rootkit	Software/program gives third-party actor remote access and control over target's computer (aka administrator rights).	*Firmware rootkit* targets computer firmware to allow the monitoring of online activity and keystrokes.

but it is predictive of face-to-face IPV perpetration among adolescents and young adults who have embraced online technology in their exploration of their sexual identity and dating. Adolescents have reported high levels of psychological (73%), physical (52%), and coercive sexual (33%) violence as a result of cyber dating (Zweig et al., 2013). Young adults (aged 18–34) experienced more online IPV psychological victimization than older adults (aged 35 and older), but these age differences were absent offline (Schokkenborek et al., 2021).

There is usually some degree of victim blaming associated with cyber IPV—by those inside (cyberpredators, victims) and outside (bystanders, friends, family) the dyadic relationship (Whiting et al., 2019). It is not surprising that perpetrators blame their victims for their own abuse as this is part of their technique for controlling the narrative and their success is demonstrated when victims accept blame. Explanations for outsiders assigning blame typically stem from their need to see the world as safe and/or denial that abusers exist (Van Prooijen & van den Bos, 2009). Christie (1986) offers another perspective—some victims are ideal and warrant support because they are weaker than their unknown perpetrator and had been engaged in a respectable activity, making them not responsible for their circumstances. An outsider may judge many of the online behaviors of victims as ambiguous or risky and therefore consider them as not engaged in a legitimate task, which would invalidate the ideal victim classification (Christie, 1986). Consider for example, the online action of someone who decides to exercise the right to post an opinion or respond to a comment and is then cyber harassed. A harasser may reason that if the person had not publicly shared, then the victimization would not have occurred. In another example, an image-based sexual abuser justifies posting a nude photograph of his ex-girlfriend as retribution for breaking off the relationship. It is the ex-girlfriend who is blamed for having taken the photograph in the first place and sharing it privately, not the perpetrator who violated her trust by distributing it online.

SEXUAL ABUSE AND EXPLOITATION ONLINE

Sexual cyberpredators target children and adults for sexual abuse and exploitation in pursuit of economic gain and/or their own sexual gratification (Briggs et al., 2011). The amount of time that potential victims spend online is proportional to the degree to which they are subjected to unwanted sexual solicitation across multiple platforms (Schulz et al., 2016) requesting them to "talk about sex, do something sexual, or to share personal sexual information" (Ybarra et al., 2007, p. 32). The internet facilitates sexual abuse and exploitation by strangers, family members, friends, acquaintances, intimate partners, traffickers, and buyers. There are four advantages of the online venue for sexual cyberpredators to engage in their deviancy (Rufo, 2011). First, cyberpredators are able to conceal their true identity onscreen—pretending to be someone the victim would like in terms of age or looks—in order to get closer to him/her than they could have gotten in real life. Second, cyberpredators are able to seek out multiple victims simultaneously, faster, and with less effort than this task would require offline. Third, cyberpredators can connect devices to the internet almost anywhere and use devices as ideal storage containers for concealing their cache of sexually explicit images. Fourth, cyberpredators can search online for victims' pictures on various social media platforms and alter them using Deep Fake apps to convert "normal" images into nudes or pornography and even insert themselves into the images.

Online sexual solicitation can be dichotomized (Seto, 2013) as *fantasy-driven* (exclusively online victimization) and *contact-driven* (victimization online initially in pursuit of offline victimization), as shown in Table 1.4. Millions of sexually explicit images of minors (aka child sexual abuse material) and nonconsenting adults (aka image-based sexual abuse material) are available through the internet and its related services. Cyber sexual offenders seeking new images of minors find a target online; gain compliance by grooming the victim; and coerce him/her through sextortion, IPV, or by paying sexual abusers to have the victim pose nude, masturbate, and/or engage in specific sex acts with one or more children or adults performed live in a pay-per-view or recorded for subsequent viewing.

Table 1.4 Two Types of Sexual Cyberpredators

Fantasy-driven sexual cyberpredators use the internet to seek and receive sexual gratification (typically climaxing through masturbation) via:

  a. *sexually explicit conversations* with minors (under age 18) and/or nonconsenting adults;

  b. upload/download/exchange of *sexual abuse and exploitation images* of minors and/or nonconsenting adults; and

  c. *online or electronic live transmission* of sexual abuse and exploitation of children and/or nonconsenting adults (Briggs et al., 2011; Wolak et al., 2008).

Contact-driven sexual cyberpredators use the internet initially to lure child and adult victims into physical meetings (offline) in order to sexually abuse and exploit them (Briggs et al., 2011; Wolak et al., 2008). Victims are used in one or more of the following ways:

  a. to provide exclusive service as a *personal sex slave*;

  b. to create *child sexual abuse material* or *non-consensual adult pornography* that is sold online and/or through live transmission venues; and

  c. trafficked for commercial sex as part of domestic and international *sex tourism, performance in sexual venues* (e.g., massage parlors, strip clubs), and *prostitution* (Development Services Group, Inc., 2014).

Cyberpredators commit other sexual offenses by:

1. coercing victims through various criminal acts (e.g., threat, sextortion, IPV) to produce and send intimate images of themselves and/or others;
2. sending (unsolicited) intimate images to juvenile or adult recipients (i.e., indecent exposure, cyber harassment);
3. soliciting juveniles to produce and send intimate images of themselves and/or others (i.e., child sexual abuse material, illicit sexting if perpetrator is minor); and/or
4. forwarding, distributing, or posting intimate images of a juvenile (i.e., child sexual abuse material) or of an adult without authorization (i.e., image-based sexual abuse).

Sexting between adult senders and receivers, if consensual, is not prohibited. In contrast, *non-consensual sexting* in which criminal coercion tactics is used to force senders into producing and sharing intimate images (e.g., cyberstalking, cyberharassment, cyber sextortion, and IPV) and/or the *unauthorized distribution and posting* of intimate images—particularly produced in the commission of a sexual crime—have been criminalized.

REFERENCES

Briggs, P., Simon, W.T., & Simonsen, S. (2011). An exploratory study of internet-initiated sexual offenses and the chat room sex offender: Has the internet enabled a new typology of sex offender? *Sexual Abuse: A Journal of Research and Treatment, 23*(1), 72–91.

Bullée, J.H., Montoya, L., Pieters, W., Junger, M., & Hartel, P.H. (2017). On the anatomy of social engineering attacks–a literature-based dissection of successful attacks. *Journal of Investigative Psychology and Offender Profiling, 15*(1), 1–26.

Bullée, J.-W., & Junger, M. (2020). Social engineering. In T. Holt and M. Bossler (eds.), *The Palgrave Handbook of International Cybercrime and Cyberdeviance* (pp. 849–875). Switzerland: Springer.

Button, M., McNaughton Nicholls, C., Kerr, J., & Owen, R. (2015). Online fraud victims in England and Wales: Victims' views on sentencing and the opportunity for restorative justice. *Howard Journal of Criminal Justice, 54*(2), 193–211.

Christie, N. (1986). The ideal victim. In E. Fattah (Ed.), *From Crime Policy to Victim Policy* (pp. 17–30). Basingstoke: MacMillan.

Clevenger, S., & Gilliam, M. (2020). Intimate partner violence and the internet: Perspectives. In T. Holt and M. Bossler (eds.), *The Palgrave Handbook of International Cybercrime and Cyberdeviance* (pp. 1333–1351). Switzerland: Springer.

Clough, J. (2010). *Principles of Cybercrime*. Cambridge: Cambridge University Press.

Development Services Group, Inc. (2014). *Commercial Sexual Exploitation of Children and Sex Trafficking*. Washington, DC: Office of Juvenile Justice and Delinquency Prevention. https://www.ojjdp.gov/mpg/litreviews/CSECSex Trafficking.pdf.

Ferreira, A., Coventry, L., & Lenzini, G. (2015). Principles of persuasion in social engineering and their use in phishing. In T. Tryfonas and I. Askoxylakis (eds.), *Human Aspects of Information Security, Privacy, and Trust* (pp. 36–47). Cham: Springer. Doi: 10.1007/978-3-319-20376-8.

Fruhlinger, J. (2019). *Malware Explained: How to Prevent, Detect, and Recover from it.* https://www.csoonline.com/article/3295877/what-is-malware-viruses-worms-trojans-and-beyond.html.

Hewitt, K. (2021). *12 Types of Phishing Attacks and How to Identify Them.* https://securityscorecard.com/blog/types-of-phishing-attacks-and-how-to-identify-them.

Kirby, S. (2020). *Different Types of Abuse and Their Impact on You.* https://www.better-help.com/advice/abuse/different-types-of-abuse-and-their-impact-on-you/.

Lee, B., & Paek, S.Y. (2020). Phishing and financial manipulation. In T. Holt and M. Bossler (eds.), *The Palgrave Handbook of International Cybercrime and Cyberdeviance* (pp. 899–916). Switzerland: Springer.

Moes, T. (2021). *Rootkit.* https://softwarelab.org/what-is-a-rootkit/.

Norton (2021). *What is the Man-in-the-Middle Attack?* https://us.norton.com/inter-netsecurity-wifi-what-is-a-man-in-the-middle-attack.html.

Payne, B., May, D.C., & Hadzhidimova, L. (2019). America's most wanted criminals: Comparing cybercriminals and traditional criminals. *Criminal Justice Studies, 32*(1), 1–15. Doi: 10.1080/1478601X.2018.1532420.

Rouse, M. (2019). *What Is Cybercrime?* https://searchsecurity.techtarget.com/definition/cybercrime.

Rufo, R.A. (2011). *Sexual Predators amongst Us*. Boca Raton, FL: Taylor & Francis Group.

Schokkenborek, J.M., Van Ouytsel, J., Hardyns, W., & Ponnet, K. (2021). Adults' online and offline psychological intimate partner violence experiences. *Journal of Interpersonal Violence*, 1–16. Doi: 10.1177/0886205211015217.

Schulz, A., Bergen, E., Schuhmann, P., Hoyer, J., & Santtila, P. (2016). Online sexual solicitation of minors: How often and between whom does it occur? *Journal of Research in Crime and Delinquency, 53*(2), 165–188.

Seto, M.C. (2013). *Internet Sex Offenders*. Washington, DC: American Psychological Association.

Shapiro, L.R. (2020). Online child sexual abuse material: Prosecuting across jurisdictions. *Journal of Internet Law, 24*(3), 3–8.

Shapiro, L.R. (2021). Corporate liability of hotels: Criminal sanctions for online sex trafficking. *Journal of Internet Law, 24*(5), 3–10.

Shapiro, L.R. & Maras, M-H. (2016). *Multidisciplinary Investigation of Child Maltreatment*. Burlington, MA: Jones & Bartlett Learning.

Stojnic, T., Vatsalan, D., & Arachchilage, N.A.G. (2021). Phishing email strategies: Understanding cybercriminals' strategies of crafting phishing emails. *Security Privacy, e165,* 1–17. Doi: 10.1002/spy2.165.

Suler, J. (2004). The online disinhibition effect. *Cyberpsychology & Behavior, 7(3),* 321–326.

U.S. Department of Justice. (1996). *Computer Crime and Intellectual Property Section, The National Information Infrastructure Protection Act of 1996.* Legislative Analysis. www.cybercrime.gov/1030analysis.html.

Van Prooijen, J. W., & Van den Bos, K. (2009). We blame innocent victims more than I do: Self-construal level moderates responses to just world threats. *Personality and Social Psychology Bulletin, 35,* 1528–1539.

Whiting, J.B., Olufuwote, R.D., Cravens-Pickens, J.D., & Whitting, A.B. (2019). Online blaming and intimate partner violence: A content analysis of social media comments. *The Qualitative Report, 24(1),* 78–94.

Willard, N. (2007). *Cyberbullying and Cyberthreats: Effectively Managing Internet Use Risks in Schools.* https://www.cforks.org/Downloads/cyber_bullying.pdf.

Witwer, A.R., Langton, L., Vermeer, M.J.D., & Banks, D. (2020). *Countering Technology-Facilitated Abuse: Criminal Justice Strategies for Combatting Nonconsensual Pornography, Sextortion, Doxing, and Swatting.* https://www.rand.org/content/dam/rand/pubs/research_reports/RRA100/RRA108-3/RAND_RRA108-3.pdfc.

Wolak, J., Finkelhor, D., Mitchell, K., & Ybarra, M. (2008). Online "predators" and their victims: Myths, realities, and implications for prevention and treatment. *American Psychologist, 63(2),* 111–128. Doi: 10.1037/0003-066X.63.2.111.

Ybarra, M.L., Espelage, D.L., & Mitchell, K.J. (2007). The co-occurrence of internet harassment and unwanted sexual solicitation victimization and perpetration: Associations with psychosocial indicators. *The Journal of Adolescent Health, 41,* S31–41.

Zweig, J. M., Dank, M., Yahner, J., & Lachman, P. (2013). The rate of cyber dating abuse among teens and how it relates to other forms of teen dating violence. *Journal of Youth and Adolescence, 42(7),* 1–15. Doi: 10.1007/s10964-013-992.

15

2

Online Romance Scammers

DEFINING ONLINE ROMANCE SCAMS

The most common and lucrative of all cyber-enabled imposter scams targeting individuals in 2020 is the online romance scam (aka sweetheart swindle)—a mass-marketing, advanced fee fraud variation of its offline postal mail fraud counterpart (Cross, 2020a; Federal Bureau of Investigation/FBI, 2020; Sorrell & Whitty, 2019; Whitty, 2018; Whitty & Buchanan, 2012). Online romance scams involve an individual or group

DOI: 10.4324/9781003092292-2

who develops fictitious online romantic relationships with one or multiple targets using fake profiles for the purpose of defrauding them of money (Buchanan & Whitty, 2014; Coluccia et al., 2020; Gregory & Nikiforova, 2021; Rege, 2009; Semenza, 2020; Sorrell & Whitty, 2019; Suarez-Tangil et al., 2020; Whitty & Buchanan, 2012). There are two types of victims in this scheme (Garren, 2021)—the target and the lure (i.e., the person whose identity is used to catfish the target). Scammers are successful in deceiving the target because the profile they use contain particularly attractive images and idyllic descriptions; additionally, they establish an intense emotionally warm and trusting connection by investing a considerable amount of time and effort into this task (Buchanan & Whitty, 2014; Coluccia et al., 2020).

The numbers of complaints filed with the Consumer Sentinel Database of the Federal Trade Commission (FTC) (Cybersecurity & Infrastructure Security Agency/CISA, 2019; FTC, 2019b, 2020) and with the Internet Crime Complaint Center (Gorham, 2018) regarding their respective financial losses from online romance scams are displayed in Figures 2.1 and 2.2, respectively. According to the figures, the number of reported online romance scam complaints in the U.S. have increased four- to six-fold from 2014 to 2020 while financial loss increased six- to nine-fold (Federal Trade Commission/FTC, 2021; Fletcher, 2021). Citizens in other Western nations have also reported victimization from online romance scam with financial losses in 2020 of £68 million in the U.K., $18.5 million in Canada, and $131 million in Australia (Australian Competition & Consumer Commission/ACCC, 2021; Royal

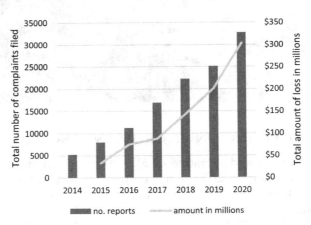

Figure 2.1 Number of reports filed with FTC and total amount of financial loss from 2014 to 2020.

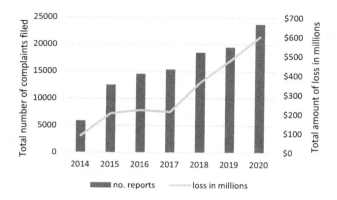

Figure 2.2 Number of online romance fraud reports filed with IC3 and total amount of financial loss from 2014 to 2020.

Canadian Mounted Police, 2021; Wakefield, 2021; Sorrell & Whitty, 2019). Financial loss from online romance scams globally is believed to be in the trillions of dollars (Cross, 2016; Garren, 2021). Yet, even this amount is likely a gross underestimation as law enforcement is not involved in 75%–80% of the cases, according to McClellan, the president of SocialCatfish.com, and because this scheme is capable of defrauding a large number of victims annually (Button et al., 2009; Nikiforova & Gregory, 2013; McClellan, 2021; Wsav.com, 2020). In addition to financial loss, victims of fraud also experience psychological suffering from shame, guilt, and social stigma of being defrauded; betrayal by a supposed loved one; and emotional loss of the romantic relationship itself (Buchanan & Whitty, 2014; Cross, 2020a; Suarez-Tangil et al., 2020; Whitty & Buchanan, 2012).

The rapid introduction of digital communication combined with creation of 1400 online dating sites in North America that now serve 32 million U.S. users, 83% of whom access these sites easily by smartphone apps, contributed significantly to inducing vulnerability to the romance scam (Coluccia et al., 2020; Semenza, 2020). The acceptance of finding mates online differs by group, with nearly half for young adults aged 18–29 and over half for LGB adults reporting this preference (Anderson et al., 2020; Cacioppo et al., 2013; Close et al., 2004; Semenza, 2020). Online dating services offer multiple benefits as they: (1) provide a platform to allow users opportunities to interact while reducing potentially crippling fears of rejection and social criticism, (2) present an (anonymous) online profile that does not have to match one's actual physical looks, (3) give access

19

through asynchronous communication to allow users a way to build relationships at their own pace and time allowances, and (4) offer profile matching to maximize the user's chances to meet others (Close et al., 2004; Coluccia et al., 2020; D'Agata et al., 2021; Semenza, 2020). The use of online dating services is the second most common method for Americans to find partners, with approximately 30%–70% of couples claiming that they met this way (Anderson et al., 2020; Semenza, 2020; Smith, 2016). The Better Business Bureau reported that lockdown loneliness due to the Corona virus pandemic increased the romance scam victimization, particularly for those in the 40–69 age group, and made it harder for targets to recognize the fraud because scammers used plausible reasons not to meet them, such as it was safer to have online dates or last-minute canceled live dates were due to positive Covid-19 tests (Schachetti, 2021).

TYPICAL ONLINE ROMANCE SCAMMERS

The typical online romance scammer may be an individual or a group. It is difficult to know the proportion of scammers who live in the U.S. versus another country, mainly because they can be anonymous, hiding behind their fake online profiles. Law enforcement believes that most perpetrators of online dating schemes, particularly those involving multistep travel scenarios, are members of Russian-Ukraine and African criminal networks (Trend Micro & INTERPOL, 2017; Rege, 2009; Steward, 2008). African syndicate crime organizations, such as the Black Axe, Yahoo Boys from Nigeria, and Sakawa Boys in Ghana operate out of 26 countries implementing not only the online romance scam using dating websites and social media platforms—but also sex and drug trafficking operations (Garren, 2021). The typical African online romance scammer is a college-educated young adult man who learns the trade from older scammers; however, women are also involved as they provide photographs, give advice on what to say, and take phone or video calls from victims (Akandle & Shadare, 2019; Aransiola & Asindemade, 2011; Lazarus, 2018). Figure 2.3 displays the proportion of the Yahoo Boys perpetrators by age group based on a report by TrendMicro & Interpol (2017). In this report (TrendMicro & Interpol, 2017), cybercriminals were asked to self-identify their role(s) in the group—44% indicated leader, 67% fraud operator, 22% financial operator, 78% IT technician, and 33% money mule.[1] Online romance scammers

---

[1] The proportion for each role does not sum to 100% because members often played more than one role.

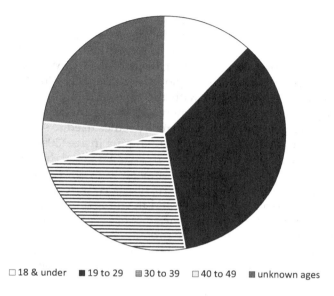

□ 18 & under   ■ 19 to 29   ▤ 30 to 39   □ 40 to 49   ■ unknown ages

Figure 2.3   Proportion of Yahoo Boys perpetrators by age group.

are ruthless, narcissistic, Machiavellian, and manipulative—characteristics that facilitate the process of getting victims to trust them (Lazarus, 2018). Three types of beliefs help scammers to justify the crime—blaming or dehumanizing the victim, minimizing their own agency in the scam, and glamorizing cyber-fraud (Lazarus, 2018; Offei et al., 2020).

ONLINE ROMANCE SCAMMERS' MOTIVES AND METHODS

The most obvious motive for online romance scams is financial gain (Cross, 2020a; Lazarus, 2018). The scammer perpetrates the online romance scheme by directly contacting the victim and deliberately maintaining communication over time using deception and persuasion to gain the target's trust and cooperation (Menard et al., 2011; Rege, 2009; Whitty, 2013). The scammers are able to stay anonymous by using virtual private networks to hide their IP addresses and smart phone apps (e.g., WhatsApp, Google Hangouts) to hide their phone numbers (Garren, 2021). They also set up fake profiles using stolen photographs of attractive people (e.g., models, military officers) on dating sites/apps and social media platforms (e.g., Facebook, Instagram) to target their victims (Anesa, 2020; Federal Trade Commission/FTC, 2021; Kopp et al., 2015; Whitty, 2013, 2015). The images and descriptions employed by scammers for their profiles (i.e., honeypots) are consistent with the type of desirable characteristics sought in potential partners by men and women (Anesa, 2020; Suarez-Tangil et al., 2020). Specifically, fake male profiles used to solicit heterosexual female targets were handsome men ranging in age (30s–50s) portrayed as educated, wealthy, and employed in a professional, business, or high ranking military position seeking someone to help him fill a particular emotional need (e.g., care for children), whereas those used for homosexual male targets depicted attractive and fit young adult men but their ethnicity/nationality and occupation varied (Anesa, 2020; Suarez-Tangil et al., 2020; Whitty, 2015). The fake female profile contained images of strikingly beautiful young adult women describing themselves as the same nationality as the target working in a low-income or non-professional job (Anesa, 2020; Suarez-Tangil et al., 2020; Whitty, 2015). There are common themes in the fake person in the profiles, such as the person is located or working outside the U.S., typically in the military, off-shore facility, or non-profit (e.g., Doctors without Borders).

Online romance scammers build a fake relationship with the target using similar power and control strategies employed by other criminals, such as sexual predators and domestic violence partners (Cross, 2020a; Shea, 2020). The effectiveness of these techniques is demonstrated by victims believing they are in a legitimate relationship with a person they never met or even saw, such as through live video-chat (Cross, 2020a; Kopp et al., 2015). Scammers reveal person information about themselves and encourage their victims to do the same (D'Agata et al., 2021; Kopp et al., 2015). To gain power and control over the victim, the scammer engages in overwhelmingly suffocating communications multiple times daily over weeks, months, or years that mimic intimacy, but really serve to socially isolate and make the target wholly dependent and compliant (Cross, 2020a; Kopp et al., 2015). The fraud is possible because the target believes s/he is in a loving, romantic relationship and expresses genuine concern and/ or compassion when the scammer spins a woeful tale to obtain financial aid (Cross, 2020b). The scam group may generate logically structured and organized templates for affiliates to use that encompass various possible ways that the victim may respond and how to respond in each situation so as to not lose the victim's trust and compliance (Anesa, 2020).

Table 2.1 displays the stages enacted by online romance scammers to commit this fraud (Buchanan & Whitty, 2014; Budd & Anderson, 2009; Button et al., 2009; Button & Cross, 2017; Cross & Blackshaw, 2015; Garren, 2021; Ross & Smith, 2011; Sofo et al., 2010; Tan & David, 2017; Whitty, 2015). Various members of the scam group will impersonate key individuals, such as bankers, doctors, and government officials, and provide victims

Table 2.1 Stages in the Online Romance Scam

Stage	Description
1	The scammer creates a fake profile on dating/social media site to lure victims into a romantic relationship by using multiple attractive photographs combined with a description consistent with the desire for a long-term relationship.
2	The scammer establishes contact with the target and convinces him/her to communicate offsite (e.g., email, instant messenger, calls).
3	The scammer uses grooming and psychological abuse to develop a relationship with the target, establishing trust and creating an exclusive and isolating bond to obtain ongoing compliance. This time-consuming manipulation process is characterized by frequent displays of affection and attention with intense declarations of love and mirroring of the target's likes and experiences (love bombing).
4	The scammer begins inventing stories, after the target indicates reciprocal affection, involving various sets of circumstances designed to elicit concern (e.g., illness, arrest, stranded overseas).
5	Building on the stories, the scammer requests small amounts of money related to dire circumstances (e.g., medicine, operation) that arose unexpectantly with a promise to repay it (i.e., *testing the water* strategy). Larger amounts are then requested, sometimes with third-party conspirators helping to establish the legitimacy of the narrative.
6 (optional)	Additional crimes: (1) the scammer convinces or forces the victim to help in various financial crimes, such as money laundering, wire fraud, and use of stolen credit cards, through extortion, blackmail, and threats to harm family and friends; (2) the scammer steals victim's identity for financial gain; (3) the scammer uses sextortion, hacking, or deep fakes to get sexually explicit photographs of the victim; and (4) the scammer convinces victim to travel abroad, then kidnaps and ransoms him/her.
7	The scammer no longer communicates with victim.

with documents (e.g., passports, hospital bills, legal papers) to make the money-soliciting scenario believable (Chang, 2008; Freiermuth, 2011). Victims do not have to progress through each stage; instead, victims may realize at any point that they were defrauded, which initiates stage 7 of ending the relationship and communication. Additionally, there are variations in the pace for implementing and proceeding through each stage with an unknown number of victims experiencing stage 6—that is, involving them as accomplices or forcing them to engage in sexual, drug, and/ or financial crimes, such as sex trafficking, drug muling (i.e., makes illegal money transfers), and money laundering (Cross, 2020a). Compliance to fulfill monetary request may also be obtained by using blackmail, extortion/sextortion, image-based sexual abuse, sex trafficking, fraud, and threats to harm the target's family/friends (Button & Cross, 2017; Cross, 2020a; Cross et al., 2016a; Foxworth, 2013). There is an app called *Virtual Cam Whore* that simulates webcam feed by using prerecorded videos of actors posing and performing flirtation and sexual acts to fool the victim (TrendMicro & Interpol, 2017, p. 19). The scammer will record any sex acts by the victim for use as blackmail (TrendMicro & Interpol, 2017). Online dating schemes involving requests for money to help with travel preparations and expenses are implemented differently depending on the scammers' country of origin (Rege, 2009; Steward, 2008; Whitty, 2015). African schemes target both men and women who become unknowing accomplices in money laundering crimes, whereas the Russian schemes focus predominantly on male targets seeking Russian brides and simple advanced fee transactions (Rege, 2009; Smirnova, 2007; Steward, 2008).

TYPICAL ONLINE ROMANCE SCAM VICTIMS

The victims in online romance scams include the "lure" or person whose photographs and identity were stolen and the target who is being catfished (Garren, 2021). In the majority of online romance scams, the fake profiles are male and catfish victims are female (Garren, 2021; Whitty & Buchanan, 2012). The male and female lures are predominantly attractive, White, unmarried young adults (women aged 20s–40s, men aged 30s–50s) whose photographs were stolen from a variety of online sites (e.g., dating services, social media platforms, news media, government, personal Webpages), but also could be deep fakes that photoshop spliced images from various people (Rege, 2009; Suarez-Tangil et al., 2020; Whitty, 2015). Social media influencer Megan Montenegro exemplifies a typical lure as her online photographs have been used in 350 fake dating site profiles over a 3-year period (WSAV.com, 2020). Military officers have also been used as lures—Retired U.S. Colonel Bryan Denny tracked his photograph and name to over 3000 fake profiles (Elliot, 2019). Table 2.2 lists the dating apps and websites reported by victims as being the online site that romance scammers used to contact them (Against Scammers, 2020; Australian Competition & Consumer Commission/ACCC, 2020).

Table 2.3 displays the number of reported complaints and amount of loss from online romance scam victims by sex and age in the U.S. in 2011 and 2014 (FBI, 2011, 2014). As indicated in the table, the proportion of men and women victims remained the same over time, yet the amount of financial loss nearly doubled for female victims while only increasing slightly for male victims. According to the FBI (2020), the U.S. has the highest number of online romance fraud complaints globally, with California (69,541) and Florida (53,793) reporting the highest number of complaints nationally. Figure 2.4 shows the number of fraud victims by age group in 2006, 2014, and 2020 (FBI, 2006, 2014, 2020). According to this figure, the over 60 group was the only one to show an increase in victimization across this timespan. There is some evidence to show that general fraud and online romance fraud affect various age groups differently. Complaints in 2014 revealed that men comprised 52% of fraud victims, whereas they made up only 31% of online romance fraud victims; the majority of fraud victims (80%) were aged 20–59, whereas online romance fraud victims were men aged 30–59 (68%) and women aged 40 to over 60 (82%).

Table 2.2 Type and Number of Fraud Complaints for Romance Scam Filed with Consumer Sentinel in 2020

Type (Number of Complaints)	Name of App/Site
Dating apps (N = 2276)	Ashley Madison, Badoo, BLK, Bumble, Chispa, Coffee Meets Bagel, eHarmony, EliteSingles, FriendFinder, Grindr, Hinge, Match.com, OkCupid, OurTime, Plenty of Fish, Seeking Arrangement, SilverSingles, Tinder, WooPlus, Zoosk
Social media/game/chat platforms (N = 5924)	Facebook, Facebook Messenger, Google Hangouts, Google Talk, Instagram, Kik, Skype, Snapchat, Twitter, WhatsApp, Words with Friends

Table 2.3 IC3 Complaints and Loss Amounts for Online Romance Scams by Sex and Age in 2011 and 2014

Age range	Complaints			
	Male		Female	
	2011 (%)	2014 (%)	2011 (%)	2014 (%)
<20	1	1	1	1
20–29	15	15	5	4
30–39	19	22	12	13
40–49	28	21	33	29
50–59	25	25	35	33
>60	12	16	14	20
Total	31 (N = 1762 out of 5663)	31 (N = 1795 out of 5883)	69 (N = 3901 out of 5663)	69 (N = 4088 out of 5883)

Age range	Loss Amounts in U.S. Dollars			
	Male		Female	
	2011 (%)	2014 (%)	2011 (%)	2014 (%)
<20	$2,575	$34,431	$28207	$3,001
20–29	$667,632	$285,750	$530617	$328,545
30–39	$955,109	$1,337,582	$2784400	$2,427,971
40–49	$2,668,066	$3,744,348	$8181733	$17,541,205
50–59	$3,645,586	$5,583,369	$18802679	$29,076,056
>60	$2,551,007	$4,438,870	$92811951	$21,911,875
Total %	21 ($10,489,976 out of $50,399, 563)	18 ($15,424,351 out of $86,713,003)	79 ($39,909,586 out of $50, 399,563)	82 ($71,288,652 out of $86,713,003)

The psychological characteristics that predispose victims to online romance scams include their romantic beliefs and idealization, which is the notion that relationships can be perfect (Whitty & Buchanan, 2012; Whitty, 2018). Researchers indicate that catfish victims set out to find the ideal romance partner and, once presented with the ideal profile, are easily seduced by the scammer (Cross, 2020a; Whitty, 2015, 2018). Scam victims had difficult regulating their emotions in response to scam offers or resisting the temptations to comply, feeling addicted to the relationship (Lea et al., 2009; Whitty, 2013, 2018). Errors in victim's decision making likely contribute to

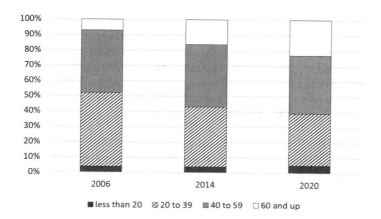

Figure 2.4 Number of fraud victims by age group in 2014 and 2020.

their gullibility to online romance scams (Lea et al., 2009; Whitty, 2013, 2018). Researchers believe that the victims gave money to the fraudsters because the fake personas were authority figures who elicit trust, such as doctors and military officers, or the scammers relied on narratives purposefully devised to activate norms for helping, such as emergencies or unexpected crisis (Lea et al., 2009; Whitty, 2013). Victims who paid scammers used the reasoning that they are already invested in the relationship of (i.e., sunk cost effect) and were close to their goal of a relationship (Lea et al., 2009; Whitty, 2013).

LAWS FOR PROSECUTING ONLINE ROMANCE SCAMS

Online romance scammers may be prosecuted for identity theft and fraud (18 USC §1028) because they used the name, photographs, and other personal information of the "lures" to create their fake profiles.

- 18 USC §1028. *Identity theft offenses*: fraud and use of the internet to knowingly attempt to commit or aid in committing identity theft through production of false identification documents or possession of such documents with intent to defraud (consistent with *Identity Theft and Assumption Deterrence Act*, 1998[2]). The penalty for producing or transferring identification or fraudulently obtaining currency or goods up to $1000 includes maximum 15 years in federal prison, fine, and criminal forfeiture of property used and profit from the crime [1028(a)(7)].

[2] Identity Theft and Assumption Deterrence Act. https://www.ftc.gov/node/119459.

Identity theft involves the misuse of another person's personal and financial identifying information (e.g., social security number, credit card account) for financial gain or to fraudulently assume the person's identity. The FTC was established to handle complaints of identity theft, which are stored in the Identity Theft Data Clearinghouse (aka Consumer Sentinel Network). Additional laws to prosecute perpetrators of identity theft and fraud (Office for Victims of Crime, 2010) include the following:

- *Identity Theft Penalty Enhancement Act of 2004* (Pub. L. 108–275 §1028A). Criminals who use another person's identity to commit felony crimes may be charged for "aggravated identity theft"; and
- *Identity Theft Enforcement and Restitution Act of 2008.* This act was used to amend 18 U.S.C. §3663(b) to allow for those convicted of identity theft to provide restitution for the value of the victim's time handling the actual or intended harm of the crime.

In general, however, people whose photographs were used to lure victims have little legal recourse, even when the scammers live in the U.S. The "injured party"—that is the person whose identity was stolen—can force websites using the image to remove it on three grounds: invasion of privacy, violation of right or publicity, and defamation.

- *Invasion of privacy*: the photograph of the person may portray him/her in a false and/or offensive manner;
- *Violation of right or publicity*: the photograph was used in a commercial manner and the public is able to identify the person depicted; and
- *Defamation*: the photograph creates a false impression and/or injures the person's reputation in a way that the public devalues him/her.

Another, now defunct option, is the *Stolen Valor Act of 2005*, which criminalized the false representation of U.S. military with medal or decoration as a federal misdemeanor, was struck down as unconstitutional by the Supreme Court because it limited First Amendment speech rights (see *United States v. Alvarez*, 2012). If the photographs used in the fake profile were taken by a professional photographer, however, then the scammer could be prosecuted for theft. Identity theft and fraud is most often prosecuted by the state, but the federal government takes jurisdiction when the charges and situations are serious (OVC, 2010).

Online romance scammers may be prosecuted for their financial crimes against catfished victims using several federal statutes ("U.S. Code: Title 18. Crimes and criminal procedure," 2019), resulting in a 30-year maximum imprisonment (Department of Justice, 2020).

- 18 USC § 1029.[3] *Credit card fraud*: includes producing, using, and trafficking in counterfeit access devices;
- 18 USC § 1030.[4] *Fraud and related activity in connection with computers;*[5]
- 18 USC § 1341.[6] *Fraud and swindles*: devised or intended to devise a scheme or artifice for obtaining money or property by means of false or fraudulent pretenses;
- 18 USC § 1343.[7] *Fraud by wire, radio, or television*: devised or intended to devise a scheme or artifice to defraud using writings, pictures, or sounds; and
- 18 USC § 1344.[8] *Bank fraud*: obtain money by means of false or fraudulent pretenses, representations, or promises;
- 18 USC §1956.[9] *Laundering of monetary instruments*: engaging in financial transactions using money from criminal activity in order to promote or conceal it;
- 18 USC § 1957.[10] *Engaging in monetary transactions*: knowingly engaging in monetary transactions exceeding $10,000 from unlawful activity.

Victims of romance scams may have some options to regain their financial loss, but the ability of law enforcement overall to recover lost funds is low (Cross, 2016). For example, the company that issued the gift cards may refund their money or they can report the fraud to their banks. The Court may also order convicted defendants to pay restitution. In *U.S. v. Amoo* (4:16-cr-00181), two Nigerians living in the U.S. pled guilty to conspiring to commit wire fraud after defrauding a woman out of $2 million and

---

[3] https://www.govinfo.gov/app/details/USCODE-2010-title18/USCODE-2010-title18-partI-chap47-sec1029.

[4] https://codes.findlaw.com/us/title-18-crimes-and-criminal-procedure/18-usc-sect-1030.html.

[5] https://codes.findlaw.com/us/title-18-crimes-and-criminal-procedure/18-usc-sect-1030.html.

[6] https://www.govinfo.gov/content/pkg/USCODE-2012-title18/pdf/USCODE-2012-title18-partI-chap63-sec1341.pdf.

[7] https://www.govinfo.gov/content/pkg/USCODE-2013-title18/pdf/USCODE-2013-title18-partI-chap63-sec1343.pdf.

[8] https://www.govinfo.gov/app/details/USCODE-2011-title18/USCODE-2011-title18-partI-chap63-sec1344.

[9] https://www.govinfo.gov/app/details/USCODE-2011-title18/USCODE-2011-title18-partI-chap95-sec1956.

[10] https://www.govinfo.gov/app/details/USCODE-2010-title18/USCODE-2010-title18-partI-chap95-sec1957.

were ordered to pay $86,581.15 in addition to their 36-month imprisonment. Also, if the scammer impersonated the victim by opening up credit cards and charging items to the point of ruining the person's credit, the following options may also be considered:

- *Fair Credit Reporting Act* provides guidelines for correcting credit records to include only legitimate charges;
- *Fair and Accurate Credit Transactions Act*, an amended version of the previous act, provides protection against identity theft;
- *Fair Credit Billing Act* established resolution procedures for resolving billing errors and limits liability for illegitimate charges; and
- *Fair Debt Collection Practices Act* prevents unfair and deceptive practices by debt collectors for collecting unpaid bills.

Unfortunately, victims who unwittingly became conspirators in multiple fraud crimes may have been prosecuted (ACCC, 2021). The scammer tricked them into becoming part of a criminal operation through compliance with requests to: open bank accounts and credit cards; engage in money laundering schemes by moving money through wire transfers and deposits; and purchase items for other victims by using stolen credit cards and mailing it to them. Consequently, they can be prosecuted for internet fraud, bank fraud, wire fraud, money laundering, identity theft, and mail fraud. Box 2.1 describes prosecution against online romance scammers.

**BOX 2.1   ONLINE ROMANCE SCAM
CASES PROSECUTED IN THE U.S.**

Case 1: In 2018, 32-year-old Kennard Banks, Boynton Beach, FL, as part of a larger cybercriminal organization, defrauded an elderly Connecticut woman out of $437,800 (NBC Universal Media, 2020). The scammer, whose fake profile identified him as Teddy Banas and was filled with images stolen from Instagram, met her on a 50+ dating site and asked for her assistance with a business deal, promising to repay her. He opened a bank account in order to receive the wired money and thus is charged with money laundering.

Case 2: Nine Nigerians aged 19–55 were arrested, a tenth person at large was charged in absentia, as part of cyber-enabled fraud schemes enacted in the U.S. and Nigeria that was investigated by law

---

enforcement in Chicago, called "Operation Gold Phish" (Department of Justice, 2018, 2019). Three types of online scams were implemented, including: (1) romance fraud using Match.com, Facebook, and Instagram to entice victims to send money to bank accounts opened using fake passports; (2) "mystery shopper" in which victims were hired to evaluate Western Union and MoneyGram by depositing fake checks wired into their bank accounts; and (3) business email compromise, which fraudulently obtained usernames and passwords and sent spoofed emails to employees instructing them to write bank payments. Criminal complaints consisted of multiple counts of wire fraud, conspiracy to commit computer intrusion, passport fraud, false statement to financial institution, and mail fraud.

Case 3: Six Nigerian nationals living in Massachusetts engaged in a series of online romance and unemployment benefits scams, defrauding victims of more than $4 million (Department of Justice, 2021). They used fake passports to open bank accounts for the purpose of collecting and laundering money, fraudulently applying for pandemic unemployment benefits unbeknownst to their victims. Three were charged with conspiracy to commit bank fraud, two were charged with conspiracy to commit wire and bank fraud, and one was charged with conspiracy to commit mail fraud.

IMPACT OF ONLINE ROMANCE SCAMS ON SOCIETY AND VICTIMS

Online romance scams are a waste of societal resources—particularly in terms of the amount of time and financial investment of criminal justice system. The investigation process requires determining the real name and location of the scammer and securing evidence of the crime (e.g., preserving social media content, and following the money) through subpoena, which may not be possible as user name and IP address may not be valid or the scam and bank is outside of the U.S. (Melton, 2019). The online romance scam differentially affects the two types of victims— the lure and the target. In some cases, lures whose images were used in the online romance scam remain blissfully unaware of their inadvertent role, mainly because online romance fraud is often not reported by catfished victims (Cross, 2020a). However, lures can become endangered and suffer emotional harm when a target tracks them down and accosts them, under the misconception that they are responsible for or involved in the scam. For example, a Polish catfished victim, believing that Sergeant Major Raymond Chandler III was actually the person who scammed her, sent an angry letter to his son (Kelly, 2015). When catfish victims report the scam to law enforcement, the superficial evidence will lead investigators to the lure as the suspect, possibly resulting in arrest and prosecution, which impose both financial and emotional harm to the innocent person.

The catfished victims of online romance scams suffer financial loss and emotional distress; the latter is true independent of whether they are duped out of money (Whitty & Buchanan, 2012, 2016). Defrauded targets may send varying amounts of money directly to the scammer, from less than $100 to as much as their entire life savings and/or the value of all of their sold possessions, to the point of becoming unable to support themselves or having to declare bankruptcy. In 2020, $2500 was the median amount of money sent, typically by gift card or wire transfer, but the eldest victims sustained median losses of $9475 (FTC, 2020; Fletcher, 2021). In some cases, the victim stops paying his/her own bills or becomes bankrupt. For example, a West Virginia widow met someone on Mingle2 claiming to be an American living abroad and her financial kindness towards helping him to return home left her homeless, carless, and without any possessions (Ogbe, 2020). The scammer may also steal the target's information to open up and max out credit card accounts, resulting in devasting debt (Cross, 2020a). A third drain of financial resources stems from victims paying private investigators to locate the scammer in an attempt to retrieve the money or an attorney to represent them in bankruptcy court. A fourth, and rarer financial burden comes from online romance victims being conned into traveling to meet the scammer who is part of an international criminal organization, thereby compromising their personal safety through kidnapping, ransom, and extortion (Powell, 2013; Whitty, 2015). In a recent incident, an American woman (age 46) traveled in February 2019 to Lagos, Nigeria to marry her online boyfriend, Chukwuebuka Obiaku (age 34), which she did in May 2019; he then held her against her will in a hotel room for 16 months and with the help of two other suspects stole $48,000 from her retirement benefits, debit cards, and credit cards (British Broadcasting Company/BBC, 2020).

Romance scam victims often feel guilt, humiliation, shame, and embarrassment that they had been deceived by the imposter suitor to the point that they no longer can trust their own judgments about people;

they also indicate they are depressed—some even contemplate or commit suicide—have poor physical health and well-being, lose their employment and/or homes, and isolate themselves from friends and family (Button et al., 2009, 2014; Cross, 2020a; Cross & Kelly, 2016; Cross et al., 2016a, 2016b; Semenza, 2020; Whitty, 2013). In some cases, even after victims cease payments to the scammers, they perceive their physical safety to be compromised so they move to a new location (Cross, 2020a; Cross et al., 2016a). Internal and external victim blaming exacerbates psychological harm and trauma (Cross, 2013, 2015, 2020a). Victims are afraid to report the fraud to law enforcement or tell anyone in their social support system they were defrauded, particularly after ignoring warnings from friends and family, because they believe they must bear the responsibility and consequences of their poor decisions (Cross, 2020a; Sorrell & Whitty, 2019). For older victims, failure to disclose may be a protective response as their family may use this incident to limit their independence; disown them; restrict access to family; and/or chastise and humiliate them for even being on dating sites (Cross, 2020a). Psychological harm is intensified when targets are defrauded multiple times by different scammers and when scammers engage in sexual crimes against the target, such as sextortion or image-based sexual abuse schemes (Cross, 2020a). Another way targets are harmed emotionally is when the scammer defrauds the victims' friends and family and/or uses them to scam others.

CYBERSECURITY TACTICS

One method for differentiating between real and fake profiles on dating sites is to use machine-learning solutions, such as the publicly available "automatic-romancescam-digger" (Suarez-Tangil et al., 2019). There are three types of attributes used in profiles: *demographics* (e.g., age, sex, ethnicity), *images*—typically a person's face in frontal position, and *description* using key traits and interests (Suarez-Tangil et al., 2020). The following discussion explains the findings from research by Suarez-Tangil et al. (2020). Table 2.4 compares demographic information portrayed in real and scam profiles. There were some interesting differences found, particularly in terms of ethnicity and average age in both types of profiles. Men in the scam profile were most likely to represent their occupations as engineer or military—at higher rates than in real profiles, whereas women in the scam profile often indicated they were students. Differences were also found in

Table 2.4 Demographic Information Typically Found in Real and Scam Profiles

Demographic Information		Real Profile	Scam Profile
Sex	Male	60%	60%
	Female	40%	40%
Ethnicity	White	44%	66%
	Hispanic	33%	2%
	Native American	1%	11%
Marital status	Single	57%	51%
	Divorced	21%	14%
	Widowed	4%	28%
Average age	Male	40	50
	Female	40	30

terms of the number and type of images used in scam and real profiles. Scam profiles contained a higher number of photographs portraying their physical appearance and interests than was present in real profiles. A generative model based on a convolutional neural network combined with a language-generating recurrent neural network revealed some content differences in the images, such as high rates of group shots in scam profiles. The descriptions used in scam profiles were constructed to gain the attention of targets by including a broad range of interests and ideal characteristics. A linguistic analysis was performed using natural language processing technology and revealed that scam profiles contained more words on average (consistent with lying), particularly emotion words; family and friend references; and formal language structures than did real profiles.

Another way to determine if the profile online is real is for users to examine the content of the descriptions and images, as well as the behavior of the online dating partner. Anyone can do a reverse image search on various search engines using your phone, computer, or other internet device to determine if the profile photograph appears on the internet elsewhere (Federal Bureau of Investigation/FBI, 2019a). Box 2.2 demonstrates how to do this type of search using Google Images. As part of a public service announcement on online dating scams, the FTC (2021) advises users to be suspicious of the following behaviors common in imposter scams:

1. Love interest encourages you to talk off of the dating site;
2. Love interest states that s/he is in love with you after a short period of time;

3. Love interest claims to be involved in international travel and/or work;
4. Love interest makes excuses for not visiting you, tied to money issues; and
5. Love interest requests money even though you have never met him/her offline (Karimi, 2019).

If you are the victim of a romance scam, you may file a complaint with the FTC at https://www.ftc.gov/faq/consumer-protection/submit-consumer-complaint-ftc or the FBI's Internet Crime Complaint Center at www.ic3. gov. Also report the scam to the dating service and/or social media website where victims met the scammer.

BOX 2.2 STEPS FOR DOING A REVERSE IMAGE SEARCH

Step 1: Open any web browser (Chrome, Firefox, Safari).
Step 2: Go to Google Images [https://images.google.com/].
Step 3: Click the camera—which will open the "search by image" box.
Step 4: Determine the method you wish to use to obtain the image—by browsing the internet for the image or by opening an image stored in a file on your computer.

1. *Paste image URL*: this is the option if you want to use an online image.
   a. Go to the website where the photograph appears;
   b. Right click on the photo;
   c. Select "copy image link";
   d. Paste link into the text box for Google Images;
   e. Click "search by image"; and
   f. A google page will list all of the online sites/pages for matching images.
2. *Upload an image*: this is the option if you want to use a photograph you already saved onto your hard drive. [Note: Alternatively, Chrome and Firefox allow you to "drag and drop" pictures rather than uploading them.]
   a. If you need to fetch the image from the website,
      i. then go to the website and locate the image;
      ii. right click on it;

      iii. select "save image as" to save it onto your hard drive;

      iv. click on "upload an image";

      v. select the image from your hard drive;

      vi. the image and a word label (e.g., man) appears in the text box; and

      vii. a google page will list all of the online sites/pages for matching images.

  b. If you *already have an image* on your hard drive,

      i. then go to upload an image;

      ii. click on "browse," select the file and click open;

      iii. the image and a word label (e.g., man) appears in the text box; and

      iv. a google page will list all of the online sites/pages for matching images.

REFERENCES

Against Scammers. (2020). *Top 5 Social Sites to Be Scammed on*. https://againstscammers.com/top-5-social-sites-to-be-scammed-on/.

Akandle, O., & Shadare, B.R. (2019). Yahoo-plus in Ibadan: Meaning, characterization and strategies. *International Journal of Cyber Criminology, 13*(2), 343–357.

Anderson, M., Vogels, E.A., & Turner, E. (2020). *The Virtues and Downsides of Online Dating*. https://www.pewresearch.org/internet/2020/02/06/the-virtues-and-downsides-of-online-dating/.

Anesa, P. (2020). Lovextortion: Persuasion strategies in romance cybercrime. *Discourse, Context & Media, 35*, 100398.

Aransiola, J. O., & Asindemade. S. O. (2011). Understanding cybercrime perpetrators and the strategies they employ in Nigeria. *Cyberpsychology, Behavior, and Social Networking, 14*(12), 759–763.

Australian Competition & Consumer Commission (ACCC). (2020). *Romance Scammers Move to New Apps, Costing Aussies More Than $28.6 Million*. https://www.scamwatch.gov.au/news-alerts/romance-scammers-move-to-new-apps-costing-aussies-more-than-286-million.

Australian Competition & Consumer Commission. (2021). *Scammers Capitalize on Pandemic as Australians Lose Record $851 Million to Scams.* https://www.accc.gov.au/media-release/scammers-capitalise-on-pandemic-as-australians-lose-record-851-million-to-scams.

BBC. (2020, July 13). *Romance Scam: US Woman Freed After Year as Hostage in Nigeria*. https://www.bbc.com/news/world-africa-53390397.

Buchanan, T., & Whitty, M.T. (2014). The online dating romance scam: Causes and consequences of victimhood. *Psychology, Crime, & Law, 20*(3), 261–283. Doi: 10.1080/1068316X.2013.772180.

Budd, C., & Anderson, J. (2009). *Consumer Fraud in Australasia: Results of the Australasian Consumer Fraud Taskforce Online Australia Surveys 2008 and 2009.* https://www.publicsafety.gc.ca/lbrr/archives/cnmcs-plcng/cn31047026-eng.pdf.

Button, M., & Cross, C. (2017). *Cyber Frauds, Scams and their Victims.* London: Routledge.

Button, M., Lewis, C., & Tapley, J. (2009). *A Better Deal for Victims: Research into Victims' Needs and Experiences.* London: National Fraud Authority.

Button, M., McNaugton Nicolls, C., Kerr, J., & Owen, R. (2014). Online frauds: Learning from victims why they fall for these scams. *Australian and New Zealand Journal of Criminology, 47*(3), 391–408.

Button, M., Nicholls, C.M., Kerr, J., & Owen, R. (2014). Online fraud victims in England and Wales: Victims' views on sentencing and the opportunity for restorative justice? *The Howard Journal of Criminal Justice, 54*(2), 193–211.

Cacioppo, J.T., Cacioppo, S., Gonzaga, G.C., Ogburn, E.L., & VanderWeele, T.J. (2013). Marital satisfaction and break-ups differ across on-line and off-line meeting venues. *Proceedings of the National Academy of Sciences, 110*(25), 10135–10140. Doi: 10.1073/pnas.1222447110.

Chang, J.J.S. (2008). An analysis of advance fee fraud on the internet. *Journal of Financial Crime, 15*(1), 71–81. Doi: 10.1108/13590790810841716.

Close, A., & Zinkhan, G. (2004). Romance and the internet. The E-Mergence of E-Dating. *Advanced Consumer Research, 31*, 153–157.

Coluccia, A., Pozza, A., Ferretti, F., Carabellese, F., Masti, A., & Gualtieri, G. (2020). Online romance scams: Relationship dynamics and psychological characteristics of the victims and scammers. A scoping review. *Clinical Practice & Epidemiology in Mental Health, 16*, 24–35. Doi. 10.2174/1745017902016010024.

Cross, C. (2016). Using financial intelligence to target online fraud victimisation: Applying a tertiary prevention perspective. *Criminal Justice Studies, 29*(2), 125–142. Doi: 10.1080/1478601X.2016.1170278.

Cross, C. (2020a). Romance fraud. In T.J. Holt and A.M. Bossler (eds.), *The Palgrave Handbook of International Cybercrime and Cyberdeviance* (pp. 917–937). Cham, Switzerland: Springer Nature.

Cross, C. (2020b). 'Oh we can't actually do anything about that': The problematic nature of jurisdiction for online fraud victims. *Criminology & Criminal Justice, 20*(3), 358–375 Doi: 10.1177/1748895819835910.

Cross, C., & Blackshaw, D. (2015). Improving the police response to online fraud. *Policing: A Journal of Policy and Practice, 9*(2), 119–128.

Cross, C., & Kelly, M. (2016). The problem of "white noise:" Examining current prevention approaches to online fraud. *Journal of Financial Crime, 23*(4), 806–818. Doi: 10.1108/JFC-12-2015-0069.

Cross, C., Richards, K., & Smith, R. (2016a). *Improving the Response to Online Fraud Victims: An Examination of Reporting and Support*. Canberra: Australian Institute of Criminology.

Cross, C., Richards, K., & Smith, R.G. (2016b). The reporting experiences and support needs of victims of online fraud. *Trends and Issues in Crime and Criminal Justice, 518*, 1–14.

Cybersecurity & Infrastructure Security Agency (2019, Feb 2). *Internet Romance Scams*. https://us-cert.cisa.gov/ncas/current-activity/2019/02/12/Internet-Romance-Scams.

D'Agata, M.T., Kwantes, P.J., & Holden, R.R. (2021). Psychological factors related to self-disclosure and relationship formation in the online environment. *Personal Relationships, 28*(2), 230–250.

Department of Justice. (2018). *9 Defendants Charged in Chicago in International Investigation Targeting "Romance Scams" and "Mystery Shopper" Schemes*. https://www.justice.gov/usao-ndil/pr/9-defendants-charged-chicago-international-investigation-targeting-romance-scams-and.

Department of Justice. (2019). *Federal Indictment Adds 10th Defendant and Expands Charges against 9 Others in International "Romance Scam" Investigation*. https://www.justice.gov/usao-ndil/pr/federal-indictment-adds-10th-defendant-and-expands-charges-against-9-others.

Department of Justice. (2020). *Identity Theft*. https://www.justice.gov/criminal-fraud/identity-theft/identity-theft-and-identity-fraud.

Department of Justice. (2021). *Six individuals Charged with Using Various Online Scams to Defraud Victims of More than $4 Million*. https://www.justice.gov/usao-ma/pr/six-individuals-charged-using-various-online-scams-defraud-victims-more-4-million.

Elliot, J.K. (2019, February 9). *'It's Been Hell': How Fraudsters Use Handsome Soldiers to Prey on Lonely Hearts over the Holidays*. https://globalnews.ca/news/4754607/military-romance-scam-bryan-denny/.

Federal Bureau of Investigation. (2006). *Internet Crime Report*. https://www.ic3.gov/Media/PDF/AnnualReport/2006_IC3Report.pdf.

Federal Bureau of Investigation. (2011). *Internet Crime Report*. https://www.ic3.gov/Media/PDF/AnnualReport/2011_IC3Report.pdf.

Federal Bureau of Investigation. (2014). *2014 Internet Crime Report*. https://www.ic3.gov/Media/PDF/AnnualReport/2014_IC3Report.pdf.

Federal Bureau of Investigation. (2019a). *Cyber Actors use Online Dating Sites to Conduct Confidence/Romance Fraud and Recruit Money Mules*. Alert No. I-080519-PSA. https://www.ic3.gov/Media/Y2019/PSA190805.

Federal Bureau of Investigation. (2019b). *2019 Internet Crime Report*. https://www.ic3.gov/Media/PDF/AnnualReport/2019_IC3Report.pdf.

Federal Bureau of Investigation. (2020). *Internet Crime Report 2020*. https://www.ic3.gov/Media/PDF/AnnualReport/2020_IC3Report.pdf.

Federal Trade Commission. (2020). *Protecting Older Consumers, 2019–2020*. https://www.ftc.gov/system/files/documents/reports/protecting-older-consumers-2019-2020-report-federal-trade-commission/p144400_protecting_older_adults_report_2020.pdf.

Federal Trade Commission. (2021). *What You Need to Know about Romance Scams.* https://www.consumer.ftc.gov/articles/what-you-need-know-about-romance-scams.

Fletcher, E. (2021). *Romance Scams Take Record Dollars in 2020.* https://www.ftc.gov/news-events/blogs/data-spotlight/2021/02/romance-scams-take-record-dollars-2020.

Foxworth, D. (2013). *Looking for Love? Beware of Online Dating Scams. The Federal Bureau of Investigations (FBI).* San Diego, CA: Federal Bureau of Investigation. Retrieved from http://www.fbi.gov/sandiego/press-releases/2013/looking-for-love-beware-of-online-datingscams.

Freiermuth, M.R. (2011). Text, lies and electronic bait: An analysis of email fraud and the decisions of the unsuspecting. *Discourse & Communication, 5*(2), 123–145. Doi: 10.1177/1750481310395448.

Garren, D.L. (2021). *The Loneliness Epidemic is Fueling the Romance Scam Epidemic.* https://www.sageinvestigations.com/blog/the-loneliness-epidemic-is-fueling-the-romance-scam-epidemic/.

Gorham, M. (2018). *2018 Internet Crime Report.* https://pdf.ic3.gov/2018_IC3Report.pdf.

Gregory, D.W., & Nikiforova, B. (2012). A sweetheart of a deal: How people get hooked and reeled in by financial scams. *Journal of Behavioral Finance & Economics, 2*(2), 96–122.

Internet Crime Complaint Center. (2018). *Internet Crime Report.* https://www.ic3.gov/media/annualreports.aspx.

Karimi, F. (2019). *Americans Lost $143 Million in Online Romance Scams Last Year. That's Way More Than Any Other Reported Fraud.* https://www.cnn.com/2019/08/23/us/online-romance-scams-losses-trnd/index.html.

Kelly, J. (2015, February 25). *Love a Man in Uniform? Online Dating Scammers Hope So.* https://www.washingtonpost.com/local/love-a-man-in-uniform-online-dating-scammers-hope-so/2015/02/25/4598a30c-bb8f-11e4-8668-4e7ba-8439ca6_story.html?utm_term=.4374e2314433.

Kopp, C., Layton, R., Sillitoe, J., & Gondal, I. (2015). The role of love stories in romance scams: A qualitative analysis of fraudulent profiles. *International Journal of Cyber Criminology, 9*(2), 205–217.

Lazarus, S. (2018). Birds of a feather flock together: The Nigerian cyber fraudsters (Yahoo Boys) and hip hop artists. *Criminology, Criminal Justice, Law & Society, 19*(2), 63–80.

Lea, S., Fischer, P. and Evans, K. (2009a). *The Psychology of Scams: Provoking and Committing Errors of Judgement. Report for the Office of Fair Trading.* www.oft.gov.uk/shared_oft/reports/consumer_protection/oft1070.pdf.

McClellan, D. (2021). *Match.com Scams: Catfishing, Romance Scams, and More.* https://socialcatfish.com/blog/catfishing-match-com-scams-learn-match-com-scams/.

Melton, P. (2019). *Military Service Members Targeted to Facilitate Romance Scams. Utica College.* ProQuest Dissertations Publishing, 22620324.

Menard, S., Morris, R.G., Gerber, J., & Covey, H.C. (2011). Distribution and correlates of self-reported crimes of trust. *Deviant Behavior, 32*(10), 877–917. Doi: 10.1080/01639625.2010.514221.

NBC Universal Media. (2020). *Suspect Charged in Online Dating Scheme that Stole $437K from Woman.* https://www.nbcconnecticut.com/news/local/suspect-charged-in-online-dating-scheme-that-stole-437k-from-woman-police/2310667/.

Nikiforova, B., & Gregory, D.W. (2013). Globalization of trust and internet confidence Emails. *Journal of Financial Crime, 20*(4), 393–405. Doi: 10.1108/JFC-05-2013-0038.

Offei, M., Andoh-Baidoo, K.F., Ayaburi, E.W., & Asamoah, D. (2020). How do individuals justify and rationalize their criminal behaviors in online romance fraud? *Information Systems Frontiers*, online. Doi: 10.1007/s10796-020-10051-2.

Office for Victims of Crime. (2010). *Identity Theft and Financial Fraud: Federal Identity Theft Laws.* https://ovc.ojp.gov/sites/g/files/xyckuh226/files/pubs/ID_theft/idtheftlaws.html.

Ogbe, V. (2020). *Weston Woman Ends up Homeless after Romance Scam.* https://www.wdtv.com/2020/10/28/weston-woman-ends-up-homeless-after-romance-scam/.

Powell, G. (2013). *Woman Believed Victim of Online Scam Found Dead. ABC News.* http://www.abc.net.au/news/2013-03-04/woman-believed-victim-of-online-scam-found-dead/4551050.

Rege, A. (2009). What's love got to do with it? Exploring online dating scams and identity graud. *International Journal of Cyber Criminology, 3*(2), 494–512.

Ross, S., & Smith, R. G. (2011). *Risk Factors for Advance Fee Fraud Victimisation* (No. 420). Canberra: Australian Government: Australian Institute of Criminology.

Royal Canadian Mounted Police. (2021). *Love is in the Air, but Beware of Romance Scam.* https://www.rcmp-grc.gc.ca/en/news/2021/love-is-the-air-beware-romance-scam.

Schachetti, L. (2021). *Better Business Bureau Warns Romance Scams Are on the Rise.* https://www.nbc29.com/2021/02/12/better-business-bureau-warns-romance-scams-are-rise/.

Semenza, D.C. (2020). Dating and sexual relationships in the age of the Internet. In T.J. Hold and A.M. Bossler (eds.), *The Palgrave Handbook of International Cybercrime and Cyberdeviance* (pp. 1067–1086). Cham, Switzerland: Springer Nature.

Shea, C. (2020). *He Stole their Hearts, then Their Money. Meet the Women Trying to Catch One of Canada's Most Prolific Romance Scammers.* https://www.chatelaine.com/living/romance-scammer-canada-marcel-andre-vautour/.

Smith, A. (2016). *15% of American Adults Have Used Online Dating Sites or Mobile Dating Apps.* Pew Research Center. http://www.pewinternet.org/2016/02/11/15-percent-of-american-adults-have-used-online-dating-sites-or-mobile-dating-apps/.

Sofo, F., Berzins, M., Ammirato, S., & Volpentesta, A.P. (2010). Investigating the relationship between consumers' style of thinking and online victimization in scamming. *Journal of Digital Content Technology and its Applications, 4*(7), 38–49.

Smirnova, N. (2007). *How the Scammers were Fooling the Foreign Grooms-to-Be.* Moskovskiy Komsomolets. http://www.russian-dating-scams.com/scams/media/mkaug07.htm.

Sorrell, T., & Whitty, M. (2019). Online romance scams and victimhood. *Security Journal, 32,* 342–361. Doi: 10.1057/s41284-019-00166-w.

Steward, W. (2008, March 28). *Scamski City, where Online "Russian Brides" Turn Out to be Mafia Conmen.* | Mail Online. Daily Mail. http://www.dailymail.co.uk/femail/article-542276/Scamski-city-online-Russian-brides-turnMafia-conmen.htm.

Suarez-Tangil, G., Edwards, M., Peersman, C., Stringhini, G., Rashid, A., & Whitty, M. (2020). Automatially dismantling online dating fraud. *IEEE Transactions on Information Forensics and Security, 15,* 1128–1137.

Tan, H.K., & David, Y. (2017). Preying on lonely hearts: A systematic deconstruction of an internet romance scammer's online lover persona. *Journal of Modern Languages, 23(1),* 28–40. https://jml.um.edu.my/article/view/3288.

TrendMicro & INTERPOL. (2017). *Cybercrime in West Africa: Poised for an Underground Market.* https://documents.trendmicro.com/assets/wp/wp-cybercrime-in-west-africa.pdf.

Wakefield, J. (2021). *Romance Fraud on Rise in Coronavirus Lockdown.* https://www.bbc.com/news/technology-55997611.

Whitty, M.T. (2013). The scammers persuasive techniques model: Development of a stage model to explain the online dating romance scam. *British Journal of Criminology, 53,* 665–684. Doi: 10.1093/bjc/azt009.

Whitty, M.T. (2015). Anatomy of the online dating romance scam. *Security Journal, 28(4),* 443–455.

Whitty, M.T. (2018). Do you love me? Psychological characteristics of romance scam victims. *Cyberpsychology, Behavior, and Social Networking, 21(2),* 105–109. Doi: 10.1089/cyber.2016.0729.

Whitty, M.T., & Buchanan, T. (2012). The online dating romance scam: A serious crime. *Cyberpsychology, Behavior, and Social Networking, 15(3),* 181–183.

Whitty, M.T., & Buchanan, T. (2016). The online dating romance scam: The psychological impact on victims –both financial and non-financial. *Criminology & Criminal Justice, 16(2),* 176–194. Doi: 10.1177/1748895815603773.

WSAV.com. (2020, November 19). *Online Dating Scammers Use Woman's Photos to Lure People Out of Thousands of Dollars.* https://www.wsav.com/now/online-dating-scammers-use-womans-photos-to-lure-people-out-of-thousands-of-dollars/.

3

Online Swatters

DEFINING ONLINE SWATTING

Swatting involves making fraudulent 911 calls to report serious-level criminal threats or ongoing violent situations (e.g., bomb threats, weapons, hostages, killings) in order to dupe law enforcement, usually a Special

DOI: 10.4324/9781003092292-3

Weapons and Tactics (SWAT) team into raiding the house or business of an innocent person (Burgess, 2018; Enzweiler, 2015; Hoeferkamp, 2019; Li, 2018; McKeigue, 2015). Often used as a prank, bragging rights, or form of revenge, callers use "spoofing" technology to disguise their phone numbers and identity (Andone, 2019; Bernstein, 2016). When the emergency operator answers the call, the number appears to be from the local area—usually the target's neighbors reporting the crime, despite the caller possibly being in another town, state, or country (Enzweiler, 2015; McKeigue, 2015).

Typically, the act of swatting results in the waste of law enforcement's time and resources, but in the worst-case scenario, death or serious injury may occur to the intended target; innocent person, family, and community members; first responders; and/or real crime victims who did not receive help because law enforcement was diverted to handle the hoax (Hoeferkamp, 2019). Swatting is terrifying to victims whose privacy is abruptly interrupted by a group of SWAT officers screaming commands at them, such as "hands up," "identify yourself," or "get down on the floor" (Calabro, 2018). It also places these first responders in an untenable situation as, per their training, they operate under the misconception that deadly force will likely be needed to disrupt this active crime, which in turn, increases the likelihood a disoriented suspect's movements will be misinterpreted as an attempt to use a weapon (Bernstein, 2016; Enzweiler, 2015). Regardless of the outcome, the strain of a swatting attack puts on both victims and law enforcement can last a lifetime (Nellist, 2018).

Swatting incidents have been recorded since 2002, but it has evolved in terms of techniques and/or targets, as shown in Table 3.1 (Enzweiler, 2015;

Table 3.1 Evolutional History of Swatting

Year	Swatting Techniques and Targets
2002	Phone service used to call 9-1-1
2005	Online video-gamers targeted other gamers
2008	Webcam used to watch live SWAT attacks
2012	Celebrities, well-known entertainers, officials, chat room users, researchers, etc. are targeted
2015	Targets include schools and public places; high-profile female video-gamers; feminists; politicians whose legislative bills promote banning swatting
2020	Targets include those opposing the Alt-Right; social media executives whose platform banned users for service violations; leaders of Black Lives Matter; etc.

Fruhlinger, 2020; Remeika, 2017). According to former FBI agent Kevin Kolbye, prevalence has increased from 400 cases in 2011 to over 1000 in 2019 (Fruhlinger, 2020). It is not uncommon for gamers to humiliate and terrorize their target by having the SWAT raid stream live while either the victim or swatter is broadcasting (Calabro, 2018). The online environment (e.g., gaming forums, social media sites) is also being used to perpetrate technology-facilitated abuse that compromises a victim's privacy in the real world (Witwer et al., 2020). Doxing or doxxing, a prerequisite for launching the swatting attack, involves obtaining and publicly displaying private and personally identifiable information (PII) of a target (MacAllister, 2017). Swatters may obtain PII from various legitimate sources (i.e., social media sites, data brokers) and/or by illegal means (i.e., hacking, social engineering) in order to set up the swatting incident. This information is then posted without permission as a means of humiliating and harassing the victim directly and/or by soliciting others to aid in the process (Department of Homeland Security/DHS, 2017; Douglas, 2016). For example, the events unfolding after Zoë Quinn's PII was maliciously posted on 4chan—having to relocate, enduring harassment from the gaming community, receiving a barrage of hateful tweets that resulted in *#gamergate*—demonstrate the severe consequences of doxing (Moyer, 2016; Nieborg & Foxman, 2018). Box 3.1 describes data brokers and their role in compiling PII. Currently, there are no federal laws criminalizing either swatting or doxing; instead, swatters and doxers are prosecuted under other laws (Ellis, 2017; MacAllister, 2017). The first federal swatting case prosecuted in 2008 involved a swatting ring who victimized 100 people in 60 cities between 2002 and 2006, disrupting emergency responders and telecommunication providers and costing the public $250,000 (Federal Bureau of Investigation/FBI, 2008).

BOX 3.1   THE ROLE OF DATA BROKERS IN GATHERING PII FOR DOXING

A variety of techniques are used (e.g., Browser Cookies, Super Cookies, Embedded Scripts) to track and understand website visitors. Internet users provide digital footprints through their online activity and many of their habits can endanger their safety, such as using the same email for every social media site; same username on multiple discussion forums; and/or posting the same/similar content across multiple sites (Christl, 2017; Federal Communications Commission/FCC, 2021; Melendez & Pasternack, 2019). Consequently, personally identifiable information (PII) is easily available to doxers simply by doing public searches for people (e.g., Spokeo, Intelius, White Pages, Whois), credit reports (e.g., Equifax, Experian, TransUnion), or advertisements (e.g., Acxiom, Oracle, Innovis). Third-party data brokers buy, license, or scrape public records as a means of gathering the American public's private information, packaging it, and then selling (and reselling) it without the owner's express permission (Christl, 2017; Melendez & Pasternack, 2019). Doxers can supplement this publicly available data by using it to gather additional information through social engineering techniques (e.g., spear-phishing, direct contact, phone calls), such as clicking on "forgot password" and then using it to answer security questions. If necessary, doxers will hack data by using *packet sniffing* to capture unencrypted information (e.g., passwords, usernames) transmitted online; *analyzing the metadata* in documents and photos from the EXIF/exchangeable image file format; and using *IP logger* to reveal a person's IP address (Rafter, 2021).

TYPICAL ONLINE SWATTERS

Data about known online swatters were derived from different sources, including news articles, research, and announcements of their arrests, charges, plea agreements, and sentencing by the Department of Justice and Attorney's Office, and then aggregated into an appendix and used for this chapter (Ellis, 2017; McKeigue, 2015; Remeika, 2017; Thomas, 2019). As displayed in Table 3.2, demographic information about arrested online swatters in the U.S. indicates that they were predominantly adolescent and young adult ($M = 21.93$ years; Mode $= 19$ years; range 15–43 years) White men. As per the appendix, swatters in 71% of the cases were part of the virtual

Table 3.2 Demographics Based on Known 48 Swatters Listed in the Appendix

Sex		Age				
Male	Female	< 18	18–25	26–43	Alone	Group
$N = 47$ (98%)	$N = 1$ (2%)	$N = 4$	$N = 34$	$N = 10$	14 cases[a]	14 cases

[a] Three swatters (Huffine, Martin, Barriss) had earlier cases that were included in the count.

gaming community acting with other co-conspirators to select and find targets (Fagone, 2015). Online swatters also demonstrated varying levels of internet-savviness, with an individual or members of the group serving in one or multiple roles as the phone phreaker (i.e., fraudulent uses telephone signal for free calls), spoofer, doxer, swatter, and/or live-streamer (Bernstein, 2016; Enzweiler, 2015). However, understanding the demographic characteristics about swatters is hampered by the fact that many of them are not in the official statistics because they were not identified, caught, charged (particularly those who were underaged), prosecuted, and sentenced (Bernstein, 2016; Krebs, 2015). For example, police linked a 12-year-old boy to swatting attacks on the residences of both Ashton Kutcher and Justin Beiber, but they suspected that he was also responsible for a series of other incidents involving high profile victims.[1] Box 3.2 describes a Canadian minor who was involved in an international series of swatting attacks.

BOX 3.2   EXAMPLE OF MINOR SWATTER

British Columbian minor swatter, B.L.A. (handle: Obnoxious), was caught through combined efforts of FBI and Royal Canadian Mounted Police after harassing, hacking, doxing, and swatting victims across North America from 2013 to 2014 (Fagone, 2015; Hurd, 2015). He targeted Disneyland, Simon Fraser University, and public schools with bombing hoaxes, but also committed numerous technology-facilitated abuses against individual players of online games—particularly League of Legends (Fagone, 2015; Shiffer, 2015; Witwer et al., 2020). Adolescent and young adult female gamers who refused his Twitch requests to "follow," chat, or provide obscene images were stalked online, harassed with constant threats, doxed, swatted, hacked, impersonated online, and subjected to distributed denial of service (DDoS) attacks that disrupted their game streaming (Fagone, 2015; Shiffer, 2015). In 2015, the then 17-year-old was sentenced by a British Columbia Judge to 16-month imprisonment and 8-month community supervision and ordered not to interact with his 25 victims in response to his guilty plea for 23 (of the 48 original) charges that included harassment, public mischief, extortion, breach of recognizance, and uttering threats (Greer, 2015).

---

[1] CBSLA.com. (2012, December 18). 12-Year-Old Boy Arrested in Celebrity 'Swatting' Incidents – https://www.cbsnews.com/losangeles/news/young-boy-arrested-in-celebrity-swatting-incidents/.

ONLINE SWATTERS' MOTIVES AND METHODS

The motives behind doxing and swatting were identified primarily as personal animosity/revenge (64%), but also included bragging rights/ego/notoriety; fun/entertaining; and voyeurism (Calabro, 2018; Hoeferkamp, 2019; MacAllister, 2017; McKeigue, 2015; Nellis, 2018). By posting PII publicly, doxers can control, intimidate, humiliate, and physically endanger the target (Moyer, 2016). Swatters who seek revenge may be jealous of another's online fame or talent; want to settle a bet or feud; or get back at someone they perceived harmed them; alternatively, many of them want to boast about the number of people they have targeted (Vogt & Goldman, 2015; Wu, 2015). Swatters may enjoy intimidating, terrorizing, and humiliating targets as a means of empowering themselves as the swatting incident unfolds live or may simply like watching the drama (Nellis, 2018).

The internet provides a platform for doxers and swatters to remain anonymous most of the time while they launch their attack (Bernstein, 2016). First, the swatter *obtains a target's PII*. This is done legally by conducting internet searches (i.e., Google search for property records, announcements, newsletters, web forums, social media pages) and purchasing information from data brokers (i.e., sites that sell compiled information from public and commercial sites) and/or illegally by social engineering strategies and hacking (DHS, 2017; Fagone, 2015; Nellist, 2018). According to Cybersecurity & Infrastructure Security Agency (CISA, 2020), social engineering attacks involve human interactions in which questions are asked to piece together a person's or company's private information and computer access. Forms of social engineering to gather information include *phishing* through email or malicious websites; *vishing* in which voice communications are performed over Internet Protocol (VoIP) and broadcasting services that spoof caller identity; and *smishing* through SMS or text messages containing links to webpages, email addresses, or phone numbers (CISA, 2020). Gamers inadvertently allow doxers and swatters to collect personal information (e.g., IP address, real name, physical location) and publish this information through deanonymizing and targeted doxing because they interact visually and verbally with each other on unprotected third-party chatting platforms, such as TeamSpeak, Skype, Discord, and Mumble (Douglas, 2016; Fagone, 2015; MacAllister, 2017; McIntyre, 2016; Nellist, 2018; Steel, 2021). For example, it is possible to identify a person's IP address by installing a network sniffer on the computer and then watching where Skype routes the communication because the message goes directly to the other party; IP address and sometimes the actual name of the party (if it was used in the registration) is exposed instantly in the packet headers.

Second, the swatter *conceals her/his identity or appears to be another individual.* There are various techniques that can be used, including a *technique* in which phone phreakers/attackers use commercially available apps (e.g., PhoneGangster, Telespoof, Spoofcard) to manipulate caller identification systems and make it appear as though they are calling from a phone number of their choice; or *relay telephone services* for the deaf, hard of hearing, or speech impaired to communicate by typing their messages (Anderson & Klos, 2018; Bernstein, 2016; Enzweiler, 2015; FCC, 2017; Nellist, 2018; Zhao et al., 2008). For example, Spoofcard is available through the Apple store and also contains voice changing technology plus the ability to record calls. Spoofing allows the swatter to pretend to be one or multiple callers—especially the victim and neighbors of the victim—to make it seem like a real emergency (Enzweiler, 2015; Nellist, 2018; Zhao et al., 2008). Alternatively, the swatter can "hide" behind voice-altering technology or even internet proxies, such as VPNs, Tor, teletypewriter/TTY, or IP relay services to obscure her/his voice and computer IP address (Bernstein, 2016).

The final step is to *dial 9-1-1 and falsely report a serious emergency,* such as a hostage situation or bomb threat, that would prompt the operators into sending SWAT. Gamer swatters often prefer their attacks to be live-streamed (e.g., Twitch, YouTube) to increase their targets' humiliation and improve their standing in that community by boasting they have the most elaborate or highest number of swatting hoaxes (Douglas, 2016; Fagone, 2015; McIntyre, 2016; Nellist, 2018; Steele, 2021). The notion of pranking someone in the real world after developing animosity in the gaming world by figuring out the target's location during streaming is called "stream sniping,"[2] and it is the type of toxic and reactionary practice that was routinized in #Gamergate (Nieborg & Foxman, 2018).

TYPICAL ONLINE SWATTING VICTIMS

Targets are typically selected by swatters purposefully, rather than randomly; however, many of the victims in the appendix dataset were not identified (typically because they are minors). Victims may be targeted simply because they are active members online, particularly in the tech or video game industry, online broadcasting community, and activists

---

[2] Witman, E. (2021, January 8). What is stream sniping? Here's what you need to know about the livestream exploitation tactic in gaming, and how to prevent it. https://www.businessinsider.com/what-is-stream-sniping

(Anderson & Klos, 2018). Minecraft server programmer, Wesley Wolfe age 25, was victimized in 2014 presumably in retaliation for issuing a takedown of CraftBukkit from Bukkit (a repository that has open-source Minecraft extension software) which infringed on his software copyright.[3] YouTube gamer Paul Denino (age 23) was victimized multiple times, but most notably he was swatted in April 2017 while live-streaming on a plane from LAX that was forced to land in the Phoenix airport because he was identified as a bombing suspect (Pearson, 2017). When targets are part of the gaming community, many of them are adolescent and young adult men. Women who have an active voice online or make a name for themselves in the gamer community are also targeted through doxing and swatting by misogynist gaming opponents. Two examples of female gamer/developers who were doxed in 2014 are Zoë Quinn, the game creator of Depression Quest and center of the #GamerGate controversy, and Brianna Wu, the co-founder with Amanda Warner of Giant Spacekat (Nieborg & Foxman, 2018).[4] Celebrities—such as Chris Brown, Rihanna, Miley Cyrus, Justin Bieber, Lil Wayne, Charlie Sheen, Russell Brand, Ashton Kutcher, Tom Cruise, Kim Kardashian, Clint Eastwood, and Paris Hilton—are also common targets for swatting (Brumfield, 2013; Burgess, 2017; Ellis, 2017). An examination of the appendix shows that in addition to residences, public schools and colleges are the second most common targets. Offline victims include dealer and trafficking rivals who use swatting as a means of reducing competition or state and federal legislatures (e.g., Rep. Katherine Clark, Senator Chuck Schumer) who became targets after introducing bills to criminalize swatting and doxing (Smith, 2016).

LAWS FOR PROSECUTING ONLINE SWATTING

The types of online harassment and threats involved in the acts of "doxing" and "swatting" can be prosecuted under various federal laws; that is, statutes covering data use and storage and information privacy are

---

[3] Hlavaty, C. (2014, September 12). Video game developer, police run afoul of "swatting" hoax. https://www.chron.com/neighborhood/bayarea/crime-courts/article/Video-game-developer-police-run-afoul-of-5750440.php

[4] Ninja, H. (2014). Game developer Brianna Wu is doxxed, blames #GamerGate. Game Developer Brianna Wu is Doxxed, Blames #GamerGate - Niche Gamer; Vincenty, S. (2014). Zoë Quinn was targeted for abuse online-here's how she's fighting back. https://www.oprah.com/inspiration/zoe-quinn-how-to-stop-online-abuse_1

relevant for doxing, whereas those involving fraud and obstruction are used for swatting (Li, 2018). Three federal laws relevant to doxing include (Doyle, 2014; Li, 2018):

1. 47 U.S.C. § 230. *Communication Decency Act* (CDA), which in its promotion of internet growth advocates a policy that encourages parents to restrict children's access to objectionable or inappropriate online material, as well enforce criminal laws to deter and punish obscenity, stalking, and harassment by means of computer;
2. 18 U.S.C. § 1030 (a)(2). *Fraud and related activity in connection with computers*: this statute criminalizes accessing someone's computer without authorization or in excess of authorization to obtain information or for the purpose of committing fraud; and
3. 18 U.S.C. § 2701. *Unlawful access to stored communications*: this statute criminalizes tampering with stored data controlled by Internet Service Providers (ISPs).

Juvenile doxers and swatters may be subjected to 18 U.S.C. §§ 5031-42 (2009), the *Juvenile Justice and Delinquency Prevention Act,* if the incidents are serious enough to be prosecuted federally instead of by the state (Bernstein, 2016; Doyle, 2018).

There are two main problems with prosecuting offenders for doxing and swatting (Fagone, 2015; Li, 2018). First, these acts often do not align with most or all of the required elements in the current statutes as written. Second, law enforcement tasked with investigating and identifying suspects are not given the necessary tools to do so, which results in victims not getting justice for the crimes perpetrated against them. For example, the current law on obstruction of state or local law enforcement (18 U.S.C. § 1511) does not have an element related to the activity most relevant in swatting—providing false police reports—except when conspiracy can be shown (Li, 2018). Despite the multitude of bills (e.g., H.R. 3670, 2669, 423 Anti-Spoofing Act of 2014, 2016, 2017; S. 1018 Swatting Won't Be Accepted or Tolerate/SWAT Act of 2015; H.R. 2031 Anti-Swatting Act of 2015; H.R. 6478 Interstate Doxxing Prevention Act of 2016; H.R. 4804 Stop Swatting in Our Schools Act of 2016; H.R. 2057 Interstate Swatting Hoax Act) introduced in the House and Senate, only one new statute was created (Li, 2018; Remeika, 2017). The *Truth in Caller ID Act* (Federal Communications Commission, 2019), passed in 2009 with modification effective in 2020, expanded the Communication Act of 1934 to criminalize caller ID spoofing when there is an intent to defraud, cause harm, or wrongfully obtain items of value.

The most successful federal prosecutions of swatting have involved cases in which several incidents were enacted across multiple jurisdictions, with charges being as idiopathic as the facts in the case (Bernstein, 2016). Relevant federal statutes for swatting include:

1. 18 U.S.C. § 875.[5] *Interstate communications*: this criminal statute can be used when the swatter's 911 communication involves threat to kidnap or injure another person (c) with a penalty of up to 5-year imprisonment; extortion of money or anything of value with threat to injure property, reputation of addressee or deceased person, or accuse someone of a crime (b or d) with a penalty of up to 20 years of imprisonment;

2. 18 U.S.C. § 844(e). *Interstate threats involving explosives*: this criminal statute can be used when the swatter's 911 communication involves threats to "kill, injure, or intimidate" or "damage or destroy any building, vehicle, or other real or personal property by means of fire or an explosive," with a penalty of up to 10 years;

3. 18 U.S.C. § 1038. *False information and hoaxes*: this criminal statute can be used when the swatter attempts "to convey false or misleading information" for the purposes of making emergency operators believe that "an activity has taken, is taking, or will take place that would constitute a violation of various statutes" including Chapter 40 § 844 and Chapter 44 § 924 (c)(1)(A) use of a firearm in a violent crime, with a penalty of up to 5 years of imprisonment, up to 20 years if it results in serious bodily harm, and up to life if death occurs.

Additional charges depend on methods used in the doxing and swatting activities, such as computer hacking (i.e., unauthorized access) and fraudulent activity, or when swatter interferes with an investigation or tampers with a witness, would likely refer to these statutes (Bernstein, 2016):

1. 18 U.S.C. § 119. *Protection of individuals performing certain official duties*: this statute criminalizes knowingly releasing private personal information of a person serving in an official capacity (e.g., witness, jury, officer, legislature), or the official's family members, to the public with the intention to threaten, intimidate, or facilitate a violent crime;

2. 18 U.S.C. § 2261A. *Stalking*: this statute criminalizes use of an electronic communication service or interactive computer service to

---

[5] 18 U.S.C. § 876 refers to criminalizing the mailing of threatening communications through post office or its authorized depository, but as it does not indicate phone, computer, or other internet device, it cannot be used to prosecute swatting.

surveil, harass, intimidate, or cause another person to experience emotional distress or fear for safety by self, family, or other;
3. 18 U.S.C. § 1029. *Access device fraud*: this statute criminalizes (a)(1) knowingly and with intent to defraud through production, use, or trafficking in counterfeit access devices; (2) uses unauthorized access devices; ...(4) defrauds through possession of device-making equipment;... (6) without authorization of the issuer of the access device, knowingly and with intent to defraud solicits a person to offer access device or sell information regarding it; (7) uses, produces, traffics in, has control or custody of, or possesses a telecommunication instrument that has been modified or altered to obtain unauthorized use; ...(10) without the authorization of the credit card system member or its agent knowingly and with intent to defraud causes or arranges for another to present... for payment...;
4. 18 U.S.C. § 1343. *Wire fraud*: this statute criminalizes the use of interstate telephone call, wire, or electronic communication in furtherance of the scheme or artifice to defraud another;
5. 18 U.S.C. § 1519. *Federal obstruction of justice*: this statute criminalizes alteration or destruction of tangible objects (aka evidence) relevant to the federal matter with the intent to influence or obstruct a potential or pending investigation; and
6. 18 U.S.C. § 1512. *Tampering with a witness, victim, or an informant*: this statute criminalizes attempts to prevent investigation and prosecution of a crime.

Like the federal statutes listed above, states use similar laws to prosecute perpetrators involved in doxing and swatting. Box 3.3 provides the most relevant California's laws for these cybercrimes (Brumfield, 2013). In addition to California, other states (e.g., Kansas, Michigan, New Jersey) have implemented sentencing guidelines that increase the charges from misdemeanor to felony, and consequently the penalties in terms of fines, restitution, and length of sentencing, when these acts result in death and serious injuries (Brumfield, 2013; Jaffe, 2016).[6] Other states use current laws to charge swatters, such as charging them in Illinois with Disorderly conduct as the statute (Chapter 720 §26-1) includes calling 911 with a false alarm as a Class 3 felony, which has penalties that include 2–5 years imprisonment, fines between $3000 and $10,000, and reimbursing the agency for reasonable costs up to $10,000.[7]

---

[6] Kansas Statutes Chapter 21. Crimes and Punishments §21.3207. https://codes.findlaw.com/ks/chapter-21-crimes-and-punishments/ks-st-sect-21-6207.html
[7] Illinois Statutes Chapter 720. Criminal Offenses § 5/26-1. https://codes.findlaw.com/il/chapter-720-criminal-offenses/il-st-sect-720-5-26-1.html.

BOX 3.3 EXAMPLES OF STATE LAWS USED TO PROSECUTE DOXING AND SWATTING

California Penal Code 646.9: *Stalking*: this statute coincides with doxing when perpetrators willfully, maliciously, and repeatedly followed or harassed another person and made a credible and intentional threat that resulted in a person fearing for safety of self or family members. Penalty is misdemeanor (fine of up to $1000 and/or maximum of 1 year in county jail).

California Penal Code 653.2: *Electronic cyber harassment*: this statute is consistent with doxing through an electronic communication device as a form of harassment (intention to place a person in reasonable fear for safety for self or family members). Penalty is misdemeanor (fine of up to $1000 and/or maximum of 1 year in county jail).

California Penal Code 148.3: *Falsely reporting an emergency*: this statute addresses swatting by criminalizing the reporting of an emergency (i.e., condition results in the first responders; jeopardizes public safety and could result in evacuation; or activation of the Emergency Alert System), or forcing someone else to file a report, knowing it is false. Penalties are a misdemeanor (fine of up to $1000 and/or maximum of 1 year in county jail), unless death or serious bodily harm occurs, in which it becomes a felony (fine up to $10,000 and up to 3 years in jail). An amendment (e), effective January 1, 2014, included liability to a public agency for the reasonable costs of that agency's emergency response (Stats. 2013, Ch. 284, Sec. 1, SB 333).[8]

California Penal Code 148.5: *False report of a criminal offense*: this statute is also relevant to swatting as it criminalizes falsely accusing a person of committing a crime; elements include—made a false statement to law enforcement; knew it was false at the time; and the knowingly false statement accused someone of committing

---

[8] Penal Code, Part 1 of crimes and punishments [25-680.41], Title 7 of crimes against public justice. https://leginfo.legislature.ca.gov/faces/codes_displaySection.xhtml?lawCode=PEN&sectionNum=148.3

a misdemeanor or felony. Penalties are a misdemeanor (fine up to $1000 and up to 6 months in jail).

Prosecutors have also included various conspiracy charges against doxers and swatters, which require proof that two or more people agreed to commit a crime (regardless if it actually occurred) and all of them understood that the crime was the intention of the agreement, typically demonstrated (but not always required) by the performance of an overt (but not necessarily illegal) act by at least one of them (Doyle, 2020). Sometimes conspiracy charges are subsumed under the federal statutes itself, for example: *conspiracy to commit device fraud* or *to use devices to modify telecommunication devices* (see 18 U.S.C. § 1029(b)(2)) and *conspiracy to tamper with a witness, victim or informant* (see 18 U.S.C. § 1512(k)). The following conspiracy charges, however, are covered under separate criminal or civil laws[9]:

1. 18 U.S.C. § 241. *Conspiracy against rights*: Civil law criminalizes conspiracy to injure, threaten, or intimidate someone's exercise and enjoyment of constitutionally protected rights;
2. 42 U.S.C. § 1985. *Conspiracy to interfere with civil rights*: Civil law criminalizes conspiracy to deter, force, intimidate, or threaten any party or witness from testifying to a matter pending; conspiracy to deprive any person from equal protection of the laws, privileges, and immunities under the law; and/or prevent a person holding office from discharging any duties required to be performed or to injure an officer while engaged in the lawful discharge of the duties of office;
3. 18 U.S.C. § 371. *Conspiracy to commit offense or to defraud United States*: broadly criminalizes conspiracy to commit another federal crime, such as §1519 for obstruction or § 875 for extortion; and
4. 18 U.S.C. § 1349. *Conspiracy to commit mail or wire fraud*: criminalizes attempts or conspiracies to commit any scheme or artifice to defraud, or for obtaining money or property by means of false or fraudulent pretenses, representations, or promises... (as related to 18 U.S.C. § 1343).

---

[9] 18 U.S. Code Title 18 –Crimes and criminal procedure. https://www.law.cornell.edu/uscode/text/18; The United States Attorney's Office. (2017). Criminal civil rights laws. https://www.justice.gov/usao-sc/criminal-civil-rights-laws.

IMPACT OF ONLINE SWATTING ON
SOCIETY AND VICTIMS

Swatting impacts society by preventing SWAT personnel from resolving legitimate crises, incurring unnecessary financial costs, and imposing trauma on the victims and SWAT teams (Enzweiler, 2015; Moore, 2020). The main danger of swatting is that it interferes with law enforcement's ability to do its job effectively by redirecting officers from real crimes and emergencies and instilling fear and distrust of law enforcement by the public (Enzweiler, 2015; McKeigue, 2015; Nellist, 2018). The financial cost of swatting cyber hoaxes in wasted resources and workforce salaries (including overtime) is estimated to be between $15,000 to $25,000 dollars (Anderson & Klos, 2018; Moore, 2020; Burgess, 2017; Enzweiler, 2015; Nellist, 2018; Remeika, 2017). A SWAT incident requires *law enforcement*, including SWAT officers to handle the emergency, patrol officers to direct traffic and close roads/highways, bomb squad and dogs to locate explosives; and detectives to investigate; *fire fighters* to assist with evacuation and other related tasks; *paramedics and emergency medical technicians* (EMTs) to render aid and transport victims; and corresponding *department chiefs* to oversee their teams (Hill, 2019; McGinnes, 2016; Marshak, 2017; Moore, 2020).

Swatting affects individual victims and their families, neighbors, and first responders—all of whom may be killed or have permanent injuries as a result (Enzweiler, 2015; Hoeferkamp, 2019; Nellist, 2018; Remeika, 2017). In addition to physical trauma and property damage from the swatting incident, victims also display emotional trauma, such as sleep disruption, suicidal thoughts, and Post Traumatic Stress Disorder (Fagone, 2015; Kershner, 2018; Lopez, 2018). There are also financial consequences in terms of loss of income and legal costs involved in defending themselves from criminal charges and arrest. Victims who earn their living online, such as gaming streamers on Twitch, will lose viewers from the DDoS and swatting attacks which interrupt the streamed game and result in a salary reduction of up to thousands of dollars per month (Fagone, 2015).

CYBERSECURITY TACTICS

The first line in prevention of swatting is educating potential victims (as discussed in Chapter 12 in this volume) and the first responders, including 911 operators. There is some guidance available by the National Emergency Number Association, such as extending the length of the call to help differentiate swatting versus real emergencies by asking specific questions and determining if responses are similar to previous genuine calls (Fruhlinger, 2020; 911.gov, 2015). To prevent victimization, gamers are encouraged to hide their IP addresses through a VPN, keep settings on private, and minimalize personal information provided to other players while engaged in a game (Fruhlinger, 2020). The disadvantage to live gamers using VPN is that it increases latency in the connection. Another fruitful and innovate technique initiated by Seattle—which may be mimicked in other cities—is to notify the police or register your concerns that you may be a potential victim of a swatting hoax (Fruhlinger, 2020).

Various government agencies have published guidelines for good cyber hygiene. The Federal Trade Commission's (FTC, 2021) website provides practical information to learn about identity theft and specific ways to protect your PII from scammers, such as using multi-factor authentication for all of your online accounts and periodically monitor credit and banking activity. The FBI's (2015) public service announcement (I-042115-PSA) describes doxing and swatting while providing advice on how to defend against hacktivism (e.g., request property records be restricted from online searches; routinely update hardware and software applications; do not open links or attachments in suspicious/unknown emails; do not provide PII over the phone or in chats; conduct online searches to determine what data of yours is public). The following steps have been suggested to protect your data:

- limit what you post online, particularly personally relevant information that could compromise you (e.g., physical location, job position) or could be used to guess your security answers;
- use "private" rather than "public" settings on your social media sites, computers and internet devices, wireless networks, etc.;
- phone settings turned in the off position should include—location services, tracking, and GPS;
- minimize your third-party applications for social media, particularly signing into other sites using your social media account, as these extract PII from your profile;
- request to be removed from data brokers;
- initiate cyber security by using two-step verification/authentication practices, use complex passwords that you change regularly, and never use the same, similar, or previous password for more than one account;
- report suspicious emails to your ISP and leaks of your PII on social media to that company with a request to remove it immediately; and
- document threatening emails or other communications and report it to the police (CISA, 2019; DHS, 2017; FBI, 2015; Federal Trade Commission/FTC, 2021).

CISA's (2020) website provides information to the public describing social engineering and phishing attacks (Security Tips ST04–014), common indicators, and advice for avoiding victimization similar to the steps listed above. There are ways you can reduce your digital footprint (Melendez & Paternack, 2019). First, check with companies such as credit bureaus (e.g., Equifax, Experian) regulated by the Fair Credit Reporting Act (FCRA) regarding what they are currently listing and correct whatever is incorrect. If a company is mishandling your data, you may file a complaint with the Federal Trade Commission. Second, opt-out whenever given this option by a company and remove yourself from any company keeping data on you by finding out how to opt-out (i.e., review "filing history," retrieve document under "data broker registration"). For a list of 121 data broker companies that registered after Vermont's law went into effect requiring them to do so, see Melendez and Paternack (2019). By 2018, one of the larger companies, Acxiom, was able to mine data with 10,000 attributes (e.g., demographics including age, sex, education, employment, socioeconomic status, religion; purchases over 2-year period; social media accounts) on 2.5 billion consumers worldwide (Christl, 2017; Melendez & Paternack, 2019).

REFERENCES

911.gov. (2015). *Public Safety Information on "Swatting."* https://www.911.gov/pdf/National_911_Program_Public_Safety_Information_Swatting_2015.pdf.

Anderson, R.B., & Klos, J. (2018). Swatting hack. In B.A. Arrigo (ed.), *The SAGE Encyclopedia of Surveillance, Security, and Privacy.* Thousand Oaks, CA: Sage Publications, Inc. Doi. 10.4135/9781483359922.

Andone, D. (2019). *Swatting is a Dangerous Prank with Potentially Deadly Consequences. Here's What You Need to Know.* CNN. https://www.cnn.com/2019/03/30/us/swatting-what-is-explained.

Bernstein, L. (2016). Investigating and prosecuting swatting crimes. *United States Attorneys' Bulletin, 64*(3), 51–56.

Brumfield, E. (2013). Chapter 284: Deterring and paying for prank 911 calls that generate swat team response. *McGeorge Law Review, 45*(3), 571–580. https://scholarlycommons.pacific.edu/cgi/viewcontent.cgi?article=1040&context=mlr.

Burgess, K. (2017). *"Swatting" is 'a Potentially Deadly Crime' that's Very Common.* https://www.police1.com/officer-shootings/articles/swatting-is-a-potentially-deadly-crime-thats-very-common-M7r3qVw3iX5OQubi/.

Calabro, S. (2018). From the message board to the front door: Addressing the offline consequences of race- and gender-based doxxing and swatting. *Suffolk University Law Review, 51*(1), 55–76.

C.C.I.T. (2020). *Crimes.* https://www.arresttracker.com/crimes.

Christl, W. (2017). *Corporate Surveillance in Everyday Life: How Companies Collect, Combine, Analyze, Trade, and Use Personal Data on Billions.* https://crackedlabs. org/en/corporate-surveillance.

Cybersecurity & Infrastructure Security Agency (CISA). (2019). *Staying Safe on Social Networking Sites.* https://us-cert.cisa.gov/ncas/tips/ST06-003.

Cybersecurity & Infrastructure Security Agency (CISA). (2020). *Avoiding Social Engineering and Phishing Attacks.* https://us-cert.cisa.gov/ncas/tips/ST04-014.

Department of Homeland Security. (2017). *How to Prevent Online Harassment from "Doxxing."* https://www.dhs.gov/sites/default/files/publications/How%20 to%20Prevent%20Online%20Harassment%20From%20Doxxing.pdf.

Douglas, D.M. (2016). Doxing: A conceptual analysis. *Ethics and Information Technology, 18,* 199–210.

Doyle, C. (2014). *Cybercrime: A Sketch of 18 U.S.C. 1030 and Related Federal Crime Laws.* https://fas.org/sgp/crs/misc/RS20830.pdf.

Doyle, C. (2018). *Juvenile Delinquents and Federal Criminal Law: The Federal Juvenile Delinquency Act and Related Matters.* https://www.everycrsreport.com/ reports/RL30822.html.

Doyle, C. (2020). *Federal Conspiracy Law: A Brief Overview. https://sgp.fas.org/crs/misc/ R41223.pdf.*

Ellis, R. (2017). *Swatting Case Poses Legal Challenged for Police, Prosecutors.* https:// www.cnn.com/2017/12/31/us/swatting-legal-ramifications/index.html.

Enzweiler, M.J. (2015). Swatting political discourse: A domestic terrorism threat. *The Notre Dame Law Review, 90*(5), 2001–2038.

Fagone, J. (2015, November 24). The Serial Swatter. *The New York Times. http://www. nytimes.com/2015/11/29/magazine/the-serial-swatter.html?_r=0.*

Federal Bureau of Investigation. (2008). *Don't Make the Call: The New Phenomenon of 'Swatting.'* https://archives.fbi.gov/archives/news/stories/2008/february/ swatting020408.

Federal Bureau of Investigation. (2015). *Hackivists Threaten to Target Law Enforcement Personnel and Public Officials.* https://www.ic3.gov/Media/PDF/Y2015/ PSA150421.pdf.

Federal Communications Commission. (2017, January 17). *Spoofing and Caller ID.* https://www.fcc.gov/consumers/guides/spoofing-and-caller-id.

Federal Communications Commission. (2019). Truth in caller id rules [47 CFR Part 64]. *Federal Register, 84*(169), 45669–45678.

Federal Communications Commission. (2021). *Consumer Information.* How To Protect Your Privacy Online. https://consumer.ftc.gov/articles/how-protect-your-privacy-online.

Federal Trade Commission. (2021). *What to Know about Identity Theft.* https://www. consumer.ftc.gov/articles/what-know-about-identity-theft.

Fruhlinger, J. (2020). *What is Swatting? Unleashing Armed Police against Your Enemies.* https://www.csoonline.com/article/3573381/what-is-swatting-unleashing-armed-police-against-your-enemies.html.

Greer, D. (2015, July 10). *Canadian Teen Who Swatted and Harassed Women Online is Going to Jail.* https://www.vice.com/en/article/ezvwew/canadian-teen-who-swatted-and-harassed-women-online-is-going-to-jail.

59

Hill, D. (2019, December 10). *Police Probe Prank SWAT Call.* http://www.greenfieldreporter.com/2019/12/10/swat-called-out-amid-reports-of-threats/.

Hoeferkamp, J. (2019). Combatting the swatting problem: The need for new criminal stature to address growing threat. *Michigan State Law Review, 2019*(4), 1133–1175.

Hurd, H. (2015, December 17). *Swatter Meets Bulldog, Swatter Loses.* https://www.northfulton.com/news/swatter-meets-bulldog-swatterloses/article_41607169-4495-594d-bc2e-3ce93a11b772.html.

Jaffe, E.M. (2016). Swatting: The new cyberbullying frontier after *Elonis v. United States. Drake Law Review, 64*, 455–553.

Kershner, S. (2018, March 1). Children and swat raids: An unintended consequence. *Worcester Magazine.* https://www.worcestermag.com/2018/03/01/feature-children-swat-raids-unintended-consequence.

Krebs, B. (2015, November 19). *Federal Legislation Targets "Swatting" Hoaxes.* https://krebsonsecurity.com/2015/11/federal-legislation-targetsswatting-hoaxes/.

Li, L.B. (2018). Data privacy in the cyber age: Recommendations for regulating doxing and swatting. *Federal Communications Law Journal, 70*(3), 317–328.

Lopez, G. (2018, June 5). David Hogg's family was swatted. That's extremely dangerous. https://www.vox.com/policy-and-politics/2018/6/5/17429258/david-hogg-swatting-parkland-shooting.

MacAllister, J. M. (2017). The doxing dilemma: Seeking a remedy for the malicious publication of personal information. *Fordham Law Review, 85*(5), 2451–2483.

Marshak, E. (2017). Online harassment: A legislative solution. *Harvard Journal on Legislation, 54*(2), 501–531.

McGinnes, M. (2016, February 18). *Police Believe 'Swatting' Hoax Caused American Legion Highway Closure.* https://www.boston.com/news/local-news/2016/02/18/police-believe-swatting-hoax-caused-american-legion-highway-closure.

McIntyre, V. (2016). Do(x) You really want to hurt me: Adapting IIED as solution to doxing by reshaping intent. *Tulane Journal of Technology and Intellectual Property, 19*, 111–134.

McKeigue, S. (2015, April 24). *Swatting Prank Gains National Attention over Last Seven Years.* University Wire. https://www-proquest-com.ez.lib.jjay.cuny.edu/wire-feeds/swatting-prank-gains-national-attention-over-last/docview/1675309944/se-2?accountid=11724.

Melendez, S. & Paternack, A. (2019, March 2). *Here Are the Data Brokers Quietly Buying and Selling Your Personal Information.* https://www.fastcompany.com/90310803/here-are-the-data-brokers-quietly-buying-and-selling-your-personal-information.

Moore, J. (2020). *Swatting: Tools for Detecting a Deadly Linguistic Prank.* Masters thesis. ProQuest #28092439 https://www.proquest.com/openview/d7b61f56eb6b9d0e1e0deb3ad96f33bd/1?pq-origsite=gscholar&cbl=44156.

Moyer, J. (2016). *Doxing: Dangers and Defenses.* https://www.cs.tufts.edu/comp/116/archive/fall2016/jmoyer.pdf.

Nellist, A. (2018). *Swatting: Protecting the Individual.* Ann Arbor, MI: ProQuest Dissertations. 10935801. ISBN: 9780438466326

Nieborg, D., & Foxman, M. (2018). Mainstreaming misogyny: The beginning of the end and the end of the beginning in gamergate coverage. In J.R. Vickery and T. Everbach (eds.), *Mediating Misogyny: Gender, Technology, and Harassment* (pp. 111–130). New York: Palgrave Macmillan.

Pearson, J. (2017). *Twitch Streamer Gets Swatted Off a Plane.* https://www.vice.com/en/article/ezyyp4/twitch-streamer-gets-swatted-off-a-plane.

Rafter, D. (2021). *What is Doxing?* Doxing: What it is and how to protect yourself | NortonLifeLock.

Remeika, R.J. (2017). *Swatting: A Crime in Search of Law.* Ann Arbor, MI: ProQuest Dissertations. ISBN: 9780355236019

Roth, D.H. (2015, December). *Culture: An Underrated Element in Security Policy.* https://www.gcsp.ch/News-Knowledge/Publications/Culture-AnUnderrated-Element-in-Security-Policy.

Shiffer, J.E. (2015, July 25). *Canadian Teen Sentenced after "Swatting," "Doxxing" across North America.* https://www.startribune.com/canadian-teen-sentenced-after-swatting-doxxing-across-north-america/318537651/.

Smith, IV, J. (2016, February 2). *Massachusetts Rep. Katherine Clark was Swatted for Trying to Criminalize Swatting.* https://ca.movies.yahoo.com/massachusetts-rep-katherine-clark-swatted-222600568.html.

Steele, B. A. (2021, January 12). *FBI Oregon Tech Tuesday: Building a Digital Defense against Smart Device Swatting.* Federal Investigations Bureau Portland. https://www.fbi.gov/contact-us/field-offices/portland/news/press-releases/fbi-oregon-tech-tuesday-building-a-digital-defense-against-smart-device-swatting.

Thomas, J.M. (2019). *Swatting Crimes and Deaths: Stories of This New and Deadly Hoax.* https://www.ranker.com/list/swatting-incidents/jessika-gilbert.

Vogt, P., & Goldman, A. (2015, March 4). *#15 I've Killed People and I Have Hostages.* https://www.gimletmedia.com/reply-all/ive-killedpeople-and-i-have-hostages#episode-play.

Witwer, A.R., Langton, L., Vermeer, M.J.D., Banks, D., Woods, D., & Jackson, B.A. (2020). *Countering Technology-Facilitated Abuse: Criminal Justice Strategies for Combating Nonconsensual Pornography, Sextortion, Doxing, and Swatting.* Santa Monica, CA: RAND Corporation. https://www.rand.org/pubs/research_reports/RRA108-3.html.

Wu, B. (2015, September 18). *Doxxed: Impact of Online Threats on Women Including Private Details Being Exposed and "Swatting."* Doi: 10.1177/0306422015605714.

Zhao, X., Chen, G., & Dong, K. (2008, November 4). *Techniques for Protecting Telephone Users from Caller ID Spoofing Attacks.* https://patents.google.com/patent/US8135119B1/e.

CASES

United States v. Hanshaw, No. 4:13-CR-40018 (D. Mass. 2013).
United States v. Neff, No. 3:1 1-cr-00152 (N.D. Tex. 2013).
United States v. Rosoff et al, No. 3:07-cr-00196 (N.D. Tex. 2008).
United States v. Tollis, No. 3:15-cr-001 10 (D. Conn. 2015).

APPENDIX

DATASET OF KNOWN SWATTERS

(C.C.I.T., 2020; Ellis, 2017; McKeigue, 2015; Remeika, 2017; Thomas, 2019)

Case 1. Desmond Babloo Singh, age 19 at time of crime (Asian)
Crime timeframe and target(s): 2020; Jane Doe.
Description, motive, and consequences: Multitude of communications, impersonation in social media profiles, swatting, and attempted to hire killer; Retribution for rejecting his interest in a romantic relationship.
Charges and sentencing: Indicted on charges of cyberstalking, intentional damage to a protected computer, aggravated identity theft, emailing a (swatting) hoax bombing threat, and murder for hire.[10]

Case 2. Jordan K. Milleson, age 18 and Kyell A. Bryan, age 16, and other unnamed co-conspirators
Crime timeframe and target(s): 2017–2020; Milleson and 6 other unknown victims
Description, motive, and consequences: From 2017 to 2020 set up a fraudulent website, engaged in various social engineering to steal six people's log-in information, and hacking schemes; in 2019 Bryan swatted Milleson for not sharing the $16846 in digital currency they stole.
Charges and sentencing: Charged with 15 counts including wire fraud and conspiracy, unauthorized access to protected computers in furtherance of fraud, intentional damage to protected computers, aggravated ID theft, wire fraud conspiracy[11]; Milleson pled guilty and was given a two-year sentence followed by one-year supervised release and $34,329.01 restitution.

---

[10] Department of Justice. (22 December 2020). New York man arrested on federal charges in Maryland for cyberstalking, attempted murder for hire, and perpetrating false information and hoaxes. https://www.justice.gov/usao-md/pr/new-york-man-arrested-federal-charges-maryland-cyberstalking-attempted-murder-hire-and

[11] Department of Justice. (28 Oct 2020). Two men facing federal indictment in Maryland for scheme to steal digital currency and social media accounts through phishing and "sim-swapping." https://www.justice.gov/usao-md/pr/two-men-facing-federal-indictment-maryland-scheme-steal-digital-currency-and-social-media

Case 3. John William Kirby Kelley, age 19; John Cameron Denton, age 27 (leader of Atomwaffen Division, White supremacist group); Kaleb Cole, age 23; Cameron Shea age 23; Taylor Ashley Parker-Dipeppe, age 19; Johny Roman Garza, age 19 [all White]

Crime timeframe and target(s): 2018–2019; Old Dominion University; other streamers; ProPublica journalist; 2 Black churches; mosque; news columnist; and Kirstjen Nielsen

Description, motive, and consequences: Did not want to go to class; racial animus; antagonize and harass religious and racial communities, LGBTQ community, journalists, and others from 2018 to 2019.

Charges and sentencing: Kelley pled guilty to conspiracy received 33-month sentence in 2021 for his role in managing online chat room where co-conspirators selected targets for 134 swatting calls.[12] Denton pled guilty and received 41-month sentence in 2021.[13] Rest charged with conspiracy to mail threatening communications, stalking, and interfering with federally protected activities: Garza and Parker-Dipeppe pled guilty and will serve 16 months.

Case 4. Sebastian Jarvison, age 25
Crime timeframe and target(s): 2018; Schools
Description, motive, and consequences: FBI received tip for school shooting and bomb threats on Facebook
Charges and sentencing: Charged with interstate commerce communications containing threats to injure[14]

Case 5. John Russell Williams, age 19
Crime timeframe and target(s): 2018; Schools.
Description, motive, and consequences: Replied "let's do it" on Facebook to school shooting threat, among other threats

---

[12] Weiner, R. (15 March 2021). College student who hosted racist online 'swatting' group is sentence to 33 months. https://www.washingtonpost.com/local/legal-issues/atom-waffen-swatting-virginia-sentence/2021/03/15/40e56be6-8277-11eb-9ca6-54e187ee4939_story.html

[13] Department of Justice. (4 May 2021). Former Atomwaffen division leader sentenced for swatting conspiracy. https://www.justice.gov/usao-edva/pr/former-atomwaffen-division-leader-sentenced-swatting-conspiracy

[14] Department of Justice. (23 Feb 2018). Two New Mexico men facing federal charges arising from social media school shooting threats. https://www.justice.gov/usao-nm/pr/two-new-mexico-men-facing-federal-charges-arising-social-media-school-shooting-threats

Charges and sentencing: Charged with interstate commerce communications containing threats to injure[15]

Case 6. Tristan H. Kelly, age 18, and Cody T. Ritchey, age 19
Crime timeframe and target(s): 2018; K.S. (minor)
Description, motive, and consequences: Created snapchat profile of K.S. to post messages suggesting active shooting was imminent at public school.
Charges and sentencing: Both pled guilty to cyberstalking and Kelly was sentenced to 21 months and Ritchey to 27 months in federal prison.[16]

Case 7. Stephen Scott Landes, age 28
Crime timeframe and target(s): 2018; School; Walmart
Description, motive, and consequences: Called in bomb threats for Georgetown school and for Walmart due online feud with Delaware man (Phipps).
Charges and sentencing: Pled guilty to interstate bomb threats and was sentenced to 27 months in federal prison.[17]

Case 8. Nathan Caleb Brown, age 19
Crime timeframe and target(s): 2018; unknown
Description, motive, and consequences: Created Twitter accounts and posted threats, referencing Columbine v2 shooting
Charges and sentencing: Charged with transmitting threats in interstate commerce, denied bail.

Case 9. Timothy Dalton Vaughn, 22 (US, White), George Duke-Cohan, 19 (UK, White), unnamed co-conspirator in UK, members of Apophis Squad, worldwide collective of hackers and swatters)
Crime timeframe and target(s): 2018; 1000s of schools in US and UK, companies, airline, unnamed others; gaming feud motivation for pipe bomb hoaxes.
Description, motive, and consequences: Collective made threatening phone calls; bogus reports of US and UK school attacks through email to

---

[15] Ibid
[16] Department of Justice. (28 Sept 2018). Nicholasville men sentenced to social media threats related to school shooting hoax. https://www.justice.gov/usao-edky/pr/nicholasville-men-sentenced-social-media-threats-related-school-shooting-hoax
[17] *United States v. Landes*, No. 19-3902 (3d Cir. Jan. 20, 2021)

86 districts; false report of hijacking of London to SF flight; and 2018 DDoS attacks on websites requesting 1.5 bitcoin ($20k).

Charges and sentencing: Duke-Cohan received 3-year sentence in the UK and faces extradition to the US; Vaughn pled guilty to one count of conspiracy to convey threats to injure, false info concerning the use of explosive device, and intentional damage a computer and one count of computer hacking and was sentenced to 60 months in 2019 (additional charge of child porn of 200 images and videos resulted in 95-month prison sentence, concurrently).[18]

Cases 10 and 11.
Crime 10. Nicholas Kyle Martino; age 16.
Crime10 timeframe and target(s): 2016; Sul Ross State University, the Big Bend Regional Medical Center, former State Representative Gallego and family.
Description, motive, and consequences: he issued bomb and death threats;
Charges and sentencing: Prosecuted as an adult and pled guilty to four felony accounts of interstate threats to injure persons and was sentenced to time served and 60-month probation.
Crime 11. Nicholas Kyle Martino; age 18.
Crime11 timeframe and target(s): 2018; unnamed girl (S.A.)
Description, motive, and consequences: harassed through hacking and swatting a "cyber girlfriend."
Charges and sentencing: 14 alleged violations of probation resulted in sentencing him to 3 years in prison and 2 years supervised release.[19]

Case 12. Nicholas Huffine, age 17, unnamed co-conspirators/gamers
Crime timeframe and target(s): 2017; unknown (C.N.).
Description, motive, and consequences: to FL Police Dept to report; purpose was revenge due to online gaming dispute; Physical damage to forced entry to residence.

---

[18] Department of Justice. (30 November 2020). Hacker collective member who made online threats against schools and airline sentenced to nearly 8 years in federal prison. https://www.justice.gov/usao-cdca/pr/hacker-collective-member-who-made-online-threats-against-schools-and-airline-sentenced
[19] Walsh, J. (16 Sept 2020). Ruling upholds prison term for Washington township man's probation violations. https://www.courierpostonline.com/story/news/2020/09/15/nicholas-kyle-martino-washington-township-swatting-alpine-texas/5808419002/

Charges and sentencing: Pled guilty to charge of interstate threats and sentenced to 2-year probation (including 8-months home detention) plus $1000 for restitution.[20]

Cases 13–17. Tyler Barriss and co-conspirators
Crime 13. Tyler Barriss, 23.
Crime13 timeframe and target(s): 2015; KABC TV station.
Description, motive, and consequences: Barriss called in a false bomb threat to KABC TV in 2015.
Charges and sentencing: Barriss served a 2-year sentence.
Crime 14–17. Tyler Barriss, 25; Casey Viner, age 18; Shane Gaskill, age 19.
Crime14 timeframe and target(s): 2017; Original target was Shane Gaskill, actual victim was Andrew Finch (age 28).
Description, motive, and consequences: Barriss was asked by Casey Viner (age 19) to swat Shane Gaskill (age 20) because of $1.50 wager in Call of Duty – Gaskill gave Barriss his old address/currently occupied by the Finch family. This hoax resulted in the death of Andrew Finch and Finch family filed civil rights lawsuit against Wichita.
Charges and sentencing: In 2019, **Barriss** pled guilty to 51 charges (bomb threats, false reports) and given 20-year sentence; **Viner** got 15 months for his involvement (conspiracy and obstruction of justice), $2500 restitution, and banned from online games; **Gaskill** received diversion.[21]
Crimes 15–17. Tyler Barriss, 25; Neal Patel, age 23; Tyler Stewart, age 19; and Logan Patten, age 19 [all White]
Crimes15–17 timeframe and target(s): 2017; no victims named plus high schools.
Description, motive, and consequences:
Crime 15. Patel co-conspired with Barriss in 2017 for swat reports in CT and TX;
Crime 16. Stewart co-conspired for false school bomb reports in IL;
Crime 17. Patten hired Barriss to swat individuals in IN and OH and high school in MO. Swatting incidents led to evacuation of high school, but no deaths or injuries reported.

---

[20] Ove, T. (28 June 2021). Dunbar man gets probation in Florida 'swatting' revenge case. https://www.post-gazette.com/news/crime-courts/2021/06/28/Dunbar-man-gets-probation-in-Florida-swatting-revenge-case/stories/202106280100

[21] Department of Justice. (29 March 2019). California man sentenced in deadly Wichita swatting case. https://www.justice.gov/usao-ks/pr/california-man-sentenced-deadly-wichita-swatting-case

Charges and sentencing: All three co-conspirators were charged with conspiracy and making threats to injure in interstate commerce; **Patel** was given 3-year probation with $33,208 in restitution and 300 hours of community service. **Stewart** is still awaiting trial; **Patten** was also charged with conveying false information concerning the use of an explosive device and is awaiting trial, *U.S. v. Patten*, (2:19-cr-00015).

Case 18. Karry Max Taylor, III, age 20
Crime timeframe and target(s): 2016; unknown and Veterans center.
Description, motive, and consequences: Contacted three people in SC and NY advising them of a bomb in the Veterans Affairs Medical Center parking lot, resulting in first responders responding and placing the hospital in lock-down for three hours.
Charges and sentencing: Pled guilty to hoax bomb threat (1038a) and sentenced to 1 year and 1 day imprisonment with 3-year supervised release; restitution to Fire and Police Depts for $1487.77 and $100 special court fee.

Case 19. Rodney Phipps, age 29 [White]
Crime timeframe and target(s): 2015–2017; Multiple unnamed victims, Landes and his wife.
Description, motive, and consequences: Made swat calls in five states; motivation was revenge.
Charges and sentencing: Pled guilty in 2020 with five counts of making interstate threats (claims of murder, shooting, arson, and hostage situations at victim residences) and one count of making a false threat involving explosives; received 37 months in prison.[22]

Case 20. Zachary Lee, age 25, and co-conspirator Robert Walker-McDaid, age 19 of England
Crime timeframe and target(s): 2015; Tyrone Dobbs.
Description, motive, and consequences: Lee asked McDaid to swat T.D. for revenge; Consequences included victim was shot with rubber bullets in chest and face, suffering injuries (e.g., bruised lungs, fractured rib, broken facial bones) requiring three facial reconstruction surgeries, and over 40 officers went to T.D.'s home, remaining there for over 2.5 hours at a cost of $10,000.00.

---

[22] Department of Justice. (4 November 2020). Georgetown man sentenced to 37 months for nationwide swatting incidents. https://www.justice.gov/usao-de/pr/georgetown-man-sentenced-37-months-nationwide-swatting-incidents

Charges and sentencing: Lee pled guilty to conspiracy to provide false information and hoax related to cause emergency service response and was sentenced to 2 years.[23]

Case 21. Zachary Lee Morgenstern, age 19 [White]
Crime timeframe and target(s): 2014–2015; Oct 7 2014 against H.M., male minor; Jan 6, 11 & 19, 2015 against D.R., male age 17; Feb 16, 2015 against I.W., male age 13; April 20, 2015 against SRO family.
Description, motive, and consequences: Pattern of swatting from 2014 to 2015 against multiple victims at their homes, school bomb threats, and death threats against the family of the School Resource Officer.
Charges and sentencing: Pled guilty to 1 count of threats to kill and sentenced on Dec 22 2015 to 41 months in prison and 3 years supervised release.[24]

Case 22. Matthew Tollis, age 21 (part of Microsoft X-Box gamer group called TCOD, TeAM CrucifiX or Die); co-conspirators live in the UK, including the founder.
Crime timeframe and target(s): 2014; UConn; Boston Convention & Exhibition Center; Boston U; 2 NJ and 1 TX high schools.
Description, motive, and consequences: At least six swatting incidents involving multiple states; UConn bomb threat caused 3-hour lockdown and response by UConn Police, CT State Police Bomb Squad, ESU, and SWAT.
Charges and sentencing: In 2015, pled guilty to conspiring to engage in malicious conveying of false info (Bomb threat hoax) and sentenced to 1 year in prison, 3 years of probation, and 300 hours of community service.[25]

Case 23. Brandon Willson, age 19
Crime timeframe and target(s): 2014; unnamed victims.

---

[23] Department of Justice. (7 November 2017). Catonsville man pleads guilty to conspiracy in "swatting" incident. https://www.justice.gov/usao-md/pr/catonsville-man-pleads-guilty-conspiracy-swatting-incident

[24] Department of Justice. (7 August, 2015). Houston, Texas-area teenager pleads guilty to swatting and making bomb threats to Minnesota high school. https://www.fbi.gov/contact-us/field-offices/minneapolis/news/press-releases/houston-texas-area-teenager-pleads-guilty-to-swatting-and-making-bomb-threats-to-minnesota-high-school

[25] U.S. Attorney's Office. (6 October 2015). Wethersfield man sentenced to prison term for involvement in multiple swatting incidents. https://www.fbi.gov/contact-us/field-offices/newhaven/news/press-releases/wethersfield-man-sentenced-to-prison-term-for-involvement-in-multiple-swatting-incidents

Description, motive, and consequences: Informed 911 that Naperville, IL house contained explosives, hostage situation, and shot girlfriend; hacked gaming consoles to obtain PII from two individuals; threatened a Naperville resident he would access bank and social security accounts to cause father to become indebted.

Charges and sentencing: Arrested in Feb 2015 and charged with computer tampering, computer fraud, and identity theft for several swatting incidents and hackings of gamers whose personal information he possessed.

Case 24. Nathan Hanshaw,[26] age 22, gamer, unemployed h.s. dropout [White]
Crime timeframe and target(s): 2012–2013; Victims in Canada and in US (CO; CA, NY) were gamers.

Description, motive, and consequences: Used spoofing, indicated he was an armed fugitive with hostages who would detonate bombs and kill hostages and law enforcement if he was not given cash and helicopter ride to Mexico; CA incident required more than 40 law enforcement, hotel was evacuated, and streets were closed for hours.

Charges and sentencing: Pled guilty to three counts of interstate threats, threats to use explosives, and threats to use a firearm and received 30-month sentence (20 months added for violating terms of juvenile case to be served concurrently) plus 3-year supervised release.[27]

Case 25. Mir Islam, age 21 (Naturalized US citizen) (with multiple, unnamed co-conspirators).

Crime timeframe and Target(s): 2013; Multiple unnamed victims, including 20 celebrities and officials who swatting victims and 50 celebrities and officials who were doxing victims (i.e., their personal identifying information/ PII was posted on Exposed.su website) and a female college student.

Description, motive, and consequences: Entertainment purposes, but also for revenge and to gain notoriety.

Charges and sentencing: July 2016, he was given 2-year sentence for guilty plea to one count of various federal offenses (identity theft, access device fraud, social security misuse, computer fraud, wire fraud, interstate

---

[26] He was previously convicted as juvenile for swatting and sentenced to 11-months in prison and was involved in hacking into corporate computer system in 2008.

[27] Croteau, S.J. (2013). Athol man gets 30 months for 'swatting.' https://www.telegram.com/article/20131029/NEWS/310299683

threats), one count of threatening and conveying false information, and one count of cyberstalking. committed Feb through Sept 2013.[28]

Case 26 Ashton Lundeby, age 18, and unnamed co-conspirators
Crime timeframe and target(s): 2009; Various colleges, schools, and FBI agents.
Description, motive, and consequences: In January 2009, Lundeby called in bomb threat to Indiana University police; In February 2009, Lundeby and others called in bomb threats to Purdue University police; January through March 2009, group called in hoax bomb threats to various colleges, schools, and FBI offices.
Charges and sentencing: Pled guilty to conspiracy to commit one or more offenses against the US by willfully making threats and maliciously conveying false info and sentenced to 22 months imprisonment and 3 years supervised release, plus restitution of $1892.70 to police, $7806.38 to prosecutor, and $19517.47 to district school.

Case 27. Randall Ellis, age 19 [White]
Crime timeframe and target(s): 2007; Doug and Stacey Bates and children; unnamed victims.
Description, motive, and consequences: Randomly selected 185 targets using Dex-line (service provides contact information) and spoofed the target's number. March 29 2007 Bates family swatting in CA cost the county $20,000.00.
Charges and sentencing: Ellis was charged with assault with a deadly weapon, false imprisonment, filing a false report, and misuse of the internet and received a three-year sentence.[29]

Case 28. Jeffrey Lynn Daniels, age 43; Matthew Weigman, age 15; Chad Ward age 32; Jason Allen Neff, age 35; Guadalupe Martinez, age 31; Stuart Rosoff, age 32; Jason Trowbridge; Angela Roberson (Trowbridge's girlfriend); Carlton Nalley, age 31; Sean Paul Benton, age 21; Bryan Barnett, and at least 9 others were part of ring (listed as: Dialtone; JDT).

---

[28] Department of Justice. (11 July, 2016). New York man sentenced to 24 months in prison for internet offenses, including "doxing," "swatting," making a false bomb threat, and cyberstalking.https://www.justice.gov/usao-dc/pr/new-york-man-sentenced-24-months-prison-internet-offenses-including-doxing-swatting; Krebs, B. (11 July 2016). Serial swatter, stalker, and doxer Mir Islam gets just 1 year in jail. https://krebsonsecurity.com/2016/07/serial-swatter-stalker-and-doxer-mir-islam-gets-just-1-year-in-jail/
[29] Garrett, R. (2009). Sighting in swatting. Sighting in swatting | Officer

Crime timeframe and target(s): 2004–2008; 250 unnamed victims mainly from the party line (SP, Beth); Stephanie Proulx.

Description, motive, and consequences: Ring is connected to at least 60 incidents, indicating motives were revenge (refusing sex) and for fun; Daniels created software for telephone chat/party line that he knowingly allowed swatting conspiracy members to use without reporting their illegal activity and advised Weigman how to swat, plus impeded FBI investigation by concealing electronic data on Ward's cellphone; Neff intimidated a witness (obstruction); Trowbridge accessed PII; Neff, Martinez, Rosoff, and Weigman were charged for their role as *phone phreakers* who used social engineering to gain PII, which was used to alter billing and service plans, discontinue service, and monitor and tape lines; Nally used spoof cards, made threats, and obtained credit cards; losses estimated to be $120,000–$250,000.

Charges and sentencing: **Daniels** received 84-month sentence in 2016 for guilty plea to swatting conspiracy and resisting arrest; **Neff** pled guilty and received 60-month sentence in 2015 and ordered to pay $79,440.00 in restitution; **Weigman** pled guilty to computer intrusion and witness intimidation and received 135- months sentence in 2009 (FBI reported he had previously swatted home of girl in 2005 who refused to have phone sex with him); **Martinez** and **Roberson** pled guilty and each received 30-month sentences in 2008; **Trowbridge** and **Rosoff** were each sentenced to 60 months in 2008; and **Ward** pled guilty and received 60-month sentence in 2008 and restitution of $24000.00. **Nalley** pled guilty of conspiracy to retaliate against a witness, conspiracy to commit access device fraud and unauthorized access of a protect computer and sentenced in 2009 to 108 months; **Barnett** received a 10-year sentence; **Benton** pled guilty to conspiring to obstruct justice and was sentenced in 2009 to 18 months.[30]

---

[30] Department of Justice.(9 Jan. 2015). Man sented to serve a total of five years in federal prison in swatting case. https://www.justice.gov/usao-ndtx/pr/man-sentenced-serve-total-five-years-federal-prison-swatting-case; Department of Justice. (3 August 2016). Man who absconded while under indictment in "swatting" case, is arrested, pleads guilty and is sentenced to serve 84 months in federal prison. https://www.justice.gov/usao-ndtx/pr/man-who-absconded-while-under-indictment-swatting-case-arrested-pleads-guilty-and; U.S. Attorney's Office (29 July 2014). Man faces five years in federal prison in 'swatting' case. https://www.fbi.gov/contact-us/field-offices/dallas/news/press-releases/man-faces-five-years-in-federal-prison-in-swatting-case; Department of Justice. (2009). Last defendant sentenced in swatting conspiracy. https://www.justice.gov/archive/usao/txn/PressRel09/nalley_swat_sen_pr.html

4

Internet Trolls

DEFINING INTERNET TROLLING

Internet trolling refers to a set of malicious practices that include baiting, provoking, agitating, luring, controlling, offending, flaming,

DOI: 10.4324/9781003092292-4

harming, and humiliating targets (Coles & West, 2016; Markey, 2013; Ortiz, 2020; Tsantarliotis et al., 2017). These strategies are effective in accomplishing the goals of forcing the victim into pointless, time-consuming defensive explanations; creating hostile environments that discourage different points of view; redirecting or interrupting the topic of conversation; influencing opinions; and causing harm to group members for the purpose of amusing the troll (Coles & West, 2016; Markey, 2013; Mihaylov et al., 2018). Trolling can be enacted by individual Internet users, bots, or state sanctioned groups (e.g., Internet Research Agency (IRA)) and is characterized by: *deception* (behaviors online are inconsistent with offline behavior), *aggression* (purposefully annoying or inciting retaliation), *disruption* (attention-seeking interference within online discussion), and *success* (achieving provocation of target or withdrawal from the site) (Aro, 2016; Bradshaw & Howard, 2017; Craker & March, 2016; Hardaker, 2010; Jalonen & Jussila, 2016; Llewellyn et al., 2019; Sest & March, 2017).

To understand prevalence of trolling, it is necessary to consider the base rate of how many users are online who could potentially be perpetrators. Social media platforms accessed through computers and apps currently allow billions of people to interact with little oversight to curb antisocial behaviors, such as those associated with trolling (Craker & March, 2016; Pew Research Center, 2016). As of January 2021, there were 4.7 billion Internet users (60% of the global population), most of whom (90%) were active on social media (Daskal et al., 2020; Johnson, 2021). Online gaming site users totaled at least 2.7 billion as of December 2020 (Newzoo, 2020) and media discussion board users were in the millions, depending on the site—such as 20 million monthly on 4chan and 52 million daily users on Reddit (Smith, 2021; Redditinc.com, 2021). Researchers indicate that 19%–28% of Americans performed acts consistent with being a troll (Golf-Papez & Veer, 2017; Kleinman, 2014). However, prevalence estimates for trolling victimization vary due to underreporting and differences in a person's recognition of trolling versus other online behaviors, such as harassment or stalking; definition and methods used for assessment; and the respondents (e.g., college students, news discussion board users) being studied (Bishop, 2013; Case & King, 2018).

TYPICAL INTERNET TROLLS

Official statistics do not exist because "trolling" itself is not illegal (Bishop, 2013; Butler et al., 2009). There is evidence that trolls in the U.S. are predominantly male, White, millennials who espouse main-stream attitudes (Ferenczi et al., 2017; Gammon, 2014; Kleinman, 2014; Phillips, 2013). Like their college student peers, high school student trolls are also likely to be users of online gaming and social media sites; for example, one-third of 14–18-year-olds admitted to trolling within the past 6 months (Case & King, 2018; Hong & Cheng, 2018; Rice, 2013). *Situational factors* influence who will become an online troll, such as being lulled by the anonymity of the Internet; lowered risk of being identified; groupthink mentality bolstered by disinhibition or the Gyges effect (i.e., lowered self-awareness and inhibition) to act in a counter-normative manner; and failure by online guardians to pun-ish attacks that dehumanize victims (Bishop, 2013; Centre for Strategy & Evaluation Services, 2019; Ekstrand, 2018; Hardaker, 2015; Paananen & Reichl, 2019; Shin, 2008; Suler, 2004). *Psychological factors* are also rel-evant as researchers indicate that trolls exhibit personality disorders and "dark tetrad" personality characteristics—sadism, psychopathy, Machiavellianism, and narcissism (Bishop, 2013; Buckels et al., 2014; Craker & March, 2016; Lopes, 2017; March & Steele, 2020; Seigfried-Spellar & Chowdhury, 2017; Sest & March, 2017; Suler, 2004; Zezulka & Seigfried-Spellar, 2016). Trolls who are sadistic enjoy physically and/or psychologically harming others, including cruelty displayed in one's culture (e.g., violent films, police brutality), whereas those who exhibit psychopathy are callous, deceitful, and irresponsible (Centre for Strategy & Evaluation Services, 2019; March & Steele, 2020). Trolls who exhibit Machiavellianism will manipulate, deceive, and exploit others to serve their own self-interested goals, whereas narcissist trolls attempt to control others due to their need to be admired and wor-shipped, sense of entitlement, and lack of empathy (Centre for Strategy & Evaluation Services, 2019; March & Steele, 2020). Table 4.1 displays common troll types, but this list is not inclusive of every possible one identified (Coles & West, 2016; Hardaker, 2013; Phillips, 2015; Sanfilippo et al., 2017; Seigfried-Spellar & Chowdhury, 2017).

Table 4.1   Description of Different Types of Trolls

Troll Types	Description
Care	Troll manufactures abusive behavior within posts against a person or animal.
Fame	Troll uses social media to provoke celebrities.
Hater	Troll fixates on an issue or person.
Kudos	Troll posts seemingly complimentary, but irrelevant information for entertainment.
Patent	Troll will post content in order to get paid.
Political	Troll posts in effort to get political candidate or incumbent to resign from office.
Professional	Public figures whose careers were developed through the posting of negative and disrespectful comments [trollumnists are professional writers who engage in this practice].
RIP	Troll will post obnoxious comments on memorial sites.
Snert[a]	Troll will post posts that violate an ISP terms of service against harassment, vulgarity, and scrolling, particularly on game sites, that ruins others' fun.
Social	Troll posts as a way of belonging to a group.
Subculture	Troll posts comments and questions for the purpose of derailing conversations and upsetting many people using various linguistic and behavioral tools.
Wikipedia	Troll revises pages in Wikipedia, an online open-source encyclopedia.

[a] Snert can refer to Someone Needing Enlightenment Regarding TOS/terms of service or Sexually Needy Emotionally Retarded Troll.

INTERNET TROLLS' MOTIVES AND METHODS

Various motives by individuals, groups, and state agents have been identified by researchers (Aro, 2016; Binns, 2012; Bradshaw & Howard, 2017;
Coles & West, 2016; Fichman & Sanfilippo, 2015; Hardaker, 2010, 2015;
Özsoy 2015; Petykó, 2018; Sanfilippo et al., 2017; Shachaf & Hara, 2010;
Thacker & Griffiths, 2012; Tsantarliotis et al., 2017), including financial;
political; attention; social (e.g., engagement with others); revenge; personal
(e.g., control and empowerment; sadism; malevolence; and fun or enter-
tainment at another's expense). Table 4.2 shows troll actions (Binns, 2012;
Ekstrand, 2018; Galán-García et al., 2014; Hardaker, 2010; Morrissey, 2010;
Thacker & Griffiths, 2012; Tsantarliotis et al., 2017) that violate interactional

Table 4.2 The Acts by Trolls Used to Fulfill Their Goals

Actions	Goals					
	Attract Attention	Trigger Negative Emotion	Disrupt Discussion, Silence Users	Deception or Manipulation	Enlist Others	Increase Conflict/ Pointless Debate
Repeat utterance	×	×	×			×
Introduce irrelevant/ meaningless content	×	×	×			×
Provide dangerous or bad advice through impersonation of experts	×	×	×	×		
Taunt, mock, and bully users	×	×	×		×	×
Make hypocritical criticism by attacking values	×	×	×	×	×	×
Flame/insult/ threaten/mock/ shock/discredit in aggressive way	×	×	×		×	×

norms to achieve their desired goals (Hardaker, 2010, 2013; Herring et al., 2002; Morrissey, 2010; Shachaf & Hara, 2010; Utz, 2005). Trolls whose comments are humorous, playful, or praising of member's insights, in seemingly *entertaining* or *supportive* ways, are tolerated by online communities (Ortiz, 2020; Phillips, 2013). For example, in frustration over House Speaker, Paul Ryan, refusing to counter President Trump on various issues, a Wikipediatroll added him as a category on the "invertebrates" page (Gilmer, 2018).

According to Markey (2013), the main strategy by trolls is harassment, which is implemented through *doxing* (releasing personal information), *googlebombing* (ensuring the terms will be in the results by repeatedly searching it), *threatening* (frightening victims with words and pictures, especially deep fakes of pornography), *hacking* (accessing the victim's Internet devices and taking information from them), and *Denial of Service* attacks launched to crash a victim's computer and/or prevent access to it. Trolls use *memes* in strategic ways to spread misinformation (false content) and disinformation (content intentionally created and spread to mislead), mainly because they are easily relatable and amusing (Klepper, 2020; Stringhini & Zannettou, 2020). For example, propaganda Russian trolls of the IRA used memes as part of a sophisticated operation to suppress African American votes and boost Trump's 2016 presidential candidacy (Barrett, 2018; Stringhini & Zannettou, 2020). Trolls manipulate public opinion by spreading lies, conspiracy theories, and exaggerations through social or political *bots* (autonomous programs) that repost their message content hundreds of times daily (Centre for Strategy & Evaluation Services, 2019; Klepper, 2020). Finally, attention-seeking trolls will *"hijack"* *hashtags* by distorting its meaning to promote a completely different concept and redirect the current audience (Campbell, 2019).

The length and intensity of the attacks depend on the troll's style. Bishop (2013) identified four types: (1) *playtime trollers* who play a simple, short game; (2) *tactical trollers* who create credible personas which they use to lure victims and induce strife in indirect and unpleasant ways; (3) *strategic trollers* who play a long game, developing and honing their strategies over time; and (4) *domination trollers* whose strategies are based on constructing and running lists and discussion forums. Trolls favor specific online locations, particularly platforms that provide a discursive element—such as media discussion forums (e.g., newspapers, magazines, encyclopedias), social networking sites, games, and government petition pages—usually as these Internet sites allow anonymous posting and/or are poorly monitored (Bratu, 2017; Cheng et al., 2017; Cook et al., 2018; Coles & West, 2016; Hardaker, 2015; Jussinoja, 2018; Mihaylov et al., 2018; Scott & Griffiths, 2012; Sest & March, 2017). Gammon (2014) reported that online trolling was found most often in chat rooms (45%), social media sites (39%), and blogs (39%). Case and King (2018) found that certain sites had high rates of trolling— YikYak (82%, now defunct) and 4chan (67%); moderate rates—Twitter (29%), Instagram (17%), Reddit (16%); or low rates—Google+ (6%), Tumblr (6%), YouTube (5%). Daily Internet trolling was indicated by 38% for social media, 23% for videos/vlogs, 15% for entertainment/ news, and 13% for blogs and for chat boards (Kunst, 2019).

TYPICAL INTERNET TROLL VICTIMS

The likelihood that someone will be targeted depends on the person's online exposure. Victims most often affected by online trolls include those who belong to one or more of these categories: women, ethnic minorities, and young adults aged 18–29 years (Case & King, 2018; Duggan, 2014; Morrison, 2015; Paananen & Reichl, 2019). Individual posters may become targets if their content is counter to mainstream stereotypes, including information that expresses liberal ideas, beliefs accepting of diversity, promotion of advancement for everyone, or any other concept that does not defer to male superiority, heterosexuality, conservative, and White entitlement (Ekstrand, 2018; Paananen & Reichl, 2019). Other potential targets include those in marginal groups, such as people with intellectual disabilities, those who identify as LGBTQI (Lesbian, Gay, Bisexual, Transgender, Queer, Intersexed), and those belonging to minority religions (e.g., Muslim); political candidates and incumbents; and companies whose competition pays trolls to attack their products (Centre for Strategy & Evaluation Services, 2019). Victims may rationalize that trolling is simply how the Internet operates and/or trolls are merely expressing their ideologies as per their first amendment rights (Sanfilippo et al., 2018). They may be lured into toxic (e.g., immune to rudeness, criticism, dark thoughts) or benign (e.g., secret fears and emotions) disinhibition, increasing the likelihood of being selected as targets (Binns, 2012).

LAWS FOR PROSECUTING INTERNET TROLLING

There are no federal or state laws criminalizing trolling. Instead, victims may use criminal laws in their states against cyber harassment, cyberstalking, and cyberbullying (Markey, 2013). Another option is to apply for civil relief, such as through torts—if these meet a prima facie standard (Markey, 2013). *Defamation* requires (1) publication of a (2) false statement that (3) causes harm to a person's reputation (§ 558[b], Restatement Second of Torts 1977). Basically, the Court must balance the first amendment rights to free speech with a person's reputation (Davis & Magaldi, 2019; Kuehl, 2016). There are four types of privacy torts (§§ 652A–652I, Restatement Second of Torts 1977). *Public disclosure* must include (1) the person publicized an aspect of the other's private life (2) to which he/she did not consent and (3) which is considered highly offensive to a reasonable person and not of legitimate public concern. *Intrusion* requires there is (1) a physical or other intrusion (2) into a zone in which the other has a reasonable expectation of privacy (3) which is highly offensive to the reasonable person. If the troll impersonates the victim, then the tort of right of *publicity infringement* or *appropriation* requires (1) unauthorized (commercial or otherwise) use (2) of a person's name, likeness, voice, or other indicia of identity resulting in injury. *False light* requires (1) a public statement (2) made with actual malice (3) placing the other in a false light before the public (4) that is highly offensive to the reasonable person. In limited circumstances, victims may be able to charge website operators who host trolls with liable (Rogers, 2015). For example, magazines have been sued when libelous attacks occurred on their online communities (Binns, 2012).

It is difficult, however, to hold social media platforms liable for third-party content on their sites as these entities are protected by the Communications Decency Act of 1996. Consequently, any attempt by the government to censor online forums is considered a violation of users' first amendment rights to free speech (Daskal et al., 2020). As shown in Box 4.1, there are three U.S. liability cases of cyberlibel against speech posted on computer bulletin boards that have guided Court decisions (Johnson & Gelb, 2002). Through these cases, the Court established that only third-party posters can be held liable for libel, except when the host serves as a publisher by its ability to modify the posts rather than a distributor. In lieu of expensive lawsuits, victims who can show that social media posts are clearly defamatory should consider alternative remedies, such as temporary restraining orders, preliminary injunctions, and/or pressure social media providers to create mechanisms to report and request removal of defamatory content (Davis & Magaldi, 2019).

**BOX 4.1 THREE CYBER LIBEL CASES
AGAINST SPEECH IN THE U.S.**

Cubby, Inc. v. CompuServe Inc., 776 F. Supp. 135 (S.D.N.Y. 1991). CompuServe owned and self-operated multiple independent sites in which Cubby, Inc. claimed defamatory comments were posted on the "Rumorville" forum of an electronic gossip magazine called "Skuttlebut." The Court ruled that CompuServe was not liable because postings by third parties were not reviewed only distributed. As per a series of landmark cases (e.g., *Smith v. California, N.Y. Times v. Sullivan*), if the carrier or distributor did not have knowledge of the libel, it cannot be held liable.

    Stratton Oakmont v. Prodigy (1995). Porush, the president of investment securities firm Stratton Oakmont, Inc., sued the network service provider for libelous claims on a public online forum. The Court agreed with the plaintiff that Prodigy was a publisher rather than a distributor as it retained its right to edit, remove, and filter posts consistent with its online "family" environment. That is, publishers are held to the same level of liability as the poster of the defamatory statement if they review, had the option of reviewing, or hold editorial control over the content.

    Zeran v. America Online (1996). Zeran, a victim of a malicious hoax in which advertisements promoting the Oklahoma City bombing were published along with his contact information on America Online. His lawsuit against American Online was the result of their failure to act after he notified the company of the hoax and had received multiple threats and harassment as a result of this impersonation. The Court ruled in America Online's favor, citing the Communications Decency Act protection of Internet Service Providers (ISPs) for hosting third-party postings. As ISPs are passive conduits that provide readers the content over which they hold not editorial control, they are not liable for false statements made by the poster.

Victims whose trolls post anonymously have difficulty pursuing online defamation suits (Kuehl, 2016; Shuntich & Vogel, 2018). Many states have short periods for statutes of limitation in defamation, all of which are likely to run the clock down (Kuehl, 2016; Shuntich & Vogel, 2018). First, as per the *single publication rule*, victims have one year after the comment was posted rather than when s/he learned about it. Second, the process of identifying the John Doe through E-discovery and serving subpoenas on technology companies have a short window as per the *Stored Communications Act*. States typically apply tests to determine whether to grant a victim's motion to identify anonymous posters, including "(1) good faith showing, (2) balancing test, and (3) summary judgment test" (Davis & Magaldi, 2019, p. 178). It must be clear that the victims can provide facts supporting their defamation claims as having merit (relevant to good faith and summary judgment); sufficient notice was made to poster (balancing identifying the troll against first amendment rights); and the identity is needed for the suit, particularly in being able to collect money judgments (Davis & Magaldi, 2019). Anonymous trolls may countersue their victims through a SLAPP (Strategic Lawsuit Against Public Participation) motion (available in 31 states and D.C. as of June 2021), claiming that they are being burdened with legal fees as a means of censoring them (Vining & Matthews, n.d.).

IMPACT OF INTERNET TROLLING ON SOCIETY AND VICTIMS

Trolls harm society by creating hostile environments in online communities by disrupting or prematurely ending the discussion, polarizing ideas in posts to limit diversity in opinions, discourage new members from joining, and instigating attacks of victims offline (Coles & West, 2016; Dahlberg, 2001; Herring et al., 2002; Markey, 2013). The danger from state-controlled (paid) trolls (e.g., China's Fifty Cent Army, Russia's IRA) to various countries' political and economic stability has become apparent as these propaganda generators have swayed people's opinions on a number of important issues (Barrett, 2018; Bradshaw & Howard, 2017; Broniatowski et al., 2018; Fedasiuk, 2021; Llewellyn et al., 2019; Mihaylov et al., 2018; Stringhini & Zannettou, 2020), such as *European referendums* (e.g., Brexit) and *U.S. elections*. Box 4.2 provides an overview of the sophisticated plan implemented by IRA to influence the 2016 U.S. presidential election (Aro, 2016; Bradshaw & Howard, 2017; DiResta et al., 2018). Trolls may also harm companies and/or their brands financially, especially by denigrating products, sullying corporate reputations, and causing mental distress to the company managers who respond to customers (The Australia Institute, 2019; Golf-Papez & Veer, 2017). Patent trolls cause companies to lose billions of dollars in Court costs for frivolous lawsuits, damages, and

BOX 4.2   INTERNET RESEARCH AGENCY PLOT FOR INFLUENCING THE 2016 U.S. PRESIDENTIAL ELECTION

In 2016, the IRA launched a three-prong attack on our democracy: (1) access voting systems; (2) cyber-attack the Democratic National Committee; and (3) coordinate social influence operation to divide U.S. citizens and affect their political decisions (DiResta et al., 2018). The latter will be described as it provides a good example of how IRA trolling in social media (e.g., Twitter; Facebook and Instagram; Google-Alphabet and YouTube; Vine; Meetup), browsers (e.g., Google and Gmail), music apps, news sites and blogs (e.g., Medium, Reddit, Tumblr), and games (Pokémon Go) impacted our society starting in January 2015 (Bradshaw & Howard, 2017; DiResta et al., 2018). The IRA, like non-state trolls, were able to create and then use their false personas to develop assets and launch attacks through, memes, conspiratorial narrative, hashtags, media, and cross-platform branding (Aro, 2016; Bradshaw & Howard, 2017; DiResta et al., 2018).

Here is the how Russian trolls influenced our 2016 election:

- Targeting candidates and political figures through Twitter and Facebook by using memes, ads, and posts
  - Posting pro-Trump messages
  - Posting anti-Hillary Clinton messages
  - Posting messages to increase/decrease support for various politicians related to media stories
- Sowing discord through hashtags and cross-platform brand building
  - Planting ideas of secession and insurrection to further dissonance among groups against the government, and
  - Eroding trust for mainstream media.
- Inducing voter suppression through Twitter, Facebook, Instagram, and YouTube
  - Misdirecting through tweets to confuse voters about rules;
  - Redirecting votes to a third-party candidate; and
  - Convincing people that their vote would not matter, which decreased voting turn out.

83

profits (Bessen, 2014). The national economy is also negatively impacted due to millions of dollars in associated costs for health care and loss of income (The Australia Institute, 2019).

As a result of online trolling, individual victims may suffer severe distress resulting in psychological and physical consequences, such as depression, sleep problems, and negative emotions and disillusionment about their identity, self-esteem, and beliefs; detrimental social effects on their personal interactions and relationships, including withdrawing from socialization; or consider suicide and other self-harm behaviors (Bentley & Cowan, 2021; Centre for Strategy & Evaluation Services, 2019; Coles & West, 2016; Hong & Chen, 2018; Markey, 2013). For example, victims suffer when the troll provokes them with mind games that induce extended and pointless arguments and escalated conflict (Hong & Chen, 2018; Tsantarliotis et al., 2017), particularly when power is the trolls endgame (Maltby, 2016). Victims lose their online voices because the fear of being targeted makes them change how they interact with community members by vetting responses, toning down the wording in discussion threads, and avoiding hot issues (Eckert, 2017). Financial costs for victims include attorney fees for civil lawsuits; physical and mental health care expenses; lost income; costs for repairing property they may have been tricked into destroying (e.g., microwaving computers to kill virus); and sometimes for defending themselves from false criminal charges (The Australia Institute, 2019; Golf-Papez & Veer, 2017; Hutchinson, 2015).

CYBERSECURITY TACTICS

Three strategies to combat online trolling include: (1) artificial intelligence mechanisms or algorithms (i.e., sorting through comments to search for key terms); (2) human-based interventions (e.g., vetting comments, ignoring flaming, reporting abuse to ISPs); and (3) legal remedies (Centre for Strategy & Evaluation Services, 2019). The technology strategy involves using an automated filtering system for detection of trolling comments or modifications to posts, typically incorporated into the social media platform, or comparisons between trolling or vandalism behaviors with benign ones, a method used in Wikipedia (Adler et al., 2011; Coles & West, 2016). Tools have been developed to detect trolling bots, such as BotOrNot employed by Twitter; however, it was not effective in differentiating human users from hybrid social bots (Grimme et al., 2017). Other mechanisms (e.g., *The Troll Filtering Process, Troll Vulnerability Rank*) operate by examining content to detect if it was created by bots, classify it as harmful to users, and determine if it is likely to draw trolls (Cambia et al., 2010).

A second strategy utilizes a human approach. The website can increase guardianship by implementing a *post moderation* mechanism that hides the content from general public until screened and a set of *moderators* are paid to control online behaviors to make it consistent with the ISPs terms of service (Binns, 2012; Coles & West, 2016). Users should be required to sign in using their own name rather than be allowed to post anonymously, as the latter encourages trolling due to de-individuation effects (Binns, 2012; Coles & West, 2016). ISPs need to make the reporting of trolls easier; train community managers to identify and respond to trolling behaviors, reduce provocation by deleting or hiding troll comments from other users, and track troll's IP addresses; establish internal policies for managing trolls; have explicit parameters in place to discourage others from "feeding the trolls"; and monitor platforms to determine when and how often trolling occurs (Golf-Papez & Veer, 2017). Ignoring a troll works for some behaviors, such as when the user spews angry words in all caps after a pet issue is encountered; escalates the attacks by questioning the target's character when s/he replies to the comment; expresses hatred toward a target or issue; extracts words and uses them out of context in the attack; or comments on others' content without adding new ideas; however, this method is the least effective (Cambia et al., 2010). Internet shaming and mild doxing has also been implemented to shame trolling and naming heretofore anonymous trolls (Phillips & Miltner, 2012).

The legal strategy involves criminalizing trolling (Bishop, 2012; Coles & West, 2016). Companies need legal recourse when their third-party content is requested by their users to be blocked or deleted as these acts, unless the content was removed due to being offensive, change their status from distributors to producers/editors and remove Section 230 protection from liability (Daskal et al., 2020; Markey, 2013). When trolling occurs across jurisdictions, another idea is to have an Internet ombudsperson serve as an ethnical moderator to resolve complaints regarding content to balance privacy, accuracy and safety concerns (Bishop, 2012; Centre for Strategy & Evaluation Services, 2019; Daskal et al., 2020). Moderators must be able to suspend, ban, or remove trolls and their content (including searches from blocked and muted accounts) reported by the community for abusive behavior (Case & King, 2018; Tsantarliotis et al., 2017). Civil suits, although time consuming and ultimately expensive, are also an alternative if trolls have inflicted distress on individual victims (Golf-Papez & Veer, 2017).

REFERENCES

Adler, B.T., de Alfaro, L., Mola-Velasco, S.M., Rosso, P., & West, A.G. (2011). Wikipedia vandalism detection: Combining natural language, metadata, and reputation features. In C.I.C. Ling (Chair), *Proceedings of the 12th International Conference on Intelligent Text Processing and Computational Linguistics*, LNCS 6609, 277–288.

Aro, J. (2016). The cyberspace war: Propaganda and trolling as warfare tools. *European View, 15*, 121–132.

The Australia Institute. (2019). *Trolls and Polls -the Economic Costs of Online Harassment and Cyberhate.* https://australiainstitute.org.au/wp-content/uploads/2020/12/P530-Trolls-and-polls-surveying-economic-costs-of-cyberhate-5bWEB5d_0.pdf.

Barrett, B. (2018). *How Russian Trolls Used Meme Warfare to Divide America.* https://www.wired.com/story/russia-ira-propaganda-senate-report/.

Bentley, L.A., & Cowan, D.G. (2021). The socially dominant troll: Acceptance attitudes towards trolling. *Personality and Individual Differences, 173*, 110628. Doi: 10.1016/j.paid.2021.110628.

Bessen, J. (2014). *The Evidence is In: Patent Trolls Do Hurt Innovation.* https://hbr.org/2014/07/the-evidence-is-in-patent-trolls-do-hurt-innovation.

Binns, A. (2012). Don't feed the trolls! Managing troublemakers in magazines' online communities. *Journalism Practice, 6*(4), 547–562. Doi: 10.1080/17512786.2011.648988.

Bishop, J. (2012). Scope and limitations in the Government of Wales Act 2006 for tackling internet abuses in the form of 'flame trolling.' *Statute Law Review, 33*(2), 207–216. Doi: 10.1093/slr/hms016.

Bishop, J. (2013). The effect of de-individuation of the internet troller on criminal procedure implementation: An interview with a hater. *International Journal of Cyber Criminology, 7*(1), 28–48. www.cybercrimejournal.com/Bishop2013janijcc. pdf.

Bradshaw, S., & Howard, P.N. (2017). *Troops, Trolls, and Troublemakers: A Global Inventory of Organized Social Media Manipulation.* University of Oxford. Working paper no. 2017.12. https://ora.ox.ac.uk/objects/uuid:cef7e8d9-27bf-4ea5-9fd6-855209b3e1f6/download_file?safe_filename=Troops-Trolls-and-Troublemakers.pdf&file_format=application%2Fpdf&type_of_work=Report.

Bratu, S. (2017). *The Inexorable Shift Towards an Increasingly Hostile Cyberspace Environment: The Adverse Social Impact of Online Trolling Behavior* (pp. 88–94). Woodside: Addleton Academic Publishers.

Broniatowski, D.A., Jamison, A.M., Qi, S., AlKulaib, L., Chen, T., Benton, A., Quinn, S.C., & Dredze, M. (2018). Weaponized health communication: Twitter bots and Russian trolls amplify the vaccine debate. *American Journal of Public Health, 108*(10), 1378–1384.

Buckels, E.E., Trapnell, P.D., & Paulhus, D.L. (2014). Trolls just want to have fun. *Personality and Individual Differences, 67*, 97–102. Doi: 10.1016/j.paid.2014.01.016.

Butler, D., Kift, S., & Campbell, M. (2009). Cyber bullying in schools and the law: Is there an effective means of addressing the power imbalance. *Electronic Journal of Law, 16*, 84–114.

Cambia, E., Chandra, P., Sharma, A., & Hussain, A. (2010). *Do Not Feel the Trolls.* https://www.researchgate.net/publication/228419623.

Campbell, A. (2019). *What is Hashtag Hijacking?* https://smallbiztrends.com/2013/08/what-is-hashtag-hijacking-2.html.

Case, C.J., & King, D.L. (2018). Internet trolling victimization: An empirical examination of incidence in undergraduate business students. *Research in Higher Education Journal, 34,* https://www.aabri.com/manuscripts/172726.pdf.

Centre for Strategy & Evaluation Services. (2019). *The Rapid Evidence Assessment: The Prevalence and Impact of Online Trolling* (ref.# 101030). https://assets.publishing.service.gov.uk/government/uploads/system/uploads/attachment_data/file/973971/DCMS_REA_Online_trolling__V2.pdf.

Cheng, J., Bernstein, M., Danescu-Niculescu-Mizil, C., & Leskovec, J. (2017, February–March). Anyone can become a troll: Causes of trolling behavior in online discussions. *CSCW Conference on Computer Support Cooperative Work,* 1217–1230. Doi: 10.1145/2998181.2998213 https://pubmed.ncbi.nlm.nih.gov/29399664/.

Coles, B.A., & West, M. (2016). Trolling the trolls: Online forum users constructions of the nature and properties of trolling. *Computers in Human Behavior, 60,* 233–244.

Cook, C., Schaafsma, J. & Antheunis, M. (2018). Under the bridge: An in-depth examination of online trolling in the gaming context. *New Media and Society, 20*(9), 3323–3340. Doi. 10.1177/1461444817748578.

Craker, N., & March, E. (2016). The dark side of Facebook®: The Dark Tetrad, negative social potency, and trolling behaviours. *Personality and Individual Differences, 102,* 79–84. Doi: 10.1016/j.paid.2016.06.043.

Dahlberg, L. (2001). Computer-mediated communication and the public sphere: A critical analysis. *Journal of Computer-Mediated Communication, 7*(1). Doi: 10.1111/j.1083-6101.2001.tb00137.x.

Daskal, E., Wentrup, R., & Shefet, D. (2020). Taming the internet trolls with an internet ombudsperson: Ethical social media regulation. *Policy & Internet, 12*(2), 207–226. Doi: 10.1002/poi3.227.

Davis, W.S., & Magaldi, J.A. (2019). "Into the bowels of hell": Examining online defamation law through the twitter account of James Wood. *Southern Law Journal, 2*(2), 157–184.

DiResta, R., Shaffer, K., Ruppel, B., Sullivan, D., Matney, R., Fox, R., Albright, J., & Johnson, B. (2018). *The Tactics and Tropes of the Internet Research Agency.* https://disinformationreport.blob.core.windows.net/disinformation-report/NewKnowledge-Disinformation-Report-Whitepaper.pdf.

Duggan, M. (2014). *5 Facts about Online Harassment.* https://www.pewresearch.org/fact-tank/2014/10/30/5-facts-about-online-harassment/.

Eckert, S. (2017). Fighting for recognition: Online abuse of women bloggers in Germany, Switzerland, the United Kingdom, and the United States. *New Media and Society, 20*(4), 1282–1302. Doi: 10.1177/1461444816688457.

Ekstrand, N. (2018). The ugliness of trolls: Comparing the strategies/methods of alt-right and the Ku Klux Klan. *Cosmopolitan Civil Societies: An Interdisciplinary Journal, 10*(3), 41–62.

Fedasiuk, R. (2021). *China's Internet Trolls Go Global.* https://www.cfr.org/blog/chinas-internet-trolls-go-global.

Ferenczi, N., Marshall, T.C., & Bejanyan, K. (2017). Are sex differences in anti-social and prosocial Facebook use explained by narcissism and relational self-contrual? *Computers in Human Behavior, 77,* 25–31. Doi: 10.1016/j.chb.2017.08.033.

Fichman, P., & Sanfilippo, M.R. (2015). The bad boys and girls of cyberspace: How gender and context impact perception of and reaction to trolling. *Social Science Computer Review, 33*(2), 163–180. Doi. 10.1177/0894439314533169.

Galán-García, P., de la Puerta, J.G., Gómez, C.L., Santos, I. & Bringas, P.G. (2014). Supervised machine learning for the detection of troll profiles in Twitter social network: Application to a real case of cyberbullying. In A. Herrero et al. (eds.), *International Joint Conference SOCO'13-CISIS'13-ICEDUTE'13. Advances in Intelligent Systems and Computer,* volume 239 (pp. 419–428). Cham: Springer. Doi. 10.1007/978-3-319-01854-6_43.

Gammon, J. (2014). *Over a Quarter of Americans have Made Malicious Online Comments.* https://today.yougov.com/topics/politics/articles-reports/2014/10/20/over-quarter-americans-admit-malicious-online-comm.

Gilmer, M. (2018). *Here Are the Most Unforgettable Wikipedia Vandalism Trolls of All Time.* https://mashable.com/article/best-wikipedia-edit-trolls/.

Golf-Papez, M., & Veer, E. (2017). Don't feed the trolling: Rethinking how online trolling is being defined and combated. *Journal of Marketing Management, 33*(15–16), 1336–1354.

Grimme, C., Preuss, M., Adam, L., & Trautmann, H. (2017). Social bots: Human-like by means of human control? *Big Data, 5*(4), 279–293. Doi: 10.1089/big.2017.0044.

Hardaker, C. (2010). Trolling in asynchronous computer-mediated communication: From user discussions to academic definitions. *Journal of Politeness Research. Language, Behaviour, Culture, 6*(2), 215–242.

Hardaker, C. (2013). "Uh… not to be nitpicky, but… the past tense of drag is dragged, not drug.": An overview of trolling strategies. *Journal of Language Aggression and Conflict, 1*(1), 58–86. Doi: 10.1075/jlac.1.1.04har.

Hardaker, C. (2015). 'I refuse to respond to this obvious troll': An overview of responses to (perceived) trolling. *Corpora, 10*(2), 201–229.

Herring, S., Job-Sluder, K., Scheckler, R., & Barab, S. (2002). Searching for safety online: Managing trolling in a feminist forum. *The Information Society, 18*(5), 371–384. Doi. 10.1080/01972240290108186.

Hong, F-Y., & Cheng, K-T. (2018). Correlation between university students' online trolling behavior and online trolling victimization forms, current conditions, and personality traits. *Telematics and Informatics, 35*(2), 397–405. Doi: 10.1016/j.tele.2017.12.016.

Hutchinson, A. (2015, September 5). *Hey Brands–if You Don't Provide Social Media Customer Service, Someone Else Will Do it for You.* http://www.socialmediatoday.com/social-business/adhutchinson/2015–09-05/hey-brands-if-you-dont-provide-social-media-customer-service.

Jalonen, H., & Jussila, J. (2016). Developing a conceptual model for the relationship between social media behavior, negative consumer emotions and brand disloyalty. *15th Conference on e-Business, e-services, and e-society* (I3E, pp. 134–145). Doi: 10.1007/978-3-319-45234-0_13.

Johnson, J. (2021). How many people use the internet? Internet users in the world 2021. https://www.statista.com/statistics/617136/digital-population-worldwide/#:~:text=How%20many%20people%20use%20the%20internet%3F%20As%20of,%284.32%20billion%29%20accessed%20the%20internet%20via%20mobile%20devices

Johnson, M., & Gelb, B.D. (2002). Cyber-libel: Policy trade-offs. *Legal Developments, 21(1),* 152–159.

Jussinoja, T. (2018). *Life-Cycle of Internet Trolls.* Master's Thesis. University of Jyväskylä, https://jyx.jyu.fi/bitstream/handle/123456789/57411/1/URN%3ANBN%3Afi%3Ajyu-201803261829.pdf.

Kleinman, A. (2014, October 20). *28 Percent of Americans Admit to Being Internet Trolls.* http://www.huffingtonpost.com/2014/10/20/internet-trolls-survey_n_601482.

Klepper, D. (2020). *Cyborgs, Trolls, and Bots: A Guide to Online Misinformation.* https://apnews.com/article/us-news-ap-top-news-elections-social-media-technology-4086949d878336f8ea6daa4dee725d94.

Kuehl, H.F. (2016). Free speech and defamation in an era of social media: An analysis of federal and Illinois norms in the context of anonymous online defamers. *Northern Illinois University Law Review, 36(3),* 28.

Kunst, A. (2019). *Witnessing Internet Trolling on Selected Media in the U.S. 2017.* https://www.statista.com/statistics/379997/internet-trolling-digital-media/

Llewellyn, C., Cram, L., Hill, R.L., & Favero, A. (2019). For whom the bell trolls: Shifting troll behaviour in the twitter Brexit debate. *Journal of Common Market Studies, 57(5),* 1148–1164.

Lopes, B. (2017). Who do you troll and why: An investigation into the relationship between the Dark Triad personalities and online trolling behaviours towards popular and less popular Facebook profiles. *Computers in Human Behavior, 77,* 69–76.

Maltby, J. (2016). *Implicit Theories of Online Trolling: Evidence that Attention Seeking Conceptions Are Associated with Increased Psychological Resilience* (pp. 448–466). Leicester: Wiley Subscription Services.

March, E., & Steele, G. (2020). High esteem and hurting others online: Trait sadism moderates the relationship between self-esteem and internet trolling. *Cyberpsychology, Behavior, and Social Networking, 23(7),* 441–446. Doi: 10.1089/cyber.2019.0652.

Markey, L.M. (2013). *Starving the Trolls: How the News Media and Harassment Victims Can Fight Harmful Speech Online.* Ann Arbor, MI: ProQuest Dissertation Publishing, 9781303154027. https://www.proquest.com/docview/1413302933?accountid=11724

Mihaylov, T., Mihaylova, T., Nakov, P., Màrquez, L., Georgiev, G.D., & Koychev, I.K. (2018). The dark side of news community forums: Opinion manipulation trolls. *Internet Research, 28(5)*, 1292–1312.

Morrissey, L. (2010). Trolling is an art: Towards a schematic classification of intention in internet trolling. *Griffith Working Papers in Pragmatics and Intercultural Communications, 3(2)*, 75–82.

Morrison, P. (2015, July 01). *Privilege Makes Them Do it - What a Study of Internet Trolls Reveals.* Retrieved from http://www.latimes.com/opinion/op-ed/la-oe-morrison-phillips-20150701-column.html

Newzoo (2020). Number of active video gamers worldwide-2015 to 2023. Number of Gamers Worldwide 2021/2022: Demographics, Statistics, and Predictions - Financesonline.com.

Ortiz, S.M. (2020). Trolling as a collective form of harassment: An inductive study of how online users understand trolling. *Social Media and Society, 6(2)*, 1–9. Doi: 10.1177/2056305120928512.

Özsoy, D. (2015). Tweeting political fear: Trolls in Turkey. *Journal of History School, 8(22)*, 535–552. Doi: 10.14225/Joh750.

Paananen, A., & Reichl, A.J. (2019). Gender trolls just want to have fun, too. *Personality and Individual Differences, 141*, 152–156. Doi: 10.1016/j.paid.2019.01.011.

Petykó, M. (2018). The motives attributed to trolls in metapragmatic comments on three Hungarian left-wing political blogs. *Pragmatics, 28(3)*, 391–416.

Pew Research Center (2016, February). *15% of American Adults have Used Online Dating Sites or Mobile Dating Sites.* http://www.pewinternet.org/2016/02/11/15- percent-of-american-adults-have-used-online-dating-sites-or-mobile-dating-apps/.

Phillips, W. (2013, January 8). *Ethnography of Trolling: Workarounds, Discipline-Jumping & Ethical Pitfalls. Ethnography of Trolling: Workarounds, Discipline-Jumping & Ethical Pitfalls (2 of 3)* | Ethnography Matters.

Phillips, W. (2015). *This is Why we Can't Have Nice Things: Mapping the Relationship between Online Trolling and Mainstream Culture.* MIT Press. http://ebookcentral.proquest.com/lib/lafayettecol-ebooks/detail.action?d.

Phillips, W., & Miltner, K. (2012, December 19). *The Internet's Vigilante Shame Army, THE AWL.* http://www.theawl.com/2012/12/the-internets-vigilante-shame-army.

Redditinc.com (2021). *Reddit by the Numbers.* https://www.redditinc.com/.

Rice, L. (2013). *It's Time for More Lolz not Trolls.* https://vinspired.com/its-time-for-more-lolz-not-trolls.

Sanfilippo, M.R., Fichman, P., & Yang, S. (2018). Multidimensionality of online trolling behaviors. *The Information Society, 34(1)*, 27–39.

Sanfilippo, M.R., Yang, S., & Fichman, P. (2017). Managing online trolling: From deviant to social and political trolls. *Proceedings of the 50th Hawaii International Conference on Systems Sciences.* https://scholarworks.iu.edu/dspace/bitstream/handle/2022/25089/Managing_Online_Trolling_Conference_Proceedings.pdf?sequence=1.

Scott, T., & Griffiths, M.D. (2012). An exploratory study of trolling in online video gaming. *International Journal of Cyber Behaviour, Psychology and Learning, 2(4)*, 17–33. Doi: 10.4018/ijcbpl.2012100102.

Seigfried-Spellar, K.C. & Chowdhury, S.S. (2017). Death and Lulz: Understanding the personality characteristics of RIP trolls. *First Monday, 22(11)*. https://first-monday.org/ojs/index.php/fm/article/download/7861/6556.

Sest, N., & March, E. (2017). Constructing the cyber-troll: Psychopathy, sadism, and empathy. *Personality and Individual Differences, 119*, 69–72. Doi. 10.1016/j.paid.2017.06.038.

Shachaf, P., & Hara, N. (2010). Beyond vandalism: Wikipedia trolls. *Journal of Information Science, 36(3)*, 357–370. Doi: 10.1177/0165551510365390.

Shin, J. (2008). Morality and internet behavior: A study of the internet troll and its relation with morality on the internet. *Society for Information Technology & Teacher Education International Conference* (Vol. 2008, pp. 2834e2840). http://www.editlib.org/noaccesspresent/27652/46654/.

Shuntich, S.L., & Vogel, K.A. (2018). Doe hunting: A how-to guide for uncovering John Doe defendants in anonymous online defamation suits. *The Computer & Internet Lawyer, 35(3)*, 17–20.

Smith, C. (2021). *4chan Statistics, User Counts and Facts*. https://expandedramblings.com/index.php/4chan-statistics-facts/.

Stringhini, G., & Zannettou, S. (2020). *We Analyzed 1.8 Million Images on Twitter to Learn How Russian Trolls Operate*. https://www.fastcompany.com/90540452/we-analyzed-1–8-million-images-on-twitter-to-learn-how-russian-trolls-operate.

Suler, J. (2004). The online disinhibition effect. *Cyberpsychology & Behavior, 7*, 321e326. Doi: 10.1089/1094931041291295.

Swenson-Lepper, T., & Kerby, A. (2019). Cyberbullies, trolls, and stalkers: Students' perceptions of ethical issues in social media. *Journal of Media Ethics, 34(2)*, 102–113. Doi: 10.1080/23736992.2019.1599721.

Thacker, S., & Griffiths, M.D. (2012). An exploratory study of trolling in online video gaming. *International Journal of Cyber Behavior, Psychology, and Learning, 2(4)*, 17–33. Doi: 10.4018/ijcbpl.2012100102.

Tsantarliotis, P., Pitoura, E., & Tsaparas, P. (2017). Defining and predicting troll vulnerability in online social media. *Social Network Analysis and Mining, 7*, 26–40.

Utz, S. (2005). Types of deception and underlying motivation. What people think. *Social Science Computer Review, 23(1)*, 49–56. Doi. 10.1177/0894439304271534.

Vining, A., & Mattews, S. (n.d.). *Overview of Anti-SLAPP Laws*. https://www.rcfp.org/introduction-anti-slapp-guide/.

Zezulka, L.A., & Seigfried-Spellar, K.C. (2016). Differentiating cyberbullies and internet trolls by personality characteristics and self-esteem. *Journal of Digital Forensics, Security, and Law, 11(3)*, 7–25.

CASES

Cubby Inc. v. CompuServe Inc. (1991), 776 F.Supp.135 (S.D.N.Y).

N.Y. Times v. Sullivan (1964), 376 US 254.

Smith v. California (1959), 361 US 147.

Stratton Oakmont Inc. v. Prodigy Services Co. (1995), 1995 WL 323710 (N. Y. Sup.Ct. May 24, 1995). Reorg. den'd by 1995 WL 805178 (N. Y.Sup. December 11).
Telecommunications Act (1996), 47 U.S.C. § 230 et seq.
Zeran v. America Online Inc. (1997), 129 F.3d 327 (4th Cir.).

5

Cyberstalkers

DEFINING CYBERSTALKING

Cyberstalking is a crime of interpersonal violence that closely resembles its offline counterpart, stalking, in its main characteristics (Burgess & Baker, 2002; Kirwan & Power, 2012; Worsely et al., 2017). Specifically, both crimes involve unwanted, willful, malicious, repeated, and persistent attempts to interact, contact, and/or communicate with a victim for the

DOI: 10.4324/9781003092292-5

purposes of manipulating, coercing, controlling, intimidating, harassing, and instilling feelings of apprehension, helplessness, and fear (Kirwan & Power, 2012; Kaur et al., 2021; Nobles et al., 2014; Ogilvie, 2000; Sheridan & Lyndon, 2012). The primary difference is that cyberstalking, albeit not exclusively, involves the use of electronic communications technology and the Internet to stalk a person or group (Goodno, 2007; Maple et al., 2011; Nobles et al., 2014; Sheridan & Grant, 2007; Tokunaga & Aune, 2017; Witwer et al., 2020). Cyberstalking, which differs from cyber harassment in that "it poses a credible threat of harm to the victim" (p. 3), is one of several types of technology-facilitated abuse—the others include swatting, doxing,[1] sextortion, and Internet-based sexual abuse (Witwer et al., 2020).

Although researchers are not sure whether cyberstalking is a different crime from stalking or merely a subset or offshoot of it (Worsely et al., 2017), they agree its online component is more difficult to prevent and/or mitigate (Kaur et al., 2021) and online attacks can easily escalate to physical assaults (Worsely et al., 2017). Vulnerability to cyberstalking is highest for those who engage often in social media sites and Internet forums, typically adolescents and young adults (Kraft & Wang, 2010; Lenhart et al., 2016). Social constraints that could typically inhibit stalkers in the real world are absent for cyberstalkers online (i.e., disinhibition effect), allowing them to engage unfettered in aggressive actions and negative emotional impulses (e.g., possessiveness, control, anger) against the victim in ways they may never do in face-to-face interactions (Burgess & Baker, 2002; Sheridan & Grant, 2007). Four factors facilitate cyberstalking: (1) there are no geographical barriers to contain it; (2) its asynchronous nature allows the crime to occur anytime; (3) perpetrators can be anonymous online, which makes it harder for a victim to identify them; and (4) the Internet is not policed (Holt & Bossler, 2009; Reyns et al., 2012; Shimizu, 2013; Tokunaga & Aune, 2017). As a result, law enforcement agencies struggle with successfully investigating and prosecuting cyberstalking, particularly as it may occur across jurisdictions with different legal requirements (Cox, 2014; Fusco, 2014).

Currently, the prevalence rates of cyberstalking reported through official statistics and research are widely variable for two reasons. First, the public was not educated about cyberstalking as a crime until the late 1990s and cyberstalking was not criminalized until 1998 when California became

---

[1] Doxing (aka doxxing) refers to the online distribution or publication of a person's private information (e.g., address, phone number).

the first state to amend its Penal Code 646.9 for stalking to include "by means of electronic communication device" (Bocij, 2003, 2004; Strawhun et al., 2013; SHouse California Law Group, 2020). Even today society does not understand cyberstalking in its varied forms, which reduces the likelihood that it will be reported consistently. The public trivializes the seriousness of cyberstalking related to someone seeking to establish or rekindle a relationship, which gaslights victims into questioning their justifiable concerns and discouraging them from reporting incidents to the police (Purcell et al., 2010). Discrepancy in prevalence rates was also due to the lengthy process for the federal government and the rest of the states to determine and pass either new cyberstalking or modified stalking using technology legislation. Second, research findings for cyberstalking in the U.S. indicate ranges of low rates, such as 6.5%–10% (Dreßing et al., 2014; Fansher & Randa, 2019; Kraft & Wang, 2010), to moderate rates, approximately 35%–46% (DeKeseredy et al., 2019; Maran & Begotti, 2019; Reyns et al., 2012). These differences can be attributed to variations in methodology, definitions, demographics of respondents, and underreporting by victims who fail to recognize the behaviors as a crime or are embarrassed by their victimization (Ahlgrim & Terrance, 2021; Kaur et al., 2021).

The need for accurate prevalence rates is two-fold. Legislation is dependent on understanding how many victims are affected (magnitude) and the impact of the crime on individuals and society (scope). The current laws seem to reflect society's belief that cyberstalking is an uncommon crime that affects only a small proportion of the population (DeMatteo et al., 2017; Purcell et al., 2010). To determine the accuracy of this assumption, the government must collect official statistics regarding the proportion of stalking versus cyberstalking cases separately; evaluate the adequacy of the current laws for prosecuting the various forms of cyberstalking; and quantify the harm to individuals and society across jurisdictions. This cannot happen without criminal justice professionals and researchers agreeing on a common definition, types, methods, behaviors, and effective punishments for cyberstalking (Dhillon & Smith, 2019). It is also important to have the public educated on this crime to allow victims, particularly minors, to recognize its occurrence and to give them training to reduce further victimization (Pensak, 2015). Victims of cyberstalking suffer significant psychological, physical, health, behavioral, social, and economical consequences beyond the fear and distress caused by their initial victimization (Fissel & Reyns, 2020). The tangible and intangible losses suffered by the victims as a result of this interpersonal violent crime also negatively impacts society beyond the misdemeanor penalty currently given to the offender (Dreßing et al., 2014; McCollister et al., 2010; Short et al., 2015).

TYPICAL CYBERSTALKERS

Law enforcement compile demographic information about exclusively online, mixed (offline and online), and exclusively offline stalkers together rather than separately (Truman & Morgan, 2021). Most stalkers/cyberstalkers (54%–85%) are single, White, college-educated adult men with moderate skills in computers (Al Mutawa, Bryce, Franqueira, & Marrington, 2016; Ashcroft, 2001; Burgess & Baker, 2002; D'Ovidio & Doyle, 2003; McFarlane & Bojic, 2003; Sheridan & Lyndon, 2010; Yar, 2006). Researchers (e.g., Al Mutawa et al., 2016; McFarlane & Bojic, 2003) have found that cyberstalkers of adult victims were more likely to be older adults aged 41 and over (42%–45%) rather than adults aged 18–30 (20%–23%) or 31–40 (35%). In contrast, studies have shown that cyberstalkers are also young adult, college students (*M* age of 24)—with equitable rates across genders (Ménard & Pincus, 2012; Spitzberg & Cupach, 2007; Strawhun et al., 2013)—and, to a lesser extent (24%), minors under age 16, who target their peers (Baker & Carreño, 2016; D'Ovidio & Doyle, 2003; Marcum et al., 2010; Pensak, 2015; Reyns et al., 2012; Rodríguez-Castro et al., 2021). Cyberstalkers demonstrate behavior patterns of deception, anger, manipulation, and aggression and have specific personality traits and attributes, such as narcissism (i.e., high self-importance and entitlement), machiavellianism, problematic attachment style (only men) or intimacy discomfort (only women), psychopathy (i.e., callous, unremorseful, antagonistic), sadism (i.e., cruel and aggressive), and egocentrism (Kircaburun et al., 2018; Ménard & Pincus, 2012; Reyns, Henson, & Fisher, 2018; Smoker & March, 2017; Strawhun et al., 2013).

Using Mishra and Mishra's (2008) typology, there are three types of cyberstalkers—*obsessive, delusional,* or *vengeful.* **Obsessive** cyberstalkers are known to the victim, such as current or previous intimate partners, family members, work colleagues, or friends. Intimate partner cyberstalkers may believe that their behavior serves as a relational maintenance tool for establishing and preserving intimacy (Duntley & Buss, 2012), particularly when the victim has terminated the relationship (Fraser et al., 2010; McFarlane & Bocij, 2003). **Delusional** cyberstalkers, due to their mental illness, believe that they are in an established, reciprocating romantic relationship even though they have not spoken to or even met the person. In some cases, the victim is a stranger to the cyberstalker, such as a celebrity or well-known figure, whereas in other cases the victim is actually in the cyberstalker's life, perhaps as an associate from work or school. **Vengeful** cyberstalkers perceive the victim[2] as committing an actual or imagined injury, humiliation, or harm against them, their families, or friends.

CYBERSTALKERS' MOTIVES AND METHODS

Motivations may be tied to the type of cyberstalker, as shown in Table 5.1 (Cavezza & McEwan, 2014; Fissel, 2021b; Kirwan & Power, 2012; McFarlane & Bocij, 2003; Spitzberg & Hoobler, 2002; Spitzberg & Cupach, 2007; Strawhun et al., 2013). Cyberstalkers use one or more form of technology to commit their crime: *email* (direct communication), *Internet* (global communication), and *computer* (unauthorized use) (Baum et al., 2009; Bocij, 2006; Fraser et al., 2010; Kirwan & Power, 2012; Ogilvie, 2000; Mishra & Mishra, 2008; Philips & Morrissey, 2004; Reyns et al., 2012; Tokunaga & Aune, 2017; Wykes, 2007). As most cyberstalkers prefer to communicate with their victims, email is their most commonly used technology, whereas social network sites are secondary (Cavezza & McEwan, 2014; McFarlane & Bocij, 2003; Truman & Morgan, 2021). A variety of technological tools have been used by cyberstalkers and are described in Box 5.1 (Eterovic-Soric et al., 2017).

Table 5.1 Motivations by Type of Cyberstalker

	Type of Cyberstalker		
Motivation	**Obsessive**	**Delusional**	**Vengeful**
Retaliation	X		x
Rejection	X	x	x
Affection	X	x	
Reconciliation	X	x	
Obsession	X	x	x
Power & control	X		x
Jealousy/anger	X		x

---

[2] Victims in this case can be individuals or corporations, but the focus of this chapter is on the former.

BOX 5.1   TECHNOLOGY USED BY CYBERSTALKERS
TO ACCESS VICTIM INFORMATION

Many commercial online services (i.e., apps, social media) require members to provide their personal identifying information (PII) as a condition of using the app or platform, consequently allowing cyberstalkers access to it through a simple Google search (Wykes, 2007). Social media users also endanger themselves through their online interactions. Facebook indirectly contributed to putting their users in jeopardy because they were collecting location data through a Google Chrome extension named "Marauders Map," which allowed people to view other people's movements (Khanna, 2015). Facebook users enjoy posting information about their lives, such as the restaurant at which they are eating or where and when they will vacation, to make it easy for their friends to engage in social surveillance (cyberstalking) by knowing what activities they are doing or even allow them to join up (Eterovic-Soric et al., 2017). A cyberstalker could easily use this information to surveille a victim's daily routine and determine the person's location throughout the day (Eterovic-Soric et al., 2017). Thus, this practice not only makes it easy for cyberstalkers to pursue their victims with very little effort, it also makes it difficult to prove that the offenders are performing "sinister" acts. Social network platforms, especially those with discussion forums, can aid cyberstalkers in locating a victim by enlisting the help of others, called "human flesh search engines" (Wang et al., 2010). Netizens (citizens online) work together to provide information through crowdsourcing techniques, sometimes called collective cyberstalking (Chang & Zhu, 2020; Eterovic-Soric et al., 2017; McFarlane & Bocij, 2003). Search engines, such as Google Image Search and TinEye, can be used to reverse search social media for a victim's image (Williams, 2012). Several apps (e.g., WeChat, Skout, Grindr, Tinder) with location-based services on Internet devices and smart phones can be used by cyberstalkers to coordinate the location of the victim (Carman & Choo, 2017; Eterovic-Soric et al., 2017; Hoang et al., 2016). For example, although "stalker app" has been marketed to parents and employees, it allows a cyberstalker to monitor the victim's phone covertly and surveil the person's location using GPS (U.S. Government Accountability Office, 2016).

The three main behaviors that characterize this crime—*pursuing, harassing,* and *terrorizing* the victim both online and offline—and their corresponding examples are shown in Table 5.2 (D'Ovidio & Doyle, 2003; Finkelhor et al., 2000; Finn, 2004; Finn & Atkinson, 2009; Fraser et al., 2010; Holt & Bossler, 2009; Jerin & Dolinsky, 2001; Marcum et al., 2010; McFarlane & Bocij, 2003; McQuade, 2006; Mishra & Mishra, 2008; Nobles et al., 2014; Philips & Morrissey 2004; Reyns et al, 2012; Sheridan & Grant, 2007; Shorey et al., 2015; Smoker & March, 2017; Spitzberg & Cupach, 2007; Tokunaga & Aune, 2017). Due to the ease of online stalking, cyberstalkers are able to pursue, harass, and terrorize more than one victim at a time across jurisdictions (Hamin & Wan Rosli, 2018). Adolescents in particular are primed to be cyberstalkers due to their high degree of synergy with technology marked by near constant connection to the Internet that allows them to seek and share information with peers, resulting in a reduced understanding of individual boundaries and expectation of privacy (King-Ries, 2011). For example, a 17-year-old girl in 2010 discovered her ex-boyfriend was dating a 15-year-old girl, so she copied photographs from the victim's MySpace account and posted them on a pornography website along with the victim's contact information. Not surprisingly, the victim began receiving calls and texts from strangers requesting sex from her. Another example involved two middle school aged girls, aged 11 and 12, who impersonated a12-year-old girl on Facebook, posting sexually explicit messages and pictures on the victim's page and sending messages to boys soliciting sex.[3]

Cyberstalkers often employ hyperintimacy strategies (e.g., expressions of affection, attempts of ingratiation, desires to repair the relationship, or messages including hypersexual overtones) to pursue relationships with their targets (Fraser et al., 2010; LeBlanc et al., 2001; Spitzberg & Hoobler, 2002; Tokunaga & Aune, 2017). Many of these offenders are also domestic violence and intimate partner violence abusers who use power and control tactics of "intimidation, coercion, threats, and emotional abuse" and isolation, often self-imposed as a protective measure, to subdue their victims (Powell, 2020, para 11). Adolescents and young adults nationwide admit to engaging regularly in cyber dating abuse behaviors, such as monitoring partner's text messages, sending/requesting sexually explicit photos, and requiring them to respond to texts immediately (Zweig et al., 2013). Abusers typically initiate relationships by *love bombing* the victims in either a

---

[3] K5. (2011). 11,12-year-old girls charged for cyberstalking classmate. https://www.king5.com/article/news/local/11-12-year-old-girls-charged-for-cyberstalking-classmate/281-331864795.

Table 5.2 Three Types of Cyberstalking Behavior with Corresponding Examples

Behavior	Examples
Pursuit	• Contact the victims directly (e.g., cell phone, email); • Contact the victims online (e.g., message board, webpage); • Send or leave gifts for the victims; and • Attempt to meet victims in real world.
Harass	• Slander and/or threaten victims on public forums (e.g., message and bulletin boards, chat rooms) using false claims; • Encourage others to harass victims and/or coordinate an attack; • Sabotage the victims by sending instant messages or unsolicited emails containing offensive messages (e.g., hate, obscenity, threats), viruses, and/or electronic junk (e.g., SPAM, mailbombing); • Dox personal information; • Impersonate the victims to create/run a business, engage in identify theft, make statements on online forums, and turn an online group against them; • Sexually harass and endanger victims by creating fake profiles on social media and dating sites; • Order goods and services for the victims to cause harm and/or embarrassment; and • Set up false personal advertisements sites to get others to contact, sexually violate, and harm the victims.
Terrorize	• Invade privacy through consistent and close monitoring of all aspects of the victims' lives, including showing up at their location physically through use of GPS or obtaining geotag information from online photos; • Surveilling victims and showing them surveillance photographs at locations visited by them that day; • Leave items in the victims' homes to demonstrate their ability to enter at will; • Be at or disclosing to the victims at their current online location (social media, discussion forum, games) obtained through use of spyware on the computer or by keylogging; • Take control of victims' computers (Window's operating system); cause damage to files, system, or equipment; • Track the victims' cars; • Steal personal information (e.g., files, photos, data); and • Obtain the content of emails, text messages, computer, cell phone logs, video chats, and offline dialogue exchanged when the victims interact with others using their computer cameras and microphones.

grandiose way through overelaborate displays of affection, adoration, and attention (e.g., love letters, flowers and candy deliveries, flattery) or a *quiet* way through oversharing emotional problems to trigger helping or nurturing responses in their victims (Andersen, 2021). Paradoxically, general or specific implicit and explicit threats of harm towards the victim (e.g., reputation, bodily injury, death) are also employed during pursuit (Spitzberg & Hoobler, 2002). Abusers maintain control over the victim by implementing harassment and terrorizing techniques, such as sabotaging his/her social and/or professional image through embarrassing messages to everyone in the victim's life (Fraser et al., 2010; Spitzberg & Hoobler, 2002). Invasion is the most disconcerting cyberstalker strategy (but the least likely as it requires a specialized skill set), involving property damage, identity theft, and surveillance (Bocij, 2004; Fraser et al., 2010; McFarlane & Bocij, 2003; Spitzberg & Hoobler, 2002; Tokunaga & Aune, 2017).

TYPICAL CYBERSTALKING VICTIMS

Cyberstalking victims tend to be young adult (aged 18–30) women, but to a lesser extent than for stalking victims (Al Mutawa et al., 2016; Paullet et al., 2009; Basile et al., 2006; Bocij, 2003; D'Ovidio & Doyle, 2003; Dreßing et al., 2014; Fissel, 2019; Hutton & Haantz, 2003; Kirwan & Power, 2012; Kraft & Wang, 2010; Moriarty & Freiberger, 2008; McFarlane & Bojic, 2003; Paullet et al., 2009; Phillips & Morrissey, 2004; Truman & Morgan, 2021). Researchers believe that men are underrepresented in this population as they fail to report or identify as victims (Alexy et al., 2005; Berry & Bainbridge, 2017; Fissel & Reyns, 2020; Strawhun et al., 2013). Discrepancies in other demographic characteristics have been indicated for race/ethnicity, marital status, and offender-victim relationship, making it difficult to generalize findings. Some studies reported mostly White victims (Kraft & Wang, 2010; McFarlane & Bojic, 2003; Truman & Morgan, 2021), whereas others found higher rates for non-White victims (Al Mutawa et al., 2016; Reyns et al., 2012). Similarly, victim relationship status has sometimes been listed as predominantly single—never married or separated/divorced (Dreßing et al., 2014; McFarlane & Bojic, 2003), whereas other studies indicated that those in relationship or married were most vulnerable due to intimate partner cyberstalking (Basile et al., 2006; Reyns et al., 2012; Truman & Morgan, 2021). As for the relationship between the cyberstalker and victim, it tends to be known or non-stranger, such as current or former intimate partners, family members, friends, work associates, classmates, and acquaintances

(Al Mutawa et al., 2016; Paullet et al., 2009; Cavezza & McEwan, 2014; Fissel, 2019, 2021a; Short et al., 2015) rather than unknown or stranger (Bocij, 2003; Phillips & Morrissey, 2004; Moriarty & Freiberger, 2008). The offender-victim relationship of stranger, however, is likely to be underestimated. Cyberstalkers not only have greater opportunities to select a stranger as a victim than do stalkers, but the anonymity of the online environments also makes it difficult for the victim to identify or trace them (Wykes, 2007).

A person may be at an increased risk for victimization depending on his/her Internet or social media use and level of engagement, such as the number hours spent online, number of social networks used daily, number of updates made, amount of information disclosed online, number of posted photos online, and daily use of apps and messenger services (Fansher & Randa, 2019; Paullet et al., 2009; Reyns et al., 2012; Welsh & Lavoie, 2012). Adolescents and young adults (usually college students) do spend more time (i.e., as moderate or heavy users) than older adults (light users) online and therefore are at increased risk for victimization (Dowdell & Bradley, 2010; King-Ries, 2011; Pensak, 2015). For example, college students experience high incidents of online pursuit behaviors due to their routine, prolonged electronic connections as their main source of communication (Buhi et al., 2009; Reyns et al., 2012). Minor victims may be at a higher risk for being cyberstalked by another minor—particularly a current or former intimate partner—than by adults and they are the least likely to report incidents for fear of losing their independence (i.e., parents removing Internet devices to lower their exposure), being teased by peers, or lack of support from parents and police (King-Ries, 2011; Pensak, 2015). According to the Youth Internet Safety Survey, 48% of adolescents aged 10–17 were being harassed by another minor versus 24% aged 18–25 and 27% undisclosed age (Burgess & Baker, 2002). A case of an adult and adolescent collaborator pair who cyberstalked three adolescent male victims over a 2-year period is described in Box 5.2.

BOX 5.2   USA V. DEMIROVIC, 2021

Ramajana Hidic Demirovic, age 46, was indicted in April 2021 on one count of cyberstalking [18 U.S.C. 2261A(2)], and one count of conspiracy to commit cyberstalking [18 U.S.C. 371] for using social media over a 2-year period to harass, intimidate, and falsely impersonate three adolescent boys.[4] Each boy had dated her co-conspirator for

---

[4] https://www.justice.gov/usao-ndca/pr/former-san-francisco-resident-charged-multi-year-campaign-cyberstalking-against-three.

varying periods of time and after the relationship ended, the vengeful cyberstalkers were motivated by retaliation to sabotage them on
multiple levels including relationships, social reputation, academic,
and work.

- Victim A (age 14) dated the co-conspirator for a few days
  in February 2016. Following the break-up, Demirovic sent
  his mother intimidating messages, showed up the victim's
  school where she asked students to help her locate him, and
  after finding him accosted and threatened him. As a result
  of the cyberstalking, the victim stopped doing activities to
  avoid being confronted by Demirovic; needed therapy to
  deal with his anxiety, depression, and fear; and he started
  receiving poor grades.
- Victim B (age 15) dated the co-conspirator for the spring of
  2016. After the relationship ended, Demirovic began sending
  multiple series of texts in the summer of 2016, man of which
  belittled and humiliated him, as well as threatening bodily
  harm. In the fall of 2016, Demirovic and the co-conspirator
  used Instagram to mock the victim and also contacted the
  victim's school and employer with false reports of substance
  abuse and physical abuse. The effects of the cyberstalking
  on the victim included changing his phone number; limiting his friendships; deleting social media; declining grades;
  sleeplessness; and seeing a therapist to deal with his fear,
  distress, and helplessness.
- Victim C dated the co-conspirator from May 2017 to
  March 2018. For the next 17 months, Demirovic and the co-
  conspirator humiliated and isolated the victim socially and
  impersonated him on social media causing his friends to
  be concerned for his well-being. They also lodged sexual
  harassment and stalking complaints to the victim's university; showed up at his home; harassed his prom dates using
  texts; and made false claims about substance abuse. The
  cyberstalking incidents caused the victim to be traumatized
  in multiple ways, resulting in permanent harm to his social
  relationships (i.e., social ostracism); needing therapy; suffering from panic attacks; and several behavioral changes,
  including deleting social media and changing his phone
  number.

LAWS FOR PROSECUTING CYBERSTALKING

Specific anti-cyberstalking wording was not introduced into federal and state statutes until after U.S. Attorney General Janet Reno released a report advocating the need for separate legislature (U.S. Department of Justice, 1999). There are three relevant federal laws criminalizing elements of cyberstalking, but government statutes do not offer civil liability (Shimizu, 2013). The Interstate Communications Act, 18 U.S.C. § 875(c) (2006), allows prosecution of cyberstalking for transmission of threats to kidnap or injure a person by interstate or foreign commerce communication. As such it is limited in cases that do not involve "credible" threats (e.g., online posts, see *United States of America v. Alkhabaz*, 1997) or those not specifying injury or kidnapping, such as harassment (e.g., *United States of America v. Ryan S. Lin)*, commonly related to domestic violence situations (Fusco, 2014; Shimizu, 2013). The Federal Telephone Harassment Statute, 47 U.S.C. § 223 (2006), criminalizes communications (i.e., abuse, threats, harassment) that attempt to cause fear in the victim through telecommunications without disclosing one's identity [223 (a)(1)(C)] or repeated communication to harass the recipient [223 (a)(1)(E)]. However, it could not be used for cyberstalking prior to 2006, as it did not directly specify interactive computer or Internet services (Goodno, 2007). This statute cannot be applied for cyberstalking when the communication is anonymous or performed through third party as it would fail the direct communication and "knowingly" requirements (Fusco, 2014; Shimizu, 2013).

The Federal Interstate Stalking Punishment and Prevention Act, 18 U.S.C. § 2261A, prohibits cyberstalking through the 2006 amendment that expanded the "scope of intent, requisite action, and mechanism of injury" (p. 126). Specifically, the intentions of harassment, intimidation, and causing emotional distress were added to "kill or injure"; action now included "causes substantial emotional distress" instead of only "reasonable fear of death or serious bodily injury"; and mechanisms now encompassed "interactive computer service" (Shimizu, 2013, p. 126). Consider the following 2017 *United States of America v. Kassandra Cruz* case to determine whether you believe the legal consequences were appropriate for the crime (i.e., provided justice for the harm rendered). Kassandra Cruz, age 23, was arrested, charged, and successfully prosecuted for cyberstalking [Title 18, U.S.C., § 2261(A)(2)(B)] resulting in a 22-month sentence. She had started cyberstalking a 33-year-old California woman using her Facebook and Instagram social media accounts after finding the actress on a pornography site in June 2015. Cruz created multiple fake media accounts, which she used to interact with the victim. After these profiles were blocked, she began to harass and threaten the victim, her family, and her friends through over 900 phone and text messages from January until April 2016, revealing a sextortion plot to expose the pornography and demanded payment to not leak the pornography video.

States have approached legislation regarding cyberstalking differently. In some states, cyberstalking is defined within its own statute, whereas in other states it is addressed as a type of stalking or other criminal behavior (i.e., harassment) with an Internet activity component (DeMatteo et al., 2017; Goodno, 2007). Additionally, states may cover cyberstalking and its criminal actions under one law (e.g., Ohio) or multiple ones (e.g., Michigan) and liability may be only criminal or covers both criminal and civil (DeMatteo et al., 2017; Shimizu, 2013). Elements of the crime—actus reus (e.g., repetitive action) and mens rea (e.g., constructive knowledge or intent to cause fear)—and grading of the crime as felony vs. misdemeanor also differ across states (DeMatteo et al., 2017; Shimizu, 2013). For example, the actus reus in the California statute (CPC 646.9) includes "follows or harasses another person" and "makes a credible threat against that person to place that individual in reasonable fear for his/her safety or the safety of his/her family, which was communicated by means of the Internet or another electronic communication device," and the mens rea of "willfully, maliciously and repeatedly." Typically, cyberstalking is considered a misdemeanor offense punishable by up to 1 year in jail, but under certain circumstances (e.g., domestic violence, minor victim, violation of protection order) it is raised to felony levels (Shimizu, 2013). If the victim is an intimate partner (i.e., fiancé/fiancée, current/former spouse, roommate/housemate, parent of your child, dating partner), then the California domestic violence law subjects cyberstalkers to additional penalties (SHouse California Law Group, 2020).

Although on the surface it seems that victims of intimate partner violence who are being cyberstalked have appropriate criminal remedies, this is not the case (see Box 5.3 for problems with the current laws). The U.S. passed the Violence Against Women Act (VAWA) of 1994, as part of the Violent Crime Control and Law Enforcement Act, to address crimes related to domestic violence and stalking (Modi et al., 2014). However, in *United States v. Morrison (2000)*, the Supreme Court struck down the civil remedy provision in the VAWA that allowed victims to sue attackers. The rationale included that (1) it failed to meet the constitutional challenge and (2) Congress could not invoke power under the Commerce Clause because

BOX 5.3 WHAT IS NEEDED TO MAKE A CYBERSTALKING STATUTE COMPREHENSIVE?

In determining the adequacy of the criminal statute, Shimizu (2013) indicated it should have five components (p. 120):

1. *Address the use of electronic communications;*
2. *Not have a physical threat requirement;*
3. *Cover anonymous communications;*
4. *Not have a requirement that communications be directed at the victim; and*
5. *Address third-party inducement by the perpetrator.*

Let's examine whether 18 U.S. Code § 2261A includes these five aspects. According to the statute, electronic communications is specified by the phrase: "uses the mail, any interactive computer service or electronic communication service or electronic communication system of interstate commerce, or any other facility of interstate or foreign commerce." A physical threat is not required for prosecutors to charge a defendant with cyberstalking as indicated by the phrasing: "(2)...in a course of conduct that – ... (B) causes, attempts to cause, or would be reasonably expected to cause substantial emotional distress to a person..." The statute seems to cover anonymous electronic communications.[5] Unfortunately, the statute in its current form does not comprise all activities associated with cyberstalking (e.g., using or suggesting lewd acts and obscene images), address impersonation of the victim, or include direct enticements or indirect website posts to engage a third party to cyberstalk the victim (Fusco, 2014; Shimizu, 2013). The federal statute fails to offer comprehensive protection to victims (Shimizu, 2013), particularly minors (King-Ries, 2011; Pensak, 2013).

In contrast, a model cyberstalking protection statute is the 2016 version of 29 Ohio Revised Code § 2903.211[6] as it contains all five requisite components (Shimizu, 2013). Below are the corresponding phrases for each item with the terms fitting the requirements underlined.

---

[5] The failure to disclose one's identity in using telecommunications devices for purposes of threats and harassment is also covered under 47 U.S.C. § 223(a)(1)(E).

[6] https://codes.ohio.gov/ohio-revised-code/section-2903.211.

1. *Electronic communication*: 2903.211 (A)(1) "No person, through the use of any form of written communication or <u>any electronic method of remotely transferring information</u>, including, but not limited to, any <u>computer, computer network computer program, computer system, or telecommunication device</u> shall post a message or use any intentionally written or verbal graphic gesture..."
2. *Non-physical threat*: "No person by engaging in a pattern of conduct shall knowingly cause another person to believe that the offender will cause physical harm to the other person or a family or household member of the other person or <u>cause mental distress</u> to the other person or a family or household member of the other person."
3. *Anonymous*: "(D) As used in this section: ...(7) "Post a message" means...whether done <u>under one's own name, under the name of another, or while impersonating another</u>."
4. *Indirect communication*: "In addition...the other person's belief or mental distress may be based on words or conduct of the offender that are <u>directed at or identify a corporation, association, or other organization</u> that employs the other person or to which the other person belongs."
5. *Third-party inducement*: "(2) No person....do either of the following: (1) Violate division (A)(1) of this section; (b) <u>Urge or incite another</u> to commit a violation of division (A)(1) of this section"; and (B)(2) "Menacing by stalking is a felony in the fourth degree if any of the following applies: ...(b)...<u>a third person induced by the offender's posted message</u> made a threat of physical harm to or against the victim"; and (h) "<u>a third person induced by the offender's posted message</u> caused serious physical harm to that premises, that real property, or any personal property on that premises."

domestic violence crimes were not "economic" in nature nor under the 14th Amendment as harm was inflicted by individuals not states (Shimizu, 2013; The Women's Legal Defense and Education Fund, n.d.). The only civil remedies available to cyberstalking victims currently are intentional infliction of emotional distress[7] and defamation[8] (Powell, 2020). In reality, however, neither are typically used because the challenges of time, financial (e.g., attorney fees), emotional (e.g., facing the perpetrator), and limited claim applicability outweigh probability of reli Unfortunately, the statute in its current ef, especially in domestic violence cases (Powell, 2020).

IMPACT OF CYBERSTALKING ON SOCIETY AND VICTIMS

Victims' responses to cyberstalking will vary depending on a number of factors. Not surprisingly, the type (e.g., property crimes, identity theft, physical attacks), severity (e.g., rape, wounds, emotional harm), frequency (e.g., daily, weekly), and duration (e.g., days, months, years) of incidents along with the offender-victim relationship (e.g., intimate partner, stranger) moderated consequences (Truman, 2010). Oftentimes, victims wait rather than report incidents, hoping to end attacks simply by ignoring them and/or not confronting or angering the cyberstalker (Alexy et al., 2005). Victims are also discouraged after their attempts to get help from police or through orders of protection or restraint do not result in their pursuers desisting (Spitzberg & Cupach, 2007). However, the reality is that the cyberstalking incidents vary–from one day to several years (Truman, 2010). A 2016 DOJ study revealed that 17% of victims were stalked less than 1 month; 45% for 1 month to nearly a year; 13% for 1 year to nearly 2 years; and 24% for two or more years (Truman & Morgan, 2021).

Common reactions to cyberstalking include psychological (e.g., depression, panic attacks), emotional (e.g., fear, anxiety, guilt), behavioral (e.g., sleeplessness, changing routines), financial (i.e., loss of income, relocation costs, medical and legal expenses; replacement costs for damaged or compromised property); social (e.g., changing identities, social withdrawal, including self-isolation); and physical/health (e.g., chronic headaches, eating disorders; gastrointestinal; conditions, stress) consequences (Buzawa

---

[7] Liability requires plaintiff to show "extreme and outrageous conduct intentionally or reckless causes severe emotional distress" (Restatement (Second) of Torts § 46(1); Am. Law Inst., 1965)).

[8] Liability requires plaintiff to show "false and defamatory statement concerning another; unprivileged publication to third-party; fault amounting to at least negligence; and either actionability of the statement irrespective of special harm or existence of special harm caused by the publication" (Restatement (Second) of Torts: Elements Stated § 558; Am. Law Inst., 1977)).

et al., 2017; Dreßing et al., 2014; Kirwan & Power, 2012; Nobles et al., 2014; Parsons-Pollard & Moriarty, 2009; Philips & Morrissey, 2004; Walker, 2017; Yar, 2006). Victims may also feel responsible for their victimization. They may comply with demands when their cyberstalkers threaten to commit suicide otherwise (Alexy et al., 2005; Philips & Morrissey, 2004). Over time, their coping strategies and emotional support networks become less effective, especially when the intensity of the attacks increase, and they are subjected to victim-blaming by society (Spitzberg & Cupach, 2007). As a result of their safety concerns and feelings of helplessness, many victims seek counseling (McFarlane & Bocij, 2003; Ngo & Paternoster, 2013; Parsons-Pollard & Moriarty, 2009). The top concerns of victims include simply not knowing when and what the stalker will do next; possibility of bodily harm; and seeing no end to the abuse (Baum et al., 2009; Parsons-Pollard & Moriarty, 2009).

Society does not understand this crime in terms of its (a) seriousness, as demonstrated by comments that portray surface behaviors like pursuit and persistence as innocuous and an overreaction by the victim; (b) prevalence; or (c) potential and actual harm to individuals and the public (Strawhun et al., 2013). Consequently, victims are loath to react to cyberstalking behaviors as being criminal, posing a danger, and needing to be reported to law enforcement, which in turn depresses actual prevalence rates as currently encapsulated in official statistics (Ashcroft, 2001; Cheyne & Guggisberg, 2018; King-Ries, 2011; Kirwan & Power, 2012). In particular, society may downplay harm from cyberstalking and consider police involvement as unnecessary when adolescents are the perpetrators or when male victims are pursued by female stalkers/cyberstalkers (Pensak, 2015; Phillips, Quirk, Rosenfeld, & O'Connor, 2004; Sheridan et al., 2003; Strawhun et al., 2013). Society also perceives verbal threats in cyberstalking as less serious and dangerous than physical ones, which in turn will likely result in victims not reporting incidents to police and the crime not being prosecuted (Sheridan & Scott, 2010). Currently, professionals in health and law enforcement fail to perceive cyberstalkers' techniques to exert power and control over victims as serious and menacing, instead conceiving these actions as merely poorly implemented romantic gestures that serve to reinforce the stalkers' own denial of responsibility and normalizes intimate partner violence (Cheyne & Guggisberg, 2018; King-Ries, 2011; Parsons-Pollard & Moriarty, 2009; Purcell et al., 2010). Without tangible harm from physical (life-threatening) threats, it is difficult for victims to get a restraining order or even for the perpetrators to receive guilty verdicts (Sheridan & Scott, 2010).

CYBERSECURITY TACTICS

The Internet provides multiple opportunities to cross paths with a potential cyberstalker. Education and training in net safety practices (e.g., NNEDV Safety Net, Technology Safety Project)[9] are common tactics to employ daily (also see Chapter 12 in this volume). To reduce the likelihood of becoming a victim, the following prevention measures should be performed when joining and using social media platforms:

1. screen names should be devoid of personal information, such as name, nickname, gender and age;
2. a new email account should be created for use only with the social media account;
3. passwords should be complex and unique to each account (i.e., email, social media) to prevent someone from guessing it and be sure to change each password every couple of months;
4. privacy options should be set to the most restrictive level, use filters to remove unwanted communications, block unknown users, and do not discuss personal information with anyone on the platform or in publicly viewable forums;
5. log out when you are not using the computer to avoid someone being able to use it or gain access to your accounts;
6. google yourself to determine how much information is publicly available;
7. do not post photos with GPS location or provide information regarding your location, vacation/travel plans, etc.; and
8. check your computer for spyware programs and keylogging devices (Canadian Resource Center for Victims of Crime, 2021; Dhillon & Smith, 2019; Kirwan & Power, 2012; Nobles et al., 2014; Ogilvie, 2000; Reyns et al., 2012; Stalking Prevention, Awareness, and Resource Center, 2018).

Technology can be used to safeguard a victim from cyberstalkers. For example, there are antivirus apps that use *heuristics* and *signatures* to detect if stalker apps are present on the device being used (Eterovic-Sori et al., 2017). *Rooting* will allow users to install security software (i.e., privacy guards) to block malicious apps from accessing private data on Android systems (Eterovic-Sori et al., 2017). *Jailbreaking*, needed for iOS devices,

---

[9] https://www.techsafety.org/resources-survivors and https://techsafetyapp.org/home; Finn & Atkinson (2009).

should only be used when the App Store does not have software to detect spyware. To reduce victimization opportunities, people can safeguard their phones by employing the *biometric factors* (e.g., fingerprint, iris scan), which aids in the device's detection of the legitimate user and prevents unauthorized users from accessing information. Currently, researchers are examining digital text forensic options for cyberstalking detection (e.g., Frommholz et al., 2016).

Victims should implement three types of protective measures, including:

1. limit their interactions:
   a. if the site they are on currently has become hostile, they should log off immediately;
   b. do not ever volunteer to meet a cyberstalker, regardless of communication indicating that it can be worked out in person;
2. employ legal remedies:
   a. contact law enforcement to determine the course of action available to them (e.g., protection order if over age 18), particularly if the stalking, harassment, and threats have begun occurring offline (Call 911);
   b. gather evidence:
      i. save all harassing and unwanted messages online and print a copy; take screenshots; record video chats; etc. for evidence to give to the authorities for investigation;
      ii. keep a hand-written log of contacts by the cyberstalker, especially if the victim's computer is compromised;
3. implement actions to ensure safety by:
   a. changing their contact information (e.g., email address, ISP, phone number) and their Internet device (if possible);
   b. developing a safety plan that evolves as needed and includes scenarios of what could possibly happen, with help from a victim services program or agency and support from their friends, family, and colleagues;
   c. contacting their own Internet Service Providers/ISPs (as well as the ISP of the cyberstalker if they know it) to file a complaint;
   d. filing a report with a third-party online service organization, such as *Working to Halt Online Abuse*/WHOA (halta-buse.org); *Stalking Prevention, Awareness, and Resource Center*/SPARC (stalkingawareness.org); *Victim Connect* (855-484-2846, https://victimconnect.org); and *Cyberangels*

(voicesfordignity.com/cyberangels), which can offer advice on prevention and assistance in evidence needed for prosecution and help in convincing law enforcement to get involved (Canadian Resource Center for Victims of Crime, 2021; Dhillon & Smith, 2019; Kirwan & Power, 2012; Nobles et al., 2014; Ogilvie, 2000; Reyns et al., 2012; Stalking Prevention, Awareness, and Resource Center, 2018).

According to Tokunaga and Aune (2017), victims use different management tactics to deal with their cyberstalking encounters—from passive measures (i.e., ignore and avoid; technology privacy management) to active ones (i.e., confrontation; delete accounts; help seeking; providing false information to cyberstalker). Victims should hold ISPs accountable by reporting incidents to the abuse and security department because harassment is considered a violation of the ISPs' *Acceptable Use Policy*. All ISPs have the ability to implement measures either to limit cyberstalkers from contacting you (e.g., assisting the victim in changing passwords, removing malicious software, or blocking the IP address in future communications) and/or terminate the violator's service (Canadian Resource Center for Victims of Crime, 2021; Kirwan & Power, 2012; Stalking Prevention, Awareness, and Resource Center, 2018).

REFERENCES

Ahlgrim, B., & Terrance, C. (2021). Perceptions of cyberstalking: Impact of perpetrator gender and cyberstalker/victim relationship. *Journal of Interpersonal Violence, 36*(7), NP4074–NP4093.

Alexy, E.M., Burgess, A.W., Baker, T., & Smoyak, S.A. (2005). Perceptions of cyberstalking among college students. *Brief Treatment and Crisis Intervention, 5*(3), 279–289. Doi: 10.1093/brief-treatment/mhi020.

Al Mutawa, A., Bryce, J., Franqueira, V., & Marrington, A. (2016). Forensic investigation of cyberstalking cases using Behavioral Evidence Analysis. Digital Investigation, 16, S96–S103. Doi: 10.1016/j.diin.2016.01.012

Andersen, C.H. (2021). *What is Love Bombing? 11 Ways to Spot this Relationship Red Flag.* https://www.thehealthy.com/family/relationships/love-bombing/.

Ashcroft, J. (2001). *Stalking and Domestic Violence: Report to Congress.* Washington, DC: U.S. Department of Justice.

Baker, C.K., & Carreño, P.K. (2016). Understanding the role of technology in adolescent dating and dating violence. *Journal of Child & Family Studies, 25,* 308–320.

Basile, K.C., Swahn, M.H., Chen, J., & Saltzman, L.E. (2006). Stalking in the United States: Recent national prevalence estimates. *American Journal of Preventive Medicine, 31*(2), 172–175.

Baum, K., Catalano, S., Rand, M., & Rose, K. (2009). *Stalking Victimization in the United States.* Washington, DC: U.S. Department of Justice.

Berry, M.J., & Bainbridge, S.L. (2017). Manchester's cyberstalked 18–30s: Factors affecting cyberstalking. *Advance in Social Sciences. Research Journal, 4*(18), 73–85. Doi: 10.14738/assrj.418.3680.

Bocij, P. (2003). Victims of cyberstalking: An exploratory study of harassment perpetrated via the internet. *First Monday, 8*(10), 1–12.

Bocij, P. (2004). *Cyberstalking: Harassment in the Internet Age and How to Protect Your Family.* Westport, CT: Praeger.

Bocij, P. (2006). *The Dark Side of the Internet: Protecting Yourself and Your Family from Online Criminals.* Westport, CT: Greenwood Publishing Group.

Buhi, E.R., & Clayton, H., & Surrency, H.H. (2009). Stalking victimization among college women and subsequent help-seeking behavior. *Journal of American College Health, 57*(4), 419–426.

Burgess, A.W., & Baker, T. (2002). Cyberstalking. In J. Boon & L. Sheridan (eds.). *Stalking and Psychosexual Obsession: Psychological Perspectives for Prevention, Policing and Treatment* (pp. 201–220). Chichester: John Wiley C Sons, Ltd.

Buzawa, E.S., Buzawa, C.G., & Stark, E.D. (2017). *Responding to Domestic Violence: The Integration of Criminal Justice and Human Services* (5th ed.). New York: Sage.

Canadian Resource Center for Victims of Crime. (2021). *Protection from Cyberstalking: Basic Advice.* https://crcvc.ca/docs/cyberstalking.pdf

Carman, M., & Choo, K.-K.R. (2017). Tinder me softly – How safe are you really on Tinder? *Proceedings of the 12th International Conference on Security and Privacy in Communication Networks. Lecture Notes of the Institute for Computer Sciences, Social Informatics and Telecommunications Engineering,* vol. 198, pp. 271–286, Springer-Verlag.

Cavezza, C., & McEwan, T.E. (2014). Cyberstalking versus off-line stalking in a forensic sample. *Psychology, Crime & Law, 20*(10), 955–970. Doi: 10.1080/1068316X.2014.893334.

Chang, L.Y.C. & Zhu, J. (2020). Taking justice into their own hands: Predictors of Netilantism among cyber citizens in Hong Kong. *Frontier Psychology.* Doi: 10.3389/fp-syg.2020.556903 https://www.frontiersin.org/articles/10.3389/fpsyg.2020.556903/full.

Cheyne, N., & Guggisberg, M. (2018). Stalking: An age old problem with new expressions in the digital age. In M. Guggisberg & J. Henricksen (eds.), *Violence against Women in the 21st Century: Challenges and Future Directions* (pp. 161–190). Hauppauge, New York: Nova Science Publishers.

Cox, C. (2014). Protecting victims of cyberstalking, cyberharassment, and online impersonation through prosecutions and effective laws. *Jurimetrics, 54*(3), 277–302.

D'Ovidio, R., & Doyle, J. (2003). Study on cyberstalking: Understanding investigative hurdles. *FBI Law Enforcement Bulletin, 72(3)*, 10–17.

DeKeseredy, W.S., Schwartz, M.D., Harris, B., Woodlock, D., Nolan, J., & Hall-Sanchez, A., 2019. Technology-facilitated stalking and unwanted sexual messages/images in a college campus community: The role of negative peer support. *SAGE Open, 9(1)*. Doi: 10.1177/2158244019828231.

DeMatteo, D., Wagage, S., & Fairfax-Columbo, J. (2017). Cyberstalking: Are we on the same (web) page? A comparison of statutes, case law, and public perception. *Journal of Aggression, Conflict, and Peace Research, 9(2)*, 83–94.

Dhillon, G., & Smith, K.J. (2019). Defining objectives for preventing cyberstalking. *Journal of Business Ethics, 157*, 137–158.

Dowdell, E.B., & Bradley, P.K. (2010). Risky internet behaviors: A case study of online and offline stalking. *The Journal of School Nursing, 26(6)*, 436–442. Doi: 10.1177/1059840510380209

Dreßing, H., Bailer, J., Anders, A., Wagner, H., & Gallas, C. (2014). Cyberstalking in a large sample of social network users: Prevalence, characteristics, and impact upon victims. *Cyberpsychology, Behavior, and Social Networking, 17(2)*, 61–67.

Duntley, J.D., & Buss, D.M. (2012). The evolution of stalking: Issues of gender in stalking research. *Sex Roles, 66(5–6)*, 311–327.

Eterovic-Soric, B., Choo, K-K. R., Ashman, H., & Mubarak, S. (2017). Stalking the stalkers—detecting and deterring stalking behaviors using technology: A review. *Computers & Security, 70*, 278–289.

Fansher, A.K., & Randa, R., 2019. Risky social media behaviors and the potential for victimization: A descriptive look at college students victimized by someone met online. *Violence Gender, 6(2)*, 115–123. Doi: 10.1089/vio.2017.0073.

Finkelhor, D., Mitchell, K.J., & Wolak, J. (2000). *Online Victimization: A Report on the Nation's Youth* (No. 6-00-020). Alexandria, VA: National Center for Missing and Exploited Children.

Finn, J. (2004). A survey of online harassment at a university campus. *Journal of Interpersonal Violence, 19*, 468–483.

Finn, J., & Atkinson, T. (2009). Promoting the safe and strategic use of technology for victims of 0intimate partner violence: Evaluation of the technology safety project. *Journal of Family Violence, 24(1)*, 53–59.

Fissel, E.R. (2019). *Victimization of the 21st Century: An Examination of Cyberstalking Victimization Using a Target Incongruence Approach*. Dissertation, University of Cinncinati. https://etd.ohiolink.edu/apexprod/rws_etd/send_file/send?accession=ucin1553613508435002&disposition=inline.

Fissel, E.R. (2021a). The reporting and help-seeking behaviors of Cyberstalking victims. *Journal of Interpersonal Violence, 36(11–12)*, 5075–5100. Doi: 10.1177/0886260518801942.

Fissel, E.R. (2021b). Victims' perceptions of cyberstalking: An examination of perceived offender motivation. *American Journal of Criminal Justice*, 1–15. Doi. 10.1007/s12103-021-09608-x.

Fissel, E.R. & Reyns, B.W. (2020). The aftermath of cyberstalking: School, work, social, and host costs of victimization. *American Journal of Criminal Justice, 45*, 70–87.

Fraser, C., Olsen, E., Lee, K., Southworth, C., & Tucker, S. (2010). The new age of stalking: Technological implications for stalking. *Juvenile and Family Court Journal, 61(4)*, 39–55. Doi: 10.1111/j.1755-6988.2010.01051.x.

Frommholz, I., al-Khateeb, H.M., Potthast, M., Ghasem, Z., Shukla, M., & Short, E. (2016). On textual analysis and machine learning for cyberstalking detection. *Datenbank Spektrum, 16*, 127–135.

Fusco, C.A. (2014). *Stalking 2.0: The Era of Cyberstalking*. Ann Arbor, MI: ProQuest Dissertations Publishing, 1571120.

Goodno, N.H. (2007). Cyberstalking, a new crime: Evaluating the effectiveness of current state and federal laws. *The Missouri Law Review, 72*, 125. https://scholarship.law.missouri.edu/cgi/viewcontent.cgi?article=3985&context=mlr

Hamin, Z., & Wan Rosli, W. (2018). Cloaked by cyber space: A legal response to the risks of cyber stalking in Malaysia. *International Journal of Cyber Criminology, 12(1)*, 316–332. Doi: 10.5281/zenodo.1467931.

Hoang, N.P., Asano, Y., & Yoshikawa, M. (2016). Your neighbors are my spies: Location and other privacy concerns in dating apps in 2016. *18th International Conference on Advanced Communication Technology (ICACT)*, IEEExplore 7423532, pp. 715–721. PyeongChang Koria (South).

Holt, T.J., & Bossler, A.M. (2009). Examining the applicability of lifestyle-rou-tine activities theory for cybercrime victimization. *Deviant Behavior, 30*, 1–25. Doi: 10.1080/01639620701876577.

Hutton, S., & Haantz, S. (2003). *Cyber Stalking*. Retrieved from National White Collar Crime Center: http://www.nw3c.org.

Jerin, R., & Dolinsky, B. (2001). You've got mail! You don't want it: Cyber-victimization and on-line dating. *Journal of Criminal Justice and Popular Culture, 9*, 15–21.

Kaur, P., Dhir, A., Tandon, A., Alzeiby, E.A., & Abohassan, A.A. (2021). A systemic literature review on cyberstalking: An analysis of past achievements and future promises. *Technological Forecasting & Social Change, 163*, 120426. Doi: 10.1016/j.techfore.2020.120426.

Khanna, A. (2015). *Facebook's Privacy Incident Response: A Study of Geolocation Sharing on Facebook Messenger*. https://techscience.org/a/2015081101/.

King-Ries, A. (2011). Teens, technology, and cyberstalking: The domestic violence wave of the future? *Texas Journal of Women and the Law, 20(2)*, 131–164.

Kircaburun, K., Jonason, P.K., & Griffiths, M.D. (2018). The Dark Tetrad traits and problematic social media use: The mediating role of cyberbullying and cyberstalking. *Personality and Individual Differences, 135*, 264–269. Doi: 10.1016/j.paid.2018.07.034.

Kirwan, G., & Power, A. (2012). *The Psychology of Cybercrime: Concepts and Principles*. IGI Global. Doi: 10.4018/978-1-61350-350-8.ch009.

Kraft, E.M., & Wang, J. (2010). An exploratory study of the cyberbullying and cyberstalking experiences and factors related to victimization of students at a public liberal arts college. *International Journal of Technoethics, 1(4)*, 74–91. Doi: 10.4018/jte.2010100106.

115

LeBlanc, J.J., Levesque, G.J., Richardson, J.B., & Berka, L.H. (2001). Survey of stalking at WPI. *Journal of Forensic Science, 46*(2), 367–369.

Lenhart, A., Ybarra, M., Zickuhr, K., & Price-Feeney, M. (2016). *Online Harassment, Digital Abuse, and Cyberstalking in America.* New York: Data & Society. https://www.datasociety.net/pubs/oh/Online_Harassment_2016.pdf.

Maple, C., Short, E., & Brown, A. (2011). *Cyberstalking in the United Kingdom: An analysis of the ECHO Pilot Survey.* Luton: National Centre for Cyberstalking Research, University of Bedfordshire.

Maran, D.A., & Begotti, T., 2019. Prevalence of cyberstalking and previous offline victimization in a sample of Italian university students. *Social Science, 8*(1), 1–10. Doi: 10.3390/socsci8010030.

Marcum, C.D., Higgins, G.E., & Ricketts, M.L. (2010). Potential factors of online victimization of youth: An examination of adolescent online behaviors utilizing routine activities theory. *Deviant Behavior, 31*(5), 1–31.

Marcum, C.D., Higgins, G.E., & Ricketts, M.L. (2014). Juveniles and cyberstalking in the United States: An analysis of theoretical predictors of patters of online perpetration. *International Journal of Cyber Criminology, 8*(1), 47–56.

McCollister, K.E., French, M.T., & Fang, H. (2010). The cost of crime to society: New crime-specific estimates for policy and program evaluation. *Drug and Alcohol Dependence, 108*(1–2), 98–109.

McFarlane, L., & Bocij, P. (2003). An exploration of predatory behaviour in cyberspace: Towards a typology of cyberstalkers. *First Monday, 8*(9), 1–10.

McQuade, S.C. (2006). *Understanding and Managing Cybercrime.* Boston, MA: Allyn & Bacon.

Ménard, K.S., & Pincus, A.L. (2012). Predicting overt and cyberstalking perpetration by male and female college students. *Journal of Interpersonal Violence, 27*(11), 2183–2207.

Mishra, D., & Mishra, A. (2008). Cyberstalking: A challenge for web security. In L.J. Janczewski and A.M. Colarik (eds.), *Cyber Warfare and Cyber Terrorism* (pp. 216–225). Hershey, PA: IGI Global.

Modi, M.N., Palmer, S., & Armstrong, A. (2014). The role of Violence Against Women Act in addressing intimate partner violence: A public health issue. *Journal of Women's Health, 23*(3), 263–259.

Moriarty, L.J., & Freiberger, K. (2008). Cyberstalking: Utilizing newspaper accounts to establish victimization patterns. *Victims & Offenders, 3*(2–3), 131–141.

Ngo & Paternoster, F.T., & Paternoster, R. (2013). Cybercrime victimization: An examination of individual and situational level factors. *International Journal of Cyber Criminology, 5*(1), 773–793.

Nobles, M. R., Reyns, B.W., Fox, K.A., & Fisher, B.S. (2014). Protection against pursuit: A conceptual and empirical comparison of cyberstalking and stalking victimization among a national sample. *Justice Quarterly, 31*(6) 986–1014, Doi: 10.1080/07418825.2012.723030.

Ogilvie, E. (2000). Cyberstalking. *Trends & Issues in Crime and Criminal Justice Canberra: Australian Institute of Criminology, 166,* 1–6.

Parsons-Pollard, N., & Moriarty, L.J. (2009). Cyberstalking: Utilizing what we do know. *Victims & Offenders, 4(4)*, 435–441. Doi: 10.1080/15564880903227644.

Paullet, K.L., Rota, D.R., & Swan, T.T. (2009). Cyberstalking: An exploratory study of students at a mid-Atlantic university. *Issues in Information Systems, 10(2)*, 640–649.

Pensak, R. (2015). Must be 18 or older: How current domestic violence policies dismiss teen dating violence. *Journal of Women & the Law in William & Mary Journal of Race, Gender, and Social Justice, 21(2)*, 499–523.

Phillips, F., & Morrissey, G. (2004). Cyberstalking and cyberpredators: A threat to safe sexuality on the internet. *Convergence, 10(1)*, 66–79.

Phillips, L., Quirk, R., Rosenfeld, B., & O'Connor, M. (2004). Is it stalking? Perceptions of stalking among college undergraduates. *Criminal Justice and Behavior, 31(1)*, 73–96. Doi: 10.1177/0093854803259251.

Powell, K. (2020). *Cyberstalking: Holding Perpetrators Accountable and Providing Relief for Victims.* https://jolt.richmond.edu/cyberstalking-holding-perpetrators-accountable-and-providing-relief-for-victims/.

Purcell, R., Pathé, M., & Mullen, P. (2010). Gender differences in stalking behaviour among juveniles, *The Journal of Forensic Psychiatry & Psychology, 21(4)*, 555–568, Doi: 10.1080/14789940903572035.

Reyns, W.B., Henson, B. & Fisher, S.B. (2012). Being pursued online: Applying cyberlifestyle–routine activities theory to cyberstalking victimization. *Criminal Justice and Behavior, 38(11)*, 1149–1169. Doi: 10.1177/0093854811421448.

Rodríguez-Castro, Y., Martínez-Roman, R., Alonso-Ruido, P., Adá-Lameiras, A., & Carrera-Fernández, M.V. (2021). Intimate partner cyberstalking, sexism, pornography, and sexting in adolescents: New challenges for sex education. *International Journal of Environmental Research and Public Health, 18*, 2180–2193.

Sheridan, L., Gillett, R., Davies, G., Blaauw, E., & Patel, D. (2003). 'There's no smoke without fire': Are male ex-partners perceived as more 'entitled' to stalk than acquaintance or stranger stalkers? *British Journal of Psychology, 94*, 87–98.

Sheridan, L., & Grant, T. (2007). Is cyberstalking different? *Psychology, Crime & Law, 13*, 627–640. Doi: 10.1080/10683160701340528.

Sheridan, L.P., & Lyndon, A.E. (2012). The influence of prior relationship, gender, and fear on the consequences of stalking victimization. *Sex Roles, 66(5–6)*, 340–350.

Sheridan, L., & Scott, A.J. (2010). Perceptions of harm: Verbal versus physical abuse in stalking scenarios. *Criminal Justice and Behavior, 37(4)*, 400–416. Doi: 10.1177/0093854809359743.

Shimizu, A. (2013). Domestic violence in the digital age: Towards the creation of a comprehensive cyberstalking statute. *Berkeley Journal of Gender, Law, & Justice, 28*, 116–137.

Shorey, R.C., Cornelius, T.L., & Strauss, C. (2015). Stalking in college student dating relationships: A descriptive investigation. *Journal of Family Violence, 30(7)*, 935–942.

Shouse California Law Group. (2020). *California Cyberstalking Laws.* https://www.shouselaw.com/ca/defense/laws/cyberstalking/#1.

Short, E., Guppy, A., Hart, J.A., & Barnes, J. (2015). The impact of cyberstalking. *Studies in Media and Communication, 3*(2), 23–37.

Smoker, M. & March, E. (2017). Predicting perpetration of intimate partner cyberstalking: Gender and the dark tetrad. *Computers in Human Behavior, 72,* 390–396. Doi: 10.1016/j.chb.2017.03.012.

Spitzberg, B.H., & Cupach, W.R. (2007). The state of art of stalking: Taking stock of the emerging literature. *Aggression and Violent Behavior, 12,* 64–86.

Spitzberg, B.H., & Hoobler, G. (2002). Cyberstalking and the technologies of interpersonal terrorism. *NewMedia & Society, 4*(1), 71–92.

Spitzberg, B.H., & Veksler, A. (2007). The personality of pursuit: Personality attribution of unwanted pursers and stalkers. *Violence and Victims, 22,* 275–289. Doi: 10.1891/088667007780842838.

Stalking Prevention, Awareness, and Resource Center. (2018). *Stalking Safety Strategies.* https://www.stalkingawareness.org/wp-content/uploads/2018/11/Safety-Strategies.pdf.

Strawhun, J., Adams, N., & Huss, M.T. (2013). The assessment of cyberstalking: An expanded examination including social networking, attachment, jealousy, and anger in relation to violence and abuse. *Violence Victims, 28*(4), 715–731.

The Women's Legal Defense and Education Fund. (n.d.). *History of Violence Against Women Act.* https://www.legalmomentum.org/history-vawa.

Tokunaga, R.S., & Aune, K.S. (2017). Cyber-defense: A taxonomy of tactics for managing cyberstalking. *Journal of Interpersonal Violence, 32*(10), 1451–1475. Doi:10.1177/0886260515589564.

Truman, J.L. (2010). *Examining Intimate Partner Stalking and the Use of Technology in Stalking Victimization.* University of Central Florida, Dissertation. etd.fcla.edu/CF/CFE0003022/Truman_Jennifer_L_201005_PhD.pdf.

Truman, J.L., & Morgan, R.E. (2021). *Stalking Victimization, 2016* (NCJ253526). U.S. Department of Justice, Bureau of Justice Statistics. https://www.bjs.gov/content/pub/pdf/sv16.pdf.

U.S. Department of Justice. (1999). *Cyberstalking: A new challenge for law enforcement and industry: A report from the Attorney General to the Vice President.* NCJ# 179575. Washington, DC: National Institute of Justice.

U.S. Government Accountability Office. (2016). *Smartphone Data: Information and Issues Regarding Surreptitious Tracking Apps that Can Facilitate Stalking.* GAO-16-317 http://www.gao.gov/assets/680/676738.pdf.

Walker, L.E.A. (2017). *The Battered Woman Syndrome* (4th ed.). New York: Springer Publishing Company.

Wang, F-Y., Zeng, D., Hendler, J.A., Zhang, Q., Feng, Z., Gao, Y., Wang, H., & Lai, G. (2010). A study of the human flesh search engine: Crowd-powered expansion of online knowledge. *Computer, 43*(8), 45–53.

Welsh, A., & Lavoie, J.A.A. (2012). Risky eBusiness: An examination of risk-taking, online disclosiveness, and cyberstalking victimization. *Cyberpsychology 6*(1), Article 4. Doi: 10.5817/CP2012-1-4.

Williams, L.Y. (2012). "Who is the virtual" you and do you know who's watching you? In D.R. Neal (ed.), *Social Media for Academics* (pp. 175–192). Sawston: Chandos Publishing.

Witwer, A.R., Langton, L., Vermeer, M.J.D., Banks, D., Woods, D., & Jackson, B.A. (2020). *Countering Technology-Facilitated Abuse: Criminal Justice Strategies for Combatting Nonconsensual Pornography, Sextortion, Doxing, and Swatting.* https://www.rand.org/content/dam/rand/pubs/research_reports/RRA100/RRA108-3/RAND_RRA108-3.pdf.

Worsely, J.D., Wheatcroft, J.M., Short, E., & Corcoran, R. (2017). Victims' voices: Understanding the emotional impact of cyberstalking and individuals' coping responses. *Sage Open, April-June,* 1–13. Doi: 10.1177/2158244017710292.

Wykes, M. (2007). Constructing crime: Culture, stalking, celebrity and cyber. *Crime, Media, Culture,* 3(2), 158–174. Doi: 10.1177/1741659007078541.

Yar, M. (2006). *Cybercrime and Society.* London: Sage Publications Ltd Doi: 10.4135/9781446212196.

Zweig, J., Dank, M., Yahner, J., & Lachman, P. (2013). The rate of cyber dating abuse among teens and how it relates to other forms of teen dating violence. *Journal of Youth and Adolescence,* 42(7), 1063–1077.

CASES

United States of America v. Alkhabaz (1997). 104 F. 3d 1492 (6th Cir.).

United States of America v. Kassandra Cruz (2017). The Southern District of Florida.

United States of America v. Demirovic (2021). Case No. 3:21-cr-00133 VC California Northern District.

United States of America v. Ryan S. Lin (2018). Case No. 118-cr-10092-WGY District of Massachusetts.

United States of America v. Morrison (2000). 529 U.S. 598

6

Cyberbullies and Cyber Harassers

DEFINING CYBERBULLYING AND CYBER HARASSMENT

Most American adults (62%) view cyberbullying and harassment as major social issues and public health hazards (Beran et al., 2012;

DOI: 10.4324/9781003092292-6

D'Auria, 2014; Duggan, 2017; Fridh et al., 2015; Van Royen et al., 2016). A comparison of the traditional and online forms of bullying and harassment is provided in **Box 6.1**. Cyberbullying and harassment are defined as the use of electronic communications to launch willful and repeated personal attacks that threaten, insult, embarrass, humiliate, harm, and/or socially exclude individuals or groups[1] (Beran & Li, 2005; Hafeez, 2014; Hinduja & Patchin, 2010; Kowalski et al., 2008; Li, 2007; Raskauskas & Stoltz, 2007; Sampasa-Kanyinga et al., 2014; Wang et al., 2009, 2010). The requirement for acts to reoccur in defining cyberbullying and harassment is problematic. Even one incident online (e.g., posting a picture, meme, or insult) can result in enormous consequences for the victim as others who have viewed it make comments and/or forward it, which increases the audience size and ensures that both the original and related postings will remain in cyberspace permanently (Fridh et al., 2015). Moreover, the occurrence of cyberbullying/harassment incidents has been found to be positively related to the amount of time bullies/harassers and victims spend engaged in online activities, which is troubling given that high schoolers average 5.5 hours/day (Celik et al., 2012; Cox, 2014; Juvonen & Gross, 2008; Kraft & Wang, 2010; Kowalski & Limber, 2013; Kowalski et al., 2014, 2018; Ybarra & Mitchell, 2004). For example, 67% of high schoolers who indicate that they are online almost constantly vs. 53% who are online up to several times a day report being bullied (Anderson, 2018).

BOX 6.1   TRADITIONAL VS. ONLINE FORMS OF BULLYING AND HARASSMENT

Researchers argue that traditional (offline) bullying and harassment share similarities with their online versions, but disagree as to whether they are the same or distinct phenomena (Antoniadou & Kokkinos, 2015). One important difference is that when offline bullies and harassers are no longer in the same physical space as their victims, the behavior stops (Watts et al., 2017). In contrast, there is no respite from cyberbullying/harassment—which provides unlimited and easy access to victims 24 hours per day/seven days

---

[1] This chapter will not address cyber harassment of organizations/businesses.

per week (Willard, 2007). Additionally, the power imbalance element that typifies the bullying/harassment dyadic relationship is less clearly defined online and likely plays a more minor role than does anonymity (Antoniadou & Kokkinos, 2015). As discussed in Chapter 1, four qualities of the online environment—toxic disinhibition, de-individuation, anonymity, and inculpability—foster cyberbullying and harassment (Antoniadou & Kokkinos, 2015; Suler, 2004; Watts et al., 2017; Willard, 2007). Victims believe they are targeted due to their perceived low status (e.g., disability, sexual orientation, gender, race, ethnicity), which may occur more frequently in cyberspace than in the physical world (Baboza & Schiamberg, 2021; Tolba et al., 2021).

Cyberbullying and harassment be differentiated first by the age of those involved (minor vs. adult, respectively) and second by the legal consequences for perpetrators (Burgin, 2012). Cyberbullying describes repeated acts of aggression or abuse by juveniles against their peers, whereas cyber harassment involves a series of repeated acts that consist of spam and/or undesirable sexual components, such as sexual solicitation, sexual harassment, obscenity, or voyeurism (Behm-Morawitz & Schipper, 2016; Wick et al., 2017) between adults whose relationship may be intimate partners, strangers, or acquaintances (Campbell, 2005; Jameson, 2008; Miller, 2006; Welsh & Lavoie, 2012). Victimization is enabled not only by the absence of systematic monitoring by popular social media platforms (e.g., Twitter, Instagram, Facebook) of their users' conduct in regard to cyber harassment and bullying, but also by their immunity from liability afforded through Section 230 of the Communications Decency Act (CDA). Americans overwhelmingly (79%) believe that Internet Service Providers (ISPs) have a duty to provide security to prevent harassment on their platforms (Duggan, 2017). Barring extreme cases (e.g., suicide), school administrators handle cyberbullying cases consistent with their policies under state law (Willard, 2007). Civil remedies for cyber harassment of adult victims by adult perpetrators are more commonly pursued than their criminal counterparts; however, the latter is dependent upon the elements of the case, such as if it involved impersonation and/or other violations under the Computer Fraud and Abuse Act (CFAA); has elements of a hate crime; involves discriminatory harassment; includes cyberstalking; and/or violates civil rights laws (Gordon, 2021; Cyberbullying Research Center, 2019; Willard, 2007).

Prevalence of cyber harassment and bullying is difficult to estimate due to (1) variations in research methodology, especially for definitions and age groups used; (2) reliance on official statistics based on prosecution charges used; (3) reluctance to admit one's role as victim and/or perpetrator; and (4) categories for roles as nonvictims/witnesses only; victims only; perpetrators only; or both victim and perpetrator (Baldry et al., 2017; Chrisholm, 2014; Dehue et al., 2008). Researchers found that online users were exposed/witnessed (5%–88%); cyberbullied (10%–52%); and/or had been the target of cyberbullying/harassment (minors: 26%–41%; college students: 10%–33%) on social media platforms and in chat rooms (Duggan, 2017; Festl & Quandt, 2013; Finn, 2004; Gahagan et al., 2016; Hamm et al., 2015; Hinduja & Patchin, 2010; Li, 2007; Lenhart et al., 2016; Melander, 2010; Vogels, 2021). In fact, 17%–23% of elementary school aged children (grades 3–5) and 15%–21% of middle schoolers and high schoolers (grades 6–12) indicated they had been cyberbullied (Centers for Disease Control and Prevention/CDC, 2020a, 2020b, 2020c; Chandler, 2015; DePaolis & Williford, 2019; Patchin & Hinduja, 2020; Seldin & Yanez, 2019; Ybarra & Mitchell, 2004). Online offending and victimization patterns are often repeated from elementary school to high school to college, but those bullied also reported becoming the offender in college (Beran et al., 2012; Chapell et al., 2006; Dilmac, 2009).

Of the 54% of high schoolers who reported witnessing cyberbullying, 35% indicated that they attempted to intervene on the victim's behalf (Cox, 2014). According to Duggan (2017), of the 66% who reported being adult bystanders to cyber harassment, only 30% intervened; additionally, 41% reporting that they had been directly targeted, with 18% indicating the incidents had been extreme (e.g., physical threats, sexual harassment). Actual prevalence rates are presumed to be higher as only 6%–35% of minors and adult victims told anyone, including parents and teachers, of their abuse (Kraft & Wang, 2010; Li, 2007; Francisco et al., 2014; United Press International/UPI, 2008; Watts et al., 2017). Cyberbullying is not limited to the U.S. as 12%–37% of minors in other countries indicate they have been victims and 3%–24% admit cyberbullying someone else (Beran & Li, 2005; Livingstone et al., 2011; Lobe et al., 2011; Microsoft, 2012; Sakellariou et al., 2012). According to the 2019 Fundamental Rights Survey (European Union Agency for Fundamental Rights, 2021) administered to 34,948 respondents (ages 16+) in 29 countries, 14% indicated they had been cyberbullied/harassed in the last year (ranging from 9% to 42%, depending on the country) through internet comments (7%) or offensive/threatening emails or texts (11%).

TYPICAL CYBERBULLIES AND HARASSERS

Research findings are inconsistent regarding the typical sex, age, and socio-economic status of cyberbullies/harassers, which may be due to perception of the respondents, the online environment, and/or the type of online bullying/harassment assessed. In some studies, boys/men are more likely than girls/women to perpetrate online bullying/harassment, whereas in others, no sex differences were found (Baldry et al., 2017; Dehue et al., 2008; Göerzig, 2011; Li, 2007; MacDonald & Roberts-Pittman, 2010; see Wilson et al., 2020, for review). Wilson et al. (2020) suggested that perpetration is positively related to socio-economic status and age, at least for minors, due to high proficiency and availability of technology and likelihood of having an online presence. Adolescents (15–17) and young adults (18–29) were more likely than children (<12) or older adults (>30) to self-identify as perpetrators (Lenhart et al., 2016; Wilson et al., 2020). Minors who cyberbully tended to be narcissistic, have low self-control, poor self-esteem, weak empathy, high impulsivity, delinquent peers, and parents who did not supervise their online activity (Kim et al., 2017; see Wilson et al., 2020, for review). Common characteristics of cyberbullies and harassers, according to Watts et al. (2017), included that they needed to exert social dominance or power over others; demonstrated poor interpersonal relationships (i.e., lacks social skills); and were vulnerable to peer pressure (i.e., overly attuned to social cues).

CYBERBULLIES' AND HARASSERS' MOTIVES AND METHODS

Common motives for cyberbullying/harassment include two **proactive** types (i.e., planful and deliberate targeting)—(1) *entertainment* or excitement, including boredom, disrupt relationships, or sadistic enjoyment at others' suffering; and (2) *prejudice* (or dislike) based on differences in appearance, ideology, etc.; and two **reactive** types (i.e., targeting based on perceived threats, insults, or provocation)—(1) *revenge* or *retaliation* out of anger, jealousy, or hatred; and (2) *social affiliation/status/acceptance*, such as peer pressure to increase or maintain power or to get attention (Abbasi et al., 2018; Calvete et al., 2010; Fluck, 2017; Schenk et al., 2013; Shapka & Law, 2013; Varjas et al., 2010). Player rank was mentioned as an important motive for cyberbullying/victimization on game sites (Ballard & Welch, 2017). Minors who engage in cyber aggression may be unaware that they

125

are being abusive (Campbell et al., 2013), often stating that their participation in the incident was part of a joke rather than motivation to cause harm (Law et al., 2012).

Langos (2012) conceptualized cyberbullying methods as *direct* (i.e., perpetrator attacks on the victim) or *indirect* (i.e., bystanders join in the attack), but insisted that specific elements must be present (i.e., repetition of intentional malicious act by perpetrator of perceived higher status). Common types of cyber harassment and bullying (some overlapping with other forms of online crime, such as trolling or hacking) and their common formats have been identified and are displayed in Table 6.1 (Abbasi et al., 2018; Ballard & Welch, 2017; Calvete et al., 2010; Chrisholm, 2014; Durkin & Patterson, 2011; Lenhart et al., 2016; Li, 2007; Watts et al., 2017; Willard, 2007). Research suggests that female and feminine adolescent cyberbullies engaged in cyber relational aggression (e.g., spread rumors, mean comments) through social networks and mobile phones, whereas male and masculine adolescent cyberbullies preferred physical aggressive forms (e.g., threats to hurt them), typically through online gaming (Patchin & Hinduja, 2020; Wright, 2020).

TYPICAL CYBERBULLY AND HARASSER VICTIMS

Cyberbullied youth are most likely to be adolescents from middle-class to upper-class families and those whose parents do not monitor their online activities (Baboza & Schiamberg, 2021; CDC, 2020b; Göerzig, 2011; Mishna et al., 2012; Rice et al., 2015). There is some evidence suggesting that victimization is highest for middle-school girls who are unpopular and middle-school boys who are currently being bullied offline (Rivers & Noret, 2010). However, risk for high schoolers is mixed, with some cyberbullying studies suggesting girls are more vulnerable than boys and others claiming the opposite (Vale et al., 2018). This inconsistency may be partially explained by whether investigators included victim-perpetrators as a third, separate category from victims and perpetrators (Vale et al., 2018).

Tables 6.2 and 6.3 provide the percentage of middle schools[2] and high schoolers from 2011 to 2019 who indicated they were electronically bullied on social media during the previous 12 months prior to completing the Youth Risk Behavior Surveillance System (YRBSS) online survey

---

[2] This dataset included 11 to 14 states, depending on the variable, but not each of these states participated in all aspects of the survey—such as race or grade.

Table 6.1 Type and Description of Cyber Harassment and Bullying in Their Typical Formats

Types	Description	Format				
		Email	Text/IM	Games	SNS	DMB
Flaming	Distributing aggressive, offensive, profane or cruel content (aka shock trolling), typically written in all capital letters and excessive punctuation marks, that insults victim's physical appearance, statements, worth, sexuality, etc. in an attempt to provoke confrontational, inane arguments.	✓	✓	✓	✓	✓
Online harassment	Offensive language used to insult, threaten, and emotionally harm victim ("slamming"), often encouraging strangers to join in the taunting process ("cyberbullying by proxy" or "brigading"); also includes bombing emails with numerous spam messages.	✓	✓	✓	✓	✓
Cyberstalking	Following person, issuing threats of harm, and use of various techniques[a] to intimidate and instill fear for one or others' safety.	✓	✓	✓	✓	✓
Denigration and Defamation	Lies, rumors, or gossip constructed to be cruel; slander one's sexual, social, or professional reputation (cybersmearing), typically by posting embarrassing and sexually explicit images; and/or harm/destroy social relationships.	✓	✓	✓	✓	✓

(Continued)

127

Table 6.1 (*Continued*) Type and Description of Cyber Harassment and Bullying in Their Typical Formats

Types	Description	Email	Text/IM	Games	SNS	DMB
				Format		
Impersonation	Either set up fake profile or catfish to gain images and information or hack into victim's computer to gain access to real profiles ("fraping"); send and post disparaging messages to friends and other users to taint reputation or social relationships; gamers may steal items from account (e.g., money, weapons).	✓		✓	✓	✓
Trickery	Tricking person into revealing embarrassing or personal information and then distributing it without permission.		✓		✓	✓
Outing	Nonconsensual distribution of embarrassing, compromising, or personal information, images, or situations in which they are attacked or humiliated (aka "happy slapping" or "exposing").	✓	✓	✓	✓	✓
Exclusion/ Ostracism	Excluding (shunning) individual from online group (e.g., delete from friendship list) and implementing plans that include "cheating, forming roving gangs, and blocking entryways" in MMOGs (Chrisholm, 2014, p. 79).		✓	✓	✓	✓

Key: MMOGs = massive multiplayer online games; IM = instant messages; SNS = social networking sites; DMB = discussion forums, message boards, and blogs.

[a] Ratting is the dominant method in which the perpetrator uses *Remote Administration Tool* software to gain control of the victim's computer or webcam via in order to spy and obtain files (Chrisholm, 2014).

Table 6.2   Percentage of Middle Schoolers Who Experienced Electronic Bullying by Sex, Race, and Grade from 2011 to 2019

	2011 (%)	2013(%)	2015(%)	2017(%)	2019(%)
Sex					
Male	15	13	15	15	17
Female	31	31	32	31	30
Race					
AI/AN	27	25	28	26	26
Asian	24	20	19	18	19
Black	15	15	16	17	18
Latinx	23	24	23	17	25
NH	—	21	24	—	25
White	15	25	25	17	24
Multiple	27	27	28	26	27
Grade					
6	19	19	19	15	20
7	23	22	24	23	23
8	24	26	26	26	26
Total	23	23	24	15	23

Key: AI/AN, American Indian/Alaskan Native; NH, Native Hawaiian/Other Pacific Islander.

Table 6.3   Percentage of High Schoolers Who Experienced Electronic Bullying by Sex, Race, and Grade from 2011 to 2019

	2011 (%)	2013(%)	2015(%)	2017(%)	2019(%)
Sex					
Male	11	9	10	10	11
Female	22	21	22	20	20
Race					
AI/AN	16	18	19	13	21
Asian	14	13	14	10	12
Black	9	9	9	11	7
Latinx	14	13	12	12	13
NH	20	16	12	15	<1

(*Continued*)

Table 6.3 (*Continued*) Percentage of High Schoolers Who Experienced Electronic Bullying by Sex, Race, and Grade from 2011 to 2019

	2011 (%)	2013(%)	2015(%)	2017(%)	2019(%)
White	19	17	18	17	19
Multiple	21	19	20	16	19
Grade					
9	16	16	17	17	17
10	18	15	17	15	16
11	16	15	15	14	14
12	15	14	14	14	15
Total	16	15	16	15	16

Key: AI/AN, American Indian/Alaskan Native; NH, Native Hawaiian/Other Pacific Islander.

(CDC, 2020b, 2020c). The data indicates both sex and grade trends: (1) twice as many girls than boys in grades 6–12 were electronically bullied and (2) middle schoolers reported gradual increase in cyberbullying from grades 6 to 8 (18%, 23%, 26%), whereas high schoolers reported a gradual decrease in cyberbullying from grades 9 to 12 (17%, 16%, 15%, 14%). Offline bullying is also an issue given that 25% of cyber victims attend the same school as their bullies (Slonje & Smith, 2008). Cyberbullying and harassment victims reported different attack behaviors (Price & Dalgleish, 2010), with *offensive name calling* being the most common (80%), followed by *abusive comments* (67%) and *spreading false rumors* (66%). Sex differences in the types of harassment have also been reported, as shown in Figure 6.1 (Lenhart et al., 2016). Vogels (2021) reported an increase in sex differences for male and female adult victims of three types of cyber harassment— offensive names (35% vs. 26%); physical threats (16% vs. 11%); and sexual harassment (5% vs. 16%).

Cox (2014) indicated that cyberbullying victims believed they were targeted primarily because of their appearance (61%) and, to a lesser extent, their intelligence/academic achievement (25%), race (17%), financial status (15%), religion (11%), or sexuality (15%). Sexual orientation has also played a role (Cassidy et al., 2009) for children and adults. The CDC (2020b) reported that 27% of non-heterosexual adolescents (Gay, Lesbian, Bi-sexual, Trans)

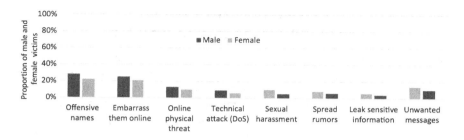

Figure 6.1 Proportion of male and female victims reporting different types of online harassment experiences.

were electronically bullied compared to 14% of heterosexual adolescents. Vogels (2021) reported that adult victims were targeted for political views (20%); gender (14%); race or ethnicity (12%); sexual orientation (7%); and religion (8%). The type of online method for cyberbullying/harassment victims differed by age, as shown in Figure 6.2 (Holfeld & Grabe, 2012; Price & Dalgleish, 2010; Vogels, 2021; Wassdorp & Bradshaw, 2015). Price and Dalgleish (2010) also reported that between ages 13 and 18, social networking sites became increasingly more prevalent as the location for cyberbullying, affecting 41% of those aged 13–14, 53% aged 15–16, and 57% aged 17–18. According to Ditch the Label (2017), Instagram leads online social media platforms in cyberbullying victimization (42%), followed by Facebook (38%), Snapchat (31%), and YouTube (10%). Adult gamers were more likely to be victims (52%) than bullies (35%), usually by unknown users (65%), while playing on MMOG sites (Ballard & Welch, 2017).

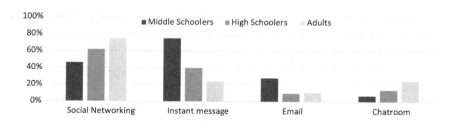

Figure 6.2 Proportion of three age groups victimized by type of online method.

LAWS FOR PROSECUTING CYBERBULLYING/HARASSMENT

Generally, communicated threats have been criminalized as a form of unprotected speech through 18 U.S.C. § 875, but in the Supreme Court's assessment of the legality and seriousness of threats in electronic media (Spitzberg & Gawron, 2016), the burden of proof falls on the prosecutor to provide the mens rea requirement rather than threats simply having a prima facie indication (Maras, 2015). Cyber harassers who encourage others to participate in the crime may be prosecuted federally for violation of a person's civil rights (Marwick & Miller, 2014). For example, it is unlawful for two or more people to conspire to injure, oppress, threaten, of intimidate anyone's free exercise of rights under the Constitution as per 18 U.S.C. § 241 (Conspiracy against rights).[3] There is no federal law criminalizing cyberbullying (Gordon, 2021), unless discriminatory harassment occurred in which the person was targeted based on one of the protected classes—race, ethnicity, color, national origin, sex, disability, or religion (Stopbullying.gov, 2019, 2021).

All 50 states have antibullying and anti-harassment legislation to guide schools; 42 states[4] have laws mandating formal school policies for bullying, 44 states[5] have criminal sanctions for cyberbullying/electronic harassment; and 45 states[6] have school sanctions for cyberbullying that allow administrators to impose appropriate discipline (Cyberbullying Research Center, 2019; Stopbullying.gov, 2019, 2021). **Box 6.2** provides cyberbullying laws in California and Missouri. Criminal charges against cyber harassment varies by state, typically require that targeted person was exposed to intentional acts that were meant not only to alarm, annoy, torment, or terrorize them, but also constituted a credible threat to their own and others' safety. Prosecution for defamation of a person's character is possible in 26 states[7] (Marwick & Miller, 2014). Harassment charges range from misdemeanors to felonies; however, the latter is most likely

---

[3] Federal Bureau of Investigation. (n.d.). *Federal Civil Rights statutes.* https://www.fbi.gov/investigate/civil-rights/federal-civil-rights-statutes.

[4] Except Arizona, Colorado, Texas, Missouri, Arkansas, Mississippi, North Carolina, and Hawaii.

[5] Except Maine, Minnesota, Nebraska, New Hampshire, New Mexico, and Wyoming.

[6] Except Alabama, Michigan, Montana, Nevada, and New Hampshire.

[7] Kenworthy, B., & Chesterman, B. (2006). *Criminal-libel statutes, state by state.* Freedom Forum Institute. https://www.freedomforuminstitute.org/first-amendment-center/topics/freedom-of-the-press/criminal-libel-statutes-state-by-state/; states included relevant to persons as victims: Alabama, Colorado, Florida, Georgia, Idaho, Iowa, Kansas, Kentucky, Louisiana, Massachusetts, Michigan, Minnesota, Mississippi, Montana, Nevada, New Hampshire, New Mexico, North Carolina, North Dakota, Ohio, Oklahoma, South Carolina, South Dakota, Utah, Virginia, and Wisconsin.

BOX 6.2   CYBERBULLYING LAWS IN
CALIFORNIA AND MISSOURI

California statutes: Anti-cyberbullying laws under **EDC § 48900,** which defines bullying in an educational facility to include by means of an electronic act (e.g., message, text, sound, video, image, posting, credible impersonation, false profile, cyber sexual bullying), by a pupil or group of pupils direct toward one or more pupils, and **EDC § 234** [Safe Place to Learn Act] which establishes students' "inalienable rights to attend class on school campuses that are safe, secure, and peaceful" (Findlaw, 2019).

- *AB 79, Chapter 646* (2001): Requires the Department of Education (DoE) to develop model policies on bullying prevention and conflict resolution, as part of school safety plan.
- **AB 9.** *Seth's Law* (2011): Specifies school policy and investigation processes.
- **AB 1156** (2011): Expanded bullying definition to include disruption and detrimental effects on students' academic performance, encourage administrator training, and removal of victims from unhealthy environment.
- **AB 746** (2011): Expanded bullying to include student behaviors on social networking sites as "electronic act" warranting suspension or expulsion [under B. 86, 2008 Code §32261 (g)].
- **AB 256,** *Chapter 700* (2013): Specifies the role of the school in intervening in off-campus bullying, with "electronic act" referring to creation and transmission either on or off school site.
- **AB 1542.** *Jordan's Law* (2017): Makes willful recording of a violent felony with intent to encourage or facilitate the offense an aggravating factor.

Cal. Pen. Code §653.2: criminalizes intent to place another in reasonable fear for safety by means of an electronic communication device; misdemeanor punishable by 1 year in jail, by fine of up to $1000, or both.

Missouri statutes: Anti-cyberbullying laws under **R.S.Mo. Title XI. Education and Libraries § 160.775 Antibullying policy (2016),** which defines bullying as repetitive intimidation, unwanted aggressive behavior, or harassment that causes a reasonable student to fear for safety or property, substantially interferes with educational performance, opportunities, or benefits, or disrupts the orderly operation of school. It includes cyberbullying and electronic communication of messages, texts, sounds, and images through social media for the purpose of bullying (specifically violent threats). There is also a requirement for each district to produce antibullying policy and procedures for reporting and investigating bullying within 2 days of incident report and an allowance for administrators to discipline students violating anti-cyberbullying rules to the greatest extent allowed by law.

R.S.Mo. 160.261.1. Written discipline policy by local board of education, includes #24 for harassment under §565.090.

R.S.Mo. 160.775 Title V. Harassment may be charged as Class A misdemeanor, but is Class D felony if victim is 17 or less and defendant is 21 or older or has a prior harassment conviction.

R.S.Mo. 565.090. Harassment, first degree may be charged as Class E felony.

R.S.Mo. 565.091. Harassment, second degree may be charged as Class A misdemeanor, unless previously found guilty or pled guilty of violation of this offense.

when offenders had been previously convicted for harassment, threats, or domestic violence offenses and when the victim was targeted based on one of the protected classes. However, criminal prosecution of the operators of social media platforms, discussion forums, and other types of websites on which cyber harassment occurred is not possible due to immunity through the CDA§ 230 (Marwick & Miller, 2014).

Civil remedies through intentional torts, despite being time consuming and expensive, are most likely the best option. Victims can sue their cyberbullies/harassers (and/or the minors' parents through parental liability laws and findings of negligence for not preventing cyberbullying when informed by the school) to recover financial damages for injuries, costs associated with removing posted material, and attorney fees (Spitzberg & Gawron, 2016; also see Chapter 11 for further explanation). Depending on the case, the following legal actions may be relevant (Marwick & Miller, 2014; Willard, 2007):

- *Defamation of character and libel,* when a false statement that is published without authorization results in damage to reputation that cause the person to be hated, ridiculed, shunned, etc.;

- *Invasion of personal privacy/false light,* right to privacy is violated by disclosure of information not known by the public, and which the public is not entitled, that is offensive to a reasonable person;
- *Invasion of privacy/public disclosure of a private fact,* when disclosed information is offensive to a reasonable person, such as health records (which meet prima facie standard);
- *Negligent and intentional infliction of emotional distress,* when extreme and outrageous behaviors result in extreme distress.

IMPACT OF CYBERBULLYING AND HARASSMENT ON SOCIETY AND VICTIMS

Cyber bullying/harassment consequences for victims are similar to their offline counterparts: **emotional responses** (e.g., anger, sadness, embarrassment, fear, terror); **internalizing symptoms** (e.g., anxiety, depression, low self-esteem); and **externalizing symptoms** affecting *health* (e.g., insomnia, suicidal ideations, psychosomatic complaints including headaches and stomachs, lower self-ratings, self-injury, suicide, substance abuse, unexplained weight gain/loss), *socialization* (e.g., delinquency, loneliness, social isolation from terminating relationships with friends, family, and significant others and avoiding school and social events), and *academic/employment* (e.g., impaired concentration, low motivation, high absenteeism, declining performance) (Akbulut & Cuhadar, 2011; Beran & Li, 2005; Beran et al., 2012; DeHue et al., 2008; Edwards et al., 2016; Fridh et al., 2015; Hinduja & Patchin, 2007, 2008, 2009; Hoff & Mitchell, 2009; Machmutow et al., 2012; Mitchell et al., 2007; Price & Dalgleish, 2010; Schenk & Fremouw, 2012; Schneider et al., 2012; Spears et al., 2009; Ybarra et al., 2007). Most of the youth (aged 11–16) in Smith et al.'s (2008) study responded that they endured cyberbullying for 1–2 weeks (57%), whereas the rest reported suffering longer—for a month (19%), 6 months (6%), 1 year (9%), or several years (10%). Long-term consequences indicated for victims (and potentially for bystanders) include substance abuse, school drop-out, delinquency, criminal convictions, and early sexual activity (Khan et al., 2020; Patchin & Hinduja, 2006).

Cyberbullies and harassers negatively impact society through their antisocial, violent, and/or criminal behaviors, which result in both social and economic costs for the community because their victims' voices are silenced and their recovery needs include health care and financial assistance (Patchin & Hinduja, 2006; Price & Dalgleish, 2010; Kulig et al., 2008). For example, Lenhart et al. (2016) reported that female adolescents and

135

young adults aged 15–29 were more likely than either their same age male counterparts to self-censor online to avoid possible harassment (41% vs. 33%) or even men and women age 30 and older (23% and 24%, respectively). Additionally, a high proportion of bystanders aged 15–29 witnessed online bullying and harassment behaviors targeting an individual (i.e., 83% person called offensive names, 80% purposefully embarrass person, 53% person physically threatened, 43% person sexually harassed), which over time is likely to lead to disinhibition (Lenhart et al., 2016). Communities whose members have been cyberbullied and harassed are tasked with providing them with mental and physical health care, financial aid, and other social services, potentially losing the benefits of productive citizens for a period of years (Hinduja & Patchin, 2010; Price & Dalgleish, 2010). News stories of cyberbullying and harassment ending with victims committing suicide have appeared over the past decade, such as occurred with Rutgers under-graduate student, Tyler Clementi, and signal societal social and health cri-ses (Schenk et al., 2013).

Box 6.3 provides the types of coping mechanisms employed by cyber-bullying victims. According to Lenhart et al. (2016), 65% of adult victims of cyber harassment employed at least one strategy to protect themselves from future attacks, including changing their personal information (43%), seeking help (33%), reporting violations to ISPs (27%), and separating themselves from online contact (26%). Orel et al. (2015) reported that while college-aged victims of cyber harassment used similar coping mecha-nisms, women were more likely than men to use blocking, threaten to report, and help seeking from family, friends, instructors, and counselors. As with other interpersonal cybercrimes, victims who had social supports were less likely to have mental health problems (Davidson & Demaray, 2007; Fridh et al., 2015; Machmutow et al., 2012). Family and friends may observe the victim reacting in anxious or stressful ways to texts and emails or after using social media and/or avoid using computers or sud-denly turning their internet device off in mid-use (Woda, 2015). Research suggests that the type of cyberbullying/harassment impacts adolescent victims differently, such that images were reported to have a more nega-tive consequence on them than words (Smith et al., 2008). For example, Price and Delagleish (2010) found that cyberbullying of adolescent victims resulted in various behavior problems—such as declining grades (35%), absenteeism (28%), and poor family relationships (19%). Additionally, girls and boys may interpret and react to cyberbullying differently resulting in stronger internalizing problems for girls vs. externalizing problems or no problems for boys (Schultze-Krumbholz et al., 2012). Lenhart et al. (2016)

also reported sex differences such that women were more likely than men to interpret online behaviors as "harassment" (53% vs. 40%), twice as likely to be worried by it, and three times more likely to be scared by it.

BOX 6.3   COPING MECHANISMS FOR DEALING WITH CYBERBULLYING

Coping mechanisms employed by cyberbullying victims include: (1) tell family, teachers, and/or friends; (2) block/ignore; (3) avoid/stay offline and/or self-isolate; (4) keep record and evidence of incidents; (5) report to ISP; (6) ask perpetrator to stop; and (7) get revenge/fight back (Hinduja & Patchin, 2007; Schenk & Fremouw, 2012; Smith et al., 2008). Girls seem to be more likely than boys to use help-seeking strategies, whereas boys are more likely than girls to use retaliation strategies (Orel et al., 2015). Hinduja and Patchin (2014) found that tweens reported strategies of seeking help (51%), blocking (60%), ignoring (43%), staying offline (30%), and reporting to ISP (30%). Juvonen and Gross (2008) indicated that minor victims commonly used blocking (75%), changing privacy setting/restricting friend list (45%), switching profile name (44%), and sending warnings (34%). In fact, most cyberbullying minors (50%–90%) do not choose strategy #1 of help-seeking and instead prefer strategies #2, #3, or #7 listed above (Cassidy et al., 2012; Juvonen & Gross, 2008; Slonje & Smith, 2008; Tokunaga, 2010). Minor victims explained their decisions not to report incidents (Juvonen & Gross, 2008) as: (1) they believed it was something best handled themselves (50%); (2) did not want to have their internet access restricted by parents (31%); and/or (3) thought they would be punished for their victimization (30%). Unfortunately, minor victims still did not report incidents even when their strategies failed to stop the abuse and/or the situation became dangerous (Hoff & Mitchell, 2009). Despite laws implemented to prevent cybervictimization, research findings suggest that minors are either unaware that the schools are supposed to be helping them with these incidents or purposefully avoiding notifying administration. Both explanations signal that anti-cyberbullying laws, policies, and programs are ineffective and suggest that students perceive their school climates as non-supportive (Cassidy et al., 2012; Parris et al., 2012).

CYBERSECURITY TACTICS

Solutions for handling online harassment include cybersecurity education (see Chapter 12), laws, and technology. Laws that criminalize cyberbullying and harassment are needed on a federal level to handle the variety of situations arising out of internet attacks on victims across multiple jurisdictions (Chrisholm, 2014; Cooper & Blumenfeld, 2012; Slonje et al., 2013). The scientific community and victims recommend that countries work together to develop effective international laws against cyberbullying/harassment (Redondo-Sama et al., 2014). Currently, online websites for blogs, discussion forums, social media, games, etc. must ensure that (a) their policies effectively protect users from digital victimization (if they do not, it should be recommended that they lose their Section 230 immunity from liability) and (b) mechanisms are in place that allow administrators responsible for making or overseeing this process to delete bullying and harassing posts; temporarily and/or permanently suspend social media users who bully or harass other users; and require users to fully disclose their real identities to prevent bullies/harassers who hide behind anonymity (Vogels, 2021). For example, Twitter suspends accounts that contain spam/fake or abusive content (Chatzakou et al., 2017). Victims need to be able to inform ISPs when cyberbullying/harassment occurs and whatever software or mechanism that is offered to users should be simple and easy to use (Redondo-Sama et al., 2014). Twitter, Instagram, and Facebook[8] have online reporting systems that include information pages and instructions for reporting violations (Lam, n.d.).

Many social media sites use various types of **simple keyword-based** approaches—such as rule-based, machine learning, lexicon-based hybrid, or deep learning (Kaur et al., 2021). Table 6.4 provides the four options from considering each type of situation and how it can be coded. *Rulebased* methods use words generated by users (e.g., Facebook, Instagram) or predefined ones (e.g., YouTube) to detect abusive content, but result in

Table 6.4   Four Options for Threat/No Threat Situations and True/False Coding

Situation	Coded as Real Threat	Coded as No Threat
Threat	True (accurate)	False negative
No threat	False positive	True (accurate)

---

[8] Twitter - https://support.twitter.com/articles/15794-online-abuse; Facebook https://www.facebook.com/help/420576171311103/; Instagram - https://help.instagram.com/527320407282978.

high false positives and false negatives[9] (Kaur et al., 2021). Another type of cybersecurity that ISPs can use to detect and/or prevent cyberbullying or harassment on their platforms is a *machine-learning algorithm*, such as online linguistic surveillance, that can determine whether online statements are harassment or simply incivility (Magarry, 2014); Näsi et al., 2014; Sengupta & Chaudhuri, 2011; Spitzberg & Gawron, 2016).

Online linguistic surveillance may be performed either by computer analysis or by expert/layperson to review the content of the message and determine whether it is a credible threat or non-threat/false threat (e.g., joke, sarcasm). This process requires the determination of intentional threats based on relevance and implications; negative valence (i.e., harm or undesirable consequence); and credibility (i.e., potential for it to be enacted), but accurate detection may be highly contextual and/or case specific (Spitzberg & Gawron, 2016). Spitzberg and Gawron's (2016) method had low reliability as only 22% of assessment accurately recognize when there was a risk (true) or not (false), whereas 60% result in false positives (i.e., claiming risk when there is none) and 18% false negatives (i.e., claiming no risk when there is risk).

Lexicon-based methods have had some success in detecting profanity, but performance is negatively affected when users misspell words, use evolving profanity, or the offensiveness of the language is context-dependent (Sood et al., 2012). *Hybrid techniques* that combine lexicon with rule and machine-learning strategies have overcome some of the previously mentioned shortcomings, resulting in efficient hate speech detection (Kaur et al., 2021). *Deep-learning strategies*, which rely on neural networks for machine learning, have demonstrated effectiveness in detecting hate speech and harassment (Tolba et al., 2018; Zhang et al., 2018). Classification of Twitter content as *aggressor* (posts 1 negative, harmful or insulting tweet), *bully* (posts multiple negative, harmful, or insulting tweets on same topic), *spammer* (posts ads), and *normal user* through deep learning demonstrated 0.71 precision, which increased to 0.91 after spam removal occurred (Chatzakou et al., 2017). Chatzakou et al. (2019) were able accurately to emulate Twitters classification system that resulted in accounts being deleted (87%) or suspended (82%). Using an *imbalanced learning* technique that first removed irrelevant elements and reduced noise, Tolba et al. (2021) reported that the *Generative Adversarial Networks* model; *cost-sensitive deep learning,* which takes into account misclassification errors; and *validation-loss strategy* based on deep-learning models all performed better than techniques assuming balanced class distribution.

---

[9] False positives refer to finding that an event (abusive content) occurred when it did not, whereas false negatives refer to indicating the event did not occur when it actually did.

Minors can also mobilize themselves to take an active stand against cyberbullying, including convincing the community and bystanders not to collude with the bullies and instead support and defend victims (Lam, n.d.).[10] There are apps that also can be used to combat cyberbullying either by providing resources (i.e., Take a stand together, Safe Eyes Mobile, Knowbullying) or identifying harassment (Bully Button, Re-think, Bully Block).[11] **Take a stand together** is an app that provides tips, resources, and supports for minors to understand cyberbullying. **Safe Eyes Mobile** is an app that parents can employ to safeguard children who should not be given full access online by using filters to customize and block specific websites. **Knowbullying** is an app that combats cyberbullying through knowledge, specifically providing adults with a guide to communicate concerns about online use with minors. **Bully Button** operates by flagging/alerting online harassment using frameworks consistent with school antibullying programs. The main benefit of this app is to reduce the "bystander effect" of being silent and instead provides users with templates for reporting what they witnessed. **Re-think**—an app created by an adolescent—employs a proactive strategy to prevent cyberbullying by signaling users that their message contains inappropriate content and offers them the opportunity to reword it. **Bully Block** is an app that provides a means for victims to record/capture evidence of cyberbullying to report it to adults.

Similar to Bully Block, **Threat Resolution & Incident Preservation Platform** (TRIPP™), created by a 2016 company called Inteliqore, is another comprehensive mechanism for identifying and preserving cyberbullying/harassment (INTELiLQORE, INC., 2021). Three elements offered include: (1) capturing and preserving legally acceptable and self-authenticating forensic evidence (i.e., identifying who, how, and why); (2) managing digital life through a centralized dashboard by defining the parameters/identifiers for the capture threshold, getting end-to-end control over online identity; and (3) collaborating with resolution entities for each incident; and resolving online harassment incidents by sharing incidents with the "Verified Help Network." As no research has been conducted using any of these mechanisms, their effectiveness is not known.

---

[10] Teens Against Cyberbullying – http://www.pacerteensagainstbullying.org/tab/; Teenangels – http://teenangels.org/internet_safety/cyberbullying.html; Peer campaign – http://preventingbullying.promoteprevent.org/cyberbullyin.

[11] *Top apps to stop cyberbullying*. The Daily Iowan. https://dailyiowan.com/2021/06/01/top-apps-to-stop-cyberbullying/.

REFERENCES

Abbasi, S., Naseem, A., Shamim, A, & Qureshi, M.A. (2018, November 21–22). An empirical investigation of motives, nature and online sources of cyberbullying. *2018 14th International Conference on Emerging Technologies (ICET)*, 1–6. Doi: 10.1109/ICET.2018.8603617.

Akbulut, Y., & Cuhadar, C. (2011). Reflections of preservice information technology teachers regarding cyberbullying. *Turkish Online Journal of Qualitative Inquiry, 2(3)*, 67–76.

Anderson, M. (2018). *A Majority of Teens Have Experienced Some Form of Cyberbullying*. A Majority of Teens Have Experienced Some Form of Cyberbullying. https://www.pewresearch.org/internet/2018/09/27/a-majority-of-teens-have-experienced-some-form-of-cyberbullying/.

Antoniadou, N., & Kokkinos, C.M. (2015). Cyber and school bullying: Same or different phenomena? *Aggression and Violent Behavior, 25*, 363–372.

Baboza, G.E., & Schiamberg, L.B. (2021). Racial and ethnic diversity in the social ecology of online harassment and cybervictimization: The adolescent-school context. In M.F. Wright & L.B. Schiamberg (eds.), *Child and Adolescent Online Risk Exposure: An Ecological Perspective* (pp. 233–254). London: Elsevier Inc. Doi: 10.1016/B978-0-12-817499-9.00012-0.

Baldry, A.C., Farrington, D.P., & Sorrentino, A. (2017). School bullying and cyberbullying among boys and girls: Roles and overlap. *Journal of Aggression, Maltreatment & Trauma, 26(9)*, 937–951.

Ballard, M.E., & Welch, K.M. (2017). Virtual warfare: Cyberbullying and cybervictimization in MMOG play. *Games and Culture, 12(5)*, 466–491.

Behm-Morawitz, E., & Schipper, S. (2016). Sexing the avatar: Gender, sexualization, and cyber-harassment in a virtual world. *Journal of Media Psychology: Theories, Methods, and Applications, 28(4)*, 161–174. Doi: 10.1027/1864-1105/a000152.

Beran, T., & Li, Q. (2005). Cyber-harassment: A study of a new method for an old behavior. *Journal of Educational Computing Research, 32(3)*, 265–277. Doi:10.2190/8YQM-B04H-PG4D-BLLH.

Beran, T.N., Rinaldi, C., Bickham, D.S., & Rich, M. (2012). Evidence for the need to support adolescents dealing with harassment and cyber-harassment: Prevalence, progression, and impact. *School Psychology International, 33(5)*, 562–576. Doi: 10.1177/0143034312446976.

Burgin, J.T., Jr. (2012). *The Frequency of Cyberharassment and Its Correlation with Emotional Management As it Relates to College Students*. Ann Arbor, MI. ProQuest Dissertations Publishing, 3510482.

Calvete, E., Orue, I., Estévez, A., Villardón, L., & Padilla, P. (2010). Cyberbullying in adolescents: Modalities and aggressors' profile. *Computers in Human Behavior, 26*, 1128–1135. Doi: 10.1016/j.chb.2010.03.017.

Campbell, M.A. (2005). Cyberbullying: An old problem in a new guise? *Australian Journal of Guidance and Counselling, 15*, 68–76.

Campbell, M.A., Slee, P.T., Spears, B., Butler, D., & Kift, S. (2013). Do cyberbullies suffer too? Cyberbullies' perceptions of the harm they cause to others and to their own mental health. *School Psychology International, 34(6),* 613–629.

Cassidy, W., Brown, K.N., & Jackson, M. (2012). "Under the radar": Educators and cyberbullying in schools. *School Psychology International, 33,* 520–532. Doi:10.1177/0143034312445245.

Cassidy, W., Jackson, M., & Brown, K. (2009). Sticks and stones can break my bones, but how can pixels hurt me? Students' experiences with cyber-bullying. *School Psychology International, 30,* 383–402. Doi: 10:1177/0143034309106948.

Celik, S., Atak, H., & Erguzen, A. (2012). The effect of personality on cyberbullying among university students in Turkey. *Egitm Arastirmalri-Eurasian Journal of Educational Research, 12(49),* 129–150.

Centers for Disease Control and Prevention. (2020a). *Adolescent and School Health.* https://www.cdc.gov/healthyyouth/data/yrbs/index.htm.

Centers for Disease Control and Prevention. (2020b). *High School Students Who Were Electronically Bullied.* https://yrbs-explorer.services.cdc.gov/#/tables?q uestionCode=H24&topicCode=C01&year=2019.

Centers for Disease Control and Prevention. (2020c). *Middle School YRBS.* https:// nccd.cdc.gov/youthonline/App/Results.aspx?TT=B&OUT=0&SID=MS&QI D=M13&LID=LL&YID=RY&LID2=&YID2=&COL=&ROW1=&ROW2=&HT= &LCT=&FS=&FR=&FG=&FA=&FI=&FP=&FSL=&FRL=&FGL=&FAL=&FIL =&FPL=&PV=&TST=&C1=&C2=&QP=&DP=&VA=CI&CS=Y&SYID=&EYID =&SC=&SO=.

Chandler, K.A. (2015). *Student Reports of Bullying and Cyber-Bullying: Results from the 2013 School Crime Supplement to the National Crime Victimization Survey.* NCES-2015-056. https://nces.ed.gov/pubs2015/2015056.pdf.

Chapell, M.S., Hasselman, S.L., Kitchin, T., Lomon, S.N., MacIver, K.W., & Sarullo, P.L. (2006). Bullying in elementary school, high school, and college. *Adolescence, 41(164),* 633–648.

Chatzakou, D., Kourtellis, N., Blackburn, J., DeCristofaro, E., Stringhini, G., & Vakali, A. (2017). Mean birds: Detecting aggression and bullying on Twitter. *Proceedings of the Association for Computer Machinery on Web Science Conference,* pp. 13–22. Doi: 10.1145/3091478.3091487 https://arxiv.org/pdf/1702.06877. pdf.

Chatzakou, D., Leontiadis, I., Blackburn, J., de Cristofaro, E., Stringhini, G., Vakali, A., & Kourtellis, N. (2019). Detecting cyberbullying and cyberaggression in social media. *Association for Computer Machinery Transactions on the Web (TWEB), 13(3),* 17–50. https://arxiv.org/pdf/1907.08873.pdf.

Chrisholm, J.F. (2014). Review of the status of cyberbullying and cyberbullying prevention. *Journal of Information Systems Education, 25(1),* 77–87.

Cooper, R.M., & Blumenfeld, W.J. (2012). Responses to cyberbullying: A descriptive analysis of the frequency of and impact on LGBT and Allied youth. *Journal of LGBT Youth, 9(2),* 153–177.

Cox. (2014). *2014 Teen Internet Safety Survey.* www.cox.com/content/dam/cox/documents/tween-internet-safety-survey.pdf.

Cyberbullying Research Center. (2019). *Bullying Laws across America.* https://cyberbullying.org/bullying-laws.

Davidson, L.M., & Demaray, M.K. (2007). Social support as a moderator between victimization and internalizing-externalizing distress from bullying. *School Psychology Review, 36*(3), 383–405.

D'Auria, J.P. (2014). Cyberbullying resources for youth and their families. *Journal of Pediatric Health Care, 28*(2), e19–e22.

Dehue, F., Bolman, C., & Vollink, T. (2008). Cyberbullying: Youngsters' experiences and parental perception. *Cyberpsychology and Behavior, 11*(2), 217–223. Doi: 10.1089/cpb.2007.0008.

DePaolis, K.J., & Williford, A. (2019). Pathways from cyberbullying victimization to negative health outcomes among elementary school students: A longitudinal investigation. *Journal of Child and Family Studies, 28*(9), 2390–2403.

Dilmac, B. (2009). Psychological needs as a predictor of cyber bullying: A preliminary report on college students. *Educational Science: Theory and Practice, 9*(3), 1307e1325. http://files.eric.ed.gov/fulltext/ EJ858926.pdf.

Ditch the Label. (2017). *The Annual Bullying Survey 2017.* https://www.ditchthelabel.org/wp-content/uploads/2017/07/The-Annual-Bullying-Survey-2017-1.pdf.

Duggan, M. (2017, July 11). *Online Harassment 2017.* https://www.pewresearch.org/internet/2017/07/11/online-harassment-2017/.

Durkin, K.F., & Patterson, D. (2011). Cyber bullying, cyber harassing, and cyber stalking. In C.D. Bryant (ed.), *The Routledge Handbook of Deviant Behavior* (pp. 450–455). London: Routledge.

Edwards, L., Kontostathis, A.E., & Fisher, C. (2016). Cyberbullying, race/ethnicity and mental health outcomes: A review of the literature. *Media and Communication, 4*(3), 71–78.

European Union Agency for Fundamental Rights (2021). *Crime, Safety and Victims' Rights.* Luxembourg: Publications Office of the European Union. Doi: 10.2811/127900 https://fra.europa.eu/sites/default/files/fra_uploads/fra-2021-crime-safety-victims-rights_en.pdf.

Festl, R., & Quandt, T. (2013). Social relations and cyberbullying: The influence of individual and structural attributes on victimization and perpetration via the Internet. *Human Communication Research, 39*(1), 101–126.

Findlaw. (2019). *California Code, Education Code – EDC § 234.* https://codes.findlaw.com/ca/education-code/edc-sect-234.html

Finn, J. (2004). A survey of online harassment at a university campus. *Journal of Interpersonal Violence, 19*, 468–483.

Fluck, J. (2017). Why do students bully? An analysis of motives behind violence in schools. *Youth & Society, 49*(5), 567–587.

Francisco, S.M., Simao, A.M.V., Ferreira, P.C., & Martins, M.J.d.D. (2014). Cyberbullying: The hidden side of college students. *Computers in Human Behavior, 43*, 167e182. Doi: 10.1016/j.chb.2014.10.045.

Fridh, M., Lindström, M., & Rosvall, M. (2015). Subjective health complaints in adolescent victims of cyber harassment: Moderation through support from parents/friends- a Swedish population-based study. *BMC Public Health, 15*, 949–959. Doi: 10.1186/s12889-015-2239-7.

Gahagan, K., Vaterlaus, J.M., & Frost, L.R. (2016). College student cyberbullying on social networking sites: Conceptualization, prevalence, and perceived bystander responsibility. *Computers & Human Behavior, 55*, 1097–1105.

Göerzig, Anke. (2011). *Who bullies and who is bullied online?: a study of 9-16 year old internet users in 25 European countries*. London, UK: EU Kids Online network. https://eprints.lse.ac.uk/39601/

Gordon, S. (2021). *Understanding the Legal Ramifications of Cyberbullying*. https://www.verywellfamily.com/cyberbullying-laws-4588306.

Hafeez, E. (2014). Cyberharassment and its implications in Pakistan. *New Horizons, 8(2)*, 29–48.

Hamm, M.P., Newton, A.S., Chisholm, A., Shulhan, J., Milne, A., Sundar, P., Ennis, H., Scott, S.D., & Hartling, L. (2015). Prevalence and effect of cyberbullying on children and young people: A scoping review of social media studies. *JAMA Pediatrics, 169(8)*, 770–777. Doi: 10.1001/jamapediatrics.2015.0944.

Hinduja, S., & Patchin, J.W. (2007). Offline consequences of online victimization: School violence and delinquency. *Journal of School Violence, 6(3)*, 89–112. Doi: 10.1300/J202v06n03_06.

Hinduja, S., & Patchin, J.W. (2008). Cyberbullying: An exploratory analysis of factors related to offending and victimization. *Deviant Behavior, 29(2)*, 129–156. Doi: 10.1080/01639620701457816.

Hinduja, S., & Patchin, J.W. (2009). *Cyberbullying Research Summary: Emotional and Psychological Consequences*. http://www.cyberbullying.us/cyberbullying_emotional_consequences.pdf.

Hinduja, S., & Patchin, J.W. (2010). Bullying, cyberbullying, and suicide. *Archives of Suicide Research, 14(3)*, 206–221.

Hinduja, S. & Patchin, J.W. (2014). *Cyberbullying Identification, Prevention, and Response*. Cyberbullying Research Center. http://cyberbullying.org/cyberbullying-fact-sheet-identification-prevention-and-response.

Hoff, D.L., & Mitchell, S.N. (2009). Cyberbullying: Causes, effects, and remedies. *Journal of Educational Administration, 47*, 652–665. Doi:10.1108/09578230910981107.

Holfeld, B., & Grabe, M. (2012). An examination of the history, prevalence, characteristics, and reporting of cyberbullying in the United States. In Q. Li, D. Cross, and P.K. Smith (eds.), *Cyberbullying in the Global Playground: Research from International Perspectives* (pp. 117–142). Chichester, UK: Blackwell Publishing Ltd.

INTELiLQORE INC. (2021). *Digital Safety is a Fundamental Human Right That Should be Accessible to Everyone*. https://www.inteliqore.com/.

Jameson, S. (2008). Cyberharassment: Striking a balance between free speech and privacy. *Common Law Conspectus, 17*, 231–266.

Juvonen, J., & Gross, E.F. (2008). Extending the school grounds? Bullying experiences in cyberspace. *Journal of School Health, 78(9)*, 496–505.

Kaur, S., Singh, S., & Kaushal, S. (2021). Abusive content detection in online user-generated data: A survey. *Procedia Computer Science, 189,* 274–281.

Khan, F., Limbana, T., Tehrim, Z, Eskander, N., & Jahan, N. (2020). Traits, trends, and trajectory of tween and teen cyberbullies. *Cureus,* 12(8), e9738. Doi: 10.7759/cureus.9738.

Kim, J., Song, H., & Jennings, W.G. (2017). A distinct form of deviance or a variation of bullying? Examining the developmental pathways and motives of cyberbullying compared with traditional bullying in South Korea. *Crime & Delinquency, 63(12),* 1600–1625. Doi: 10.1177/0011128716675358.

Kowalski, R.M., Giumetti, G.W., Schroeder, A.N., & Lattanner, M.R. (2014). Bullying in the digital age: A critical review and meta-analysis of cyberbullying research among youth. *Psychological Bulletin, 140,* 1073–1137. Doi: 10.1037/a0035618.

Kowalski, R.M., & Limber, S.P. (2013). Psychological, physical, and academic correlates of cyberbullying and traditional bullying. *Journal of Adolescent Health, 53(1 Suppl.),* S13–S20. Doi: 10.1016/j.jadohealth.2012.09.018.

Kowalski, R.M., Limber, S.P., & Agatston, P.W. (2008). *Cyber Bullying: Bullying in the Digital Age.* Malden: Blackwell Publishing.

Kowalski, R., Limber, S.P., & McCord, A. (2018). A developmental approach to cyberbullying: Prevalence and protective factors. *Aggression and Violent Behavior.* Doi: 10.1016/j.avb.2018.02.009.

Kraft, E.M., & Wang, J. (2010). An exploratory study of the cyberbullying and cyber-stalking experiences and factors related to victimization of students at a public liberal arts college. *International Journal of Technoethics, 1(4),* 74–91. Doi: 10. 4018/jte.2010100106.

Kulig, J.C., Hall, B.L., & Kalischuk, R.G. (2008). Bullying perspectives among rural youth: A mixed methods approach. *Rural and Remote Health, 8(2),* 923. Doi: 0.22605/RRH923.

Lam, H. (n.d.). *Cyberbullying Among Students.* Information resource. cyber.pdf.

Langos, C. (2012). Cyberbullying: The challenge to define. *Cyberpsychology, Behavior, and Social Networking, 15(6),* 285e289. Doi:10.1089/ cyber.2011.0588.

Law, D.M., Shapka, J.D., Hymel, S., Olson, B.F., & Waterhouse, T. (2012). The changing face of bullying: An empirical comparison between traditional and Internet bullying and victimization. *Journal of Computers and Human Behavior, 28,* 226–232.

Lenhart, A., Ybarra, M., Zickuhr, K., & Price-Feeney, M. (2016). *Online Harassment, Digital Abuse, and cyberstalking in America.* Data & Society Research Institute. https://datasociety.net/wp-content/uploads/2016/11/Online_Harassment_2016.pdf.

Li, Q. (2007). Bullying in the new playground: Research into cyberbullying and cyber victimization. *Australasian Journal of Educational Technology, 23(4),* 435–454.

Livingstone, S., Haddon, L., Görzig, A., & Ólafsson, K. (2011). *Risks and Safety on the Internet: The Perspective of European Children.* London: EU Kids Online.

Lobe, B., Livingstone, S., Ólafsson, K., & Vodeb, H. (2011). *Cross-National Comparison of Risks and Safety on the Internet: Initial Analysis from the EU Kids Online Survey of European Children.* London, England: EU Kids Online, LSE. https://www.researchgate.net/publication/313022362_Cross-national_comparison_of_risks_and_safety_on_the_internet_initial_analysis_from_the_EU_Kids_Online_survey_of_European_children.

MacDonald, C.D., & Roberts-Pittman, B. (2010). Cyberbullying among college students: Prevalence and demographic differences. *Procedia Social and Behavioral Sciences, 9,* 2003e2009. Doi: 10.1016/j.sbspro.2010.12.436.

Machmutow, K., Perren, S., Sticca, F., & Alasker, F. D. (2012). Peer victimisation and depressive symptoms: Can specific coping strategies buffer the negative impact of cybervictimisation? *Emotional & Behavioural Difficulties, 17,* 403–420. Doi:10.1080/13632752.2012.704310.

Magarry, J. (2014). Online incivillity or sexual harassment? Conceptualizing women's experiences in the digital age. *Women's Studies International Forum, 47,* 46–55.

Maras, M.-H. (2015). Unprotected speech communicated via social media: What amounts to a true threat? *Journal of Internet Law, 19,* 3–9.

Marwick, A., & Miller, R. (2014). *Online Harassment, Defamation, and Hateful Speech: A Primer of the Legal Landscape.* https://ir.lawnet.fordham.edu/cgi/viewcontent.cgi?article=1002&context=clip.

Melander, L.A. (2010). College students' perceptions of intimate partner cyber harassment. *Cyberpsychology, Behavior, and Social Networking, 13*(3), 263–268.

Microsoft. (2012). *WWW Online Bullying Survey: Final Executive Summary.* http://www.microsoft.com/en-us/download/confirmation.aspx?id=3014.

Miller, C. (2006). Cyber harassment: Its forms and perpetrators. *Law Enforcement Technology, 33,* 26–30.

Mishna, F., Khoury-Kassabri, M., Gadalla, T., & Daciuk, J. (2012). Risk factors for involvement in cyber bullying: Victims, bullies and bully–victims. *Children and Youth Services Review, 34*(1), 63–70.

Mitchell, K.J., Ybarra, M. & Finkelhor, D. (2007). The relative importance of online victimization in understanding depression, delinquency and substance use. *Child Maltreatment, 12*(4), 314–324.

Näsi, M., Räsänen, P., Oksanen, A., Hawdon, J., Keipi, T., and Holkeri, E. (2014). Association between online harassment and exposure to harmful online content: A cross-national comparison between the United States and Finland. *Computers in Human Behavior, 41,* 37.

Orel, A., Campbell, M., Wosencroft, K., Leong, E., & Kimpton, M. (2015). Exploring university students' coping strategy intentions for cyberbullying. *Journal of Interpersonal Violence, 32*(3), 446–462. Doi. 10.1177/0886260515586363.

Parris, L., Varjas, K., Meyers, J., & Cutts, H. (2012). High school students' perceptions of coping with cyberbullying. *Youth & Society, 44,* 284–306. Doi:10.1177/0044118X11398881.

Patchin, J.W., & Hinduja, S. (2006). Bullies move beyond the schoolyard: A preliminary look at cyberbullying. *Youth Violence and Juvenile Justice, 4*(2), 148–169.

Patchin, J.W., & Hinduja, S. (2020). *Tween Cyberbullying in 2020*. Cyberbullying Research Center and Cartoon Network. https://i.cartoonnetwork.com/stop-bullying/pdfs/CN_Stop_Bullying_Cyber_Bullying_Report_9.30.20.pdf.

Price, M., & Dalgleish, J. (2010). Cyberbullying: Experiences, impacts and coping strategies as described by Australian young people. *Youth Studies Australia, 29(51)*, 59.

Raskauskas, J., & Stoltz, A.D. (2007). Involvement in traditional and electronic bullying among adolescents. *Developmental Psychology, 43(3)*, 564–575. Doi: 10.1037/0012-1649.43.3.564.

Redondo-Sama, G., Pulido-Rodriguez, M.A., Larena, R., & de Botton, L. (2014). Not without them: The inclusion of minors' voices on cyber harassment. *Qualitative Inquiry, 20(7)*, 895–901.

Rice, E., Petering, R., Rhoades, H., Winetrobe, H., Goldbach, J., Plant, A., & Kordic, T. (2015). Cyberbullying perpetration and victimization among middle-school students. *American Journal of Public Health, 105(3)*, e66–e72.

Rivers, I., & Noret, N. (2007). I h8 u: Findings from a five-year study of text and email bullying. *British Educational Research Journal, 36*, 643–671.

Sakellariou, T., Carroll, A., & Houghton, S. (2012). Rates of cyber victimization and bullying among male Australian primary and high school students. *School Psychology International, 33(5)*, 533–549. Doi: 10.1177/0143034311430374.

Sampasa-Kanyinga, H., Roumeliotis, P., & Xu, H. (2014). Associations between cyberbullying and school bullying victimization and suicidal ideation, plans and attempts among Canadian schoolchildren. *PLoS One, 9(7)*, e102145.

Schenk, A.M., & Fremouw, W.J. (2012). Prevalence, psychological impact, and coping of cyberbully victims among college students. *Journal of School Violence, 11(1)*, 21–37. Doi: 10.1080/15388220.2011.630310 https://doiorg.ez.lib.jjay.cuny.edu/10.1016/j.chb.2013.05.013.

Schenk, A.M., Fremouw, W.J., & Keelan, C.M. (2013). Characteristics of college cyberbullies. *Computers in Human Behavior, 29(6)*, 2320–2327.

Schneider, K., O'Donnell, L., Stueve, A., & Coulter, R.W.S. (2012). Cyberbullying, school bullying, and psychological distress: A regional census of high school students. *American Journal of Public Health, 102(1)*, 171–177. Doi: 10.2105/AJPH.2011.

Schultze-Krumbholz, A., Jäkel, A., Schultze, M., & Scheithauer, H. (2012). Emotional and behavioral problems in the context of cyberbullying: A longitudinal study among German adolescents. *Emotional and Behavioral Difficulties, 17(3–4)*, 329–345. Doi: 10.2080/13632752.2012.704317.

Seldin, M., & Yanez, C. (2019). *Student Reports of Bullying: Results from the 2017 School Crime Supplement to the National Crime Victimization Survey*. Web Tables. NCES 2019-054. Washington, DC: National Center for Education Statistics. https://nces.ed.gov/pubs2019/2019054.pdf

Sengupta, A., & Chaudhuri, A. (2011). Are social networking sites a source of online harassment for teens? Evidence from survey data. *Children and Youth Services Review, 33(2)*, 284–290.

Shapka, J.D., & Law, D.M. (2013). Does one size fit all? Ethnic differences in parenting behaviors and motivations for adolescent engagement in cyberbullying. *Journal of Youth and Adolescence, 42*, 723–738. Doi: 10.1007/s10964-013-9928-2.

Slonje, R., & Smith, P. (2008). Cyberbullying: Another main type of bullying? *Scandinavian Journal of Psychology, 49*, 147–154. Doi: 10.1111/j.1467-9450.2007.00611.x.

Slonje, R., Smith, P.K., & Frisén, A. (2013). The nature of cyberbullying and strategies for prevention. *Computers in Human Behavior, 29(1)*, 26–32.

Smith, P.K., Mahdavi, J., & Carvalho, M. (2008). Cyberbullying: Its nature and impact in secondary school pupils. *Journal of Child Psychology and Psychiatry, 49(4)*, 376–385.

Sood, S.O., Churchill, E.F., & Antin, J. (2012). Automatic identification of personal insults on social news sites. *Journal of the American Society for Information Science and Technology, 63(2)*, 270–285.

Spears, B.A., Slee, P., Owens, L., & Johnson, B. (2009). Behind the scenes and screens: Insights into the human dimension of covert and cyberbullying. *Zeitschrift für Psychologie/Journal of Psychology, 217*, 189–196.

Spitzberg, B.H., & Gawron, J.M. (2016). Toward online linguistic surveillance of threatening messages. *Journal of Digital Forensics, Security, and Law, 11(3)*, 43–77.

Stopbullying.gov. (2019). *Key Components in State Anti-Bullying Laws, Policies, and Regulations*. https://www.stopbullying.gov/resources/laws/key-components.

Stopbullying.gov. (2021). *Federal Laws*. https://www.stopbullying.gov/resources/laws/federal.

Suler, J. (2004). The online disinhibition effect. *Cyberpsychology & Behavior, 7(3)*, 321–326.

Tokunaga, R.S. (2010). Following you home from school: A critical review and synthesis of research on cyberbullying victimization. *Computers in Human Behavior, 26*, 277–287. Doi: 10.1016chb.2009.11.014

Tolba, M., Oudfel, S., & Meshoul, S. (2018). Deep learning for online harassment detection in tweets. *Third Annual International Conference on Pattern Analysis and Intelligent Systems* (PAIS). Doi: 10.1109/PAIS.2018.8598530.

Tolba, M., Oudfel, S., & Meshoul, S. (2021). Hybrid ensemble approaches to online harassment detection in highly imbalanced data. *Expert Systems with Applications, 175*, 114751. Doi: 10.1016/j.eswa.2021.114751.

United Press International. (2008, April). *Survey: Cyberbullying Affects U.S. Teens*. United Press International. http://www.upi.com/Health_News/2008/04/09/Survey-Cyber-bullying-affects-US-teens/38231207776077/.

Vale, A., Pereira, F., Concalves, M., & Matos, M. (2018). Cyber-aggression in adolescence and internet parenting styles: A study with victims, perpetrators, and victim-perpetrators. *Children and Youth Services Review, 93*, 88–89. Doi: 10.1016/j.childyouth.2018.06.021.

Van Royen, K., Poels, K., & Vandebosch, H. (2016). Help, I am losing control! Examining the reporting of sexual harassment by adolescents to social networking sites. *Cyberpsychology, Behavior, and Social Networking, 19(1)*, 16–22. Doi: 10.1089/cyber.2015.0168.

Varjas, K., Talley, J., Meyers, J., Parris, L., & Cutts, H. (2010). High school students' perceptions of motivations for cyberbullying: An exploratory study. *Western Journal of Emergency Medicine, XI(3)*, 269–273.

Vogels, E.A. (2021). *The State of Online Harassment*. The State of Online Harassment. https://www.pewresearch.org/internet/2021/01/13/the-state-of-online-harassment/.

Wang, R.J. Iannotti, J.W. Luk, T.R., & Nansel, T.R. (2010). Co-occurrence of victimization from five subtypes of bullying: Physical, verbal, social exclusion, spreading rumors, and cyber. *Journal of Pediatric Psychology, 35(10)*, 1103–1112.

Wang, J., Iannotti, R.J., & Nansel, T.R. (2009). School bullying among adolescents in the United States: Physical, verbal, relational, and cyber. *Journal of Adolescent Health, 45*, 368–375J.

Wassdorp, T.E., & Bradshaw, C.P. (2015). The overlap between cyberbullying and traditional bullying. *Journal of Adolescent Health, 56*, 483–488. Doi: 10.1016/j.jadohealth.2014.12.002.

Watts, L.K., Wagner, J., Velasquez, B., & Behrens, P.I. (2017). Cyberbullying in higher education: A literature review. *Computers in Human Behavior, 69*, 268–274.

Welsh, A., & Lavoie, J.A. (2012). Risky ebusiness: An examination of risk-taking, online disclosiveness, and cyberstalking victimization. *Cyberpsychology, 6(1)*, 1–12.

Wick, S.E., Nagoshi, C., Basham, R., & Jordan, C. (2017). Patterns of cyber harassment and perpetration among college students in the United States: A test of routine activities theory. *International Journal of Cyber Criminology, 11(1)*, 24–38. Doi: 10.5281/zenodo.495770.

Willard, N. (2007). *Cyberbullying and Cyberthreats: Effectively Managing Internet Use Risks in Schools*. https://www.cforks.org/Downloads/cyber_bullying.pdf.

Wilson, D., Witherup, K., & Payne, A.A. (2020). Risk and protective factors for cyberbullying perpetration and victimization. In T. Holt and A.M. Bossler (eds.), *The Palgrave Handbook of International Cybercrime and Cyberdeviance* (pp. 1257–1282). Switzerland: Springer. Doi: 10.1007/978-3-319-90307-1_56-1.

Woda, T. (2015, January). Cyberbullying: Children as victims and predators. *USA Today, 143(2836)*, 32+.

Wright, M.F. (2020). The role of technologies, behaviors, gender, and gender stereotype traits in adolescents' cyber aggression. *Journal of Interpersonal Violence, 35*, 1719–1738. Doi: 10.1177/0886260517696858.

Ybarra, M.L., Diener-West, M., & Leaf, P. (2007). Examining the overlap in internet harassment and school bullying: Implications for school intervention. *Journal of Adolescent Health, 41(6)*, S42–S50.

Ybarra, M.L., & Mitchell, K.J. (2004). Online aggressor/targets, aggressors, and targets: A comparison of associated youth characteristics. *The Journal of Child Psychology and Psychiatry, 45*, 1308–1316. Doi: 10.1111/j.1469-7610.2004.00328.x.

Zhang, Z., Robinson, D., & Tepper, J. (2018). *Hate Speech Detection Using a Convolution-LSTM Based Deep Neural Network*. https://irep.ntu.ac.uk/id/eprint/34022/1/11440_Tepper.pdf.

7

Minor Online Sexual Activity Offenders

DEFINING ILLEGAL ONLINE SEXUAL ACTIVITY

Online sexual activity (OSA), a phenomenon that spans at least 30 years, refers to the exchange of sexually explicit content—both images and messages—by electronic means, such as cell phones, email, Internet devices, and social media platforms (Kopecký, 2014, 2015; Kopecký & Szotkowski, 2019; O'Sullivan, 2014; Shaughnessy et al., 2017; Silva et al., 2016; Ngo et al., 2017; Villacampa, 2017). OSA is illegal when minors are involved in the sending or receiving of sexually explicit content (e.g., partial or full nudes, suggestive or obscene images) as it constitutes child sexual abuse material (CSAM). In the early 1990s, OSA occurred between users in virtual environments called *MUDs* (multi-user dimensions/dungeons) and *MOOS* (Mud, Object Oriented)[1] as these spaces allowed synchronous text-based communication (Bright, 1992). Most people were unaware that these spaces existed, however accessibility to OSA was mainstreamed with the advent of *instant message* (IM) service (circa 1997–1999) that used various email communication platforms (AOL, Yahoo, MSN/Windows Live) to share texts, photos, and videos. Research indicated that adolescents were more active users of IMs than adults overall in 2000 (74% vs. 44%) and again in 2004 (75% vs. 42%), although three-quarters of both groups owned personal computers (Lenhart et al., 2001, 2005; Madden et al., 2013). The next metamorphosis of OSA occurred in 2003 when *Second Life*—a website-based, three-dimensional virtual fantasy world—provided opportunities for its presumably adult "residents,"[2] visually represented as avatars, to engage in sexual activities together and/or with objects (e.g., kink and fetish play) in various sites in the game (Federal Trade Commission/FTC, 2009). According to VR Reporter (n.d.), future OSA will combine virtual and augmented reality (VR/AR) with motion-sensitive suits and synced teledildonics (i.e., sex toys that simulate genitalia).

Around the timeframe when IM technology emerged in the late 1990s to early 2000 (Lenhart et al., 2005), *texting* using a very small keypad (e.g., 2 represented ABC) on a cellphone became possible in the U.S. via a 2G network, but it was cumbersome (i.e., you had to select a number, then click to choose the letter you wanted—twice for B, thrice for C) and expensive (e.g., charged per text, per minute for calls, roaming charges, overuse of data fees). After major changes were implemented, from the mid-2000s through 2010s, texting increased in popularity. Most importantly, structural modifications of the cellphone, such as keyboards, touchscreens, and cameras

---

[1] These sites were created to allow users to engage in role-playing games, such as Dungeons & Dragons, but the creators realized that members enjoyed sitting in taverns and talking or playing board games. Although it was possible to build homes and use objects in the MOOs and MUDS, it was text based.

[2] According to FTC (2009), it is not difficult for minors to pretend to be adults in order to enter "adult only" locations on Second Life.

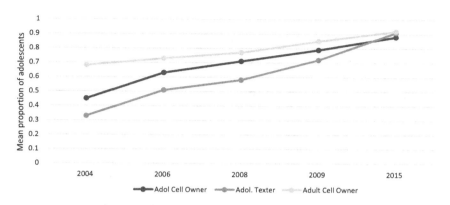

Figure 7.1 Mean Proportion of adolescent and adult cell phone owners and adolescent texters.

becoming standard; improvement in connectivity occurred by linking services and media streaming through 3G networks;[3] and reasonably pricing of mobile plans offered unlimited texting, calls, and data (Chowdhury, 2014; Rearson, 2008). Secondarily, the cost of cellphones decreased or were offered at no or low cost with 2-year contracts[4] while quality and ease-of-use improved (Chowdhury, 2014). Apps were preloaded on smart phones, starting with Apple iPhone in 2007, and third-party apps associated with websites, email services, and social media platforms became available in 2008—making it simple to text and exchange self-portraits called "selfies" (Shah, 2021).

As shown in Figure 7.1, increases occurred from 2004 to 2015 in the proportion of American adults and adolescents (ages 13–17) who owned cell phones, reducing the gap between the two groups, and in the proportion of adolescents who were cell phone owners and texters (Anderson, 2015; Lenhart, 2012, 2015; Lenhart et al., 2005, 2010b; Madden et al., 2013; Rideout & Robb, 2019). A report by Pew Research (2019) found that 96% of American adults (99% aged 18–49; 95% aged 50–64; 91% aged 65+) owned cellphones, of which 81% were smart phones. Figure 7.2 displays the proportion of 2019 smart phone ownership by age group (Pew Research, 2019; Rideout & Robb, 2019). Not

---

[3] As of 2019, smart phones in the U.S. operate on a 5G network.
[4] In 1990s, cellphones cost $900–1000, but could be purchased for $200 with cell service contract; in 2000s, the price was $350–700 (but was free or up to $199 with contract).

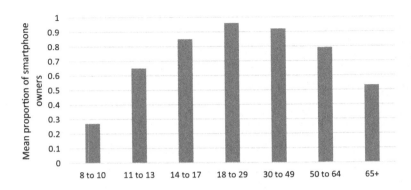

Figure 7.2 Mean proportion of 2019 smartphone owners by age group.

surprisingly, the figure shows that ownership was highest among millennials (ages 18–29), who were raised with cell phones, and secondarily by middle aged adults (aged 30–49), which in turn promoted juvenile ownership (aged 8–13). In particular, although it may seem like an expensive indulgence to purchase smartphones for children as young as age 8 (19%) or 9 (26%), keep in mind that anyone born in 2007 or later were raised surrounded by this technology. Rideout and Robb (2019) indicated that the acquisition of smart phones by juveniles jumped at two points corresponding to transition from elementary to middle school—36% at age 10 (fifth grade) compared to 53% at age 11 (sixth grade)—and from middle to high school—72% at age 13 (eighth grade) compared to 81% at age 14 (ninth grade). Box 7.1 compares 2019 use/ownership of Internet devices and SM profiles by U.S. and U.K. youth ages 3–15 (Ofcome, 2020; Rideout & Robb, 2019; Tankovska, 2021).

BOX 7.1   ONLINE ACCESS OF MINORS BY AGE, DEVICE, AND SM PROFILE IN THE U.K. VS. THE U.S.

Table 7.1 compares 2019 availability of Internet-ready devices and social media profiles of minors from the U.K. (Ofcome, 2020) and the U.S. (Auxier et al., 2020; Rideout & Robb, 2019; Tankovska, 2021). From an early age, minors have access to the Internet (ranging from *somewhat limited and supervised* to *unlimited and unsupervised*), predisposing them to a variety of online harms, including increased exposure

Table 7.1 Comparison of 2019 Availability of Internet-Ready Devices and Social Media Profiles of Minors By Developmental level and Country (U.K. and U.S.)

Developmental Level and Country	Tablet		Smart Phone		Other Device Use (%)	Social Media Account (%)
	Use (%)	Own (%)	Use (%)	Own (%)		
Preschoolers U.K. (Ages 3–4)	49	24	20	0	15 LT; 11 SS	1
Preschoolers U.S. (Ages 3–4)	64	13	62	8	21 LT; 30 SS	1
School-age U.K. (Ages 5–7)	63	37	27	5	20 SS	4
School-age U.S. (Ages 5–8)	81	26	59	35	54 LT; 47 SS	2
Preadolescents U.K. (Ages 8–11)	72	49	49	37	25 SS	21
Preadolescents U.S. (Ages 9–11)	78	52[a]	67	34–51	23[a]LT; 45 SS; 73 C	5
Adolescents U.K. (Ages 12–15)	69	59	81	83	36 SS	71
Adolescents U.S. (Ages 12–14)	19	35[+]	-	76	49 [+] LT	34

Key: LT = laptop; SS = smart speaker; C = computer.
[a] Ages 8–12.; [+]Ages 13–18.

to inappropriate sexual content and vulnerability to sexual predators and decreased inhibition to online sexual activity (Auxier et al., 2020). Although parents in both countries limit SM profiles prior to adolescence, acceptance of preadolescents' and adolescents' presence on social media was higher in the U.K. than in the U.S. (Auxier et al., 2020; Ofcome, 2020). This may be due to U.K. parents not knowing the minimum age is at least 13 for most SM profiles (e.g., awareness was 27% for Facebook, 20% for Instagram, 15% for Snapchat) and at least 16 for WhatsApp (awareness was 5%) (Ofcome, 2020).

Table 7.2 Social Media Platforms and Apps Used to Exchange Photos and Texts or Livestream

		Multi-Level Interaction	
Dating	Video Chat	Short-term	Long-term
HotOrNot, 2000; MeetMe, 2005; Badoo, 2006; Grindr, 2009; Tinder, 2012	Skype, 2003; Zoom, 2011; Facebook Messenger, 2011; Google hangouts, 2013; Facebook Live, 2015; LiveMe, 2016; GoogleDuo, 2016	Twitter, 2006; Tumblr, 2007; WhatsApp, 2009; Instagram, 2010; Kik, 2010; Snapchat, 2011; WeChat, 2011; TikTok, 2016	Facebook, 2004; Google, 2006

The launching of social media platforms and availability of dating and communication Apps starting in 2000 and growing significantly thereafter (see Table 7.2) offered its members/owners[5] easy and multiple opportunities to share, post, and exchange IMs, photographs, and videos, as well as to livestream video chat. Social networking sites became a common and popular vehicle for presenting and expressing one's identity (or at least, an ideal self) by posting content (e.g., comments, photographs, status updates) in a strategically controlled and constructed profile, which was further encouraged by the number of "likes," "Wall posts and comments," "followers," and "friends" users had (Del Ray et al., 2019; Hinduja & Patchin, 2016; Kim et al., 2020). Minors' comfort with digitally sharing almost all aspects of themselves—particularly through selfies—contributed to normalizing the OSA phenomenon called "sexting"—a term that blended *sex* with *texting* (Lenhart, 2009; Sacco et al., 2010; Vandan Abeele et al., 2014; Wood, 2009)

Four types of sexting have been identified. *Primary sexting* occurs between consenting adults and, as such, is the only type not prohibited at the state or federal level in the U.S. (Ngo et al., 2017; Paravecchia, 2011). On the other hand, *experimental* sexting occurs between minors (i.e., under age 18) as producers, possessors, senders, and/or receivers of sexually explicit images (Barnes, 2012; Wolak & Finkelhor, 2011; Wolak et al., 2012) and thus is always illegal in the U.S. This is true even when both parties have reached the legal age to consent to sex and engaged in all acts voluntarily because such content by definition is still CSAM. By 2009, adolescents in ten states across the country had been arrested for sexting (Wood, 2009, 2010). The legislation in place at that time was a byproduct of society's belief that youth, due to their immaturity and

---

[5] There is a presumption that users are adults, as most of these sites require new members to acknowledge that s/he is at least 18 or have specific regulations for minors (often with a minimum age of 13), but the government does not oversee whether compliance is checked.

short-sightedness, must be protected from long-term sexually exploitative consequences (i.e., harm principle) that occur as a result of sharing digital CSAM (Paravecchia, 2011; Primack, 2018; Wood, 2009). In sexting cases involving an adult as one party and a minor as the other party, the charge of CSAM is consistent with the intended law. In contrast, when sexting involves minors as the sending and receiving parties, each state has decided either to charge them with violating current CSAM laws or instituted special "sexting" laws (shown in subsequent section).

Two other types of sexting—aggravated and secondary—are prohibited by federal and/or state legislation, regardless if the parties involved are minors and/or adults. *Aggravated sexting* involves the receiving party coercing the sending party to provide sexually explicit images through threats or pressure (Drouin et al., 2015; Drouin & Tobin, 2014; Kernsmith et al., 2018; Lemke & Rogers, 2020; Ross et al., 2016; Wolak et al., 2018). *Secondary sexting* is defined as the nonconsensual sharing, forwarding, and/or posting of sexts (Morelli et al., 2016; Vitis, 2019; Wolak & Finkelhor, 2011). Multiple cases have been reported in which minors, whose sexts had been shared without permission and led to relentless taunting by peers, committed suicide (Wood, 2009). Victim advocates raise concerns that even primary sexting predisposes adults to potential victimization, including being unable to prevent aggravated sexting, secondary sexting, and/or cybervictimization through societal responses, such as online shaming, harassing, bullying, threating, stalking, and unwanted sexual solicitations (Reyns et al., 2013). As cybercrimes resulting from aggravated and secondary sexting are already discussed in other chapters within this volume, the current chapter focuses solely on experimental sexting.

TYPICAL MINOR OSA OFFENDERS

Minor OSA—whether they are sending or receiving parties in experimental sexting—are offenders and not victims. This is because the content they produce, exchange, and/or possess violate federal and state child sexual abuse material laws. Prevalence rates for OSA through sexting differ due to a variety of factors, including *sample size and participant demographics*; *definition* of sexting, particularly **which acts** were included (i.e., sending, receiving, or exchanging), **type** of sexually explicit content (i.e., messages, images, or both), and **when** (e.g., 1 month ago, ever) and **how often** sexting occurred (e.g., once, weekly); *timeframe* of data collection and the correspondence to proportion of participants who owned cellphones and texted; and various aspects of *data collection,* including timeframes and locations (Barrense-Dias et al., 2017; Harris et al., 2014; Madigan et al., 2018;

Table 7.3 Proportion of Adolescents Who Sent and Received Sext Images and Messages

Act	Type of Content	
	Images	Messages
Sexts sent	$M=16\%$ Range 4%–55% $N=36{,}180$	$M=19\%$; Range 5%–30% $N=6889$
Sexts received	$M=26\%$ Range 7%–41% $N=24{,}914$	$M=36\%$ Range 29%–48% $N=2764$

Mitchell et al., 2012; National Campaign to Prevent Teen and Unplanned Pregnancy, 2008; Shafer, 2019; Ybarra & Mitchell, 2014). Table 7.3 shows data averaged across 22 studies for sexting of images, five of which also indicated sexting of messages (AP & MTV, 2009; Houck et al., 2014; Murray, 2014; Peskin et al., 2013; Ybarra & Mitchell, 2014). The studies, described in detail in Appendix A, consisted of predominantly White,[6] American, heterosexual[7] adolescents ages 10–18 (50% female), most of whom owned cellphones (65%–100%). Regardless of type of content, a higher proportion of adolescents reported receiving than sending sexts.

The studies described in Appendix A were examined for differences in the sex and age of the adolescent parties involved in sending and receiving sext images. For sending sext images, although most of the studies indicated no significant sex differences, investigators in three studies (Cox, 2009; Maheux et al., 2020; Mitchell et al., 2012) reported a higher proportion of girls than boys sent them ($M=62\%$ vs. $M=41\%$). Limited support from five studies (Hinduja & Patchin, 2010; Mitchell et al., 2012; Strassberg et al., 2013, 2017;[8] Murray, 2014) indicated a higher proportion of boys than girls received sext images ($M=44\%$ vs. $M=32\%$). This finding, based on predominantly heterosexual adolescents, may be due to fewer boys than girls self-producing sexually explicit images (Reed et al., 2020) and/or because boys were more likely than girls to request such images (Temple et al., 2012). Age differences were also found in the proportion of adolescents aged 13–17 who sent and received sext images averaged across nine studies[9] and is

---

[6] Ethnicity information was not provided in all 20 studies: White ($M = 54\%$, 15 studies, range 15%–87%); Latinx ($M = 36\%$, 11 studies, range 10%–72%); Black ($M = 11\%$, 11 studies, range 9%–43%).

[7] The average proportion was 92% based on five studies (range 87%–96%).

[8] Velarde (2014) used the same dataset as Strassberg et al. (2017).

[9] Data collection in these studies spanned from 2009 to 2019.

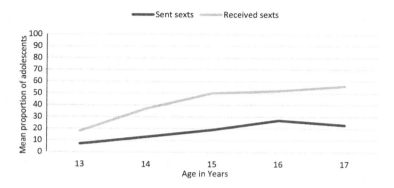

Figure 7.3 Mean proportion of adolescents who sent and received sext images.

displayed in Figure 7.3 (Cox, 2009; Dake et al., 2012; Lenhart, 2009; Mitchell et al., 2012; Patchin & Hinduja, 2019; Steinberg et al., 2019; Strassberg et al., 2013; Temple et al., 2012; Ybarra & Mitchell, 2014). The mean prevalence rates for sending and receiving sext images increased steadily with age and is likely a reflection of the higher proportion of older adolescents—aged 16 and 17—who owned smartphones and were heavy daily texters in comparison to younger adolescents—aged 13–15 (Hinduja & Patchin, 2016; Lenhart, 2012; Rice et al., 2014, 2018; Rideout & Robb, 2019).

Specific individual factors have been determined to moderate whether minors will engage in sexting. Juveniles who have sexted reported that their own and others' experiences with it had been pleasant and their peers (particularly the popular ones) perceived it to be acceptable behavior (Burén & Lunde, 2018; Maheux et al., 2020; Van Ouytsel et al., 2017). Low parental monitoring of adolescents' use of technology also contributed to sexting (Campbell & Park, 2014; Confalonieri et al., 2020; Klettke et al., 2014; Maheux et al., 2020; Romo et al., 2017; Walrave et al., 2014; West et al., 2014). Sexting was also most likely among youth who were dating and sexually active (Handschuh et al., 2018; Houck et al., 2014; Kosenko et al., 2017; Mori et al., 2019; Rice et al., 2012; Temple et al., 2012, 2014; Ybarra & Mitchell, 2014). Similarly, juvenile decisions to sext coincided with their performance of a number of high-risk activities related to (1) *health,* such as smoking, drinking, and drugs (Temple et al., 2014; Titchen et al., 2019); (2) *sex,* such as transactional sex, unprotected sex, and multiple partners (Dake et al., 2012; Döring, 2014; Temple et al., 2012); and (3) *aggression,* such as cyberbullying and IPV (Dake et al., 2012; Drouin et al., 2015; Lee et al., 2016; Titchen et al., 2019).[10]

---

[10] Similar positive correlations were also found between sexting and high-risk health and sexual behaviors in young college students (Benotsch et al., 2013).

MINOR OSA OFFENDERS' MOTIVES AND METHODS

The term *experimental* aptly describes sexting between minors for a number of reasons. First, adolescents today are completely enmeshed in the digital world—they are on their cellphones or Internet devices during most of their waking hours (Anderson & Jiang, 2018; Campbell & Park, 2014). Second, adolescents are social creatures who crave contact and communication with their peers, relying on them to provide feedback, establish norms, and help them resolve problems (Anderson & Jiang, 2018; Campbell & Park, 2014; Shapiro & Maras, 2016). In fact, peer approval and rejection—ultimately shaped by media and culture—become strong motivators in their risk-taking decisions (Arain et al., 2013; Rhyner et al., 2018). Third, a natural part of normative socio-emotional development is exploring identity, self-expression, sexuality, and intimacy (Doornwaard et al., 2015; Shapiro & Maras, 2016). Adolescents' ability to modulate their behaviors within peer, friend, and intimate partner relationships is depending upon both cognitive and physical development. Adolescent brains are immature and incomplete until age 25, particularly in regard to the prefrontal cortex, which is involved in decision making, self-control and impulse regulation, risk and reward assessment, and planning (Arain et al., 2013; Rhyner et al., 2018; Shapiro & Maras, 2016). Their ability to think logically and abstractly is tenuous, as is their ability to visualize potential behavioral outcomes, whereas their emotionally ladened limbic system stimulates their motivation to seek and obtain pleasurable options (Arain et al., 2013; Doornwaard et al., 2015; Raine et al., 2020; Rhyner et al., 2018). Thus, it is not surprising that adolescents succumb to the short-term (immediate) rewards associated with sexting—a risky behavior—while giving little heed to its possible negative long-term consequences (e.g., unauthorized forwarding/posting, arrest).

Research examining motives for experimental sexting reveal they can be categorized under *personal* (Cooper et al., 2016; Lenhart, 2009; Ringrose et al., 2012; Vandan Abeele et al., 2014). First, adolescents use sexts to *enhance connections* to **friends**, by sharing jokes, chatting/gossiping, getting advice, and bonding through shared experiences; **peers**, by increasing status and acceptance; and **intimate partners**, by signaling romantic attraction to potential ones and expressing intimacy to current ones, particularly when they are not able to be together (Del Ray et al., 2019; Drouin et al., 2015; Lippman & Campbell, 2014; Walker et al., 2011). Second, sexts serve to *express adolescent development and agency*—individuals feel thrills; explore, demonstrate, and test their sexuality; fulfill sexual desires; and compete with peers over physical attractiveness (Lenhart et al., 2010a; Lippman & Campbell, 2014; Vandan Abeele et al., 2014; Van Ouytsel et al., 2017; Walker et al., 2011).

160

Consistent with motivation, the relationship between the sexting parties affects incidence rates. As shown in Table 7.4, adolescents predominantly engaged in sexting with current intimate partners and secondarily with potential partners (Cox, 2009; Harris et al., 2013; Lenhart, 2009; Lenhart et al., 2010a; Lippman & Campbell, 2014; Martinez-Prather et al., 2014; Strohmaier et al., 2014; Temple et al., 2012).[11] These rates for sexting are not surprising given that adolescents involved in romantic relationships reported that they texted (72%), instant messaged (29%), messaged by App (20%) or social media (21%), and video chatted (12%) daily with their partners—which likely compensated for the low rates (21%) of in-person meeting (Lenhart et al., 2015).

Methods for non-abusive OSA include producing exchanging content *asynchronously* (e.g., IMs/texts, photos, videos) and *synchronously* by camming (e.g., Facetime, Skype, WhatsApp). A variety of Internet-connecting devices with digital cameras may be used, including tablets, laptops, and smartphones, which operate through service provider plans, social media platforms, websites, and Apps (Dowdell et al., 2011). Sexting can be conceptualized as a dichotomy of *active acts*, when a party creates, sends, and/or posts content, and *passive acts*, when a party is *asked* to send, *asks someone* to send, and/or *receives* content (Barrense-Dias et al., 2017). Based on longitudinal research by Temple and associates (Temple & Choi, 2014; Temple et al., 2012), the percentage of adolescents who were asked to provide sext images is double those who actively solicit them from others ($M=59\%$ vs. $M=31\%$).

Table 7.4 Mean Proportion of Sext Images Sent and Received by Relationship between Parties

	Relationship between Sext Party						
Sext Act	Boyfriend/ BF Girlfriend/ GF (%)	Crush (%)	Ex-BF/ GF (%)	Best Friend (%)	Friend (%)	Classmate (%)	Stranger (%)
Sent	42	25	19	12	22	4	6
Received	57	43	20	20	23	18	14

[11] Data in each category were comprised of information from one or more studies.

LAWS FOR PROSECUTING ONLINE
SEXUAL ACTIVITY OFFENSES

Primary and experimental sexting are differentiated solely by the age of the parties and those portrayed—adults vs. adolescents. The First Amendment protects both adult ownership of obscene images depicting adults[12] and adult exchange of non-obscene, sexually explicit messages and images depicting adults (Hessick, 2018). In contrast, *depiction* of minors in the sext content designates it as *CSAM,* and the acts of minors *producing, possessing, sending, and receiving* of sexually explicit messages and/or images constitute *status offenses* (i.e., noncriminal acts considered to be law violations due to their underage status). Many states adhere to the notion that, consistent with *New York v. Ferber* and *Osborne v. Ohio,* the acts and content in experimental sexts violate CSAM laws and thus do not qualify as protected speech (Grasz & Pfaltzgraff, 1998; Hessick, 2018). Unfortunately, even when adolescents understand that production, possession, and distribution of CSAM is illegal and these laws are in place to protect sexual abuse and exploitation of children, they are unlikely to conceive of experimental sexting as CSAM (Lorang et al., 2016). Box 7.2 examines the paradox of minors' consent to have sex versus legally exchange sexually explicit images with their romantic partner.

BOX 7.2   PARADOX OF MINORS'
CONSENT FOR SEX VS. SEXTING

Consistent with *New York v. Ferber,* society must protect children from sexual abuse, the images derived from it, and the distribution of child sexual abuse images. Yet, the government's interest in protecting youth from harm limits adolescents' sexual rights, including viewing sexual content and expressing themselves in a sexual manner through sext images. In the U.S., the minimum age at which one can legally consent to sexual conduct varies by state—age 16 in 31 states and D.C.; age 17 in 8 states; and age 18 in 11 states (Age of Consent.net, 2021). However, there are sexual consent exceptions in 26 states that allow those younger than the minimum age to engage in consensual sex with those "close" in age (Romeo

---

[12] Supreme Court decision in *Stanley v. Georgia*, 394 U.S. 557 (1969).

and Juliet laws) to protect them from extreme consequences (e.g., sex offender registry). This means that minors are able to engage in sex in most states, but are prohibited from producing recordings of those legal, consensual acts. Spooner and Vaughn (2016) argue that experimental sexting images by adolescents who meet the consent age requirements should be protected by the First Amendment because, in line with *United States v. Stevens* (2010), they are not derived from criminal activity.

Marriage exceptions offer another way to skirt the sexual consent issue (as well as statutory rape charges for the spouse) because 46 states allow marriage of minors, under specific circumstances (i.e., parental permission; judicial review and approval; pregnancy/birth). A person can legally consent to marriage at age 18 in 48 states and D.C., but age 19 in Nebraska and age 21 in Minnesota (World Population Review, 2021). The minimum age for marrying under an exception is as low as age 14 in one state, age 15 in five states, age 16 in 22 states and D.C., and age 17 in 11 states, whereas no minimum age is quantified in eight states (Find Law, 2020). The concern in marriage exemptions is that it predisposes minors to abuse and coercion, particularly when minors engage in sex below the age of consent. In Maryland, for example, parents of a 15-year-old who is pregnant or has given birth may permit her to marry her rapist. These conflicting laws make it difficult for minors to determine what can or cannot do in their resident state—consent to sex, get married, or encapsulate and exchange their consensual sexual acts in images.

Two acts were created with the goal of protecting children from harm online:

- *Communications Decency Act* (CDA) *of 1996* [47 U.S.C. §230. Protection for private blocking and screening of offensive material] criminalized knowingly transmitting obscene or indecent messages to minors and displaying patently offensive materials without verifying viewer with at least 18; and
- *Child Online Privacy Protection Act* (COPPA) of 1998 [15 U.S.C. § 6501–6505] criminalized commercial distribution of material deemed harmful to minors.

However, the American Civil Liberties Union in separate cases argued that both Acts were unconstitutionally overbroad, in that to protect minors they were suppressing protected adult speech, and the Courts agreed.[13]

In 2008, the criminal justice system was forced to consider the legal aspects of experimental sexting when Pennsylvanian school administrators[14] turned over confiscated cellphones to the local prosecutor, Mr. Skumanick (Wood, 2009, 2010). He then threatened to charge 20 students as violators or accomplices for the possession and distribution of CSAM[15] if they did not accept a plea deal requiring attendance of a re-education program, writing a letter that admitted wrongdoing, and 6-month probation (Wood, 2009, 2010). The actions by administrators and the prosecutor were deemed in *Miller v. Skumanick*[16] to be an overreach: forcing students to take the re-education program violated parents' 14th Amendment substantive due process rights to rear and manage their children as they see fit (*Troxel v. Granville*, 2000), whereas compelling students to write the letter under threat of felony conviction violated the First Amendment right to free speech (Spooner & Vaughn, 2016; Wood, 2009, 2010). The issue of whether the content (e.g., photographs of girls partially or completely nude; clothed in bras, underwear, bathing suits) met the criteria for CSAM[17] as defined by statute was not addressed.

At the federal level, there is no sexting offense because it simply never occurred to legislatures that minors would engage in self-producing and consensual exchanging of intimate images, either as part of non-criminally intended reasons, such as sexual experimentation, or for nefarious ones, such as revenge, bully, shame, humiliate, or intimate partner violence (Barry, 2010; Ngo et al., 2017). Thus, minors who engage in OSA may face one or more federal charges related to CSAM, as shown in Table 7.5 (Seto, 2013). The intention behind these laws, however, was to prosecute adult

---

[13] National Coalition Against Censorship. (2021). Supreme Court won't revive Child Online Protection Act. https://ncac.org/news/blog/copa-is-dead; Zeigler, S.L. (2009). Communications Decency Act of 1996. https://www.mtsu.edu/first-amendment/article/1070/communications-decency-act-of-1996.

[14] Administrators, as mandatory reporters, may have feared that they could be charged with 18 USC §2258 if they failed to report this possible child abuse.

[15] 18 Pa. Cons. Stat. §6312 (possession or distribution of child pornography) and 18 Pa. Cons. Stat. §7514 (criminal use of a communication facility).

[16] 605 F. Supp.2d.634, 2009; Skumanick was replaced by Mitchell, see *Miller v. Mitchell*, 598 F.3d. 139.

[17] Although 18 Pa. Cons. Stat. §6312(g) includes nudity in its definition of CSAM, it is only relevant if the purpose for producing the image was for sexual stimulation or gratification.

Table 7.5 Federal Criminal Laws Relevant When Sexually Explicit Images of Minors Are Exchanged

Federal Law	Explanation of Statute Relevant to Sexting
18 USC §2251	*Sexual exploitation of children*: A person persuades/induces/entices a minor to engage in sexually explicit conduct[a] for the purpose of producing any visual depiction of such conduct or for the purpose of transmitting a live visual depiction of such conduct (i.e., CSAM) shall be punished… knowing that such visual depiction produced using a computer will be transmitted.
18 USC §2252	*Materials depicting sexual exploitation of minors*: A person knowingly transmits visual depiction of a minor engaged in sexually explicit conduct.
18 USC §2422b	*Coercion and enticement*: A person, using interstate commerce, knowingly persuades/induces/entices (including attempts) any individual who has not attained the age of 18 to engage in prostitution or any sexual activity.
18 USC §2425	*Transmit information about a minor*: A person knowingly initiates transmission of the personally identifiable information (PII) of an individual who has not attainted the age of 16 years with the intent to entice/encourage/solicit to engage in sexual activity, including production of CSAM.
18 USC §1466A	*Obscene representation so children*: A person who knowingly produces, distributes, receives, or possesses with intent to distribute a visual depiction of any kind of a minor engaging in sexually explicit conduct and is obscene or engaging in sexual intercourse with same/opposite sex persons.
18 USC §1470	*Transfer of obscene material to minors*: A person using interstate commerce knowingly transfers obscene material to any individual who has not attained the age of 16 years.

[a] As per the definition in 18 USC §2256, *sexually explicit conduct* includes actual or simulated sexual intercourse (genital-genital, oral-genital, anal-genital, or oral-anal) between persons of the same/opposite sex; bestiality; masturbation; sadistic or masochistic abuse; or lascivious exhibition of the anus, genitals, or pubic areas.

sexual predators who exploited children for their own prurient interests (O'Conner et al., 2017; Vitis, 2019). In OSA cases involving sexting between an adult predator and a minor victim resulting in charges of child sexual abuse, child sexual exploitation for production and distribution of CSAM, and obscenity are unquestioningly appropriate (see Chapters 8 and 9 for further discussions). However, applying these offenses and their associated, severe consequences (e.g., registering as sexual offenders, felony charges, mandatory prison sentences) to experimental sexting contexts are inconsistent with the spirit of the law—that is, to protect juveniles from harm by adult sexual predators (Eraker, 2010; Holoyda et al., 2017; Mills, 2019; Ricketts et al., 2015;[18] Strohmaier et al., 2014; Vitis, 2019; Wood, 2010).

States have taken different stances for dealing with minors who produce, possess, send, and receive their own and others' intimate images (Grasz & Pfaltzgraff, 1998). Table 7.6 indicates which criminal charges are used by each state (Hinduja & Patchin, 2016; O'Connor et al., 2017). Without legislative exceptions, prosecutors are obligated to charge minor parties with CSAM offenses and enforce their registration as sexual predators because, consistent with the laws as written, neither the context of the offense or the age of the perpetrator is considered (Holoyda et al., 2017; Vitis, 2019). At present, 25 states have either enacted specific sexting laws or have designated age-based affirmative defenses within pre-existing laws involving possession or dissemination of child sexual abuse material (Vitis, 2019; Westlake, 2018). Current sexting laws typically punish minors by charging them with a misdemeanor (sometimes increasing to a felony when caught again), requiring

Table 7.6 Criminal Charges for Experimental Sexting by State

Law	Penalty	States
Sexting	Felony	GA,* NE, NY
	Misdemeanor	AZ+, CO, CT+, HI, IN, KS, LA+, ND, PA, SD+, TX, UT, WA
	Non-criminal	AR+,[1] FL, ^^IL, NV, [a]NJ+, [d]NM, RI+, [s]VT, [d]WV+[d]
CSAM	Felony	AL, CA, DE, ID,* IA, MA, MI, MN, MS, MT, NH, NC, OH, OR, SC, TN, VA, WI, WY
	Misdemeanor	AK, KY,^ ME,* MD,^ MO, OK

Key: *misdemeanor if defenses met; [a]only when aged 14–18; [s]status offense; [d]delinquent act; ^only for first offense, then felony; ^^misdemeanor for second offense, felony for third offense; [1]first offense only, then misdemeanor; +sexually explicit text.

---

[18] Also true for Marcum et al. (2014) as they used the same dataset.

them to take educational or diversion programs, and/or charging them civilly (Hinduja & Patchin, 2016). However, felony charges for CSAM force minors to register as sex offenders and result in life-altering consequences that significantly limit their future in terms of employment, education, and housing (Eraker, 2010; Holoyda et al., 2017; Leary, 2007).

The failure of state legislatures to reach consensus on what content constitutes CSAM; how to handle sexting cases to optimize deterrence; and which legal defenses are appropriate has resulted in adolescent sexting defendants receiving wholly inequitable consequences (Holoyda et al., 2017; Ngo et al., 2017). Box 7.3 exemplifies the problem of having different responses to the same experimental sexting incident. Legal scholars propose the use of structured prosecutorial discretion to allow consideration of factors in each case to distinguish mutually consensual experimental sexting from intentionally harmful aggravated sexting (Holoyda et al., 2017; Leary, 2010).

BOX 7.3   COMPARISON OF TWO STATES' LEGISLATION APPLIED TO THE SAME SEXTING SITUATION

A 16-year-old girl takes a photograph of herself wearing a bikini from the front and another from the back, revealing her butt cheeks. She texts the photographs to her 15-year-old friend, accompanied by the following words, "u think my bf 💧"

Colorado Revised Statute §18-7-109 (2019). *Posting, possession, or exchange of a private image by a juvenile.*

> §18-7-109 (1)(b) A juvenile over age 14 knowingly distributed a sexually explicit image of herself to another juvenile over age 14 who had not requested it (but did not suffer emotional harm).[19]
> §18-7-109 (2) The juvenile friend now possesses the private image of someone at least age 14 (unless it is deleted within 72 hours after viewing) and §18-7-109 (3)(b) believes the sender agreed to the transmittal of the image.
> §18-7-109 (8a) The content would be considered of a juvenile under age 18 and §18-7-109 (8b) sexually explicit nudity as her buttocks are exposed.

---

[19] *Class 2 misdemeanor* charge for producer/sender if unrequested selfie causes emotional distress to receiver.

Charges: *Petty offense* (civil infraction) for sender and receiver.
Code of Virginia §18.2–374.1. *Production, publication, sale, financing, etc. of child pornography* and **§18.2–374.1:1.** *Possession, reproduction, distribution, solicitation, and facilitation of child pornography.*

> §18.2–374.1 (A)The statute defines sexually explicit visual material in §18.2–390 as a photograph depicting lewd exhibition of nudity as defined (exposed buttocks) or sexual excitement symbolized by the tent emoji (the condition of human male genitals when in a state of sexual arousal).
> §18.2–374.1 (B)(2) The juvenile is guilty of production as she self-produced the image.
> §18.2–374.1:1. A. Both the friend and the sender would be guilty of knowingly possessing child pornography.
> §18.2–374.1:1.C. The juvenile knowingly electronically transmitted the child pornography.

Charges: *Class 3 Felony* for producer of CSAM (depicted aged 15–17) is 1–20 years prison and for sender is 5–20 years; *Class 6 Felony* for possessor of CSAM, 1–5 years prison ($2500 fine). Mandatory registration as sex offenders, but if both are under 18, they may be processed in Juvenile Court and receive delinquency instead of a conviction.

IMPACT OF MINOR ONLINE SEXUAL ACTIVITY ON SOCIETY AND SENDING/RECEIVING PARTIES

In determining the effect of online sexual activity by adolescents on society and on themselves, it is important to consider this voluntary and intentional "cybercrime" of experimental sexting in the appropriate context. During adolescence, youth seek to establish themselves as individuals; however, they are vulnerable to the influence of their culture and to the attention and feedback provided by their peers, both online and offline (Hinduja & Patchin, 2016; Valkenburg et al., 2017; Wolfe et al., 2016). American minors have been indoctrinated from a young age to use a variety of Internet-connecting devices for education, entertainment, and socialization (Hinduja & Patchin, 2016). By 2019, most preadolescents (aged 8–12) and adolescents (aged 13–18) reported they have access to TVs (87%), Video game consoles (78%), computer laptops (79%), tablets (75%), desktops

168

(52%), and smart speakers (30%) in their homes (Rideout & Robb, 2019). As shown in Figure 7.4, a significant number of them also own Internet devices with digital cameras, giving them easy access to send and receive sext images through Apps, social media platforms, email, and phone services (Rideout & Robb, 2019).

Adolescents' prolonged and near constant access to digital information and communication has transformed how they experience three psychosocial developmental tasks and corresponding abilities (Shafer, 2019; Valkenburg & Peter, 2011; Valkenburg et al., 2017)—*intimacy* (e.g., peer relationships, socially responsibleness); *identity* (e.g., social roles, self-esteem, emotional independence); and *sexuality* (e.g., sexual orientation, body image acceptance). Although adolescents learned and developed socialization skills that shaped their identity in the past through daily offline interactions with peers and friends, these experiences typically occur today via online activities (Valkenburg & Peter, 2011; Valkenburg et al., 2017). The online environment of instant messaging and social networking, and even online sexual activity through experimental sexting, offers adolescents "anonymity, asynchonicity, and accessibility" to help them modulate "self-presentation and self-disclosure" in an effort to optimize favorable responses from peers as they explore their "identity, intimacy, and sexuality" (Valkenburg & Peter, 2011, p. 122; Valkenburg et al., 2017). Anonymity in online chat rooms, IMs, and social network sites increases opportunities for users to respond quickly and emotionally. This environment is problematic for adolescents, who often act impulsively in pursuit of approval and acceptance, because they rely on their peers to regulate the amount and type of information they disclose and present in forming their online identity (Valkenburg & Peter, 2011). In

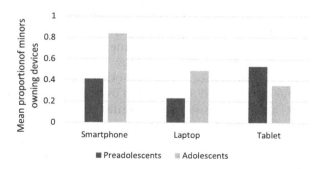

Figure 7.4 Mean proportion of minors owning different Internet devices in 2019.

contrast, it may be easier for them to discuss potentially sensitive and embarrassing aspects of sex, sexual orientation, and sexuality, as well as explore their sexual identity, under the cloak of invisibility (Hinduja & Patchin, 2016; Valkenburg & Peter, 2011; Valkenburg et al., 2017). The disinhibiting characteristics of electronic devices likely contribute to adolescents' willingness to communicate their sexual desires asynchronically and anonymously through the exchange of sexually explicit images (Van Ouytsel et al., 2017).

The public first learned about *sexting* from sensationalized media coverage of adolescent suicides (e.g., Jessica Logan in 2008; Hope Witsell in 2009) following a protracted period of cyberbullying and humiliation when their sexually explicit images were shared/forwarded to peers without their consent (Livingstone & Görzig, 2014; Hinduja & Patchin, 2016; Ringrose et al., 2013). Society associates sexting with multiple risks, including adolescents becoming sexually active, getting exploited by online sexual predators, and being victimized by peers (Klettke et al., 2014; Livingstone & Görzig, 2014; O'Connor & Drouin, 2020; Ringrose et al., 2013; Valido et al., 2020). According to longitudinal (Steinberg et al., 2019; Temple & Choi, 2014) and cross-sectional research (Dake et al., 2012; Jewell & Brown, 2013; Rice et al., 2012, 2014; Strassberg et al., 2013), there is a correlation between adolescents who exchange sext images and are sexually active. However, it is not clear if adolescents engage in experimental sexting as a precursor action or as a signal that they are now ready to experience sexual intimacy (Temple & Choi, 2014). Developmental psychologists conceive of sexting as ranging along a continuum—on one end is *experimental sexting* comprised of typical, normative behavior by consenting, romantically inclined/committed adolescents who are exploring their sexuality and/or intimacy through digital communication and on the other end are *aggravated* and *secondary sexting* involving adolescents who intentionally victimize, exploit, and harm other adolescents through online/offline harassment, stalking, and coercion (Hinduja & Patchin, 2016; Valido et al., 2020; Walrave et al., 2014; Wolak & Finkelhor, 2011). Nonetheless, legislators, parents, and educators feel frustration and concern over their inability to supervise and protect minors whose use of digital communication technology makes them vulnerable to legal, socio-emotional, and academic repercussions (Livingstone & Görzig, 2014; O'Connor & Drouin, 2020).

As revealed by prevalence rates reported in this chapter, only a small proportion of minors engage in experimental sexting and this behavior has both positive and negative outcomes. Online sexual activity allows adolescents to foster their psychosocial skills—particularly for identity, as well as for intimacy between romantically involved individuals who are the most likely to be sexting (Drouin et al., 2015; Englander, 2012; Mori et al, 2019). Sexting may also result in negative consequences for individuals and their families when it is discovered by parents, school administrators, and law enforcement (Reyner et al., 2018), including punishment by parents (e.g., loss of privileges, removal of devices); academic repercussions (e.g., suspension or expulsion, low grades); legal costs, prosecution, and, depending on the state of residence, associated consequences of conviction (e.g., sex offender registry, prison sentence); and adverse social and reputational problems when peers gossip about who was caught sexting. In some cases, sexting coincides with socio-emotional (e.g., poor self-esteem; emotion dysregulation); behavioral (e.g., conduct problems, substance use/abuse); and psychological problems (e.g., depression and anxiety disorders), but not necessarily in a cause-and-effect way (Cox Communications, 2009; Gassó et al., 2020; Gómez & Ayala, 2014; Harris et al., 2013; Judge, 2012; Klettke et al., 2018, 2019; Kopecký, 2014, 2015; Rhyner et al., 2018; Strohmaier et al., 2014; Temple et al., 2012, 2014; Van Ouytsel et al., 2019; Walrave et al., 2014; Ybarra & Mitchell, 2014).

Acceptance of experimental sexting is the result of adolescents internalizing American values in which sexually explicit content portrayed through various online media sources is condoned, resulting in sexual norms, behaviors, language, and concepts being perverted (Hinduja & Patchin, 2016). These unhealthy sexuality standards tie adolescents' self-worth to physical attractiveness (Hinduja & Patchin, 2016). Heterosexual boys are subjected to peer pressure to receive and view sexts, which increases their sexual reputation and masculinity image (Titchen et al., 2019). In contrast, heterosexual girls experience a double standard for sexual reputation, similar to peer pressure experienced in real life to engage in sexual activities, resulting in moral condemnation for complying to sexting requests (Confalonieri et al., 2020; Jewell & Brown, 2013; Lippman & Campbell, 2014; Ringrose et al., 2013). Consistent with the American Psychological Association (APA, 2007), girls and women are disproportionately targeted through socialization to act in ways that please others; objectification of their bodies to equate them with commodities; and consumerism to purchase products aimed at enhancing their physical appeal—all of which sexualizes them. Society is harmed by augmenting social problems that further continue and increase victimization and sexualization of girls and women—including sexual violence, exploitation, and harassment—while decreasing their aspirations for higher education and high paying occupations in science, technology, engineering, and math (APA, 2007).

CYBERSECURITY TACTICS

Carrier services offer parents *usage control* options that regulates tools used for sexting by either partially (e.g., shut off picture messaging) or completely (i.e., phone can only make calls) restricting them (Silver, 2010). Although phone settings provide the least invasive technique, most parents opt to use technology that allows them to monitor their adolescents' phones for sexting. SMobile offers a software program that examines children's incoming and outgoing emails; messages—text and pictures; and phone calls—however, it cannot monitor social media platforms or Apps (Silver, 2010). The *Gallery Guardian* App notifies parents when a photo in the child's gallery is suspicious, rather than displaying it, such as poses in the nude, lingerie, underwear, or swimsuit (Dredge, 2017). However, in order to detect sexting on Snapchat, parents would need to download mSpy onto their children's phones[20] and pay a monthly fee to see every message; it also monitors messages from WhatsApp and Skype calls (Lobosco, 2014). Annual parent control services can also be purchased (e.g., Bark, Oustodio), which cover multiple Internet devices (e.g., tables, smartphones, computers), and alert parents to potential concerns based on examination of photos and videos in device storage and in social media chats; displays the amount of time the child spent on various social networks; allows SMS messages to be read; and lists the child's logs from calls, Chrome browsing, and YouTube videos (Edwards, 2020). Table 7.7 displays five Apps that work on all Androids and iPhones and do not require a monthly subscription to use (Stanley, 2019). This technology allows parents to apply the App through an over-the-air link which downloads it remotely onto the Target phone, where it is undetectable. Then the App will remotely connect with the monitored device to upload the data onto a secure online account.

---

[20] Parents do not need permission to download spy software if the phone belongs their minor child and the App does not appear on the phone, making it undetectable.

Table 7.7 Five Parental Monitoring Apps and What They Do

App	What Can be Examined?
Auto Forward Spy—includes free customer service support	Text messages; Social media monitored in real time; Keylogger (records keystroke entries); Internet browser history; Calls (incoming/outgoing log); Monitor and record email; Remote listening; Remote command to snap picture
Highster Mobile—includes free customer service support	Text messages; Social media messages; Keylogger Internet browsing history; Photos and videos
PhoneSpector	Text messages (including deleted texts); social media messages [But not Viber]; Keylogger; Internet Browser history; Calls; Email; Photos; Videos; Installed and running Apps
DDI Utilities	Text messages; Social media messages; Keylogger; Calls (incoming/outgoing log); Emails; Photos (new, old, deleted); Videos taken on/received by phone; iMessages; Remote command to snap picture
Easy spy	Text messages (included deleted ones); Calls; Internet Browsing history; Emails; Social media

REFERENCES

Abraham, A.E. (2015). *Sexting Uncensored: An Exploratory Study on the Behaviors, Experiences, and Perceptions of Sexting among College Students.* Thesis, Fresno, CA: California State University. ProQuest No. 1601678.

Age of Consent.net. (2021). *United States Age of Consent.* https://www.ageofconsent.net/states.

American Psychological Association. (2007). *Report of the APA Task Force on the Sexualization of Girls.* https://www.apa.org/pi/women/programs/girls/report-full.pdf.

Anderson, M. (2015). *Technology Device Ownership: 2015.* https://www.pewresearch.org/internet/2015/10/29/technology-device-ownership-2015/.

Anderson, M., & Jiang, J. (2018). *Teens, Social Media & Technology 2018.* Pew Research Center. https://www.pewresearch.org/internet/2018/05/31/teens-social-media-technology-2018/.

Arain, M., Haque, M., Johal, L., Mathur, P., Nel, W., Rais, A., Sandhu, R., & Sharma, S. (2013). Maturation of the adolescent brain. *Neuropsychiatric Disease Treatment, 9,* 449–461. Doi: 10.2147/NDT.S39776.

173

Associated Press and MTV. (2009). *A Thin Line. 2009 AP-MTV Digital Abuse Study.* http://www.athinline.org/MTV-AP_Digital_Abuse_Study_Executive_Summary.pdf

Auxier, B., Anderson, M., Perrin, A., & Turner, E. (2021). *Parenting Children in the Age of Screens.* https://www.pewresearch.org/internet/2020/07/28/parenting-children-in-the-age-of-screens/

Barnes, S.P. (2012). Responding to self-produced child pornography: Examining legislative successes and shortcomings to reach an appropriate solution. *Journal of Law, Technology, & The Internet, 4*(1), 1–39.

Barrense-Dias, Y., Berchtold, A., Suris, J-C., & Akre, C. (2017). Sexting and the definition issue. *Journal of Adolescent Health, 61*(5), 544–554. Doi: 10.1016/j.jadohealth.2017.05.009

Barry, J.L. (2010). The child as victim and perpetrator: Laws punishing juvenile "sexting." *Vanderbilt Journal of Entertainment and Technology Law, 13*(1), 129–153.

Benotsch, E.G., Snipes, D.J., Martin, A.M., & Bull, S.S. (2013). Sexting, substance use, and sexual risk behavior in young adults. *Journal of Adolescent Health, 52*(3), 307–313.

Bright, S. (1992). *Susie Bright's Sexual Reality: A Virtual Sex World Reader.* Berkley, CA: Cleis Press.

Burén, J. & Lunde, C. (2018). Sexting among adolescents: A nuanced and gendered online challenge for young people. *Computers in Human Behavior, 85*, 210–217.

Campbell, S.W., & Park, Y.J. (2014). Predictors of mobile sexting among teens: Toward a new explanatory framework. *Mobile Media & Communication, 2*(1), 20–39.

Chowdhury, R. (2014). *Evolution of Mobile Phones:1995–2012.* https://www.hongkiat.com/blog/evolution-of-mobile-phones/.

Confalonieri, E., CuccÃ, G., Olivari, M.G., Parise, M., Borroni, E., & Villani, D. (2020). What are you sexting? Parental practices, sexting attitudes and behaviors among Italian adolescents. *BMC Psychology, 8*(1), 63–73. Doi: 10.1186/s40359-020-00425-1.

Cooper, K., Quayle, E., Jonsson, L., & Svedin, C.G. (2016). Adolescents and self-taken sexual images: A review of the literature. *Computers in Human Behavior, 55*, 706–716.

Cox Communications. (2009). *Teen Online & Wireless Safety Survey: Cyberbullying, Sexting, and Parental Controls.* http://ww2.cox.com/wcm/en/aboutus/datasheet/takecharge/2009-teen-survey.pdf?campcode=takecharge-research-link_2009-teen-survey_0511.

Dake, J., Price, J., Maziarz, L., & Ward, B. (2012). Prevalence and correlates of sexting behaviour in adolescents. *American Journal of Sexuality Education, 7*, 1–15.

Del Rey, R., Ojeda, M., Casas, J.A., Mora-Merchán, J.A., & Elipe, P. (2019). Sexting among adolescents: The emotional impact and influence of the need for popularity. *Frontier Psychology, 10*, 1828.

Doornwaard, S.M., Ter Bogt, T.F., Reitz, E., & Van Den Eijnden, R.J. (2015). Sex-related online behaviors, perceived peer norms and adolescents' experience with sexual behavior: Testing an integrative model. *PloS One, 10*(6), e0127787.

Dowdell, E.B., Burgess, A.W., & Flores, J.R. (2011). Original research: Online social networking patterns among adolescents, young adults, and sexual offenders. *American Journal of Nursing, 111*(7), 28–36. Doi: 10.1097/01. NAJ.0000399310.83160.73.

Dredge, S. (2017, November 6). *Gallery Guardian App Polices the Photos on Your Child's Smartphone.* https://medium.com/contempoplay/gallery-guardian-app-polices-the-photos-on-your-childs-smartphone-343b6e3c6da1.

Drouin, M., Ross, J., & Tobin, E. (2015). Sexting: A new, digital vehicle for intimate partner aggression? *Computers in Human Behavior, 50,* 197–204.

Drouin, M., & Tobin, E. (2014). Unwanted but consensual sexting among young adults: Relations with attachment and sexual motivations. *Computers in Human Behavior, 31,* 412–418, Doi: 10.1016/j.chb.2013.11.001.

Edwards, R. (2020, December 9). *The Best Parental Control Apps of 2021.* https://www.safewise.com/resources/parental-control-filters-buyers-guide/.

Englander, E. (2012). *Low Risk Associated with Most Teenage Sexting: A Study of 617 18- Year-Olds.* Massachusetts Aggression Reduction Center, Bridgewater State University. https://vc.bridgew.edu/cgi/viewcontent. cgi?article=1003&context=marc_reports

Eraker, E.C. (2010). Stemming sexting: Sensible legal approaches to teenagers' exchange of self-produced pornography. *Berkeley Technology Law Journal, 25,* 555–596.

Federal Trade Commission. (2009). *Virtual Worlds and Kids: Mapping the Risks. A Report to Congress.* https://www.ftc.gov/sites/default/files/documents/reports/virtual-worlds-and-kids-mapping-risks-federal-trade-commission-report-congress/oecd-vwrpt.pdf

Find Law. (2020). *State-by-State Marriage "Age of Consent."* www.findlaw.com/family/marriage/state-by-state-marriage-ages-of-consent-laws.html.

Gassó, A.M., Mueller-Johnson, K., & Montiel, I. (2020). Sexting, online sexual victimization, and psychopathology correlates by sex: Depression, anxiety, and global psychopathology. *International Journal of Environmental Research and Public Health, 17,* 1018.

Gómez, L.C., & Ayala, E.S. (2014). Psychological aspects, attitudes and behaviour related to the practice of sexting: A systematic review of the existent literature. *Procedia-Social and Behavioral Sciences, 132,* 114–120.

Grasz, L., & Pfaltzgraff, P.J. (1998). Child pornography and child nudity: Why and how states may constitutionally regulate the production, possession, and distribution of nude visual depictions of children. *Temple Law Review, 71*(3), 609–606.

Handschuh, C., LaCross, A., & Smaldone, A. (2019). Is sexting associated with sexual behaviors during adolescence? A systematic literature review and meta-analysis. *Journal of Midwifery & Women's Health, 64*(1), 88–97. Doi: 10.1111/jmwh.12923.

Harris, A.J., Davidson, J., Letourneau, E., Paternite, C., & Tusinski Miofsky, K. (2013). *Building a Prevention Framework to Address Teen "Sexting" Behaviors.* https://www.ojp.gov/pdffiles1/ojjdp/grants/244001.pdf.

175

Henry, N., & Powell, A. (2015). Beyond the "sext": Technology-facilitated sexual violence and harassment against adult women. *Australian & New Zealand Journal of Criminology, 48,* 104–118.

Hessick, C.B. (2018). The expansion of child pornography law. *New Criminal Law Review, 21(3),* 321–344. https://scholarship.law.unc.edu/cgi/viewcontent.cgi? article=1462&context=faculty_publications

Hinduja, S., & Patchin, J.W. (2010). Bullying, cyberbullying, and suicide. *Archives of Suicide Research, 14(3),* 206–221. Doi: 10.1080/13811118.2010.494133

Hinduja, S., & Patchin, J.W. (2016). *School Climate 2.0: Preventing Cyberbullying and Sexting One Classroom at a Time.* Thousand Oaks, CA: Corwin Press/Sage. Online ISBN:9781506335438.

Holoyda, B., Landess, J., & Sorrentino, R. (2018). Trouble at teens' fingertips: Youth sexting and the law. *Behavioral Sciences & the Law, 36,* 170–181. Doi: 10.1002/bsl.2335.

Houck, C.D., Barker, D., Rizzo, C., Hancock, E., Norton, A., & Brown, L.K. (2014). Sexting and sexual behavior in at-risk adolescents. *Pediatrics, 133(2),* e276–282. Doi: 10.1542/peds.2013-1157.

Huang, E. T.-Y., Williams, H., Hocking, J.S., & Lim, M.S. (2016). Safe sex messages within dating and entertainment smartphone apps: A review. *JMIR mHealth and uHealth, 4(4).* Doi: 10.2196/mhealth.5760.

Jewell, J.A., & Brown, C.S. (2013). Sexting, catcalls, and butt slaps: How gender stereotypes and perceived group norms predict sexualized behavior. *Sex Roles, 69(11),* 594–604.

Judge, A.M. (2012). "Sexting" among U.S. adolescents: Psychological and legal perspectives. *Harvard Review of Psychiatry, 20,* 86–96.

Kernsmith, P.D., Victor, B.G., & Smith-Darden, J.P. (2018). Online, offline, and over the line: Coercive sexting among adolescent dating partners. *Youth & Society, 50(7),* 891–904. Doi: 10.1177/0044118X18764040.

Kim, S., Martin-Storey, A., Drossos, A., Barbosa, S., & Georgiades, K. (2020). Prevalence and correlates of sexting behaviors in a provincially representative sample of adolescents. *The Canadian Journal of Psychiatry, 65(6),* 401–408. Doi: 10.1177/0706743719895205.

Klettke, B., Hallford, D.J., Clancy, E., Mellor, D.J., & Toumbourou, J.W. (2019). Sexting and psychological distress: The role of unwanted and coerced sexts. *Cyberpsychology, Behavior, and Social Networking, 22,* 237–242.

Klettke, B., Hallford, D.J., & Mellor, D.J. (2014). Sexting prevalence and correlates: A systematic literature review. *Clinical Psychology Review, 34,* 44–53.

Klettke, B., Mellor, D., Silva-Myles, L., Clancy, E., & Kumar, M. (2018). Sexting and mental health: A study of Indian and Australian young adults. *Cyberpsychology: Journal of Psychosocial Research on Cyberspace, 12,* 2. Doi: 10.5817/CP2018-2-2

Kopecký, K. (2014). Cyberbullying and sexting between children and adolescents—Comparative study. *Procedia Social and Behavioral Sciences, 149,* 467–471. Doi: 10.1016/j.sbspro.2014.08.292.

Kopecký, K. (2015). Sexting among Slovak pubescents and adolescent children. *Procedia Social and Behavioral Sciences, 203,* 244–250.

Kopecký, K. & Szotkowski, R. (2019). Sexting in the population of children and its risks: A quantitative study. *International Journal of Cyber Criminology, 12(2)*, 376–391. Doi: 10.5281/zenodo.3365620.

Kosenko, K., Lurrs, G., & Binder, A.R. (2017). Sexting and sexual behavior, 2011–2015: A critical review and meta-analysis of a growing literature. *Journal of Computer-Mediated Communication, 22(3)*, 141–160.

Leary, M.G. (2007). Self-produced child pornography: The appropriate societal response to juvenile self-sexual exploitation. *Virginia Journal of Social Policy & the Law, 15(1)*, 1–50.

Leary, M.G. (2010). Sexting or self-produced child pornography? The dialog continues— structured prosecutorial discretion within a multidisciplinary response. *Virginia Journal of Social Policy & the Law, 17(3)*, 486–566.

Lee, C-H., Moak, S., & Walker, J. (2016). Effects of self-control, social control, and social learning on sexting behavior among South Korean youths. *Youth & Society, 48(2)*, 242–264. Doi: 10.1177/0044118X13490762.

Lemke, M., & Rogers, K. (2020). When sexting crosses the line: Educator responsibilities in the support of prosocial adolescent behavior and the prevention of violence. *Social Science, 9(9)*, 150–164. DOI: 10.3390/socsci9090150.

Lenhart, A. (2009). *Teens and Sexting: How and Why Minor Teens Are Sending Suggestive Nude or Nearly Nude Images Via Text Messaging*. Pew Research Center. https://www.pewresearch.org/internet/2009/12/15/teens-and-sexting/.

Lenhart, A. (2012). *Teens, Smartphones, & Texting*. https://www.pewresearch.org/internet/wp-content/uploads/sites/9/2012/03/PI_2012.03.19_teens-smart-phones-texting_REPORT.pdf.

Lenhart, A. (2015). *Teens, Social Media & Technology Overview 2015*. Pew Research Center: http://www.pewinternet.org/2015/04/09/teens-social-media-technology-2015/.

Lenhart, A., Madden, M., & Hitlin, P. (2005). *Youth are Leading the Transition to a Fully Wired and Mobile Nation*. https://www.immagic.com/eLibrary/ARCHIVES/GENERAL/PEW/P050727L.pdf.

Lenhart, A., Ling, R., & Campbell, S. (2010a). *Teens, Adults & Sexting: Data on Sending & Receipt of Sexually Suggestive Nude or Nearly Nude Images by American Adolescents and Adults*. https://www.pewresearch.org/internet/2010/10/23/teens-adults-and-sexting-data-on-sendingreceiving-sexually-suggestive-nude-or-nearly-nude-photos-by-americans/.

Lenhart, A., Ling, R., Campbell, S., & Purcell, K. (2010b). *Teens and Mobile Phones*. Pew Internet and American Life Project. http://pewinternet.org/Reports/2010/Teens-and-Mobile-Phones.aspx,

Lenhart, A., Rainie, L., & Lewis, O. (2001). *Teenage Life Online: The Rise of the Instant-Message Generation and the Internet's Impact on Friendships and Family Relations*. https://www.pewresearch.org/internet/wp-content/uploads/sites/9/media/Files/Reports/2001/PIP_Teens_Report.pdf.pdf.

Lippman, J.R., & Campbell, S.W. (2014). Damned if you do, damned if you don't…If you're a girl: Relational and normative contexts of adolescent sexting in the United States. *Journal of Children Media, 8*, 371–386. 10.1080/17482798.2014.923009.

177

Livingstone, S., & Görzig, A. (2014). When adolescents receive sexual messages on the internet: Explaining experiences of risk and harm. *Computers in Human Behavior, 33,* 8–15. Doi: 10.1016/j.chb.2013.12.021.

Lobosco, K. (2014, September 3). *How to Find Out if Your Kids Are Sexting on Snapchat.* CNN Business. https://money.cnn.com/2014/09/03/technology/social/spy-on-snapchat/.

Lorang, M.R., McNiel, D.E., & Binder, R.L. (2016). Minors and sexting: Legal implications. *Journal of American Academy of Psychiatry Law, 44,* 73–81.

Madden, M., Lenhart, A., Duggan, M., Cortesi, S., & Gasser, U. (2013). *Teens and Technology 2013.* Pew Internet & American Life Project. https://heartmdinstitute.com/wp-content/uploads/2015/04/PIP_TeensandTechnology2013.pdf

Madigan, S., Ly, A., Rash, C.L., Van Ouytsel, J., & Temple, J.R. (2018). Prevalence of multiple forms of sexting behavior among youth: A systematic review and meta-analysis. *JAMA Pediatrics, 172(4),* 327–335.

Maheux, A.J., Evans, R., Widman, L., Nesi, J., Prinstein, M.J., & Choukas-Bradley, S. (2020). Popular peer norms and adolescent sexting behavior. *Journal of Adolescence, 78,* 62–66.

Marcum, C.D., Higgins, G.E., & Ricketts, M.L. (2014). Sexting behaviors among adolescents in rural North Carolina: A theoretical examination of low self-control and deviant peer association. *International Journal of Cyber Criminology, 8(2),* 68–78.

Martinez-Prather, K., & Vandiver, D.M. (2014). Sexting among teenagers in the United States: A retrospective analysis of identifying motivating factors, potential targets, and the role of a capable guardian. International Journal of Cyber Criminology, 8(1), 21–35.

Mills, A. (2019). Juvenile sexting: A harsh reality. *Thurgood Marshall Law Review, 43* Online 3.

Mitchell, K.J., Finkelhor, D., Jones, L.M., & Wolak, J. (2012). Prevalence and characteristics of youth sexting: A national study. *Pediatrics, 129(1),* 13–20. Doi: 10.1542/peds.2011-1730.

Morelli, M., Bianchi, D., Baiocco, R., Pezzuti, L., & Chirumbolo, A. (2016). Notallowed sharing of sexts and dating violence from the perpetrator's perspective: The moderation role of sexism. *Computers in Human Behavior, 56,* 163–169. Doi: 10.1016/j.chb.2015.11.047.

Mori, C., Cooke, J.E., Temple, J.R., Ly, A., Lu, Y., Anderson, N., Rash, C., & Madigan, S. (2020). The prevalence of sexting behaviors among emerging adults: A meta-analysis. *Archives of Sexual Behavior, 49,* 1103–1119.

Mori, C., Temple, J.R., Browne, D., & Madigan, S. (2019). Association of sexting with sexual behaviors and mental health among adolescents: A systematic review and meta-analysis. *JAMA Pediatrics, 173(8),* 770–779. Doi:10.1001/jamapediatrics.2019.1658.

MTV–AP. (2009). *Digital Abuse Study* [online]. http://www.athinline.org/MTVAP_Digital_Abuse_Study_Full.pdf.

Murray, D.L. (2014). *A Survey of the Practices and Perceptions of Students in One Catholic High School on the Use of the Internet in Relation to Safety, Cyberbullying, and Sexting* [dissertation]. https://repository.usfca.edu/diss/89/.

National Campaign to Prevent Teen and Unplanned Pregnancy. (2008). *Sex and Tech: Results from a Survey of Teens and Young Adults.* Cosmogirl.com. https://powertodecide.org/what-we-do/information/resource-library/sex-and-tech-results-survey-teens-and-young-adults

Ngo, F., Jaishankar, K., & Agustina, J.R. (2017). Sexting: Current research gaps and legislative issues. *International Journal of Cyber Criminology, 11*(2), 161–168. Doi: 10.5281/zenodo.1037369.

Ofcome. (2020). *Children and Parents: Media Use and Attitudes Report, 2019.* https://www.ofcom.org.uk/__data/assets/pdf_file/0023/190616/children-media-use-attitudes-2019-report.pdf.

O'Connor, K., & Drouin, M. (2020). Sexting and social concerns. In T.J. Holt and A.M. Bossler (eds.), *The Palgrave Handbook of International Cybercrime and Cyberdeviance* (pp. 1088–1108). Switzerland: Palgrave Macmillan. Doi: 10.1007/978-3-319-78440-3.

O'Conner, K., Drouin, M., Yergens, N., & Newsham, G. (2017). Sexting legislation in the United States and abroad: A call for uniformity. *International Journal of Cyber Criminology, 11*(2), 218–245. Doi: 10.5281/zenodo.1037397.

O'Sullivan, L.F. (2014). Linking online sexual activities to health outcomes among teens. In E.S. Lefkowitz & S.A. Vasilenko (Eds.), *Positive and Negative Outcomes of Sexual Behaviors. New Directions for Child and Adolescent Development, 144,* 37–51.

Paravecchia, J. (2011). Sexting and subsidiarity: How increased participation and education from private entities may deter the production, distribution, and possession of child pornography among minors. *Ave Maria Law Review, 10*(1), 235–259.

Patchin, J.W., & Hinduja, S. (2019). The nature and extent of sexting among a national sample of middle and high school students in the U.S. *Archives of Sexual Behavior, 48,* 2333–2343.

Patchin, J.W., & Hinduja, S. (2020). Sextortion among adolescents: Results from a national survey of U.S. youth. *Sexual Abuse, 32*(1), 30–54. Doi: 10.1177/1079063218800469.

Peskin, M.F., Markham, C.M., Addy, R.C., Shegog, R., Thiel, M., & Tortolero, S.R. (2013). Prevalence and patterns of sexting among ethnic minority urban high school students. *Cyberpsychology, Behavior, and Social Networking, 16*(6), 454–459.

Pew Research Organization (2019, June 12). *Mobile Fact Sheet.* https://www.pewresearch.org/internet/fact-sheet/mobile/#ownership-of-other-devices.

Primack, A.J. (2018). Youth sexting and the first amendment: Rhetoric and child pornography doctrine in the age of translation. *New Media & Society, 20*(8), 2917–2933.

Raine, G., Khouja, C., Scott, R., Wright, K., & Sowden, A.J. (2020). Pornography use and sexting amongst children and young people: A systematic overview of reviews. *Systematic Reviews, 9,* 283–294. Doi: 10.1186/s13643-020-01541-0.

Rearson, M. (2008). *Text Messaging Explodes in America*. https://www.cbsnews. com/news/text-messaging-explodes-in-america/.

Reed, L.A., Boyer, M.P., Meskunas, H., Tolman, R.M., & Ward, L.M. (2020). How do adolescents experience sexting in dating relationships? Motivations to sext and responses to sexting requests from dating partners. *Children and Youth Services Review, 109*, 104696. Doi: 10.1016/j.childyouth.2019.104696.

Reyns, B.W., Burek, M.W., Henson, B., & Fisher, B.S. (2013). The unintended consequences of digital technology: Exploring the relationship between sexting and cybervictimization. *Journal of Crime and Justice, 36(1)*, 1–17.

Rhyner, K.J., Uhl, C.A., & Terrance, C.A. (2018). Are teens being unfairly punished? Applying the dual systems model of adolescent risk-taking to sexting among adolescents. *Youth Justice, 18(1)*, 52–66. Doi: 10.1177/143225417741227.

Rice, E., Craddock, J., Hemler, J., Rusow, J., Plant, A., Montoya, J., & Kordic, T. (2018). Associations between sexting behaviors and sexual behaviors among mobile phone-owning teens in Los Angeles. *Child Development, 89(1)*, 110–117.

Rice, E., Gibbs, J., Winetrobe, H., Rhoades, H., Plant, A., Montoya, J., & Kordic, T. (2014). Sexting and sexual behavior among middle school students. *Pediatrics, 134*, e21–e28. Doi: 10.1542/peds.2013-2991.

Rice, E., Rhoades, H., Winetrobe, H., Sanchez, M., Montoya, J., Plant, A., & Kordic, T. (2012). Sexually explicit cell phone messaging associated with sexual risk among adolescents. *Pediatrics, 130(4)*, 667–73. Doi: 10.1542/peds.2012-0021.

Ricketts, M.L., Maloney, C., Marcum, C.D., & Higgins, G.E. (2015). The effect of Internet related problems on the sexting behaviors of juveniles. *American Journal of Criminal Justice, 40(2)*, 270–284.

Rideout, V., & Robb, M.B. (2019). *The Common Sense Census: Media Use by Tweens and Teens*. https://www.commonsensemedia.org/sites/default/files/uploads/research/2019-census-8-to-18-full-report-updated.pdf.

Ringrose, J., Gill, R., Livingstong, S., & Harvey, L. (2012). *A Qualitative Study of Children, Young People and 'Sexting:' A Report Prepared for the NSPCC*. https://www.researchgate.net/publication/311806257_A_qualitative_study_of_children_young_people_and_%27sexting%27_English.

Ringrose, J., Harvey, L., Gill, R., & Livingstone, S. (2013). Teen girls, sexual double standards and 'sexting': Gendered value in digital image exchange. *Feminist Theory, 14(3)*, 305–323. Doi: 10.1177/1464700113499853.

Romo, D.L., Garnett, C., Younger, A.P., Stockwell, M.S., Soren, K., & Catallozzi, M.J. (2017). Social media use and its association with sexual risk and parental monitoring among a primarily Hispanic adolescent population. *Journal of Pediatric and Adolescent Gynecology, 30*, 466–473.

Ross, J.M., Drouin, M., & Coupe, A. (2016). Sexting coercion as a component of intimate partner polyvictimization. *Journal of Interpersonal Violence, 34(11)*, 2269–2291. Doi: 10.1177/0886260516660300.

Sacco, D., Argudin, R., Maguire, J., & Tallon, K. (2010). *Sexting: Youth Practices and Legal Implications* (SSRN Scholarly Paper No. ID 1661343). Rochester, NY: Social Science Research Network. https://papers.ssrn.com/abstract=1661343.

Seto, M.C. (2013). *Internet Sex Offenders*. Washington, DC: American Psychological Association.

Shafer, A. (2019). Advancing research on adolescent sexting. *Journal of Adolescent Health, 65(6)*, 711–712.

Shah, N. (2021). *The Evolution of Mobile Apps –1994 through 2016*. https://arkenea.com/blog/evolution-of-mobile-apps/.

Shapiro, L.R. & Maras, M-H. (2016). *Multidisciplinary Investigation of Child Maltreatment*. Burlington, MA: Jones & Bartlett Learning.

Shaughnessy, K., Fudge, M., & Byers, E.S. (2017). An exploration of prevalence, variety, and frequency data to quantify online sexual activity experience. *Canadian Journal of Human Sexuality, 26(1)*, 60–75. Doi: 10.3138/cjhs.261-A4.

Silva, B.R., Teixera, C.M., Vascolncelos-Raposo, J., & Bessa, M. (2016). Sexting: Adaptation of sexual behavior to modern technologies. *Computers in Human Behavior, 64*, 747–753.

Silver, C. (2010, April 6). *"Sexting" and Texting Teens Need Parental Controls*. Wired. https://www.wired.com/2010/04/sexting-texting-teens-need-parental-controls/.

Spooner, K., & Vaughn, M. (2016). Youth sexting: A legislative and constitutional analysis. *Journal of School Violence, 15(2)*, 213–233.

Stanley, P. (2019). *Top 5 Best Cell Phone Spy Apps*. https://bestcellphonespy-apps.com/?gclid=cjwkcaiam-2bbhaneiwae7eyfoe2v5zrxafr6wrqlw0iqz-ni1cbqddocowacey4hat1hvrtckq7kqbocylgqavd_bwe.

Steinberg, D.B., Simon, V.A., Victor, B.G., Kernsmith, P.D., & Smith-Darden, J.P. (2019). Onset trajectories on sexting and other sexual behaviors across high school: A longitudinal growth mixture modeling approach. *Archives of Sexual Behavior, 48(8)*, 2321–2331. Doi: 10.1007/s10508-019-1414-9.

Strassberg, D.S., Cann, D., & Velarde, V. (2017). Sexting by high school students. *Archives of Sexual Behavior, 46*, 1667–1672.

Strassberg, D.S., McKinnon, R.K., Sustaíta, M.A., & Rullo, J. (2013). Sexting by high school students: An exploratory and descriptive study. *Archives of Sexual Behavior, 42*, 15–21.

Strohmaier, H., Murphy, M. & DeMatteo, D. (2014). Youth sexting: Prevalence rates, driving motivations, and the deterrent effect of legal consequences. *Sexuality Research and Social Policy, 11*, 245–255. Doi: 10.1007/s13178-014-0162-9.

Tankovska, H. (2021). *Acceptable Age for Kids to Use Social Media According to U.S. Parents 2020*. https://www.statista.com/statistics/1153880/share-us-parents-acceptable-social-media-child-age/.

Temple, J.R., & Choi, H. (2014). Longitudinal association between teen sexting and sexual behaviour. *Pediatr Off Journal American Academy of Pediatrics, 134(5)*, 1–6.

Temple, J.R., Le, V.D., Berg, P.V.D., Ling, Y., Paul, J.A., & Temple, B.W. (2014). Brief report: Teen sexting and psychosocial health. *Journal of Adolescence, 37*, 33–33.

Temple, J.R., Paul, J. a, Van den Berg, P., Le, V.D., McElhany, A., & Temple, B.W. (2012). Teen sexting and its association with sexual behaviors. *Archives of Pediatrics & Adolescent Medicine, 166*, 1–6. Doi: 10.1001/archpediatrics.2012.835.

Titchen, K.E., Maslyanskaya, S., Silver, E.J., & Coupey, S.M. (2019). Sexting and young adolescents: Associations with sexual abuse and intimate partner violence. *Journal of Pediatric and Adolescence Gyncology, 32,* 481–486. Doi: 10.1016/j.jap.2019.07.004.

Valido, A., Espelage, D.L., Hong, J.S., & Rivas-Koehl, M. (2020). Social-ecological examination of non-consensual sexting perpetration among U.S. adolescents. *International Journal of Environmental Research and Public Health, 17,* 9477–9495. Doi: 10.3390/ijerph17249477.

Valkenburg, P.M., Koutamanis, M., & Vossen, H.G.M. (2017). The concurrent and longitudinal relationships between adolescents' use of social network sites and their social self-esteem. *Computers in Human Behavior, 76,* 35–41. Doi: 10.1016/j.chb.2017.01.008.

Valkenburg, P.M., & Peter, J. (2011). Online communication among adolescents: An integrated model of its attraction, opportunities, and risks. *Adolescent Health, 48(2),* 121–127. Doi: 10.1016/j.jadohealth.2010.08.020.

Vandan Abeele, M., Campbell, S.W., Eggermont, S., & Roe, K. (2014). Sexting, mobile porn use, and peer group dynamics: Boys' and girls' self-perceived popularity, need for popularity, and perceived peer pressure. *Media Psychology, 17,* 6–33. Doi: 10.1080/15213269.2013.801725.

Van Ouytsel, J., Van Gool, E., Walrave, M., Ponnet, K., & Peeters, E. (2017). Sexting: Adolescents' perceptions of the applications used for, motives for, and consequences of sexting. *Journal of Youth Studies, 20(4),* 446–470. Doi:10.1080/136 76261.2016.1241865

Van Ouytsel, J., Walrave, J., & Ponnet, K. (2019). An exploratory study of sexting behaiors among heterosexual and sexual minority early adolescents. *Journal of Adolescent Health, 65,* 621–626.

Velarde, V. (2014). *The Exchange of Sexually Explicit Cell Phone Pictures (Sexting) Among High School Students* [senior honors thesis]. Salt Lake City: University of Utah.

Villacampa, C. (2017). Teen sexting: Prevalence, characteristics, and legal treatment. *International Journal of Law, Crime, and Justice, 29,* 10–21.

Vitis, L. (2019). Victims, perpetrators and paternalism: Image driven sexting laws in Connecticut. *Female Legal Studies, 27,* 189–209.

VR Reporter. (n.d.). *Future of Cybersex: Virtual Reality Porn, 3D Sex Game, Smart Interactive Sex Toys.* https://virtualrealityreporter.com/future-cyber-sex-virtual-reality-porn-3d-sex-game-smart-interactive-sex-toys/.

Walker, S., Sanci, L., & Temple-Smith, M. (2011). Sexting and young people: Experts' views. *Youth Studies Australia, 30(4),* 8–16.

Walrave, M., Heirman, W., & Hallam, L. (2014). Under pressure to sext? Applying the theory of planned behavior to adolescent sexting. *Behaviour & Information Technology, 33,* 86–98.

West, J.H., Lister, C.E., Hall, P.C., Crookston, B.T., Snow, P.R., & Zvietcovich, M.E. (2014). Sexing among Peruvian adolescnets. *BMC Public Health, 14,* 811.

Westlake, B.G. (2018). Delineating victims from perpetrators: Prosecuting self-produced child pornography in youth criminal justice systems. *International Journal of Cyber Criminology, 12(1),* 255–268.

Wolak, J., & Finkelhor, D. (2011). *Sexting: A Typology.* http://www.unh.edu/ccrc/pdf/CV231_Sexting%20Typology%20Bulletin_4-6-11_revised.pdf

Wolak, J., Finkelhor, D., & Mitchell, K. J. (2012). How often are teens arrested for sexting? Data from a national sample of police cases. *Pediatrics, 129(1),* 4–12. Doi: 10.1542/peds.2011-2242a2.

Wolak, J., Finkelhor, D., Walsh, W., & Treitman, L. (2018). Sextortion of minors: Characteristics and dynamics. *Journal of Adolescent Health, 62(1),* 72–79.

Wolfe, S.E., Marcum, C.D., Higgins, G.E., & Ricketts, M.L. (2016). Routine cell phone activity and exposure to sext messages: Extending the generality of routine activity theory and exploring the etiology of a risky teenage behavior. *Crime Delinquency, 62(5),* 614–644.

World Population Review. (2021). *Marriage Age by State 2021.* https://worldpopulationreview.com/state-rankings/marriage-age-by-state.

Wood, R.H. (2009). The failure of sexting criminalization: Plea for the exercise of prosecutorial restraint. *Michigan Telecommunications and Technology Law Review, 16(1),* 151–178.

Wood, R.H. (2010). The First Amendment implications of sexting at public schools: A quandary for administrators who intercept visual love notes. *Journal of Law & Policy, 18,* 701–737.

Wood, M., Barter, C., Stanley, N., Aghtaie, N., & Larkins, C. (2015). Images across Europe: The sending and receiving of sexual images and associations with interpersonal violence in young people's relationships. *Children and Youth Services Review, 59,* 149–160. clok.uclan.ac.uk/13214/8/13214 Image accross Europe article CYSR Final 3 11 15.pdf.

Ybarra, M.L., & Mitchell, K.J. (2014). "Sexting" and its relation to sexual activity and sexual risk behavior in a national survey of adolescents. *Journal of Adolescent Health, 55,* 757–764.

CASES

Miller v. Mitchell (2010), 598 F.3d. 139.
Miller v. Skumanick (2009), 605 F. Supp.2d.634
New York v. Ferber (1982), 458 US 747
Osborne v. Ohio (1990), 495 U.S. 103
Stanley v. Georgia (1969), 394 U.S. 557
Troxel v. Granville (2000), 530 US 57
United States v. Stevens (2010), 559 U.S. 460

APPENDIX A: STUDIES EXAMINING
SENT AND RECEIVED SEXTS

Study	Risk Correlates with Sexting	Data Findings	Sent	Received
Cox Communication (2009)	*Sext Senders Risks:* 43% sent & received with 81% cellphone ownership; 86% SM profile user	**Sext Image Prevalence**	9% overall; 6%M; 12%F	17%
Data collected: April 2009 National study N = 655 Age: 13–18 50% Female 54% White (18% Latinx; 14% Black) 60% IM users 72% Social Media profiles 73% Cell phone owners 80% posting selfies		**Sex differences**	65%F> 35% M	NONE
		Age differences	61% Aged 16–18 > 39% Aged 13–15	NONE
Lenhart (2009) Data collected: June to September 2009 National study N = 800 Age: 12–17 46% Female 77.5% White 75% Cell phone (unlimited plans) 66% Text	*Sext Senders Risks:* 17% sext prevalence rate if pay themselves for services vs. 3% if pay some or nothing; 16% prevalence rate if texters vs. 7% if non-texters; 18% if have unlimited texting plan v 8% if limited plan vs 4% if pay per message	**Sext Image Prevalence**	4% of cell phone owners	15% of cell phone owners
		Sex differences	NONE	NONE
		Age differences	8% age 17 vs. 4% age 12; 14–17 > 12–13	18% age 14–17 vs. 6% age 12/13; 4% of age 12; 20% age 16; 30% age 17

(Continued)

Study	Risk Correlates with Sexting	Data Findings	Sent	Received
Dake et al. (2012) Data collected: 2009 Regional: Ohio middle and high schools N = 1289 Age: 12–18 (54% middle school, 47% high school) 48% Female 87% White 61% 2-parent home	*Sext Senders Risks:* Higher sexting associated with sexually active (47%) and victims of IPV (43%), including forced sexual intercourse (52%)	**Sext Image Prevalence**	17%	N/A
		Sex differences	19%Male> 16% Female[1]	N/A
		Age differences	31% Older (16–18) > 15% Younger (13-15)	N/A
Maheux et al.2020 Data collection: April 2016 Regional/ longitudinal study, SE U.S. N = 626 Grades 11 and 12 Female 54% 47% White, 23% Latinx, 22% Black 64% sexually active		**Sext Image Prevalence**	55%	N/A
		Sex differences	61%Female > 50%Male	N/A
		Age differences	NONE	N/A
Hinduja and Patchin (2010) Data collected: 2010 National study N = 4365 Age: 11–18 49.5 Female		**Sext Image Prevalence**	8%	13%
		Sex differences	NONE	16%M > 10%F
		Age differences	NONE	61% age 16–18 > 39% age 13–15

(Continued)

Study	Risk Correlates with Sexting	Data Findings	Sent	Received
Patchin and Hinduja (2019)		**Sext Image** Prevalence	12%	19%
Data collected: 2016 National study		**Sex** differences	NONE	NONE
N = 5569 Age 12–17 50% Female 66% White 93% Heterosexual		**Age** differences	9% age 13; 14% age 15; 19% age 17	5% age 13; 22% age 15; 26% age 17
Patchin and Hinduja (2020)		**Sext Image** Prevalence	14%	23%
Data collected: 2019 National study		**Sex** differences	NONE	NONE
N = 5000 Age 12–17		**Age** differences	NONE	NONE
MTV-Associated Press (2009)	*Sext Senders Risks:*	**Sext Image** Prevalence	10%	18%
Data collected Sept 2009	45% sexually active sext;	**Sex** differences	NONE	NONE
N = 1247 Age: 14–24 38% 14–17 62% 18–24 50% Female	53% received a naked image from intimate partner. Also: impact, risks and dating violence	**Age** differences	24% age 14–17 < 33% 18–24	NONE
Peskin et al. (2013) Data collected: 2009–2010 Regional study, Texas urban h.s.		**Sext image** prevalence	21% images; 25% msg [4% posted]	31% images; 32% msg
N = 1034 Age: 10th grade		**Sex** differences	NONE	NONE
63% Female 57% Latinx, 43% Black 55% used cell more than 10 hours/weekly		**Age** differences	NONE	NONE

(Continued)

Study	Risk Correlates with Sexting	Data Findings	Sent	Received
Mitchell et al. (2012) Data collected: 2010–2011 National study N = 1560 Age: 10–17 49.3% Female 73% White, 15% Black, 10% Latinx 78% two-parent home (66% biological)		**Sext image prevalence**	3%; 10% create, sent/ received	7%
		Sex differences	61%F > 39%M	56% F > 44% M
		Age differences	6% ages 10–12, 10% ages 13–14, 13% age 15 < 31% age 16 < 41% age 17	0% age 10–12 < 26% age13–14, 19% age 15 < 27% age 16, 28% age17
Houck et al. (2014) Data collected: 2009 to 2012 Regional study, RI, at-risk 7th graders; 5 urban middle schools N = 410 Age: 12–14 46% Female 38% White, 35% Black		**Sext image prevalence**	22% image; 17% message	N/A
		Sex differences	NONE	N/A
		Age differences	NONE	N/A
Ybarra and Mitchell (2014) Data collected: 2010–2011 National study N = 3715 Age 13–18 57% Female 75% White, 10% Black 96% Heterosexual	*Sext Senders Risks:* Sexually active (63%) sext > not active (14%)	**Sext image prevalence**	7% image; 5% message	N/A
		Sex differences	Tendency for female > male	N/A
		Age differences	17 (11%); 16 (9.75%); 15 (6.4%); 14 (3%)	N/A

(Continued)

187

Study	Risk Correlates with Sexting	Data Findings	Sent	Received
Strassberg et al. (2013)		**Sext image prevalence**	18%	41%
Data collected: 2009		**Sex differences**	NONE	49.7%M > 30.9F
Regional study, SW USA N = 606 Age: 14–18 46% Female 75% White, 14% Latinx, 9% Black 96% Cell phone (text sent/M = 91; received/M = 95) 83% Social Media profile		**Age differences**	Grade: 9th, 9.2% male, 14% female; 12th, 26.5% male, 24.2% female. 6% 10–12 vs. 15% 15–17	Grade: 9th 38.5% male, 25% female; 10th 57% male, 24% female; 11th 43%male, 28% female; 12th 65% male, 46% female
Strassberg et al. (2017) (Velarde, 2014, same dataset)		**Sext image prevalence**	15%	36%
		Sex differences	NONE	40%M > 31%F
Data collected: 2013 Regional study, Utah, Suburban, private high school. N = 622 Grades: 9–12 46% Female 75% White, 15% Latinx 95% Cell phone; 88% Social Media		**Age differences**	NONE	NONE

(Continued)

Study	Risk Correlates with Sexting	Data Findings	Sent	Received
Murray (2014) Data collected: Feb 2014 N = 483 Age: 14–19 51% Female 87% post selfies 85% images of friends 75% post messages; 75% IM; 75% use webcam	*Sext senders risks:* 20% have 1 Social Media Accounts, 27% have 2 SMA, 26% have 3 SMA, 22% have 4+ SMA, 3% have no SMA	**Sext image prevalence**	18% image; 30% message	41% image; 48% message
		Sex differences	N/A	58%M > 43%F image
		Age differences	N/A	N/A
Ricketts et al. (2015) **(Marcum et al.,** 2014 same dataset) Data collected: 2014 Regional study, Western NC rural N = 1617 Grade:9th–12th 51% Female 72% White		**Sext Image Prevalence**	13%	N/A
		Sex differences	NONE	N/A
		Age differences	NONE	N/A
Rice et al. (2012) Data collected: 2011 Regional study, Los Angeles high schools N = 1839 (**1714** have cell) Age: 14–17 (LA high school) 48% Female 72% Latinx, 12% Black, 9% White 87% Hetero 75% Cell phone, daily users 54% peers sext	*Sext senders risks:* 41% sexually active	**Sext image prevalence**	15% of 1714 cell owners	N/A
		Sex differences	NONE	N/A
		Age differences	NONE	N/A

(Continued)

Study	Risk Correlates with Sexting	Data Findings	Sent	Received
Rice et al. (2014) Data collected: 2012 Regional study, Los Angeles high schools N = 1285 (of which **841** had text-capable phones Age: 10–15 (LA middle school) 48% Female 61% Latinx (18% Black, 15% White) 96% Heterosexual	*Sext Senders Risks:* Sex active, text over100 > likely sext	**Sext Image Prevalence**	5% of 841	20% of 841
		Sex differences	N/A	N/A
		Age differences	N/A	N/A
Rice et al. (2018) Data collected: 2013 Regional study, Los Angeles high schools N = 1208 Grades 9–12 Female: 51% 68% Latinx (7% White, 6% Black) 88% Heterosexual 100% cell owners; 46% friends sexting 28% sent 24 or less text/daily vs. 20%>300; 34% sexuallyactive		**Sext image prevalence**	19%	41%
		Sex differences	N/A	N/A
		Age differences	N/A	N/A
Temple et al. (2012) Data collected: Spring 2011 Regional/longitudinal study (2nd wave) 7 Texas high schools N = 948 from original 1042 (spring 2010) Age 14–19 56% Female 32% Latinx (30% White, 27% Black)	*Sext senders risks:* 76% are sexually active	**Sext image prevalence**	28%	N/A
		Sex differences	NONE	N/A
		Age differences	33% age 17 > 20% age 16	N/A

(*Continued*)

Study	Risk Correlates with Sexting	Data Findings	Sent	Received
Temple & Choi (2014) Data collected: Spring 2012 Regional/ longitudinal study (3rd wave) N = 947 Age 14–18 [73%10th grade] Female 56% 31% Black, 29% White, 28% Latinx		**Sext image prevalence**	28%	N/A
		Sex differences	NONE	N/A
		Age differences	NONE	N/A
Reed et al. (2020) Data collected: December 2013 to March 2014 Regional study, Michigan suburban high school N = 964 Age 13–19 56% Female 7% Black, 72% White, 2% Latinx 96% owned cellphones (91% smartphones) 100% home computer access	*Sext senders risks:* If dating, 28%Female>20%Male *Sext receivers risks:* If dating, 45%Female < 52%Male	**Sext image prevalence**	18%	40%
		Sex differences	21%F > 15%M	44%M > 36%F
		Age differences	N/A	N/A

8

Online Domestic Commercial Sexual Traffickers

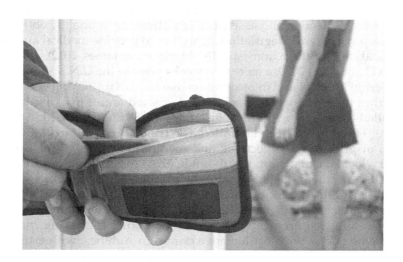

DEFINING ONLINE DOMESTIC COMMERCIAL SEX TRAFFICKING

Modern-day slavery concerns globally had prompted the United Nations in 2000 to hold a convention for the purpose of developing the Palermo Protocol (anti-trafficking law), which set the definition and obligations of

DOI: 10.4324/9781003092292-8

member states under international law to prevent, protect, and prosecute trafficking. Pursuant with the Palermo Protocol, trafficking for sexual exploitation consists of three core elements (United Nations Office on Drugs and Crime, n.d):

1. The **actions**, which refer to the recruitment, transportation, transfer, harboring or receipt of persons;
2. The **means**, which refer to threat or use of force, coercion, abduction, fraud, deception, abuse of power or vulnerability, or giving payments or benefits (e.g., political, social gains) to a person in control of the victim;[1] and
3. The **purpose**, which refers to exploiting the prostitution of others and sexual exploitation.

This agreement extended the original (but limited) concern of forced trafficking for prostitution that had been addressed in the 1949 Convention (Marinova & James, 2012; Office of Juvenile Justice and Delinquency Prevention/OJJDP, 2014). The Trafficking Protocol now provides specifications for the protection and assistance of victims, including the obligation to develop policies and legislation, as well as to provide medical and psychological care for them domestically (Marinova & James, 2012).

On October 28, 2000, a mere two weeks prior to the U.N.'s adoption of the Palermo Protocol and in recognition that human trafficking was growing within its own borders, the U.S. had enacted anti-trafficking legislation called the *Trafficking Victims Protection Act*/TVPA (discussed in a later section). The U.S. has been identified as a triple threat country—because it is an **origin** (source of locating and recruiting victims), **transit** (intermediary location that supports the industry), and **destination** (location best suited for the industry) of sexually exploited and trafficked victims (Godoy et al., 2016; Gregorio, 2015). Despite being a Tier 1 country based on the 2021 Trafficking in Persons Report rankings (i.e., compliant with U.N. anti-trafficking requirements), the domestic sexual trafficking industry has become one of the most lucrative crimes in America, with estimated annual profits in the multi-millions (International Labor Organization/ ILO, 2014, U.S. Department of State, 2021).

This criminal enterprise is considered to be more profitable than selling drugs because no capital investment is needed and victims, as

---

[1] When the victim is a minor, however, there is no other proof needed for trafficking beyond actions and purpose as defined in #1 and #3 above under both the Palermo Protocol and Trafficking Victims Protection Act (TVPA).

commodities, can be sold and resold online numerous times daily (Finklea et al., 2015). Revenue generated from the commercial sex trade in 2007 within eight U.S. cities ranged from $40 to $290 million dollars, depending on the location (Dank et al., 2014). Similarly, the commercial sex trade in 2013 within San Diego was estimated to be $810 million, with third-party controllers each earning an annual average of $670,625 by trafficking two to 30 victims (Carpenter & Gates, 2016). Moreover, this underground market caters to buyers, such that traffickers charge "above market" prices to those who prefer having sex with minors—which could be as high as $1000 on weekend nights in some locations (Farley et al., 2009; ILO, 2005; U.S. DOJ, 2010). Based on their research of buyers from 2016 to 2017, Demand Abolition (2018) valued the U.S. commercial sex market to be $5.7 billion dollars. Annual earnings today can be estimated based on typical charges—ranging from $25 to $400 (average of $100/transaction) per sexual encounter for 15–60 minutes—multiplied by imposed daily quotas of $500–$2000 per victim, forcing them to service from 5 to 45 buyers per day (Belser, 2005; Belser et al., 2005; Just Facts, 2022; Polaris Project, 2015a, 2015b). Combining these sex act rates and daily number of buyers, the annual earnings from one victim working everyday could range from $45,625 to $6,570,000.

Individual governmental (e.g., law enforcement) and non-governmental (e.g., nonprofit, service providers) agencies collect statistics based on reports, investigations, research, and treatment of identified children and adults forced into the commercial sex trade (Franchino-Olsen, 2021). Most of the rescued victim-survivors (68%–83%) identified in sex trafficking conviction cases were U.S. citizens and legal permanent residents, rather than foreign nationals as originally assumed (Banks & Kyckkelhan, 2011; U.S. Department of Justice, 2010). The U.S. Human trafficking hotline is an important source for determining prevalence rates because it provides help to victims, collects statistics, and connects callers (including those reporting trafficking schemes) with law enforcement partners (Polaris Project, 2020). In 2019, the hotline confirmed that 11,500 of the 48,426 contacts via email, webchat, call, text, and report were human trafficking situations; 76% involved commercial sex exploitation and trafficking in which 1,912 suspicious businesses, 15,645 victims, and 4384 traffickers were identified (Polaris Project, 2020). Due to the secretive nature of this crime and the resulting challenges that preclude large-scale, national studies from being conducted (e.g., Gerassi, 2015 using datasets from 2003 to 2013), it is difficult to determine good estimates for victim prevalence. Many victims do not seek assistance because they are afraid, believe they have no other alternative, or do not realize they are being exploited (Clawson et al., 2009; Greenbaum, 2014). For these reasons, researchers suggest that the number of victims in the U.S. being sex trafficked is likely higher than what has been reported and discovered by nonprofit agencies, law enforcement, and/or human services (IOM and NRC, 2013; Jimenez et al., 2015; Polaris Project, 2020).

Domestic commercial sex trafficking contains aspects of both online and offline components, but it would be impossible to tease the two apart. Contrary to common belief, less than 10% of trafficking victims are abducted; instead, victims have been subjugated through a psychological coercion process by their recruiters to believe that they have no other choice (Polaris Project, 2020). In some cases, the victims—typically socially vulnerable minors—remain in their homes and make themselves accessible to offenders upon demand (Polaris Project, 2020). Once these predators have control over their victims, they may be kept to start or increase the size of the trafficking victims or for other sex venues; sold to other third-party controllers; or purchased by predators interested in owning personal sex slaves (Polaris Project, 2017). Most victims become part of the underground commercial sexual exploitation and trafficking trade in which sexual activity is exchanged for something of value (e.g., money, food, shelter, drugs, protection), including: *sex tourism,* especially for large sporting and entertainment events;[2] *live performance in physical* (e.g., massage parlors, peep shows, strip clubs) *and online, pay-per-view sexual venues* (e.g., remote interactive sexual activity, electronic transmission of victims engaged in sexual acts); *prostitution* in various locations (e.g., hotels/ motels, cars, truck stops, brothels, residences, bars, drug dens, cantinas, streets[3]); and *child sex abuse material or non-consensual adult pornography* (Development Services Group, Inc., 2014; Institute of Medicine/IOM and National Research Council/NRC, 2013; OJJDP, 2014).[4] Polaris Project (2017) used hotline calls reported between December 2007 and 2016 to determine the proportion of 12,500 victim-survivors who were forced to engage in one of 9 types of sex trafficking activities. This distribution, shown in Figure 8.1, indicated that most provided sex primarily as escorts and secondarily in illicit massage parlors.

---

[2] This is a non-traditional way to consider sex tourism, which usually refers to travel to foreign countries for the purpose of having sex.

[3] Truck/rest stops are typical for rural areas, whereas streets (also called *strolls* or *tracks*) are common for urban areas.

[4] Early and forced marriages are also part of this list, but these were excluded from examination in this chapter.

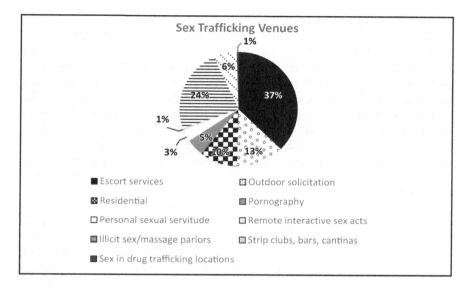

Figure 8.1 Sex trafficking venues.

TYPICAL ONLINE DOMESTIC COMMERCIAL SEXUAL TRAFFICKING OFFENDERS

Domestic commercial sex trafficking offenders include *buyers* who purchase sex acts performed by victims, *third-party controllers* who directly exploit victims, *associates* who contribute directly to maintaining the trafficking enterprise by working in partnerships or supportive roles with controllers; and *facilitators* who indirectly benefit financially from the victims' exploitation—including corporations (e.g., hospitality, transportation, finance, communication) and their employees—but may also be independent contractors.[5] Buyers of commercial sex acts—based on research using arrest record and attendance of court-ordered John school data; interviews and self-reports, including online message boards or forums; and Internet

---

[5] Very few attempts have been made to criminally prosecute facilitators, such as hotels, for their role in sex trafficking (exception, *U.S. v. Bhimani et al.*), although there are hundreds of cases awaiting civil trial initiated in 2019 and later by victim-survivors (Shapiro, 2021). Independent contractors are market facilitators in a mutually beneficial, non-financial relationship, such as hotel concierge who recommend sex workers to guests or sex workers recommend drug dealers to buyers (Swaner et al., 2016).

CYBERPREDATORS AND THEIR PREY
sex advertisements—are predominantly male, White, aged 25–55 years, well-educated, and employed with disposable income (Farley et al., 2009, 2017; Milrod & Monto, 2012; Monto & Milrod, 2013; Morris et al., 2012; Nichols, 2016; Roe-Sepowitz et al., 2019; Shelton et al, 2016; Shively et al., 2008). In one study (Williamson et al., 2012), buyers who purchased sex from coerced victims in Ohio worked in a variety of jobs—criminal justice and law, such as lawyers, police, judges, politicians (27%); postal workers and government employees (9%); businessmen and managers (17%); drug dealers (9%); sports and military (10%); social workers, teachers, and pastors (8%); and working-class jobs, such as construction and factory workers (20%). Men are the predominant buyers of commercial sex from both male and female victims (Tyler & Beal, 2010).

Commercial sex exploitation and trafficking controllers (aka traffickers or pimps) vary in both the *size* (small, medium, large) and *composition* (individual vs. group) of their business. In addition to controllers working alone, there are organized crime sex trafficking offenders ranging from small informal networks to large hierarchically organized groups (Bouché, 2017; Finkenauer, 2019; Roe-Sepowitz et al., 2016, 2017; Williamson & Prior, 2009). Demographic information regarding controllers and associates convicted of trafficking (Banks & Kyckelhahn, 2011; Dank et al., 2014; Motivans, 2018; Roe-Sepowitz et al., 2017; Shelton et al., 2016) include that they are predominantly single (50%), Black (37%–66%), young adult (aged 18–34 years, 61%–77%), men (75%–85%), U.S. citizens or permanent residents (69%–94%), with a basic level of education (35%–43% had high school diploma/GED; 27% had some college). Roe-Sepowitz et al. (2017) noted the average age of women ($M=26.34$ years) convicted of minor sex trafficking in their sample was younger than men ($M=29.2$ years).

Bouché (2017) used 862 federal cases from 2000 to 2015 to create a typology of five organizations involved in human trafficking (see Table 8.1). She determined that 58% of the predominantly U.S. defendants were part of organized crime groups, of which 24% engaged in commercial sex trafficking of only minors (92% of victims were U.S. citizens), 17% only adults (45% of victims were U.S. citizens), and 34% both minors and adults (56% adult victims and 77% minor victims were U.S. citizens). Denton (2016) indicated that 79% of the perpetrators convicted for sex trafficking between 2006 and 2011 were part of a group or network. Other researchers similarly indicated that organized crime groups were involved in sex trafficking. For example, gangs have sophisticated networks that facilitate the domestic commercial sex trafficking trade, including loaning minor victims to gangs in other states to maximize profits (Carpenter & Gates,

198

Table 8.1 Typology of Crime Group Traffickers

Type of Crime Group	Self-Identification	Sex Trafficking	Venues	Federal Statistics
Mom & Pop	Family; family/friend connections. Some have hierarchy, most are decentralized.	All venues: minor only; adult only; both	33% Brothels and massage parlors; 12% street prostitution; 12% escort services; 25% Internet prostitution; 4% personal sexual slave[a]	Sample=35% cases with 71% only sex trafficking Average # victims=17.6 Average # of defendant/case=5.30
Crime ring	Friends or accomplices. Operate nationally (40%) or in one locality (36%); somewhat to very decentralized.	INTERNET: 81% minors, 29% adult	47% Internet prostitution; 3% strip club; 17% street prostitution; 9% escort services	Sample=33% cases with 95% only commercial sex trafficking Average # victims=7 Average # of defendant/case=5.30
Gang	All members of the same gang. Hierarchy and chain of command.	Street: 70% Minors, 30% Adults; Internet: 81% Minors, 29% Adults.	58% street prostitution; 42% Internet prostitution	Sample=6% cases with 100% commercial sex trafficking Average # victims=8.8 Average # of defendant/case=14.5
Cartel and crime syndicate	Hierarchy and chain of command.	All venues: both minors and adults	Brothels/massage parlors; Internet prostitution	*0% cases, instead filed 10 mafia suspected cases under Mom & Pop
Illegal enterprise	Employees run illicit business under the guise of a legal one. Hierarchy and chain of command.	All venues: mainly adult	50% Brothels/massage parlors;19% strip clubs; 3% Internet prostitution; 13% escort services; 19% personal sex slave	Sample=26% cases with 64% commercial sex trafficking Average # victims=65.7 Average # of defendant/case=7.02

[a] See *United States v. Bagley, et al.* (2011) and *United States v. Soto-Huarto, et al.* (2003).

2016; Frank & Terwilliger, 2015; Roe-Sepowitz et al., 2017). Additionally, crime syndicates have also been implicated in sex trafficking. Finckenauer (2019) reported a case in which seven members of the Gambino crime family pled guilty in 2011 to sex trafficking of a minor as part of their interstate sex trafficking network from 2008 to 2009. The evidence against the Gambino defendants included recruitment of adolescents aged 15–19, advertisement of sexual services on the Internet, and transportation of victims to clients in different New York City boroughs and New Jersey.

Williamson and Prior (2009) described seven roles with specific duties in the domestic sex trafficking group organizations—connectors, recruiters, groomers, controllers/traffickers,[6] bottoms, watchers, and wife-in-laws (see Table 8.2). Although this table and prosecutors still use the original terms for involuntary roles played by the victims, the terminology is problematic given the sex trafficking victim-offender intersectionality. Specifically, the prosecution of these survivors as equal offenders to their exploiter fails to recognize how their own victimization contributed to their complicity in roles they were forced to play (Shared Hope International, 2020).

The number of roles played by members in each sex trafficking organization depends on its size. Solo traffickers who have control over the victims will play multiple roles, but will likely require trafficking victims to perform tasks to aid the controller. However, depending on the size of the group, the controller, associates, and victim-offenders each play one or more roles. Conviction records for sex trafficking showed that victim-offenders had played core roles (i.e., connectors, recruiters, groomers, bottoms, wife-in-laws) in 47%–56% of the cases (Denton, 2016; Roe-Sepowitz et al., 2017, 2019), but they received no compensation indicating that they had limited agency (i.e., under directions of controller rather than their own decisions). In a study with 49 predominantly White women convicted of sex trafficking minors (37% had history of being a sex trafficked as minors), 74% were part of a trafficking ring with a male controller—the woman was a relative (26%), business partner (18%), intimate partner (21%), part of the trafficking victims (16%), or victim-offender (13%)—vs. 15% independent of a male controller (Roe-Sepowitz et al., 2016). It would not be unusual for young adult victims who were exploited and trafficked since they were adolescents to conceive of themselves as "willing" participants who contribute their share to the controller, gang, or family (Mapp, 2020). Moreover,

---

[6] The term trafficker, used by Williamson and Prior (2009), was adapted for this discussion as technically, all of the players are considered to be engaged in sex trafficking and thus are "traffickers" under the law.

Table 8.2   Seven Roles Played in the Domestic Sex Trafficking Group Organization

Controller: This player maintains control over sex trafficking victims (when part of a group, this leader decides which associate or victim plays specific roles), determines what sex acts and where victims will perform them, and retains the money earned by victims. To gain compliance over victims—male traffickers may use a *Romeo* tactic (i.e., uses false romance/boyfriend con), whereas female traffickers use a *Mother* tactic (i.e., helping the child feel connected in a family way); alternatively, male and female traffickers may use *Guerrilla* tactics (i.e., brute force).

[a]*Connector*: This player locates potential victims and introduces them to the controller, who can give them a better life—one with money, fame, love, etc. Connectors can be associates or sex trafficking victims, are compensated with cash or other benefits (e.g., drugs, club entry).

[a]*Recruiter*: This player, often a current sex worker, convinces new victims to join the current group of sex trafficking victims (called, "knocking a bitch") under the controller.

[a]*Groomer*: This player teaches new victims about the business—from *how to dress* to *how to negotiate the fees* per sex act with customers. Groomers often are current sex trafficking victims, but may also be associates paid a fee by controllers to train new victims.

[a]*Bottom*: This player is a current sex worker, but one who has been with the controller the longest, knows the most about the business, and is the most trusted of the sex trafficking victims. As the second in command, she typically controls the rest of the sex trafficking victims—including administering punishments, advertising victims online, and ensuring victims meet their quotas. Most victims perceive the bottom and trafficker to be in an *intimate partner relationship*.

Watcher: This player, typically an associate (but may be the controller or bottom), transports new and current sex workers, ensures they safely make it to/from their sexual venue (e.g., truck stop, strip club, hotel), and collects money earned by them to give to the controller.

[a]*Wife-in-laws*: These players are sex workers "owned" by same controller and are informally paired together for housing purposes—they give all of their earnings to the controller, who in turn "takes care of their needs."

[a]   All of these roles are played by victim-offenders.

the experience of trauma, both prior and subsequent to being forced into commercial sex, impacts victims' ability to understand or even escape their situation (Mapp, 2020). Box 8.1 provides a sex trafficking case describing the roles different people played using the original terms.

> **BOX 8.1   *U.S. V. DAVILA*, 8:15-CR-00233-GJH-1, 17-4036[7]**
>
> This case—part of the FBI's *Project Safe Childhood*—involved co-defendants originally charged with three counts: 18 U.S.C. § 1594 *conspiracy to engage in sex trafficking of a minor*, 18 U.S.C. § 1591(a), (b)(2) *sex trafficking of a minor, and* 18 U.S.C. § 2423(a) *transportation of a minor for prostitution.*
>
> Michael Andrew Davila, age 27, was arrested in April 2015, pled guilty in April 2016 to transportation of a minor for prostitution, 18 U.S.C. § 2423(a), and sentenced in August 2016 to 175 months in prison followed by 25 years of supervised release and must register as a sex offender. During the 3 months he had the minor, he played four roles, including **recruiter** by contacting the minor on Instagram and convincing her to meet him; **groomer**, by teaching her how to arrange dates and set prices; **controller**, by forcing the minor to engage in prostitution, by advertising the minor for sexual services online and communicated with victim using Kik and Pinger, and arranging for and buying hotel rooms; and **watcher** by transporting and arranging for transportation of the minor.
>
> John David Hamlett, age 33, pled guilty to 18 U.S.C. § 1552(a)(3) (A) *Travel in Interstate Commerce in Aid of Unlawful Activity* and was sentenced to 30 months in prison. His primary role was **watcher**, in which he was paid $50–$100 per night to transport the minor and other victims to engage in commercial sex acts in Maryland, D.C., and Virginia.
>
> Elsie Lisbeth Pazmino, age 29, who was a sex-trafficked worker under Davila, pled guilty to using telephone and Internet to facilitate the prostitution of a minor and was sentenced in June 2016 to time served followed by 6 months of home detention as part of her 3 years of supervised release. She played two roles—**bottom**, by answering text messages, arranging dates, arranging and paying for hotels, and **groomer**, by teaching the victim how to talk to customers and set up dates.

---

[7] U.S. Attorney's Office. (2017, January 9). *Prince George's county pimp sentenced to over 14 years in federal prison for prostitution 15-year-old child first contact through the internet.* District of Maryland news release. https://www.justice.gov/usao-md/pr/prince-george-s-county-pimp-sentenced-over-14-years-federal-prison-prostituting-15-year.

After Michael Davila's arrest, he contacted his mother, Maria Davila, age 51, in April 2015. At his behest, Maria tampered with evidence by accessing and erasing contents of Kik accounts (and attempting to do the same with the Pinger account) that contained communications with victim regarding proceeds earned, locations prostitution occurred, and posting of online ads. Maria Davila, was charged and pled guilty to 18 U.S.C. § 1512(k) *Conspiracy to Commit Evidence Tampering* and was sentenced in August 2016 to 2 years in prison.

ONLINE DOMESTIC COMMERCIAL SEXUAL TRAFFICKERS' MOTIVES AND METHODS

It has been estimated that between 10% and 20% of men in the U.S. have purchased commercial sex in their lifetime (Demand Abolition, 2018). Motivations for sex predator buyers would be *personal*, specifically (1) thrill-seeking or fulfilling sexual desires—particularly pathological ones outside of societal norms (e.g., fetishes, compulsions, addictions) and/or which are not likely to be performed by intimate partners; (2) male entitlement (misogyny) aligned with desire to dominate and control women (e.g., insatiable male sex drive paired with purpose of women to serve them) and/or desire for variety; (3) girlfriend experience of intimacy without the obligation; and (4) delusion that they are providing desperate women with financial aid (Janson, 2013; Miller-Perrin & Wertele, 2017; Sanders, 2008). For example, buyers of commercial sex who posted discussions in online forum called *USA Sex Guide* boasted to other members how they exploited and brutalized the women (Janson, 2013). Buyers who prefer to purchase sex from minors may do so because they are aroused by them or they believe minors are less likely than adults to carry sexually transmitted diseases (Adams et al., 2010; Kosloski et al., 2017). Nonetheless, almost half of buyers were cognizant that the trafficking victim was not consenting to sexual acts and 67% believed that the majority of them were forced, tricked, exploited, and/or is a minor; nonetheless, they still engaged in the purchased sex act (Farley et al., 2009, 2011, 2017). Janson (2013) reported that buyers' online discussion posts included the realization that the girls/women were likely younger than legal age, offering sex for survival, under the influence of drugs, being physically controlled and exploited by a third-party, and being mistreated, but it did not stop them from engaging in the sexual acts they purchased. Methods for buyers include answering online advertisements, referrals from online discussion forums, driving the known prostitution track, and going to legitimate businesses that have illicit sex, such as cantinas and massage parlors (Demand Abolition, 2018; Janson, 2013; Kosloski et al., 2017).

Motivations for controllers, associates, and facilitators are predominantly *financial*; however, controllers may also have *personal* motives, including attaining power and control that comes with leadership or through manipulation and control over others; or *revenge* motives for being denied the lifestyle from parents and others that they believed they should have had as children and/or as adults (Bouché, 2017; Dank et al., 2014). Research on controllers and associates (Carpenter & Gates, 2016; Gotch, 2016; Raphael & Myers-Power, 2010) indicated that as children they had experienced physical abuse (19%–88%), sexual abuse (26%–76%), family members were in the sex trade (11%–60%), sold sex themselves (68%), gang involvement (22%–26%), and/or had been removed from their homes/placed in foster care (24%–41%). Family members (and their paramours) who exploit victims have *financial* or *personal* (e.g., drugs) motives, whereas peers (who are also victims) have *personal* motives, specifically they are often required to find and recruit others or suffer severe consequences (Raphael & Myers-Powell, 2010).

Sexual predators (connectors, recruiters, groomers, controllers) engage in a four-step method to lure vulnerable and marginalized victims (particularly minors and young adults who have low self-esteem, family problems, etc.) into the commercial sexual exploitation and sex trafficking industry—(1) locate, (2) groom, (3) recruit, and (4) control.

> They **locate** victims online predominantly through *social media* platforms (e.g., Facebook, MySpace), *interactive game* platforms (e.g., Fortnite, Minecraft, Discord), *microblogging* apps (e.g., Twitter, Tumblr), and *dating* apps (e.g., Tinder, Grindr, MeetMe, Yubo) (Briggs et al., 2011; Latonero, 2011; Schulz et al., 2016; Wolak et al., 2008).

Controllers operating in a group also rely on associates—typically from the same community (e.g., teachers, coaches) as the victim—and sex trafficking victims of the same age and/or gender to find others who are ripe for exploitation (Denton, 2016; Thorn, 2019). High-risk, troubled youth who live at home are targeted in schools, parks, and malls, whereas those who are runaways, throwaways, or in the foster care system are approached at bus and train stations, shelters, and group homes by "friendly" strangers convincing them that the controller will provide for their needs (Kiensat et al., 2014; Schulz et al., 2016; Shared Hope International, 2021).

> Next, sexual predators engage in **online grooming** (i.e., a psychological process of manipulation), which is similar to offline grooming (Shapiro & Maras, 2016). This process involves five stages: (1) *friendship*—patiently developing rapport by expressing common interests; (2) *relationship*—increasing attention and interactions to make the target feel special; (3) *risk assessment*—testing willingness to engage secretly in increasingly explicit sexual discussions; (4) *exclusivity*—gaining control over them, often by increasing familial conflict, isolating them from peers and family, and creating emotional dependance on the predator; and (5) *sexual*—requesting sexually explicit images and arranging offline meetings for sex (De Santisteban et al., 2018; Dombrowski et al., 2004; Kirwan & Power, 2012; O'Connell, 2003; Polaris Project, 2019; U.S. Department of Justice, 2010).

Online predators rely on the fact that victims are less cautious and wary of strangers online than they would be offline, and are able to progress through the stages under the Internet's cloak of anonymity to establish a relationship (Seto, 2013). The advent of the smart phone makes it easier for predators to build relationships with victims (and bypass guardian supervision) by using *photo and video sharing* apps (e.g., Snapchat, Whisper, TikTok, Instagram) which deletes content immediately or after 24 hours; Wi-Fi *untraceable message* apps (e.g., Kik, WhatsApp, Chatlive), and *vault* apps that hide photos and files (e.g., Fake Calculator; Secret Photo Vault) (Shared Hope International, 2019b). Interviews with 260 domestic sex-trafficked minor victim-survivors initially enslaved from 2015 to 2017 revealed that 55% had they met and built a relationship with their traffickers online, most of them (63%) communicated through text, website, or app and some (25%) by phone call (Thorn, 2019). Online recruitment is facilitated by people's beliefs that the Internet is a safe way to meet and get to know others (as promoted by the apps),[8] allowing traffickers to earn their trust and convince them to meet in person after 1–4 months (Bouché, 2015; Shared Hope International, 2019). Additionally, predators are aware that social media platforms do little to monitor their users' content as they have immunity from liability through Section 230 of the Communications Decency Act, so the ones most popular with minors are used as tools to enlist them. In 2020,

---

[8] For example, the defined purpose of several apps (e.g., Yubo; ChatLive; Omegle; Down) is to encourage users to talk to strangers and make new friends (Shared Hope International, 2017b).

Facebook was reported to be responsible for 59% of online sex trafficking recruitment of child victims (Feehs & Wheller, 2021, p. 4).

> Sexual predators **recruit** victims by preying on their needs, while normalizing selling sex as contributing to the shared living expenses, such as *desire for a romantic partner* by offering an intimate partner relationship or proposing marriage; *family and belonging* by offering to include them in their family consisting of sex trafficking victims who have a glamorous lifestyle; and *being loved and cared for by an adult* pretending to be a benefactor (e.g., pay for housing, education), giving addicts drugs and alcohol, providing them with a high paying job, and falsely promising them careers as models or movie stars (Polaris Project, 2019; Roe-Sepowitz et al., 2017, 2019). Figure 8.2 shows the proportional use of the top five tactics for recruiting for a sample of victim-survivors (Polaris Project, 2019).

Actual victim relationships with the controller (Currier & Feehs, 2019; Dank et al., 2014; Gragg et al., 2007; Greenbaum, 2014; Polaris, 2019; Raphael, 2020; Reid, 2016; Roe-Sepowitz et al., 2017) are categorized as: intimate partner (14%–60%), family member (3%–44%), friend/acquaintance (15%–58%), adult stranger (28%–75%), or employer (2%–5%).

> The final stage is **control** over victims (aka "seasoning"). Controllers, often with help from their associates, use the following techniques to ensure victim participation in commercial sexual exploitation and trafficking: inducing/exploiting substance abuse; physical abuse; sexual abuse; emotional abuse; violence and threats of violence; isolation from friends and family; and economic abuse—all which, combined with humiliation, shame, fear, and trauma bonding from being victimized—prevents them

Figure 8.2 Top recruitment tactics.

from escaping even when unsupervised (Mitchell et al., 2010; Polaris Project, 2020; Raphael & Ashley, 2008).

As is typical in domestic abuse situations, victims are kept in a perpetual state of psychological danger—sensing tension from the controller and fearing an unprovoked abusive attack. In addition to the seasoning methods listed above, victims may be unfamiliar with the area in which they are being sex trafficked. It would not be unusual for victims to be transported from *origin* to *destination* states (e.g., Minnesota Pipeline to NY) or across state lines for "dates," sex tourism opportunities (e.g., Superbowl), or to follow one of the prostitution circuits, such as down the Pacific west coast states and across to Hawaii (Dank et al., 2014; Roe-Sepowitz et al., 2017). Law enforcement has difficulty convincing victims to admit when they have been coerced or forced into prostitution rather than consenting, as is required by law (U.S. Dept of State, 2021). This is due to a variety of reasons, including they are not aware of alternatives to the lifestyle in which they are trapped, have no other way to make money legally due to limits in their education and finances and/or restrictions from disadvantaged social structures; do not classify themselves as victims, instead believing themselves to be in love with the abuser; are ashamed of what they have done and believe no one will love them; and/or stay with the abuser as a means of protecting their family from harm (Berman, 2008; Polaris Project, 2020; Raphael & Ashley, 2008; Swaner et al., 2016; Thorn, 2019; Tyler & Johnson, 2006).

Once the victim is submissive and compliant, the Internet again plays a prominent role by soliciting buyers through online advertising (indicated in 75%–88% conviction cases), scheduling victims for "dates" (aka purchased sex acts) with buyers, getting payments for dates, and booking hotels for dates (Briggs et al., 2011; Currier & Feehs, 2019; Latonero, 2011; Roe-Sepowitz et al., 2017; Wolak et al., 2008). The most common online commercial sites used for advertising has been Backpage, Craigslist, Redbook, Adam4Adam, and SugarDaddy and social networking sites like Facebook, Twitter, and MySpace (which 90% indicated they had access and used during enslavement)—a process simplified by web-enabled smart phones (Latonero, 2011; Swaner et al., 2016; Thorn, 2019).[9] The trafficker lowers his/her criminal risk by providing Internet access to the victims for

---

[9] In 2018, closure of some sites (e.g., Myredbook, Backpage) or at least their personal ads section (e.g., Craiglist) has not impacted other websites used to advertise commercial sexual services, including Adam4Adam, Eros, AdultSearch, TheEroticReview, Tagged, and Cityvibe, as well as communities such as Livelinks and LiveJasmin (Dank et al., 2014; Dubrawski et al., 2015).

posting advertisements and communicating with buyers (often by text), who then make transactions online prior to meeting for sex (Latonero, 2011; Thorn, 2019). An examination of commercial sex consumers showed that online advertisements encouraged 41% of low-frequency buyers and 89% high-frequency buyers to purchase sex from trafficking victims (Demand Abolition, 2018). Victim-survivors reported that online advertising increased the daily number of buyers they serviced, such that at least 25% reported having 10 or more (Thorn, 2019). **Box 8.2** provides case examples in which victims were advertised online.

BOX 8.2   ONLINE ADVERTISING OF SEX TRAFFICKING VICTIMS

Technology is instrumental for controllers to sell their sex trafficking victims, either through advertising or live, webcam-based performances of commercial sexual services that are distributed on personal websites. Backpage was the biggest marketer for online commercial sex trafficking from 2004 until 2018 when it was seized and shut down by the FBI (Krell, 2021; Maras, 2017). Backpage lost its CDA Section 230 immunity and the CEO plead guilty to trafficking (Manchester, 2018); civil suits against it are pending (Krell, 2021). Other sites have since replaced it, including Facebook. In response to three lawsuits by adolescent victims indicating Facebook's role in recruiting them, the Texas Supreme Court ruled that Facebook lost its' Section 230 immunity as it did not protect them from federal human trafficking (Dangor, 2021).

In the criminal cases listed below, sex trafficking victims were advertised online.

United States v. Tate and Merritt: Mr. Tate, the leader of a sex trafficking ring (Merritt was a bottom), posted advertisements in the adult escort section on various websites and forced a female minor to engage in commercial sex acts in multiple hotels. His other accomplices, Dominque and Garon, were charged separately.

United States v. Dominque: Ms. Dominque forced a female minor (her niece) to post advertisements on Backpage.com and engage in commercial sex acts out of her residence in Louisiana and elsewhere.

United States v. Tillman: Ms. Tillman advertised a minor and herself on Backpage.com for prostitution services.

United States v. Williams: Mr. Williams and Mr. Davis, Jr., who ran a sex trafficking ring with accomplice Ms. Canterbury, advertised three minors for commercial sex on Backpage.com.

United States v. Omuro and Lanoce: Mr. Omuro was the operator of the website myRedBook.com which hosted advertisements for services by sex workers, including 50 minors.

TYPICAL ONLINE DOMESTIC COMMERCIAL SEXUAL TRAFFICKING VICTIMS

Early sex trafficking research indicated that most victims were female (e.g., 94%), but subsequent studies estimated the proportion of male victims—particularly minors—may be equal or almost equal (40%–50%) to the total number of female victims (Banks & Kyckkelhan, 2011; Bryan, 2014; Curtis et al., 2008; Greenbaum, 2014; O'Brien et al., 2017; Reid, 2012; Walker, 2013). Gender disparity may be explained by: (1) lack of awareness—few non-governmental organizations have identified boys (and male victims are loath to self-identify) as "at risk for commercial sexual exploitation and trafficking" nor provided services for them; (2) differences in the style of exploitation for male and female victims—boys/men are more likely than girls/women to be exploited through survival sex than through third-party trafficker; and (3) variations by locality for the buyers' predominant preference for female vs. male victims (Curtis et al., 2008; Reid, 2012; Reid & Piquero, 2016; Walker, 2013).

The race/ethnicity of victims in sex trafficking conviction cases indicated 21%–24% were Latinx, 22%–27% were White, and 35%–45% were Black (Banks & Kyckkelhan, 2011; Thorn, 2019; United Nations Office of Drugs and Crime/UNODC, 2018). In general, however, the racial/ethnic backgrounds of victims are most likely going to be a reflection of the population in the area of the U.S. from which they originated, such as Latinx in the West, White in the Midwest, and Black in the East (Estes & Weiner, 2001). Sex trafficking victims are also overrepresented in comparison to their population, such as Native American victims (40% even though only 8% of the population) in South Dakota (Furguson, 2016). Victims of the same race may also be represented differently within the same state, such as 47% in upstate New York versus 6% in NYC of victims are White (Gragg et al., 2007).

As indicated in cases from 2008 to 2010 (Banks & Kyckkelhan, 2011), a higher proportion of online sex trafficking victims were minors (54%) rather than young adults aged 18–24 years (31%); this is probably because commercial sex buyers prefer youths and traffickers find minors to be easier than adults to control and manipulate due to their immature reasoning ability and focus on short-term rewards (Konrad et al., 2013). Age is a contributing factor in predisposing a minor victim to the lure of sexual predators because the prefrontal cortex is not fully formed until age 25, affecting the ability to analyze risks and consequences, control impulsive behaviors, make logical decisions, and plan appropriately (Konrad et al., 2013). The minor victims of commercial sexual exploitation and trafficking are typically between 12 and 17 years of age, with less than 20% younger than age 12 (Polaris Project, 2015b; Thorn, 2019).

Research shows that male victims (particularly gay and transgendered minors) first enter sex trafficking between 11 and 13 years, whereas female victims typically enter between ages 12 and 14 years—but they are considered at greatest risk between 15 and 19 years (Clawson et al., 2009; De Santisteban et al., 2018; Greenbaum, 2014; Hardy et al., 2013; UNICEF, 2014). The age of entry is believed to be even younger (e.g., less than 10 years) for victims whose controller is a family member than non-relative (Reid et al., 2015; Raphael, 2020). As shown in Table 8.3, three types of risk factors—individual characteristics, family factors, and maltreatment history—have been linked to adults' and minors' vulnerability to sexual exploitation and trafficking victimization (De Santisteban et al., 2018; Dombrowski et al., 2004; Franchino-Olsen, 2021; Gerassi, 2015; Kirwan & Power, 2012; Marcus et al., 2014; Polaris Project, 2020; Smith et al., 2009). These risk factors predispose individuals to victimization, but are merely correlates rather than casual factors.

Table 8.3 Risk Factors Associated with Commercial Sexual Exploitation and Trafficking

Type of Factors	Risks
Individual characteristics	Impaired cognitive function
	Academic problems
	Mental or physical disability
	LGBTQ+
	Substance abuse and addiction
	Undiagnosed and/or untreated Mental illness
	Untreated behavioral problems

(Continued)

Table 8.3 (*Continued*)   Risk Factors Associated with Commercial Sexual Exploitation and Trafficking

Type of Factors	Risks
	Runaway
	Thrown-away[a]
	Low self-esteem
	Juvenile Justice system involvement
	Socially awkward/poor peer relationships
	Gang/crime delinquency
	Physical/cognitive impairment
	Emotionally insecure (seeking affection and attention)
	Risky/endangering behaviors
	Early onset puberty/precocious transition
	Stigma/discrimination
Maltreatment history	Prior/current sexual abuse
	Prior/current sexual assault
	Prior/current psychological abuse
	Prior/current physical abuse
	Prior/current emotional abuse
	Prior/current neglect
	Prior/current intimate partner violence
Family factors	Dysfunctional family
	Unstable home life/recent relocation
	Impoverished/economic vulnerability
	Child Protection Services involvement[b]
	Little/no online supervision
	Compromised parenting[c]
	Homeless
	Lack of social support system
	Dangerous neighborhood (gangs, crime, drugs, prostitution)
	Domestic violence
	Conflict with parents
	Family involvement with gangs/crime/drugs/sex work

[a] Minors are told by family to leave for various reasons, but are not given a safe housing alternative.

[b] Formally investigate reports of maltreatment, which may result in placing the minor into foster care.

[c] Parents' capacity to safeguard and care for children appropriately is compromised due to domestic abuse, mental illness, and/or substance misuse.

LAWS FOR PROSECUTING ONLINE DOMESTIC COMMERCIAL SEXUAL TRAFFICKING

The first federal law aimed at criminalizing trafficking was the *Mann Act* of 1910, sometimes referred to as the White Slave Traffic Act, in response to claims that girls and women were being held captive and forced into prostitution (Fisher, 2012).

> The **Mann Act of 1910** (18 U.S.C. §2421 et seq.) prohibited abduction for the purpose of forced prostitution[10] as part of interstate or foreign commerce and for sexual relations with underage girls[11] and women (Find Law, 2019). It was primarily used to prosecute men who transported girls or women across state lines for the purpose of debauchery or for any other "immoral purpose." In addition to its racist application (i.e., charging Black men for consensual sex with White women), it was also used to punish those considered "immoral," such as homosexuals, polygamists, adulterers, or unmarried adults. The initial amendment in 1978 included gender-neutral protection and criminalized exploitation, such as child pornography. Later amendments (1986, 1994) were aimed at protecting children from "slavery-like" practices, but most importantly prohibited transportation of minors (defined as under age 18), and extended prosecution from "any other immoral purpose" to include "any sexual activity." The Mann Act could still be used today to prosecute someone who transported an adult or minor across state lines for the purpose of commercial sex exploitation and trafficking, particularly if the person was coerced or kidnapped and when electronic communications facilitated the act.

The Mann Act was a precursor for the *Trafficking Victims Protection Act* (TVPA) of 2000, and each statute has different advantages in terms of prosecution. The former does not require proof that force, fraud, or coercion were used, whereas the latter does not require proof of transportation across state lines (or any movement whatsoever) and its language reduces the potential for prosecutorial (morality) misuse as has been seen under the Mann Act (Mattar, 2011; Miller-Perrin & Wertele, 2017).

> The **Trafficking Victims Protection Act** (TVPA, Title 18 Sec. 112 Chapter 77) **of 2000** prohibited human trafficking (slavery) of U.S. and non-U.S.

---

[10] There was no federal law for prostitution, instead each state created its own statute (Fisher, 2012).

[11] Legal consent was raised from age 10 to 16 in most states by 1900.

citizens using a three-pronged approach—*prevention* (Sec. 106—includes educational programs in anti-trafficking, employment options, and business training; public awareness), *protection* (Sec. 107—provides victims access to benefits and social services, including T-visa), and *prosecution* (Sec. 108—punishes traffickers severely enough to deter and sufficiently to reflect the gravity and heinousness of offenses) and established Interagency Task Force to monitor and combat trafficking (Sec. 105).

A partial list of relevant definitions for the TVPA appears below. Sec. 103. Definitions:

(2) COERCION: (a) threats of serious harm to or physical restraint against any person; (b) any scheme, plan or pattern intended to cause a person to believe that failure to perform an act would result in serious harm to or physical restraint against any person, or (c) abuse or threated abuse of the legal process.

(3) COMMERCIAL SEX ACT: any sex act on account of which anything of value is given to or received by any person.

(8) SEVERE FORMS OF TRAFFICKING IN PERSONS: (A) sex trafficking in which a commercial sex act is induced by force, fraud, or coercion, or in which the person induced to perform such act has not attained 18 years of age; or (B) the recruitment, harboring, transportation, provision, or obtaining of a person for labor or services, through the use of force, fraud, or coercion for the purpose of subjection to involuntary servitude, peonage, debt bondage, or slavery.

(9) SEX TRAFFICKING: the recruitment, harboring, transportation, provision, or obtaining of a person for labor or services, through the use of force, fraud, or coercion for the purpose of a commercial sex act.[12]

There were multiple reauthorizations of this act, each of which remedied perceived inadequacies (based on new information about trafficking) and expanded the original scope. The key changes relevant to sex trafficking are indicated below (Alliance to End Slavery & Trafficking/ATEST, 2017; Farrell, & Reichert, 2017; U.S. Department of Justice, 2017). Table 8.4 provides the list and definition of each section, with terms in bold representing modifications as per the most recent reauthorization. Additional legal mechanisms were put in place to prosecute traffickers who sexually abuse and exploit children through production and distribution of child sexual

---

[12] 22 USC § 7102, Title 22, Chapter 78: "Trafficking Victims Protection – Definitions."

Table 8.4 Federal Statutes Relevant for Prosecuting Commercial Sexual Exploitation and Trafficking

Statute	Intended Meaning of Section
18 U.S.C. §1590 (Chapter 77). Trafficking with respect to peonage, slavery, involuntary servitude, or forced labor	This section provides a standardized definition for two types of human trafficking, distinguished by use of victim for purposes of labor and/or sex. Sentencing is increased when death occurs or if victim was kidnapped or attempts were made to kidnap, attempt or engage in aggravated sexual abuse, or attempt to kill victim. Also criminalized are obstruction, attempts to obstruct or interfere with/prevent enforcement. The following acts are criminalized: knowingly *recruits, harbors, transports, provides, or obtains by any means, any person for labor or services.*
18 U.S.C. §1591 (Chapter 77). Sex trafficking of children or by force, fraud, or coercion	This section describes the sex trafficking offense, which allows prosecution of traffickers, buyers, and facilitators. The following acts are criminalized: knowingly *recruits, entices, harbors, transports, provides, obtains,* **advertises, maintains, patronizes, or solicits by any means.**[a] Additional acts criminalized include: knowingly *benefits, financially or by receiving anything of value,* **from participation in a venture** *which has engaged in an act described...or* **advertising, in reckless disregard of the fact,** *that* **means of force, threats of force,** *fraud, coercion described in subsection (e)(2)*[b] **or any combination of such means** *will be used to cause the person to engage in a commercial sex act, or that the person has not attained the age of 18 years and will be caused to engage in a commercial sex act.*

(Continued)

[a] *United States v. Jungers,* was instrumental in codifying §1591 to include "patronizes" and "solicits" to punish buyers (Gregorio, 2015).

[b] According to the TVPA, 18 U.S.C. §1591(a), defines sex trafficking as "to cause the person to engage in a commercial sex act," which is "any sex act, on account of which, anything of value is given to or received by any person" (18 U.S. C. §1591(a) (e)(3)).

214

Table 8.4 (*Continued*) Federal Statutes Relevant for Prosecuting Commercial Sexual Exploitation and Trafficking

Statute	Intended Meaning of Section
18 U.S.C. §1593 (Chapter 77). Mandatory restitution	This section provides the Court a mechanism of mandatory restitution for the victim-survivor (beyond 3663/3663A or other penalties imposed), allowing the person to transition from bondage to freedom and in recognition that trafficking imposes emotional, social, educational/vocational, mental, and physical health costs. The victim's full losses are determined by the Court (consistent with § 2259).[c]
18 U.S.C. §1594 (Chapter 77). General provisions	This section provides the Court with a mechanism by which the forfeited assets of those convicted—real and personal property that was employed or traceable to commit or facilitate trafficking, or derived from proceeds of trafficking—could be used for mandatory restitution to compensate victims in the full amount of their past, current, and future losses (i.e., greater of gross income or value to convicted defendant of victims' services).
18 U.S.C. §1595 (Chapter 77). Civil remedy	This section allows victims, following pending criminal action, to bring civil suit against perpetrator or facilitator who benefited from trafficking venture to recover damages and attorney fees. Victims have 10 years to file suit subsequent to onset of trafficking, however victims who were minors are allowed to start the 10-year clock subsequent to turning 18.
18 U.S.C. §2421 (Chapter 117). Transportation	This section criminalizes *transporting* victims for purposes of commercial sex acts (i.e., engage in prostitution or any illegal sexual activity).

(Continued)

[c] Losses included for restitution: *medical services* (physical psychiatric, psychological); *physical or occupational therapy or rehabilitation; transportation, temporary housing, and child care expenses; lost income; attorney fees;* and other losses, which could include education expenses and vocational training (U.S. Sentencing Commission, 2016). The calculations can be reasonable estimates based on the facts presented in the case, such as *U.S. v. Lundquist.*

Table 8.4 (*Continued*) Federal Statutes Relevant for Prosecuting Commercial Sexual Exploitation and Trafficking

Statute	Intended Meaning of Section
18 U.S.C. §2422 (Chapter 117). Coercion and enticement	For this section, 2422 (a) criminalizes knowingly *persuading, inducing, enticing, or coercing victims to travel for the purposes of commercial sex acts,* whereas 2422 (b) criminalizes knowingly *using mail or interstate commerce to persuade, induce entice, or coerce a minor to engage in commercial sex acts.*
18 U.S.C. §2423 (Chapter 117). Transportation of minors	For this section, 2423 (a) criminalizes knowingly *transporting minors with the intent have them engage in commercial sex acts,* whereas 2423(b) *prohibits traveling[d] for the purpose of engaging in illicit sexual conduct.*
18 U.S.C. §3014 (Chapter 201). Additional special assessment	This section imposes a mandatory $5000 assessment on nonindigent person or entity convicted of sex trafficking related offenses—Chapters 77 (trafficking), 109A (sexual abuse), 110 (child sexual abuse and exploitation), and 117 (transportation for illegal sex) to be paid into Domestic Trafficking Victims' Fund for victim services and deterrence programs.[e] However, court-ordered fines, restitution orders, and other victim compensation must be paid before this assessment can be implemented.

[d]Includes interstate, into the U.S., or into foreign country.

[e]In a recent decision by 2nd Circuit Appellate Court for *U.S. v Haverkamp,* the Court interpreted sentencing to mean that the $5000 assessment fee was not per count (as interpreted by the Third Circuit in *U.S. v Johnson*) but rather per offender. The legislatures must revise the wording to be consistent in future interpretation, particularly if the intention was to provide a fee per victim—then the current interpretation of per offender is less than desirable.

abuse material (see Chapter 9 for use of 18 U.S.C. §2251, §2251A, §2252, §2252A, §2253, §2257, §2260, §2425).

Trafficking Victims Protection Reauthorization Act (TVPRA) of 2003 included (1) categorization of trafficking under Racketeer Influenced and Corruptions Act/RICO (criminal operations associated with organized crime groups); (2) mandated annual reports to Congress; (3) disseminating material alerting travelers that sex tourism is illegal; and (4) civil remedy provided for victims to recover damages and attorney fees (§1595(a), but required plaintiffs to wait until after the pendency of the criminal action (§1595 (b)(1)). A special report (*Trafficking in Persons*) grades countries in terms of anti-trafficking laws and enforcement is provided annually to the State Department.

Another legal tool developed by the federal government around this time was the **Prosecutorial Remedies and Other Tools to End the Exploitation of Children Today (PROTECT) Act of 2003**, which (1) provided an alert system (Amber) to inform the public of missing, exploited, and abducted children; (2) provided grants for transitional housing for children who had been sexually assaulted; and (3) enhanced penalties for child sex offenders who engage in sex tourism within/outside of the U.S.

William Wilberforce Trafficking Victims Protection Reauthorization Act (TVPRA) of 2005 included a new crime, *trafficking in persons offenses committed by federal contractors outside the United States*. Also, in recognition that US citizens and Legal Permanent Residents were also victims of sex trafficking, added measures included the creation and offering of: (1) grant programs to assist law enforcement in combatting trafficking and expanding assistance to victim-survivors, and (2) comprehensive services and rehabilitative facilities for victims (such as shelters for minors).

Trafficking Victims Protection Reauthorization Act (TVPRA) of 2008 extended and modified programs for the prevention, protection, and prosecution of trafficking, particularly for unaccompanied alien minors and those entering the U.S. lawfully. It provided *criminalized obstruction* into trafficking, created a penalty for conspiring to commit trafficking and added *facilitator liability*, such as corporations that indirectly, but knowingly, profited from the venture in **reckless disregard** to use of force, fraud, and coercion against the victim for purposes of criminal and civil charges (Shapiro, 2021). Importantly, it eliminated the requirement that the government prove the defendant knew the person was a minor, replaced with having a reasonable opportunity to observe the minor. Finally, it required the Uniform Crime Reporting (UCR) unit of the FBI to collect data on human trafficking.

Trafficking Victims Protection Reauthorization Act (TVPRA) of 2013, was amended as a part of the **Violence Against Women Act**. It strengthened the law enforcement partnerships with private entities for purposes of assisting in the investigation and prosecution of sex traffickers, while providing resources and mandatory restitution for victim-survivors plus enhanced enforcement and prosecution of U.S. citizens living abroad who commercially sexually exploit children (under the **2003 PROTECT Act**). The statute of limitations for civil actions by victims who were trafficked as minors was extended.

The Justice for Victims of Trafficking Act (JVTA) of 2015 expanded the TVPRA by: (1) §1591(a) including new acts of *patronizing* and *soliciting* and new means of commission, *advertising*; (2) amending §1594 to direct assets forfeited for use in the victim restitution order; (3) including in §2423(f) transportation and travel for purposes of production of child pornography as "illicit sexual conduct;" (4) not requiring proof that defendant knew or recklessly disregarded that victim was a minor, if there had been a reasonable opportunity to observe the victim; and (5) creating a $5000 special assessment fee per conviction to support a fund intended to provide trafficking victim services (set forth in Chapters 77, 110, and 117). In sum, the offenses covered are trafficking, sexual abuse, sexual exploitation and other abuse of children, production of child pornography, and transporting for illegal sexual activity and related crimes.

Frederick Douglass Trafficking Victims Prevention and Protection Reauthorization Act (TVPRA) of 2017 (signed 2018) limited the number of consecutive years countries on the watch list may remain (penalties result in aid restrictions and reductions). It also reauthorized grant programs, including child centered grant programs (e.g., Create Hope through Outreach Options, Services, and Education for children and youth/CHOOSE Children & Youth),[13] through various government agencies and grant funding to train School Resource Officers to identify trafficking victims. It also extended the use of child advocates appointed for trafficking victims and Unaccompanied Alien Children (Section 301) plus requirements for data reporting, including the status of the *Innocence Lost National Initiative* (Section 401).

Trafficking Victims Protection Reauthorization Act (TVPRA) of 2019 (signed 2020) combined four bills in order to strengthen efforts to combat trafficking through (1) existing programs; (2) new enforcement through identification, prosecution (using a designated prosecutor per district), and sentencing tools (increasing maximum sentences for offenses §1583, §1587, §1591(d) and §2426) and applying mandatory restitution to Mann Act offenses; (3) accountability of corporations and government entities through programs; and (4) prevention, including training of flight attendants, judges, and school staff to identify victims.

---

[13] 34 U.S. Code § 12451 sets up "grants to enhance the safety of youth and children who are victims or, or exposed to, domestic violence, sexual assault, stalking, or sex trafficking and prevent future violence." It also provides programs that include services, education, and protection.

After the TVPA of 2000 was created, state laws were given a limited amount of time to modify their current laws (e.g., removing the term "child prostitutes" in recognition that minors are unequivocally victims not perpetrators) or create new ones to reflect accurately the trafficking definitions and components in the federal law. Unfortunately, many states have not yet aligned their laws with the current TVPRA in regard to implementing *Safe Harbor laws* (i.e., prevents prosecuting victims for prostitution and provides services to sex trafficking victims) and *Vacatur laws* (i.e., permits Court to vacate—make legally void—non-violent and prostitution-related convictions) for sexually exploited victims (National Council of Jewish Women, 2016a, 2016b).

Table 8.5 indicates the level of protection allotted to minor victims by states, demonstrating that as of 2019 only 29 states and D.C. prohibit charging child sex trafficking victims with prostitution (Bendtsen, 2019; Gies et al., 2019; Shared Hope International, 2017a, 2018). Although all states criminalize child sex trafficking and purchasing children for sex, laws and practices in some states still charge minors with prostitution and/or their laws narrowly define CSEC in conflict with the federal definition, such as requiring proof that minors were controlled by a third party as affirmative defenses against prostitution and/or juvenile delinquency charges, diversion, or referral in lieu of arrest (Shared Hope International, 2019a).[14] Consequently, without child victims being properly identified, the corresponding measures in place to protect them are not triggered, including expunging criminal records; obtaining justice, mandatory fees ($5000), and restitution against buyers, traffickers, and facilitators; and receiving specialized victim assistance services, such as housing, medical treatment, mental health, food (Love, 2021; Shared Hope International, 2017a, 2019a). Box 8.3 provides an example of how the process for obtaining mandatory fee and restitution for victims is not functioning as intended.

---

[14] A child can only qualify in Maryland if a trafficker is identified, whereas in Alaska even when the trafficker is identified, the victim must prove force or coercion (National Conference of State Legislatures, n.d.). These additional qualifications are not aligned with the federal requirements.

Table 8.5 Safe Harbor and Vacatur Protection by States and D.C.

Safe Harbor Laws	States	Vacatur Laws	States
Minors charged as prostitutes: a.) *unless affirmative defense of CSEC* (third party) used (N=17); b.) *age-limited protection* (N=4)	Alaska, Arizona, Arkansas, Hawaii, Idaho, Iowa, Kansas, Louisiana, Maryland, Massachusetts, Missouri, New York, Oregon,[a] Virginia, Washington,[a] Wisconsin, Wyoming Only if under 16: Michigan, Ohio,[a] South Dakota[a] Only if under 14: Texas	Expungement and sealing of juvenile delinquency records Expungement of prostitution and related charges	49 states (excludes Hawaii) plus D.C. California (+nv), Connecticut (po), Delaware (prostitution, loitering, obscenity), Florida (+nv), Georgia (sex crimes only), Indiana (+nv), Kentucky, Louisiana (pro), Michigan, New Hampshire (+nv), New Mexico, Ohio (pro), Texas, Washington (po), Wisconsin (po)
Safe Harbor Laws protect minors from prosecution, adjudication, or conviction as delinquent for prostitution (N=29+D.C.)	Alabama, California, Colorado, Connecticut, Delaware, Florida, Georgia, Illinois, Indiana, Kentucky, Maine, Minnesota, Mississippi, Montana, Nebraska, Nevada, New Hampshire, New Jersey,[a] New Mexico, North Carolina,[a] North Dakota, Oklahoma, Pennsylvania, Rhode Island, South Carolina, Tennessee, Utah,[a] Vermont, West Virginia,[a] D.C.	Vacatur provision for trafficking victims	Arizona, California, Connecticut, Delaware, Florida, Georgia, Hawaii, Idaho, Illinois, Indiana, Kentucky, Louisiana, Maryland, Michigan, Mississippi, Montana, Nevada, New Hampshire, New Jersey, New Mexico, New York, North Carolina, North Dakota, Ohio, Oregon, Pennsylvania, Rhode Island, South Carolina, Texas, Utah, Vermont, Washington, West Virginia, Wisconsin, Wyoming

Key: +nv=non-violent; po=prostitution only; pro=prostitution related only.
[a] Entered into Child and Family Services or into the juvenile justice system as "child in need of supervision" or as status offender.

220

BOX 8.3 SPECIAL ASSESSMENT FEE AND MANDATORY RESTITUTION FOR TRAFFICKING VICTIMS

The Trafficking Victims Protection (Reauthorization) Act provides two financial mechanisms in which convicted traffickers (e.g., controllers, associates, facilitators) would pay a special assessment fee of $5000 into a fund for victims and mandatory restitution directly to victims to cover their full losses. Unfortunately, only a small percentage of those convicted of trafficking offenses are being ordered by the Court to pay the fee and/or restitution, despite its requirement as stated in the federal law (Levy, 2018; Murphy, 2019). Nonindigent defendants convicted of offenses under Chapter 77 (trafficking), Chapter 109A (sexual abuse), Chapter 110 (sexual exploitation/abuse of children), and Chapter 117 (transportation for illegal sexual activity/other crimes) are required by the 2015 JVTA to pay the $5000 special assessment into the Domestic Trafficking Victims Fund [18 U.S.C. § 3014]. The purpose of the fund is to assist criminal justice professionals and victim service organizations in rescuing and restoring victims' lives during investigation and prosecution of their cases. Since the fee's enactment, the number of defendants paying into the fund over 4 years has slowly increased: 6 in 2016, 24 in 2017, 31 in 2018, and 34 in 2019 (Human Trafficking Institute, 2020). At this rate, even with the initial $2 million dollars from the Office for Victims of Crime (2017), the $475,000 collected from the 95 convicts is financially unsustainable to support its' function. Compliance by the Courts to award mandatory restitution under 18 U.S.C. § 1593 and with issuance and enforcement of restitution under 18 U.S.C. § 3664 is also dysfunctional.[15] As shown in Table 8.6, only a small percentage of those convicted were ordered to pay their victims mandatory restitution and compliance rates are similarly low for restitution collected (Office of the Attorney General/ OAG, 2016, 2017, 2018, 2020). In summary, the failure of these mechanisms to render aid to victims as dictated in the TVPRA starts at the investigation level with law enforcement failing to identify victims as such and proceeds to the judicial level with judges not requiring those pleading guilty or convicted to pay the special assessment, not awarding mandatory restitution for every victim, and not guaranteeing that awards are paid from the forfeited property.

---

[15] *U.S. v. Charles* indicated that restitution can be sought for defendants who attempted victimization by soliciting online.

Table 8.6 Restitution Awards for Defendants Convicted by DOJ in Sex Trafficking Cases

Defendants	FY2018	FY2017	FY2016	FY2015
# Convicted	501	471	428	291
# Ordered to pay restitution	77	60	75	32
Percentage ordered	15%	12.7%	17.5%	11%
Total amount of original awards	$9,565,137.00	$10,551,540.9	$9,166,689	$4,018,988
Amount still owed	$8,612,179.00 as of Sept. 25, 2019	$10,396,366.57 as of April 19, 2018	$8,909,190 as of November 17, 2017	$4,018,001 as of 2016
Percentage paid	10%	1.5%	2.8%	0.025%

IMPACT OF ONLINE DOMESTIC COMMERCIAL SEXUAL TRAFFICKING ON SOCIETY AND VICTIMS

There are short-term and long-term problems for victims, their families, and communities (IOM and NRS, 2013). Victims often suffer multiple forms of exploitation (e.g., prostitution and child sexual abuse material) and are enslaved on average 2 years (range is 1 day to 11 years) before escaping or being freed by law enforcement when the controllers and associates are arrested (International Labour Organization and Walk Free Foundation, 2017; Roe-Sepowitz et al., 2017). Unfortunately, most of the programs geared toward victim-survivors are ill-equipped to handle their unique needs, mainly because they are uninformed, uncoordinated, underfunded, and insufficient (OJJDP, 2014). The commercial sex exploitation and trafficking trade places a large financial burden on both the criminal justice system and public health and social services (e.g., medical, psychological)—in the millions of dollars (Shively et al., 2012). Currently, the financial aid mechanisms in place through legislation have not been operating as planned, specifically the $5000 special assessment fee for victim services or mandatory restitution for each victim, which would have reduced this burden on the community (Shapiro, 2021).

The residents and businesses in communities where commercial sex acts occur also suffer due to increases in drugs and violence; disturbances of the peace through loud screaming, cursing, fighting, and beatings of victims; littering of sexual, alcohol, and drug paraphernalia in public parks, school years, and sidewalks; and social modeling of criminal activities in front of children (Shively et al., 2012). Victim services must strive to improve their understanding of the victim-survivors' predispositions for and experiences of trafficking through research, data, and evidence-based practices; align efforts for identifying victims and matching them with programs at all governmental levels with education, training, and technical assistance, as well as ensuring protection through state safe harbor and vacatur laws consistent with federal guidelines; ensure that the legal mechanisms already in place for mandatory fees, restitution for victims, and allotted funding for victim services, grants, and research are properly enacted; and meet victims' short- and long-term health, safety, and well-being in order to transition them back into society (OJJDP, 2014). Society must provide funding for services at no cost to victims when compensation is not provided by the Court to allow them to pay for themselves.

The *physical health* of victims suffers due a variety of problems: long-term malnutrition; multiple physical and sexual abuse traumatic injuries (e.g., facial deformities, broken bones, anogenital trauma/infection, brain damage); complications from limited access to comprehensive and preventative medical and dental care; substance use/abuse problems; and gynecological associated issues, such as loss of bowel control, sexually transmitted infections/HIV, discharge, pelvic pain, bleeding, multiple pregnancies, and multiple or unsafe abortions (Greenbaum, 2018; Jimenez et al., 2015; Shively et al., 2012). It is difficult for medical professionals to connect the injuries to the commercial sex trade, particularly when medical care is obtained in multiple states (Roe-Sepowitz et al., 2017). Victims also exhibit *socio-emotional and psychological* problems, including post-traumatic stress disorder (PTSD), mental health problems (e.g., depression, anxiety), poor attachment, and/or inability to form relations with others; *educational/vocational* problems, including no high school diploma and no legitimate work experiences; and various *behavioral* problems, such as self-harm, lack of life-skills, and hyper-sexualization (Hardy et al., 2013; Miller-Perrin & Wurtele, 2017; Shively et al., 2012).

There is a bi-directional effect of sex trafficking such that societal attitudes, norms, and values are communicated to citizens, which in turn, are reshaped and amplified back to society (Mapp, 2020). American society contributes to the acceptance and facilitation of the commercial sex exploitation and trafficking trade by: (1) allowing the objectification and sexualization of children, especially girls; (2) promoting sexual objectification

223

of women, especially in pornography; (3) accepting and promoting gender inequality;[16] (4) accepting, tolerating, and normalizing gender-based violence; and (5) failing to prioritize resources (i.e., financial, services, education) to protect potential victims, prevent their victimization, and prosecute those who profit or gain from the commercial sexual exploitation and trafficking trade (IOC and NRC, 2013). Our culture, as portrayed through music and the media, glorifies the pimp culture—encouraging people to accept the symbolism (e.g., pimping your ride); using women as objects to sell items (e.g., cars) or as symbols of success; and assigning high status to those who excel at controlling others (Franchino-Olsen, 2021; Gerassi, 2015; Greenbaum, 2014). As a result, it is easier for vulnerable and/or marginalized individuals to succumb to the controller's manipulation and exploitation. The only way for society to combat commercial sex exploitation and trafficking trade effectively is to recognize its influence in promoting it, ensure partnerships between private and public sectors, enhance legislation that enforces the mandatory fees and victim restitution is paid, and make changes in society and criminal justice itself to reduce the rewards currently gained by buyers, controllers, associates, and facilitators while increasing the consequences for them (Shapiro, 2021).

CYBERSECURITY TACTICS

The fourth prong in the comprehensive approach to combat trafficking, *partnership*, acknowledges the need for the public and private sectors globally to work together by combining diverse experiences and expertise and sharing resources. Private companies have developed a variety of tech tools for use by anti-trafficking stakeholders that focus on prevention, protection, and prosecution. Microsoft has a prevention tool called *Project Artemis* used to detect grooming in chats and report flagged conversations to moderators (Office of the Special Representative and Coordinator for Combating Trafficking in Human Beings/OSRCCTHB, 2020). Thorn (2014) created a guide for use by website companies consisting of tools, resources, and policies (e.g., prescreen photographs in photo sharing and classified sites) that could help them to identify, report, and remove exploitation content. Global search engine and social media firms also have corporate

---

[16] This includes laws and societal beliefs that limit women's control over their own bodies related to sex and pregnancy.

social responsibility policies in place to combat users attempting to post child sexual exploitation content (Godoy et al., 2016). To reduce demand, buyers are targeted in different ways. *Project Intercept,* which uses chatbots as decoys to interrupt buyers from purchasing sex from ads or redirects them to deterrence websites, while gathering insights about buyer patterns and behaviors (Simonite, 2017). Another short-term method is the use of nuisance telephone *denial of service attacks.* Malaga (2015) suggested using a Web crawler to find the online commercial sex ads, harvest the phone number, and launch the attack by flooding the number with continuous calls and/or text messages so as to prevent buyers from making contact. There are also anti-money laundering protocols in place by major financial institutions through the United States Bank Alliance Against Human Trafficking. The tools scan internal systems to uncover trafficking operations by detecting attempted credit card transactions made during nonbusiness hours and prevent buyers from completing suspicious purchases (OSRCCTHB, 2020).

For parents seeking preventative measures to detect online predators, Bark and Qustodio are parent control services they can purchase annually to monitor their children's social networks, common apps, messages, and photographs for potential problems (Edwards, 2020). There are also tools for victims to use to connect them with services or with law enforcement who investigate and prosecute offenders. When the mainstream Internet is used by online criminals, such as controllers posting ads and buyers answering ads for commercial sex, evidence in the form of digital footprints remain and are used by investigators to prosecute them (Godoy et al., 2016). *TraffickCam* is an application that uses a crowdsourced database of hotel rooms photographed by travelers to allow anti-trafficking agencies and law enforcement to determine the location based on comparisons with image background details shown in ads and online photographs (Couch, 2016).

Technology tools are also needed to sift through the large amount of online data (aka web data extraction or AI web scraping) to make the investigation process for law enforcement manageable (Thorn, 2014). The *Sex Trafficking Operations Portal* converts data into reports regarding possible human trafficking activity online for law enforcement to investigate (OSRCCTHB, 2020). Thorn (2015) designed a tool called *Spotlight,* which examines online commercial sex ads and aggregates data, to help law enforcement agencies reduce the amount of time needed for examining content (e.g., images, contact information, sex acts in each case). Lexis Nexis developed a tool called *Social Media Monitor* that helps law enforcement in detecting and gathering digital evidence of crimes on various platforms (Godoy et al., 2016). The Defense Advanced Research Projects Agency constructed the *Memex* program, which is accessed through a *Tellfinder* or *Domain-specific Insight Graphics* interface, to help its anti-trafficking partners search escort ads and online sexual exploitation content for information; organize information for use in analyzing patterns, trends, and dynamics of victimization (e.g., financial transactions); and determine the scope of the trafficking network in the surface, deep, and dark web using knowledge graphs (DIG, 2016; Sneed, 2015; Szekely et al., 2016). Marinus Analytics created *Traffic Jam*, which trawls online commercial sex ads to locate photos of suspected victims and then uses Amazon Web Services' facial recognition to match them to missing persons (in partnership with National Center for Missing & Exploited Children (NCMEC) or social media accounts. Another facial recognition tool called *idTraffickers* can also match photographs of missing persons with those in online ads using biometric technology (OSRCCTHB, 2020).

The Special Technologies & Applications Office at the FBI uses a tool, *FANTOM* (originally created to examine terrorist relationships), to find patterns in communication data across trafficking suspects and their relationship to victims and solidify intel for their operations (Godoy et al., 2016; Kronfeld, 2020). It is also possible using Spotlight or Traffic Jam to apply linguistics to determine whether the writing style across advertisements can be traced to a particular author—including the victim or the trafficking associate tasked with post them (Couch, 2016). Two tech-based companies in 2013, Palantir Technologies and Salesforce.com (supported by a grant from Google) provided software to develop a multi-modal solution, *The Global Human Trafficking Hotline*, that standardized and aggregated data records for Polaris (U.S.), La Strada International (Europe), and Liberty Asia to share and access (Grothaus, 2013). Hotline specialists use a single dashboard to locate trafficking victims who contact them by mapping the location (Google Maps) to determine the closest NGO and/or LEA resources (Grothaus, 2013; Sneed, 2015). The system is also able to discern trafficking patterns that could ultimately help LEAs, NGOs, and legislators in understanding how best to fight this crime by sharing each victim's story (e.g., locations used for trafficking, number of buyers, names and demographics of controllers and associates) to determine the most effective strategies and policies (Grothaus, 2013; Sneed, 2015).

Victims may obtain help by texting *BeFree*, which uses an SMS-based program developed by Polaris, Twilio, Thorn, and Salesforce, connecting them with the National Center for Missing and Exploited Children hotline (Petronzio, 2013).

REFERENCES

Adams, W., Owens, C., & Small, K. (2010). Effects of Federal legislation on the commercial sexual exploitation of children. *Juvenile Justice Bulletin*. Office of Juvenile Justice and Delinquency Prevention, U.S. Department of Justice. https://www.ojp.gov/pdffiles1/ojjdp/228631.pdf

Alliance to End Slavery & Trafficking/ATEST. (2017). *Summary of the Trafficking Victims Protection Act (TVPA) and Reauthorizations FY2017*. https://endslaveryandtrafficking.org/summary-trafficking-victims-protection-act-tvpa-reauthorizations-fy–2017–2/.

Banks, D., & Kyckkelhahn, T. (2011). *Characteristics of Suspected Human Trafficking Incidents, 2008–10*. Washington, DC: U.S. Department of Justice, Office of Justice Programs, Bureau of Justice Statistics. http://www.bjs.gov/content/pub/pdf/cshti0810.pdf.

Belser, P. (2005). *Forced Labor and Human Trafficking: Estimating the Profits*. Geneva: International Labour Office. https://ecommons.cornell.edu/bitstream/handle/1813/99623/Forced_labor_no__17_Forced_labour_and_human.pdf?sequence=1&isAllowed=y.

Belser, P., de Cock, M., Mehran, F. (2005). *An ILO Minimum Estimate of Forced Labour in the World*. Geneva: International Labour Office. https://www.ilo.org/wcmsp5/groups/public/---ed_norm/---declaration/documents/publication/wcms_081913.pdf.

Bendtsen, S. (2019). *States' Laws Say "kids Are Not Prostitutes." So Why Are They Still Being Punished?* https://sharedhope.org/2019/12/03/states-laws-say-kids-are-not-prostitutes-so-why-are-they-still-being-punished/.

Berman, H. (2008). William Wilberforce Trafficking Victims Protection Reauthorization Act of 2008. *Congressional Record, 154(185)*, 20–36.

Bouché, V. (2015). *A Report on the Use of Technology to Recruit, Groom, and Sell Domestic Minor Sex Trafficking Victims*. https://www.thorn.org/wpcontent/uploads/2015/02/Survivor_Survey_r5.pdf.

Bouché, V. (2017). *An Empirical Analysis of the Intersection of Organized Crime and Human Trafficking in the United States*. https://www.ojp.gov/pdffiles1/nij/grants/250955.pdf.

Briggs, P., Simon, W.T., & Simonsen, S. (2011). An exploratory study of internet-initiated sexual offenses and the chat room sex offender: Has the internet enabled a new typology of sex offender? *Sexual Abuse: A Journal of Research and Treatment, 23(1)*, 72–91.

Bryan, C. (2014). *What judges need to know about human sex trafficking: Screening and assessment and matching to empirically based treatment*. NCJFCJ Annual Conference, Chicago, Ill.

Carpenter, A., & Gates, J. (2016). *The Nature and Extent of Gang Involvement in Sex Trafficking in San Diego County.* www.ncjrs.gov/App/Publications/abstract.aspx?ID=272017.

Chiu, M.M., Seigfried-Spellar, K.C., & Ringenberg, T.R. (2018). Exploring detection of contact vs. fantasy online sexual offenders in chats with minors: Statistical discourse analysis of self-disclosure and emotion words. *Child Abuse & Neglect, 81,* 128–138.

Clawson, H.J., Dutch, N., Solomon, A., & Grace, L.G. (2009). *Human Trafficking into and within the United States: A Review of the Literature.* U.S. Department of Health and Human Services. https://aspe.hhs.gov/report/human-trafficking-and-within-united-states-review-literature.

Couch, C. (2016, September 21). *How Artificial Intelligence Can Stop Sex Trafficking.* http://www.pbs.org/wgbh/nova/next/tech/sex-trafficking/.

Currier, A & Feehs, K.E. (2019). *2018 Federal Human Trafficking Report. Report from the Human Trafficking Institute.* Accessed at https://www.traffickingmatters.com/2018-federal-human-trafficking-report/.

Curtis, R., Terry, K., Dank, M., Dombrowski, K., & Khan, B. (2008). The commercial sexual exploitation of children in New York City: Vol. 1. *The CSEC Population in New York City: Size, Characteristics, and Needs (NCJ 225083).* New York: Center for Court Innovation and John Jay College of Criminal Justice. https://www.ncjrs.gov/pdffiles1/nij/grants/225083.pdf.

Dangor, G. (2021, June 25). *Ruling against Facebook in Sex Trafficking Case Threatens Key Legal Shield for Social Media Platforms.* https://www.forbes.com/sites/graisondangor/2021/06/25/ruling-against-facebook-in-sex-trafficking-case-threatens-key-legal-shield-for-social-media-platforms/?sh=25b6186d3acc.

Dank, M., Khan, B., Downey, P.M., Kotonias, C., Mayer, D., Owens, C., Pacifici, L., & Yu, L. (2014). *Estimating the Size and Structure of the Underground Commercial Sex Economy in Eight Major U.S. Cities.* Retrieved from the Urban Institute website: http://www.urban.org/research/publication/estimating-size-and-structure-underground-commercial-sex-economy-eight-major-us-cities/view/full_report.

Demand Abolition. (2018). *Who Buys Sex: Understanding and Disrupting Illicit Market Demand.* https://www.demandabolition.org/wp-content/uploads/2019/07/Demand-Buyer-Report-July-2019.pdf.

Denton, E. (2016). Anatomy of offending: Human trafficking in the United States, 2006–2011. *Journal of Human Trafficking, 2*(1), 32–62.

de Santisteban, P., del Hoyo, J., Alcázar-Córcoles, M.A., & Gámez-Guadix, M. (2018). Progression, maintenance, and feedback of online child sexual grooming: A qualitative analysis of online predators. *Child Abuse & Neglect, 80,* 203–215.

Development Services Group, Inc. (2014). *Commercial Sexual Exploitation of Children and Sex Trafficking.* Washington, DC: Office of Juvenile Justice and Delinquency Prevention. https://www.ojjdp.gov/mpg/litreviews/CSECSexTrafficking.pdf.

DIG. (2016). *What is DIG.* http://usc-isi-i2.github.io/dig.

Dombrowski, S.C., LeMasney, J.W., Ahia, C.E., & Dickson, S.A. (2004). Protecting children from online sexual predators: Technological, psychoeducational, and legal considerations. *Professional Psychology: Research and Practice, 35(1),* 65–73.

Dubrawski, A., Miller, K., Barnes, M., Boecking, B., & Kennedy, E. (2015). Leveraging publicly available data to discern patterns of human-trafficking activity. *Journal of Human Trafficking, 1(1),* 65–85. Doi: 10.1080/23322705.2015.1015342.

Edwards, R. (2020, December 9). *The Best Parental Control Apps of 2021.* https://www.safewise.com/resources/parental-control-filters-buyers-guide/.

Estes, R.J., & Weiner, N.A. (2001). *The Commercial Sexual Exploitation of Children in the U.S., Canada, and Mexico.* Philadelphia: University of Pennsylvania. https://abolitionistmom.org/wp-content/uploads/2014/05/Complete_CSEC_0estes-weiner.pdf.

Farley, M., Bindel, J., & Golding, J.M. (2009). *Men Who Buy Sex: Who They Buy and What They Know.* Prostitution Research & Education. http://www.prostitutionresearch.com/c-prostitution-research.html.

Farley, M., Golding, J., Matthews, E., Malamuth, N., & Jarrett, L. (2017). Comparing sex buyers with men who do not buy sex: New data on prostitution and trafficking. *Journal of Interpersonal Violence, 32(23),* 3601–3625. Doi: 10.177/0886260515600874.

Farley, M., Macleod, J. Anderson, A. & Golding, J. (2011). Attitudes and social characteristics of men who buy sex in Scotland. *Psychological Trauma: Theory, Research, Practice and Policy, 3–4,* 369–383. Doi: 10.1037/a0022645.

Feehs, K., & Wheeler, A.C. (2021). *The 2020 Federal Human Trafficking Report.* https://www.traffickinginstitute.org/wp-content/uploads/2021/06/2020-Federal-Human-Trafficking-Report-Low-Res.pdf.

Ferguson, D. (2016). *Law enforcement, Native Communities focus on sex trafficking prevention training.* https://www.argusleader.com/story/news/crime/2016/08/27/law-enforcement-native-communities-focus-sex-trafficking-prevention-training/89273822/

Finkenauer, J.O. (2019). Human trafficking, modern day slavery and organized crime. In J.B. Clark and S. Poucki (eds.), *The Sage Handbook of Human Trafficking and Modern Day Slavery* (pp. 215–231). London: Sage Publications. Doi: 10.4135/9781526436146.n11

Find Law. (2019). *What is the Mann Act?* https://criminal.findlaw.com/criminal-charges/what-is-the-mann-act.html.

Finklea, K.M., Fernandes-Alcantara, A.L., & Siskin, A. (2015). *Sex trafficking of children in the United States: Overview and issues for Congress.* https://sgp.fas.org/crs/misc/R41878.pdf

Fisher, T. (2012). Traffic stop: How the United States can improve its efforts to halt sex trafficking. *Journal of International and Comparative Law, 2(2),* 1–37.

Franchino-Olsen, H. (2021). Vulnerabilities relevant for commercial sexual exploitation of children/domestic sex trafficking: A systematic review of risk factors. *Trauma, Violence, & Abuse, 22(1),* 99–111.

Frank, M.J., & Terwilliger, G.Z. (2015). Gang-controlled sex trafficking. *Virginia Journal of Criminal Law, 3*, 342–434. http://sharedhope.org/wp-content/uploads/2015/08/Gang-Sex-Trafficking-Article.pdf.

Ferguson, D. (2016, August 27). Law enforcement, Native Communities focus on sex trafficking prevention training. *Argus Leader.* https://www.argusleader.com/story/news/crime/2016/08/27/law-enforcement-native-communities-focus-sex-trafficking-prevention-training/89273822/.

Gerassi, L. (2015). From exploitation to industry-definitions, risks, and consequences of domestic sexual exploitation and sex work among women and girls. *Journal of Human Behavior in the Social Environment, 25*, 591–605. Doi: 10.1080/10911359.2014.991055.

Gies, S., Bobnis, A., Cohen, M., & Malamud, M. (2019). Safe harbor laws: Changing the legal response to minors involved in commercial sex, phase 1. *The Legal Review.* https://www.ncjrs.gov/pdffiles1/ojjdp/grants/253146.pdf.

Godoy, S., Sadwick, R., & Baca, K. (2016). *Shedding Light on Sex Trafficking: Research, Data, and Technologies with the Greatest Impact.* https://innovation.luskin.ucla.edu/wp-content/uploads/2019/03/Shedding_Light_on_Sex_Trafficking.pdf.

Gotch, K. (2016). Preliminary data on a sample of perpetrators of domestic trafficking for sexual exploitation: Suggestions for research and practice. *Journal of Human Trafficking, 2(1),* 99–109.

Gragg, F., Petta, I., Bernstein, H., Eisen, K., & Quinn, L. (2007). *New York Prevalence Study of Commercially Sexually Exploited Children.* A WESTAT Report prepared for the New York State Office of Children and Family Services. http://www.ocfs.state.ny.us/main/reports/csec-2007.pdf.

Greenbaum, V.J. (2014). Commercial sexual exploitation and sex trafficking of children in the United States. *Current Problems in Pediatric and Adolescent Health Care, 44,* 245–269. Doi: 10.1016/j.cppeds.2014.07.001.

Greenbaum, J. (2018). Child sex trafficking and commercial sexual exploitation. *Advances in Pediatrics, 65,* 55–70.

Gregorio, H.C. (2015). More than "johns," less than traffickers: In search of just and proportional sanctions for buyers of sex with trafficking victims. *New York Law Review, 90,* 626–670.

Grothaus, M. (2013, May 14). How Google is fighting sex trafficking with big data. *Fast Company.* https://www.fastcompany.com/3009686/how-google-is-fighting-sex-trafficking-with-big-data.

Hardy, V.L., Compton, K.D., & McPhatter, V.S. (2013). Domestic minor sex trafficking. *Affilia, 28,* 8–18. Doi: 10.1177/0886109912475172.

Human trafficking state laws. https://www.ncsl.org/research/civil-and-criminal-justice/human-trafficking-laws.aspx

Institute of Medicine and National Research Council. (2013). *Confronting Commercial Sexual Exploitation and Sex Trafficking of Minors in the United States.* Washington, DC: The National Academies Press. https://ojjdp.ojp.gov/sites/g/files/xyckuh176/files/pubs/243838.pdf.

International Labour Organization. (2005). *A Global Alliance Against Forced Labour. Global Report under the Follow-up to the ILO Declaration on Fundamental Principles and Rights at Work.* Geneva. https://www.ilo.org/wcmsp5/groups/public/---ed_norm/---declaration/documents/publication/wcms_081882.pdf.

International Labour Organization. (2014). *Profits and Poverty: The Economics of Forced Labour.* https://www.ilo.org/wcmsp5/groups/public/---ed_norm/---declaration/documents/publication/wcms_243391.pdf ISBN: 9789221287810. 9789221287827.

International Labour Organization and Walk Free Foundation. (2017). *Global Estimates of Modern Slavery.* https://www.ilo.org/wcmsp5/groups/public/---dgreports/---dcomm/documents/publication/wcms_575479.pdf. ISBN 978-92-2-130132-5.

Janson, L. (2013). *Our great hobby: An analysis of online networks for buyers of sex inIllinois.* https://www.caase.org/wp-content/uploads/2020/06/OurGreatHobby.pdf

Jimenez, M., Jackson, A.M., & Deye, K. (2015). Aspects of abuse: Commercial sexual exploitation of children. *Current Problems Pediatric Adolescent Health Care, 45,* 80–85. Doi.org/10.1016/j.cooeds, 2015.02.003.

Just Facts. (2022). *Be informed: Sex trafficking.* https://www.justfacts.com/sexuality

Kiensat, J., Lakner, M., & Neulet, A. (2014). Role of female offenders in sex trafficking organizations. Regional Academy on the United Nations (RAUN). http://www.raun.org/uploads/4/7/5/4/47544571/the_role_of_female_offenders_in_sex_trafficking_organizations.pdf.

Kirwan, G., & Power, A. (2012). Online child predators: Does internet society make predation easy? In *The Psychology of Cyber Crime: Concepts and Principles* (pp. 133–152). Hershey, PA: Information Science Reference.

Konrad, K., Firk, C., & Uhlhaas, P. J. (2013). Brain development during adolescence: Neuroscientific insights into this developmental period. *Deutsches Ärzteblatt International, 110*(25), 425–431.

Kosloski, A., Bontrager Ryon, S., & Roe-Sepowitz, D. (2017). Buying the girl next door: A study of solicitations for sex online. *Family & Intimate Partner Violence Quarterly, 9*(4), 53–59.

Krell, A. (2021). *Woman Who Was a Victim of Sex Trafficking at Age 14 Sues Backpage.com and Salesforce.* https://www.thenewstribune.com/news/local/article248174885.html.

Kronfeld, M.J. (2020). Trafficking, technology and public health: The malignant malady of modern slavery. In P. Murthy and A. Ansehl (eds.), *Technology and Global Public Health* (pp. 219–240). Switzerland: Springer Nature.

Latonero, M. (2011). *Human Trafficking Online: The Role of Social Networking Sites and Online Classifieds.* https://technologyandtrafficking.usc.edu/files/2011/09/HumanTrafficking_FINAL.pdf.

Levy, A.F. (2018). *United States Federal Courts' Continuing Failure to Order Mandatory Criminal Restitution for Human Trafficking Victims.* https://www.htlegalcenter.org/wp-content/uploads/2018-Mandatory-Restitution-Report.pdf.

Love, M.C. (2021). *Restoration of Rights Project.* https://ccresourcecenter.org/state-restoration-profiles/50-state-comparisonjudicial-expungement-sealing-and-set-aside/.

Malaga, R.A. (2015). Using nuisance telephone denial of service to combat online sex trafficking. *Open Journal of Information Systems, 2*(1), 1–7. https://www.ronpub.com/OJIS_2015v2i1n01_Malaga.pdf.

Manchester, J. (2018). *Backpage.com Pleads Guilty to Human Trafficking.* https://thehill.com/policy/technology/382962-backpagecom-pleads-guilty-to-human-trafficking.

Mapp, S.C. (2020). Domestic sex trafficking. In J. Winterdyk and J. Jones (eds.), *The Palgrave International Handbook on Human Trafficking* (pp. 1–18). Cham, Switzerland: Palgrave Macmillan. Doi: 10.1007/978-3-319-63192-9_21-1.

Maras, M-H. (2017). Online classified advertisement sites: Pimps and facilitators of prostitution and sex trafficking? *Journal of Internet Law, 21*(5), 17–21.

Marinova, N.K., & James, P. (2012). The tragedy of human trafficking: Competing theories and European evidence. *Foreign Policy Analysis, 8*(3), 231–253.

Marcus, A., Horning, A., Curtis, R., Sanson, J., & Thompson, E. (2014). Conflict and agency among sex workers and pimps: A closer look at domestic minor sex trafficking. *The Annals of the American Academy of Political and Social Science, 653,* 225–246. Doi: 10.1177/0002716214521993.

Mattar, M.Y. (2011). Interpreting judicial interpretations of the criminal statutes of the Trafficking Victims Protection Act: Ten years later. *American University Journal of Gender Social Policy and Law, 19*(4), 1247–130.

Miller-Perrin, C., & Wurtele, S.K. (2017) Sex trafficking and the commercial sexual exploitation of children. *Women & Therapy, 40*(1–2), 123–151. Doi: 10.1080/02703149.2016.1210963.

Milrod, C., & Monto, M.A. (2012) The hobbyist and the girlfriend experience: Behaviors and preferences of male customers of internet sexual service providers. *Deviant Behavior, 33*(10), 792–810, Doi: 10.1080/01639625.2012.70750.

Mitchell, K., Finkelhor, D., & Wolak, J. (2010). Conceptualizing juvenile prostitution as child maltreatment: Findings from the National Juvenile Prostitution Study. *Child Maltreatment, 15*(1), 18–36.

Monto, M., & Milrod, C. (2014). Ordinary or peculiar men? Comparing the customers of prostitutes with a nationally representative sample of men. *International Journal of Offender Therapy and Comparative Criminology, 58*(7), 802–820.

Morris, M., Dahl, B., Breslin, L., Berger, K., Finger, A., & Alejano-Steele, A., (2012). *Prostitution and Denver's criminal justice system: Who pays?* https://combathumantrafficking.org/report-downloads/LCHT-WhoPays_Full.pdf

Motivans, M. (2018). *Federal Prosecution of Human-Trafficking Cases, 2015.* Report from the U.S. Department of Justice Bureau of Justice Statistics. https://www.bjs.gov/content/pub/pdf/fphtc15.pdf.

Murphy, C.J. (2019). *Human Trafficking Restitution Resource Guide for Judges.* https://www.traffickingmatters.com/wp-content/uploads/2019/02/Restitution-Article_Updated-2019-05-WEB.pdf.

National Council of Jewish Women. (2016a). *Fact Sheet: Safe Harbor Laws*. https://www.ncjw.org/wp-content/uploads/2017/07/Fact-Sheet_Safe-Harbor_Updated-2016.pdf.

National Council of Jewish Women. (2016b). *Fact Sheet: Vacatur Laws*. https://www.ncjw.org/wp-content/uploads/2017/07/Fact-Sheet_Vacatur-Laws_Updated-2016.pdf.

Nichols, A. (2016). *Sex Trafficking in the United States: Theory, Research, Policy, and Practice*. New York: Columbia University Press.

O'Brien, J. E., White, K., & Rizo, C. F. (2017). Domestic minor sex trafficking among child welfare-involved youth: An exploratory study of correlates. *Child Maltreatment, 22*, 265–274. Doi: 10.1177/1077559517709995.

O'Connell, R. (2003). *A Typology of Child Cybersexploitation and Online Grooming Practices*. http://image.guardian.co.uk/sys-files/Society/documents/2003/07/17/Groomingreport.pdf.

Office of the Attorney General. (2016). *Attorney General's Annual Report to Congress on U.S. Government Activities to Combat Trafficking in Persons, Fiscal Year 2015*. https://www.justice.gov/humantrafficking/page/file/948601/download.

Office of the Attorney General. (2017, November 17). *Attorney General's Annual Report to Congress on U.S. Government Activities to Combat Trafficking in Persons, Fiscal Year 2016*. https://www.justice.gov/humantrafficking/page/file/1103086/download.

Office of the Attorney General. (2018, April 19). *Attorney General's Annual Report to Congress on U.S. Government Activities to Combat Trafficking in Persons, Fiscal Year 2017*. https://www.justice.gov/humantrafficking/page/file/1103081/download.

Office of the Attorney General. (2020, April 28). *Attorney General's Annual Report to Congress on U.S. Government Activities to Combat Trafficking in Persons, Fiscal Year 2018*. https://www.justice.gov/humantrafficking/page/file/1276166/download.

Office of Juvenile Justice and Delinquency Prevention. (2014). *Commercial Sexual Exploitation of Children and Sex Trafficking*. Washington, DC: OJJDP. https://permanent.fdlp.gov/gpo122626/CSECSexTrafficking.pdf.

Office of the Special Representative and Co-ordinator for Combating Trafficking in Human Beings. (2020). *Leveraging Innovation to Fight Trafficking in Human Beings: A Comprehensive Analysis of Technology Tools*. https://www.osce.org/files/f/documents/9/6/455206_1.pdf.

Office of Victims of Crime. (2017). *OVC Report to the Nation, Fiscal Years 2015–2016*. https://ovc.ojp.gov/sites/g/files/xyckuh226/files/pubs/reporttonation2017/programs-to-combat-human-trafficking.html.

Petronzio, M. (2013). *'BeFree' Text Shortcode Helps Victims of Human Trafficking*. http://mashable.com/2013/03/29/befree-text-shortcode/#FxSOLR2BYqqC.

Polaris Project. (2015a). *Human Trafficking Brief: Safe Harbor*. https://polaris-project.org/sites/default/files/2015%20Safe%20Harbor%20Issue%20Brief.pdf.

Polaris Project. (2015b). *Sex Trafficking in the United States: A Closer Look at U.S. citizen Victims.* https://polarisproject.org/sites/default/files/us-citizen-sex-trafficking.pdf.

Polaris Project. (2017). The typology of modern slavery: Defining sex and labor trafficking in the United States. https://polarisproject.org/wp-content/uploads/2019/09/Polaris-Typology-of-Modern-Slavery-1.pdf

Polaris Project. (2019). *Sex Trafficking in the U.S.: A Closer Look at U.S. Citizen Victims.* https://polarisproject.org/wp-content/uploads/2019/09/us-citizen-sex-trafficking.pdf.

Polaris Project. (2020). *What We Know About How Child Sex Trafficking Happens.* https://polarisproject.org/blog/2020/08/what-we-know-about-how-child-sex-trafficking-happens/.

Raphael, J. (2020). Parents as pimps: Survivor accounts of trafficking of children in the United States. *Dignity: A journal of Sexual Exploitation and Violence, 4*(4), 1–34. https://digitalcommons.uri.edu/cgi/viewcontent.cgi?article=1137&context=dignity.

Raphael, J. & Ashley, J. (2008). *Domestic Sex Trafficking of Chicago Women and Girls.* A Report from the Schiller DuCanto & Fleck Family Law Center, DePaul University College of Law, and the Illinois Criminal Justice Information Authority. https://www.ojp.gov/ncjrs/virtual-library/abstracts/domestic-sex-trafficking-chicago-women-and-girls

Raphael, J., & Myers-Powell, B. (2010). *From Victims to Victimizers: Interviews with 25 Ex-pimps in Chicago.* https://www.ojp.gov/ncjrs/virtual-library/abstracts/domestic-sex-trafficking-chicago-women-and-girls.

Reid, J. A. (2012). Exploratory review of route-specific, gendered, and age-graded dynamics of exploitation: Applying life course theory to victimization in sex trafficking in North America. *Aggression and Violent Behavior, 17,* 257–271. Doi: 10.1016/j.avb.2012.02.005.

Reid, J.A., Huard, J., & Haskell, R.A. (2015). Family-facilitated juvenile sex trafficking. *Journal of Crime & Justice, 38*(3), 361–376.

Reid, J.A., & Piquero, A.R. (2016). Applying general strain theory to youth commercial sex exploitation. *Crime & Delinquency, 62*(3), 341–367.

Roe-Sepowitz, D., Bontrager Ryon, S., Hickle, K., Gallagher, J.M., & Hedberg, E.C. (2016). Invisible offenders: Estimating online sex customers. *Journal of Human Trafficking, 2*(4), 272–280, Doi: 10.1080/23322705.2015.1107711.

Roe-Sepowitz, D., Gallagher, J., Hogan, K., Ward, T., Denecour, N., & Bracky, K. (2017). *A Six-Year Analysis of Sex Traffickers of Minors: Exploring Characteristics and Sex Trafficking Patterns.* Arizona State University, School of Social Work, Office of Sex Trafficking Intervention Research and McCain Institute for International Leadership. https://socialwork.asu.edu/sites/default/files/ASU-Sex-Traffickers-of-Minors-Six-Year-Study-Full-Report-April-2017.pdf.

Roe-Sepowitz, D., Gallagher, J., Hogan, K., Ward, T., Denecour, N. & Bracky, K. (2019). A six-year analysis of sex trafficking of minors: Characteristics and sex trafficking patterns. *Journal of Human Behavior in the Social Environment, 29*, 608–629.

Roe-Sepowitz, D., Gallagher, J., Risinger, M., & Hickle, K. (2015). The sexual exploitation of girls in the United States: The role of female pimps. *Journal of Interpersonal Violence, 30*(16), 2814–2830.

Sanders, T. (2008). Male sexual scripts: Intimacy, sexuality, and pleasure in the purchase of commercial sex. *Sociology, 42*(3), 400–417.

Schulz, A., Bergen, E., Schuhmann, P., Hoyer, J., & Santtila, P. (2016). Online sexual solicitation of minors: How often and between whom does it occur? *Journal of research in Crime and Delinquency, 53*(2), 165–188.

Seto, M.C. (2013). *Internet Sex Offenders.* Washington, DC: American Psychological Association.

Shapiro, L.R. (2021). Corporate liability of hotels: Criminal sanctions for online sex trafficking. *Journal of Internet Law, 24*(5), 3–10.

Shapiro, L.R. & Maras, M-H. (2016). *Multidisciplinary Investigation of Child Maltreatment.* Burlington, MA: Jones & Bartlett Learning.

Shared Hope International. (2017a). *National State Law Survey: Expungement and Vacatur Laws.* https://sharedhope.org/wp-content/uploads/2016/03/NSL_Survey_Expungement-and-Vacatur-Laws.pdf.

Shared Hope International. (2017b). *Internet Safety Guide.* http://sharedhope.org/wp-content/uploads/2017/05/Internet-Safety-Guide-Love-146.pdf.

Shared Hope International. (2018). *Seeking Justice: Legal Approaches to Eliminate Criminal Liability for Child Sex Trafficking Victims.* https://sharedhope.org/wp-content/uploads/2018/08/ANALYSIS-OF-STATUTORY-APPROACHES_ver7.pdf.

Shared Hope International. (2019a). *2019 State Report Cards—Protected Innocence Challenge.* https://sharedhope.org/what-we-do/bring-justice/reportcards/2019-reportcards/.

Shared Hope International. (2019b). *Microblogging Apps.* https://sharedhope.org/wpcontent/uploads/2019/10/Apps-Factsheet.pdf.

Shared Hope International. (2020). *Victim-Offender Intersectionality: A Guide for Criminal Justice Stakeholders.* https://spopy1bvira2mldnj1hd926e-wpengine.netdna-ssl.com/wp-content/uploads/2020/04/SH_Responding-to-Sex-Trafficking-Victim-Offender-Intersectionality2020_FINAL_updatedApril2020.pdf.

Shared Hope International. (2021). *What is Sex Trafficking? FAQs.* https://sharedhope.org/the-problem/faqs/.

Shelton, J., Eakin, J., Hoffer, T., Muirhead, Y., & Owens, J. (2016). Online child sexual exploitation: An investigative analysis of offender characteristics and offending behavior. *Aggression and Violent Behavior, 30*, 15–23.

Shively, M., Kliorys, K., Wheeler, K., & Hunt, D. (2012). *A National Overview of Prostitution and Sex Trafficking Demand Reduction Efforts, Final Report.* https://www.ncjrs.gov/pdffiles1/nij/grants/238796.pdf.

Shively, M., Kuck-Jalbert, S., Kling, R., Rhodes, W., Flygare, C., Finn, P., Tierney, L., Squires, D., & Dyous, C. (2008). *Final Report on the Evaluation of the First Offender Prostitution Program*. U.S. Department of Justice, Office of Justice Programs, National Institute of Justice. https://www.ncjrs.gov/pdffiles1/nij/grants/238796.pdf

Simonite, T. (2017). Microsoft Chatbot Trolls Shoppers for Online Sex. https://www.wired.com/story/microsoft-chatbot-trolls-shoppers-for-online-sex/

Smith, L., Vardaman, S., & Snow, M. (2009). *The National Report on Domestic Minor Sex Trafficking: America's Prostituted Children*. Vancouver, WA: Shared Hope International (SHI). http://sharedhope.org/wp-content/uploads/2012/09/SHI_National_Report_on_DMST_2009.pdf.

Sneed, T. (2015). *How Big Data Battles Human Trafficking*. U.S. News. https://www.usnews.com/news/articles/2015/01/14/how-big-data-is-being-used-in-the-fight-against-human-trafficking.

Sprang, G. & Cole, J. (2018). Familial sex trafficking of minors: Trafficking conditions, clinical presentation, and system involvement. *Journal of Family Violence, 33*(3), 185–195.

Swaner, R., Labriola, M., Rempel, M., Walker, A., & Spadafore, J. (2016). *Youth Involvement in the Sex Trade: A National Study*. Center for Court Innovation. https://www.courtinnovation.org/sites/default/files/documents/Youth%20Involvement%20in%20the%20Sex%20Trade_3.pdf.

Szekely, P., Knoblock, C., Slepicka, J., Philpot, A., Singh, A., Yin, C., Kapoor, D., Natarajan, P., Marcu, D., Knight, K., Stallard, D., Karunamoorthy, S.S., Bojanapalli, R., Minton, S., Amanatullah, B., Hughes, T., Tamayo, J., Flytn, D., Artiss, R., Change, S-F., Chen, T., Hiebel, G., & Ferreira, L. (2016). *Building and Using a Knowledge Graph to Combat Human Trafficking*. https://usc-isi-i2.github.io/papers/szekely15-iswc.pdf.

The Human Trafficking Institute. (2020). *2019 Federal Human Trafficking Report*. https://www.traffickinginstitute.org/wp-content/uploads/2020/05/2019-Federal-Human-Trafficking-Report_High-Res.pdf.

Thorn. (2014). *Sound Practices Guide to Fight Child Sexual Exploitation Online*. http://www.thorn.org/wp-content/uploads/2016/08/Thorn_Sound_Practices_Guide.pdf.

Thorn. (2019). *Survivor Insights: The Role of Technology in Domestic Minor Sex Trafficking*. https://www.thorn.org/wp-content/uploads/2019/12/Thorn_Survivor_Insights_090519.pdf.

Tyler, K.A., & Johnson, K.A. (2006). Trading sex: Voluntary or coerced? The experiences of homeless youth. *Journal of Sex Research, 43*(3), 208–216.

Tyler, K.A., & Beal, M.R. (2010). The high-risk environment of homeless young adults: Consequences for physical and sexual victimization. *Violence and Victims, 25*(1), 101–115. Doi: 10.1891/0886–6708.25.1.101.

United Nations Office on Drugs and Crime. (n.d.). *Human trafficking FA Qs*. https://www.unodc.org/unodc/en/human-trafficking/faqs.html

United Nations Children's Fund (UNICEF). (2014). *Hidden in Plain Sight: A Statistical Analysis of Violence Against Children.* http://www.unicef.org/publications/files/Hidden_in_plain_sight_statistical_analysis_EN_3_Sept_2014.pdfl.

United Nations Office on Drugs and Crime. (2018). *Global Report on Trafficking in Persons.* https://www.unodc.org/documents/data-andanalysis/glotip/2018/GLOTiP_2018_BOOK_web_small.pdf.

United States Department of Justice. (2010). *The National Strategy for Child Exploitation Prevention and Interdiction.* https://www.justice.gov/psc/docs/natstrategyreport.pdf.

United States Department of Justice. (2017). *Key Legislation.* https://www.justice.gov/humantrafficking/key-legislation.

United States Department of State. (2021). *Trafficking in Persons Report.* https://www.state.gov/wp-content/uploads/2021/09/TIPR-GPA-upload-07222021.pdf.

United States Sentencing Commission. (2016). *Sex Trafficking Overview: Statutes, Guidelines, and Restitution Issues.* 2016 Annual National Seminar. https://www.ussc.gov/sites/default/files/pdf/training/annual-national-training-seminar/2016/backgrounder_sex-trafficking.pdf.

Walker, K. (2013). *Ending the Commercial Sexual Exploitation of Children: A Call for Multisystem Collaboration in California.* Sacramento, CA: California Health and Human Services Agency, California Child Welfare Council. http://www.chhs.ca.gov/CWCDOC/Ending%20CSEC%20-%20A%20Call%20for%20Multi-System%20Collaboration%20in%20CA%20-%20February%202013.pdf.

Williamson, C., & Prior, M. (2009). Domestic minor sex trafficking: A network of underground players in the Midwest. *Journal of Child & Adolescent Trauma, 2,* 46–61, Doi: 10.1080/19361520802702191.

Williamson, C., Perdue, T., Belton, L., & Burns, O. (2012). *Domestic Sex Trafficking in Ohio.* A report of the Ohio Human Trafficking Commission. https://www.researchgate.net/publication/260339717_Domestic_Sex_Trafficking_in_Ohio.

Wolak, J., Finkelhor, D., Mitchell, K.J., & Ybarra, M.L. (2008). Online "predators" and their victims: Myths, realities, and implications for prevention treatment. *American Psychologist, 63,* 111–128.

CASES

United States v. Bagley et al. (2011), 10-00244-01/02/04-CR-W-DW (w.D.MO.).

United States v. Bhimani et al. (2021), 3:17-324.

United States v. Charles (2018), 895 F.3d 560.

United States v. Davila (2017), 8:15-cr-00233-GJH-1, 17-4036.

United States v. Dominque (2019), 15-112-SDD-RLB.

United States v. Haverkamp (2020), 18–3735 (2d Cir.).

United States v. Johnson (2020), 948 F.3d 612 (3d Cir.).

United States v. Jungers (2011), 834 F. Supp. 2d 930 (D.S.D).

United States v. Lundquist (2013), F.3d —, No. 11–5379-CR, 2013 WL 4779644, at *12 (2d Cir.)

United States v. Omuro and Lanoce (2014), 3:14-cr-00336.

United States v. Soto-Huarto et al. (2003), 7:03-CR-00341-S3–008

United States v. Tate and Merritt (2020), 3:19-cv-00146-RJC 3:15-cr-00265-RJC-DCK-1.

United States v. Tillman (2020), No. 4:19-cr-06007-SMJ-01.

United States v. Williams (2019), No. 18-4361 (4th Cir.).

9

Online Child Sexual Abuse Material Offenders

DEFINING ONLINE CHILD SEXUAL ABUSE MATERIAL (AKA CHILD PORNOGRAPHY) OFFENSES

The original term for this offense was child pornography and is defined as content portraying sexually explicit activities involving minors (Canadian Centre for Child Protection, Inc., 2016; U.S. Department of Justice, 2020).

DOI: 10.4324/9781003092292-9

To reinforce the fact that crimes of sexual abuse and exploitation of children occurred in the production of the content, the terms *child sexual abuse material* (CSAM), *child sexual exploitation material*, or combination thereof (*child sexual abuse/exploitation material*) are currently used to discuss this offense (Canadian Centre for Child Protection, Inc., 2016; Kloess et al., 2019). However, "child pornography" still appears in U.S. legislation. This chapter will focus on crimes committed by *fantasy-driven cybersexual predators* who use computers to upload/download/exchange CSAM for their own sexual gratification and by *contact-driven online sexual predators* who produce CSAM for personal and financial reasons.

According to U.S. laws, both the luring of a minor into sexual encounters and "production, distribution, importation, reception, or possession of any image of child pornography" are prohibited (U.S. Department of Justice, 2020, para 2). The wording of the current federal statutes (*18 U.S.C. § 2251, 2252, 2260*) for CSAM makes the laws applicable for prosecuting online and offline offenders who live in different states. The most common problem, however, is when the offenders (and victims) live in different parts of the world because to have successful prosecution would require a uniform definition for CSAM and for "minors."

Although desirable from a legal perspective (International Centre for Missing and Exploited Children/ICMEC, 2018), there are three problems in worldwide acceptance of a single CSAM definition.

Problem 1: Most people have never seen CSAM nor do they understand what was involved in producing it (Gillespie, 2018; O'Donnell & Miller, 2007).

In determining whether the depiction constitutes CSAM, many countries indicate that a *reasonable adult* would find it to be *offensive*. Yet, the content of CSAM must be left to one's imagination in terms of its repugnancy because downloading, possessing, and viewing it is in itself illegal,[1] making it theoretically impossible for a jury-eligible citizen to truly understand the heinousness of this crime, which encompasses "rape, abuse, and torture" of children (Gillespie, 2018).

---

[1] The ruling in *R v Bowden* (1999) that downloading indecent images was illegal also applied to law enforcement. To resolve this dilemma, amendments to the wording of the Protection of Children Act by the Sexual Offenses Act 2003 were made allowing the statutory defense for law enforcement to obtain CSAM "for the purposes of the prevention, detection or investigation of crime, or for the purpose of criminal proceedings" (Internet Watch Foundation, 2020). Similar exceptions have been made in Australia for possession of CSAM by law enforcement officers for purposes of investigation and evidence (Krone, 2004).

The reality of producing (and distributing) CSAM requires that an abuser engage in the following actions:

1. locates child victims and uses a series of techniques (i.e., grooming, threats) to remove them from their (actual or believed) place of safety;
2. commits abusive acts—including (but not limited to) forcing them once or multiple times to:
   a. pose in unnatural and uncomfortable ways,
   b. perform masturbation,
   c. watch sexual acts performed live or on video,
   d. have sexual acts performed on them,
   e. perform sexual acts on or with other children, adults, and/or animals,
   f. endure physical abuse (beyond the sexual acts) as part of masochism and/or as punishment for perceived resistance—all of which will scar them emotionally, physically, socially, and psychologically;
3. gaslights the victims into believing they deserved this treatment and/or that they are supposed to engage in these acts (normalizing); and
4. threatens harm to them and/or their loved ones to prevent them from recounting what happened, particularly to law enforcement.

These actions by sexual cyberpredators are themselves crimes in most countries through legislation, such as the *sexual abuse of a minor (penetration)* described in *18 U.S.C. § 2253* for the United States, and could be prosecuted as separate indictments or in conjunction with CSAM. There is also secondary harm (i.e., psychological revictimization) to the child victims knowing that these CSAM exist (or learning about them afterwards) and neither they nor the authorities are able to remove CSAM permanently from offenders' possessions or the Internet where it can be down-loaded, distributed, purchased, and traded in perpetuity (Gillespie, 2018; U.S. Department of Justice, 2020).

> *Problem 2*: The conceptualization of what constitutes child sexual abuse and exploitation material will differ in accordance to the laws in each country in regard to specificity of the legislation in how the terms of "child" and "offensive" are defined (Kloess et al., 2019).
> A minor is typically differentiated from adults by age, but there is no universal consensus demarcating when a child becomes an adult

(Gillespie, 2018). The U.S. defines a "minor child" as being under age 18 (*18 U.S.C. § 2256* Definitions), but the victim's actual age is not always known. Therefore, the police use a digital forensics analysis on the images to estimate the age of those victims who have not been previously identified in the Child Abuse Image Database. It is usually easier to determine that the portrayed victims are "children" when the physical signs indicate they are prepubescent, whereas even medical experts struggle to determine ages of victims who are postpubescent or sexually mature (Gillespie, 2018; Kloess et al., 2019; National Center for Missing & Exploited Children/NCMEC, 2017; Wells et al., 2007).

Consistent with the U.S. definition of children as being under 18, *Article 1 of the United Nations Convention on the Rights of the Child* (UNCRC, 1989), a legally binding international agreement that determined the scope of protecting children's rights (e.g., to be free from sexual exploitation), was confirmed by its member countries.[2] *Article 9(c)* by *The Council of Europe Convention on Cybercrime* (2001, entered into force in 2007) also agreed to the "under 18" definition, but allowed its contracting parties (e.g., Switzerland) to lower the age to 16.[3] Similarly, the *Directive 2011/92/EU* of the European Parliament and of the Council of the European Union on combatting the sexual abuse and sexual exploitation of child and child pornography in *Article 2 (a)* also used the "under age 18" framing (Astinova, 2013); however, *Article 2 (b)* permitted its member states to determine their own national law for the minimum age of sexual consent (e.g., 14 in Hungary, Germany, Austria, Italy, and Portugal, 15 in Czech Republic). The rationale is that citizens can make sexual consent decisions at a younger age than they can understand the consequences of agreeing to being photographed or filmed and thus must be protected from sexual exploitation. Yet, this does not ensure that underage girls will not be sexually exploited, pressured into having sexual relations, and/or forced to marry, particularly when pregnant as the result of rape or incest (Tahirih Justice Center, 2020).

Also, allowing countries to have discrepant legislation for the age of being a child for CSAM purposes versus minimal legal age for sexual

---

[2] The U.S. signed the Convention on the Rights of the Child in 1995 and had signed and ratified the Optional Protocol on the sale of children, child prostitution, and child pornography (Unikowski, 2019).

[3] The U.S. signed and ratified the Council of Europe's Convention on Cybercrime (Unikowski, 2019).

consent and even for marriage complicates the prosecution of CSAM across jurisdictions (Pew Research Center, 2016). For example, a country may have legislation allowing a girl, who cannot legally consent to engage in sex, to be married nonetheless without adverse consequences for the spouse, such as statutory rape charges (Pew Research Center, 2016; Tahirih Justice Center, 2020). Yet, the husband's photographing of her in alluring poses—even when fully clothed—constitutes CSAM (and exceptions should not be made). The *Directive* also dictates consequences for crimes delineated in *Articles 3* (sexual abuse), *4* (sexual exploitation), and *5* (child pornography) that rely on whether the victim reached the minimum legal age of sexual consent.

Consider *Article 4 (3)* which states that the maximum imprisonment for coercion of a child to participate in pornographic performances is 8 years *if under the age of sexual consent*, but 5 years *if over that age*. There are no justifications to support the upward/downward adjustments to the punishment for the same crime due to a victim's age. Any modification negates the fact that the victim's rights were violated because coercion by definition precludes consent. It also assumes the degree of harm to the child is ameliorated simply because the victim is considered capable of giving sexual consent (O'Donnell & Miller, 2007).

Another concept, determining whether the material being viewed is *offensive*, is also problematic as it relies on a subjective evaluation rather than objective assessment (Gillespie, 2018; Wells et al., 2007). The *Protection of Children Act 1978* in the U.K. used the term "indecent" material, which at the time was held at a lower standard within obscenity laws (Clark & Hyland, 2007; Gillespie, 2018). Similarly, *18 U.S.C. § 2256* in the U.S. determines child pornography by "lascivious exhibition of the genitals or pubic area," which had been interpreted by Courts to mean "sexually suggestive" (*United States v Dost*), as a "sexual object" (*United States v Wiegand*), and in a "sexualized context" (*United States v. Rayl*). For laws against CSAM to be effective, they cannot be overly broad or at odds with their intended purpose of protecting children from abuse and exploitation from its production, possession, and distribution (Gillespie, 2018). Additionally, without an agreed upon, universal definition, it is almost impossible to prosecute online CSAM offenders given the number of jurisdictions in which the images were produced, viewed, and/or distributed (Astinova, 2013; U.S. Department of Justice, 2020). Yet the need to do so is essential given today's advanced technology. Online CSAM offenders can (re)produce child sexual abuse images easily, almost undetectably, due to accessible digital production of photographs and video on smart phones and computers that allow private sharing through mobile apps, texts, gaming devices, Internet forums and chatrooms, file-sharing sites, social networking websites, and livestreaming worldwide (Kloess et al., 2019; U.S. Department of Justice, 2020).

Problem 3: Standards differ in each country due to variations in the cultural, social, and moral beliefs of the citizens (Astinova, 2013).

Each nation decides the specifics regarding whether the subject in the image must be an actual child, the act must be real, and which modes of portrayal should be prohibited, although these three issues are interconnected. It is generally accepted that real children are harmed and exploited in the production, possession, and distribution of child sexual abuse/exploitation material (Gillespie, 2018). Disagreement, on the other hand, occurs in regard to whether artificial (e.g., morphed child face imposed on body) and virtual (e.g., drawings, cartoons) representations of children (under 18 or younger than the age of sexual consent) engaged in sexual actions should also be prohibited due to their potential to cause harm (albeit indirectly). The U.S. requires the child to be "real" for the offender to be charged with child sexual abuse/exploitation material. In *Ashcroft vs. the Free Speech*, the Court struck down the original wording for the Child Pornography Prevention Act of 1996 that allowed depiction of a virtual child to qualify as CSAM. The exception to the "actual child" requirement is morphing (Prosecutorial Remedies and Other Tools to end the Exploitation of Children Today Act/PROTECT of 2003), in which an image of a real child's face is superimposed on the body of an adult (which may be further modified to appear childlike), and it is illegal in the U.S., Canada, and the U.K. because having one's image used in this (obscene) sexually exploitative manner violates both the privacy and dignity of a child (Astinova, 2013; Gillespie, 2018; Steinberg, 2019). Australia uses the broadest interpretation as it includes fictitious children portrayed in morphed and pseudo-photographs (i.e., digitally altered and sexualized images; combined pictures that superimpose body parts to appear together; and montage) and those described in text (see *Dodge v. R*, 2002) in its classification of child sexual abuse/exploitation material (Krone, 2004).

Each nation further decides whether classification as CSAM applies depending upon the format of the representations—visual, audio, drawn/

computer-generated, and text (Gillespie, 2018). The Optional Protocol on the Sale of Children (OPSC), Child Prostitution and Child Pornography at the 1996 convention entered into force in 2002, is upheld in 2019 by 179 countries. Article 2(c) of the OPSC indicated child sexual abuse/exploitation material represented "by whatever means," which would include all four types and obviously not require a "real" child be involved (according to iii, can be realistic images of non-existent child engaged in the conduct), however, most countries (e.g., United States) restrict child sexual abuse/exploitation material to visual formats (Astinova, 2013; Gillespie, 2018). Australia (Crimes Act 1900 sections 64 and 65) and Canada (Government of Canada, 2020; Criminal Code R.S.C. 1985, c. C-46, section 163.1) have legislation that prosecutes online CSAM offenders who use audio, text, visual, or digital depictions of children—defined by these jurisdictions as under 16 and under 18, respectively (Krone, 2004). The U.K. prosecutes virtual representations in drawings and cartoons through the Coroners and Justice Act (2009), rationalizing that exposure to this material of an imaginary child is harmful to children (Gillespie, 2018). Reasons given for not prosecuting audio materials as CSAM stems from the difficulty most people have in differentiating between actual sounds emanating from sexually abused children and imitated ones (Astinova, 2013; Gillespsie, 2017). Similarly, international laws and enforcement of prohibition against CSAM have failed to include written materials—alone or alongside "legal" photographs—that promote abuse against children, particularly when it is (loosely) disguised as artistic expression covered under the First Amendment (Gillespie, 2018).

TYPICAL ONLINE CSAM OFFENDERS

According to official statistics and self-report studies (Adams & Flynn, 2017; Burgess et al., 2008; Burke et al., 2002; Frei et al., 2005; Henshaw et al., 2017; McCarthy, 2010; NCMEC, 2017; O'Brien & Webster, 2007; Seto, 2013; Shelton et al., 2016; Siegfried et al., 2008; U.S. Sentencing Commission, 2019; Webb et al., 2007; Wolak et al., 2005; Wortley & Smallbone, 2006), the typical online CSAM offender is White (79%–92.2%); male (92.7% to 100%); aged 26–40 (46%–86%); single, never-married (41%–63.3%); and college educated (77%–82.1%). CSAM offenders' relationships are rarely described as involving romantic or cohabiting relationships, being married, or having a family, all of which is indicative of interpersonal functioning deficits, including intimacy avoidance, inadequate social skills, and disinterest in adult socialization (Shelton et al., 2016; Webb et al., 2007).

It is also not uncommon for CSAM offenders to have cognitive and emotional disorders (i.e., cognitive distortions; lack of victim empathy; increased fantasy; and under assertiveness) allowing them to rationalize their behavior as justification to continue offending (Eke et al., (2011; Kirwan & Power, 2012; Laulik et al., 2007; Reijnen et al., 2009). Three types of cognitive distortions facilitate their engagement in this online offense:

1. children enjoy sexual activities—sex is a natural and healthy aspect of their lives;
2. children are willing participants—they are learning about sexuality "safely" through adult-led guidance; and
3. children are "disposable objects"—viewing of the images in itself is not abusive or harmful.

Further, the reasoning by CSAM offenders is that if there is any harm to children portrayed in the images, it would be the responsibility of the producers not them because they fail to acknowledge product demands regulate the flow of supply (Burke et al., 2002; Howitt & Sheldon, 2007; Kirwan & Power, 2012).

CSAM offenders may have a paraphilic disorder, even if they were never officially diagnosed. Diagnosis requires that the person with atypical sexual interests either be personally distressed by these interests or their desires/behaviors involve harm resulting in another person's death, injury, or psychological distress or involve partners who cannot or do not consent (American Psychiatric Association/APA, 2013a). According to the DSM-5 (APA, 2013b), Paraphilic Disorders (PD) refer to "any intense and persistent sexual interest other than sexual interest in genital stimulation or preparatory fondling with phenotypically normal, physiologically mature, consenting human partners." One classification of PD, Paraphilic Coercive Disorders (i.e., Voyeuristic,[4] Exhibitionistic,[5] Frotteuristic,[6] Sexual Sadism[7]), involves sexual arousal in response to coerced or non-consenting sexual behavior. A second classification of PD, Pedophilic Disorder, which involves anomalous target preferences, is defined as "recurrent, intense sexually arousing fantasies, sexual urges, or behaviors involving sexual activities with a prepubescent child or children (generally aged 13 years and younger)."

---

[4] Refers to obtaining sexual pleasure from observing unclothed people and those engaging in sexual activity.
[5] Refers to act of exposing genitals to non-consenting people.
[6] Refers to the act of rubbing genitals against a non-consenting person for sexual pleasure resulting in orgasm.
[7] Refers to obtaining sexual excitement and orgasm from inflicting physical or psychological pain on another.

ONLINE CSAM OFFENDERS' MOTIVES AND METHODS

As shown in Figure 9.1, the motives of online CSAM offenders can be conceptualized along a continuum from situational to preferential (Beech et al., 2008; Lanning, 2010; Merdian et al., 2013; Wortley & Smallbone, 2006). Child sexual cyberpredators victimize minors because they are easily controlled, manipulated, subdued, and available, whereas Pedophiles prefer children as their sexual partners. The motives of the three types of CSAM offenders—producers, distributors, and collectors—sometimes overlap because the categories are not exclusive; for example, producers can also be collectors and/ or distributors and collectors can also be distributors (Burgess & Hartman, 2005; Elliott & Beech, 2009; Krone, 2004). The motives of producers are deliberate due to their deviant sexual interests in children or in general (e.g., engage in pseudosexual contact or online conversation/role-play; exhibitionists; perverted pleasure from harming children), whereas the motives of distributors are opportunistic, commercial exploitation as they seek financial gain (NCEMC, 2017). Collectors' prurient motives in seeking sexually explicit images for their own gratification due to attraction to children (deliberate) or indiscriminately to whomever is available (opportunistic).

Online CSAM offenders may be involved in one or more methods of producing, distributing, and collecting images through a variety of Internet mechanisms (Shapiro, 2020; Wortley & Smallbone, 2012), including emails, e-groups, discussion/newsgroups, web cams, web pages/websites, chat

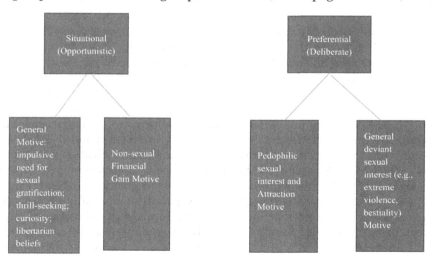

Figure 9.1 Motives of online CSAM offenders.

rooms, bulletin board systems, peer-to-peer networks (PPN), or Internet relay chat. Table 9.1 describes the method for different categories of CSAM offenders (Krone, 2004; McCarthy, 2010; Merdian et al., 2013; NCMEC, 2017; O'Donnell & Milner, 2007). The five subcategories of *producers* engage in the highest level of networking in order to directly and actively engage in sexual abuse and exploitation of children, including finding, grooming, maltreating, threatening, and recording for personal use and/or sale. The four subcategories of *distributors* are responsible indirectly for the sexual abuse and exploitation of children by trafficking CSAM and engage in networking as a means to sell their product. The four subcategories of *collectors* contribute indirectly to the abuse and exploitation of children by creating the demand for images that result in harm and by exchanging them through networking channels in a quid pro quo manner that further harms victims.

Male offenders typically use non-familial-related victims to produce CSAM, whereas female offenders (including those working with male offenders) often sexually abuse and exploit their own family members or those under their direct care to produce CSAM (NCMEC, 2017; Seto et al., 2018). Based on the CyberTipline reports, NCMEC (2017) reported that offenders solicit children for producing CSAM by contacting pubescent minors directly online (91% offenders initiating communication; 2% children initiating contact; 6% posted ads or memes; 1% children postings), whereas third-party contacts (74%) are used to find prepubescent minors indirectly (73% communication with other offenders; 13% posting ads; 13% soliciting those with access to children). This difference in online enticement is probably due to the high amount of unsupervised time and unlimited access to the Internet by the adolescents. Webcam child sex tourism emerged as another method for producing pay-per-view specialized CSAM. The customer pays a fee to have the adult perform acts on the child(ren) or directs the child actors to perform specific sexual activities on each other or on the adult (Terre des Hommes, 2013; Varrella, 2017).

CSAM offenders use different online platforms to entice victims, but often stay on one platform (78%) unless they are terminated due to user complaints to ISP or children refuse to continue communication with them (NCMEC, 2017). As part of the grooming process, offenders engage in sexual role-play and conversations through messaging and social media apps and in private chat rooms; requested reciprocal or mutually exchanged sexually explicit images or livestream sites/apps/cams; developing rapport through positive comments, empathy, shared interests, offering goods and financial incentives; providing sexually explicit selfies of themselves and of other children to normalize the concept; and arrangements to meet the child (Gottfried et al., 2020; NCMEC, 2017).

Table 9.1 Online CSAM Method, Offender Category, Description, and Networking

CSAM Method	Offender Category	Description	Interaction with Other Offenders (Networking)
Produce	Online groomers	Groom children through exposure to child porn; initiate sexual relationship;	Varies; physical contact with individual children introduced online or in real life; networking to solicit requests
	Photographers, cam recorders, and home video makers	Create CSAM, including digital and morphing images	
	Private fantasy	Create CSAM fantasy in text or digital format	
	Publishers	Record abuse or induces child to provide selfies	
	Physical/ sexual abusers	Abuse of child using pornography as lure	
Distribute	Advertisers	Obtain CSAM for dissemination purposes; may or may not have sexual interest	Varies; some sites are not secure; solicit for sales
	Hosts of web sites		
	Administrators of web sites		
	Individual traders		
Collect	Secure collectors	Internet only searches on secure and encrypted sites	High networking with members of child porn rings
	Non-secure collectors	Internet searches/purchase/ download/exchange of CSAM on non-secure, and open content sites	High: networking through chat services message boards, PPN
	Browsers/ Lurkers	Response to spam, accidental find but knowingly saves CSAM	None
	Trawlers	Internet searches on openly available browsers	Low networking; online services with no interactive communication tools

TYPICAL ONLINE CSAM VICTIMS

Researchers (Canadian Centre for Child Protection, Inc., 2016; InHope, 2019) examining the demographics of typical victims identified in CSAM reported: 62%–91% are female children (2%–4% have male and female children together), 56%–90% are prepubescent under age 11 (2%–4% are infants and toddlers; 20%–49% are pubescent), and 77%–87% are Caucasian (10% Hispanic, 8%–10% Asian). In order to escape detection, CSAM producers have increasingly been using very young, preverbal minors, including infants and toddlers, who are unable to alert care-givers of their dire circumstances (U.S. Department of Justice, 2020). Vulnerability characteristics of sexually abused and exploited children include being from economically disadvantaged families, with sexual abuse histories, and little to no Internet supervision and restrictions imposed by family (Fanetti et al., 2014).

The Canadian Centre for Child Protection, Inc. (2016, p. 11) uses a four-point scale to determine the severity of child sexual abuse acts appearing in the images—from *sexual posing* (*Level 1*: unclothed; and *Level 2*: focused on genitalia and anus) to *sexual activity and assaults* (*Level 3*: non-penetrative sexual activity and masturbation or explicit, penetrative sexual acts between adults and children; and *Level 4*: extreme acts "involving bestiality, bondage, weapons, defecation/urination, etc."). Table 9.2 shows the proportion of children by age and sex being subjected to posing and abuse in a sample of 33,375 images (Canadian Centre for Child Protection, Inc., 2016). When CSAM portrayed multiple victims and/or offenders, infant/toddler only content was the most actively traded (Seto et al., 2018) and often consisted of explicit and extreme sadistic and violent sexual assaults (Canadian Centre for Child Protection, Inc., 2016). The environment in which CSAM is produced appears to be predominantly "home" (68.7%), particularly with the explicit and extreme sexual activity/assaults, more than "outdoor" (15.3%) or "studio" (10.8%) settings (Canadian Centre for Child Protection, Inc., 2016).

Seto et al. (2018) reported that when only one victim was portrayed in the CSAM (N=1965 images), a higher proportion of infant and toddler victims were shown being abused by familial rather than non-familial offenders (58.9% vs. 41.1%), whereas prepubescent (57.4% vs. 42.6%) and pubescent victims (85.6% vs. 14.4%) were portrayed being abused by non-familial rather than familial offenders. Although most of the CSAM was not traded, three conditions dictated when it was traded (Seto et al., 2018). First, familial (nuclear member) offenders were more likely to trade CSAM than those produced by non-familial (unknown) offenders. Second, CSAM containing images of prepubescent victims were more likely than those

250

Table 9.2 Severity of Abuse Level by Age and Sex of Child Depicted

	Ages of Children			
Severity of Abuse Level	**0–4** (%)	**4–8** (%)	**8–11** (%)	**12–17** (%)
Sexual posing	40.28	44.18	50.35	56.06
Sexual activity and assault	59.72	55.82	49.65	43.94
Total	**926**	**16,953**	**9324**	**6172**
	Sex of Children			
Severity of Abuse Level	**Female** (%)	**Male** (%)	**Both** (%)	
Sexual posing	49.12	40.59	24.75	
Sexual activity and assault	50.88	59.41	75.25	
Total	**27,342**	**5578**	**1119**	

containing images of infant/toddler or pubescent victims to be traded (15.8% vs. 8.9% vs. 2.6%, respectively). Third, cases portraying Level 4 severity abuse content, typically produced by familial offenders, were more likely to be traded than lower-level content.

LAWS FOR PROSECUTING ONLINE CSAM OFFENSES

The laws for CSAM offenses in the United States have undergone refinement over the past 50 years or so. In 1978, the U.S. outlawed manufacturing and commercial distribution of obscene material portraying minors under age 16 (Sexual Exploitation of Children Act). Previously, the *Miller v. California* ruling required a three-prong test to determine obscenity (i.e., appeals to prurient interest; patently offensive; lacks scientific, literary, artistic, or political value), which is not protected by the First Amendment. The Court in *New York v. Ferber* (1982) concluded, consistent with the government's responsibility for protecting children, that prohibiting CSAM distribution did not violate the First Amendment as its production causes harm to children. CSAM was codified in the 1984 Child Protection Act and the age of minors was raised to 18.[8] By 1988, legislation specified use of computers in regard to producing or advertising CSAM (Child Protection and Obscenity Enforcement Act). Moreover, the 1990 ruling in *Osborne v. Ohio*

---

[8] As per 18 U.S.C. § 2257, records of names and ages of actors portrayed in pornographic films must be kept to prove they are of legal age instead of minors.

confirmed that possession and viewing of CSAM contributed to children's exploitation and continuing harm as it serves as a record of their abuse.

Currently, federal laws (*18 U.S. Code § 2251, 2252, 2260*) make it illegal to produce, distribute, import, receive, or possess child pornography images is their various formats—photograph, video, livestream, and digital (Shapiro, 2020; U.S. Department of Justice, 2020). Prosecution of CSAM offenses is judged using the *Dost* test [see **Box 9.1**] to determine whether alleged violations meet the 18 U.S.C. standards. As shown in Table 9.3, the U.S. online CSAM offense statues are consistent with the principles outlined in both the *Lanzorate Treaty* and the *OPSC* (Unikowski, 2019). Criminal liability for CSAM in the U.S. is comprised of four elements: (1) the actus reus of "possessing, importing, distributing, publishing, or otherwise issuing child pornography using a computer"; (2) the mens rea of "knowingly possessing or purposefully importing, distributing, or issuing child pornography"; (3) attendance circumstances include the material portrays child sexual abuse and exploitation; and (4) two harms include that "minors are used to create" it and that CSAM is "disseminated through the Internet to those finding it appealing and stimulating" (Brenner, 2001 as cited in Schell et al., 2007, p. 53).

BOX 9.1 *UNITED STATES V. DOST (1986)*, 636 F. SUPP. 828 – DIST. COURT, SD CALIFORNIA

The defendants (Dost and Wiegand) in the case were being tried for alleged violations of:

- 18 U.S.C. § 2251(a) (using a minor to engage in sexually explicit conduct for the purpose of producing visual depictions of such conduct);
- 18 U.S.C. § 2252(a)(2) (knowing receipt or distribution of visual depictions of minor engaging in sexually explicit conduct); and
- 18 U.S.C. § 371 (conspiracy).

The defendants stipulated to inducing, enticing, and using minor children for the purpose of producing visual depictions of those minors. The government submitted 22 photographs, 21 were of a 14-year-old girl in various supine and sitting poses and the other was of a 10-year-old girl sitting nude on a beach.

The Court had to determine whether the pictures were consistent with the definition in 18 U.S.C. § 2255 of minors engaging in sexually explicit conduct (i.e., actual or simulated)—sexual intercourse (i.e., genital-genital, oral-genital, anal-genital, or oral-anal), whether between same or opposite sex persons; bestiality; masturbation; sadistic or masochistic abuse; or lascivious[9] exhibition of the genitals or pubic area of any person. Consistent with *New York v. Ferber* (1982), the wording of the law was intended by Congress to allow judgment to be at a lower standard than that for obscenity.

To determine whether the images constituted "lascivious exhibition," the Court as the trier of fact employed a criterion in which six possible factors were relevant (aka *Dost* test):

1. "whether the focal point of the visual depiction is on the child's genitalia or pubic area;
2. whether the setting of the visual depiction is sexually suggestive, i.e., in a place or pose generally associated with sexual activity;
3. whether the child is depicted in an unnatural pose, or in inappropriate attire, considering the age of the child;
4. whether the child is fully or partially clothed, or nude;
5. whether the visual depiction suggests sexual coyness or a willingness to engage in sexual activity;
6. whether the visual depiction in intended or designed to elicit a sexual response in the viewer."

The Court did not require that all of the factors be present and suggested other factors may also be relevant; instead, determination was recommended to be made on the basis of the overall content (i.e., combined effect of setting, attire, pose, emphasis on the genitals) and the age of the minor. The Court found the defendants guilty on all counts of the indictment.

---

[9] The amendment in Child Protection Act of 1984 replaced "lewd" (equated with obscene) with "lascivious" as shown here to make it clearer that the obscenity standard does not have to be met for the exhibition to be unlawful. The word substitution allowed the federal law to conform to the Supreme Court's holding in *New York v. Ferber*, 458 U.S. 747, 102 S.Ct. 3348, 73 L.Ed. 2d 1113 (1982).

Table 9.3 U.S. Federal Laws Relevant for Prosecuting Online CSAM Offenses

Category	U.S. Federal Law	Explanation
Lanzorate Treaty/Article 20. Offences concerning child pornography: production; offering/making available; distributing/transmitting; procuring; possessing; knowingly obtaining access to CSAM.	*18 U.S.C. § 2252*—Certain activities relating to material involving the sexual exploitation of minors (possession, distribution, and receipt of child pornography).	Prohibits possession, receipt and transportation of CSAM in interstate or foreign commerce (i.e., U.S. mail, carriers, Internet, computer download of image for storage).
Optional Protocol on the sale of children, child prostitution, and child pornography, Article 3.1(a) (ii)(c): Improperly inducing consent for producing, distributing, disseminating, importing, exporting, offering, selling, or possessing for child pornography	*18 U.S.C. § 2252A*—Certain activities relating to material constituting or containing child pornography.	Prohibits person from advertising, promoting, presenting, distributing, or soliciting through mail or other means of interstate or foreign commerce, including computer, containing CSAM.
	18 U.S.C. § 1466A—Obscene visual representations of the sexual abuse of children.	Prohibits knowing production, distribution, receipt, or possession with intent to distribute obscene visual representations of the sexual abuse of children (includes bestiality, sadistic/masochistic abuse, sexual intercourse and lacks literary, artistic, political, or scientific value)

(Continued)

Table 9.3 (*Continued*) U.S. Federal Laws Relevant for Prosecuting Online CSAM Offenses

Category	U.S. Federal Law	Explanation
Lanzorate Treaty/Article 21. Offences concerning the participation of a child in pornographic performances: recruiting/causing participation; coercing participation; and knowingly attending child performances.	*18 U.S.C. § 2251*—Sexual exploitation of children (production of child pornography).	Prohibits person from attempting or conspiring to persuade, induce, entice, or coerce a minor to engage in sexually explicit conduct for the purposes of producing visual depictions of that conduct or live transmission of it; also prohibits minor self-produced CSAM.
Optional Protocol on the sale of children, child prostitution, and child pornography, Article 3.1 (a) (i)a: in the context of the sale of a child: offering, delivering or accepting, by whatever means, a child for the purpose sexual exploitation	*18 U.S.C. § 2251A*—Selling and Buying of Children.	Also, prohibits parent, guardian, or custodian in control of minor (under 18) from buying, selling, or transferring custody of that minor or knowingly permitting minor to engage in these acts for the purposes of producing child pornography.
	18 U.S.C. § 2260—Production of sexually explicit depictions of a minor for importation into the U.S.	Applies prohibition of § 2251 to anyone outside of the U.S. with intent to import or transmit the visual depiction into the U.S.
Lanzorate Treaty/Article 23. Solicitation of children for sexual purposes: Criminalize intentional communication of adult to meet child.	*18 U.S.C. § 2425*—Use of interstate facilities to transmit information about a minor.	Prohibits transmission of personally identifiable information (PII) about a child under age 16 with the intent to facilitate a criminally punishable sexual activity (including the production of child pornography, per 18 U.S.C. § 2427)

As indicated previously in this chapter, successful prosecution of CSAM across jurisdictions can only occur when the laws in place to prohibit offenders' possession, reception, importation, production, and distribution are the same worldwide. Not all countries are recognized by every member state of the United Nations, but may be considered sovereign states. The United Nations universally recognizes 194 countries—193 member states and one nonmember observer state of Holy See/Vatican (Kershner, 2020).[10] According to the ICMEC (2018, p. 5), however, only 118 out of these 194 UN Interpol member countries had comprehensive legislation to combat CSAM, whereas: (1) 16 do not have any CSAM laws; (2) 51 fail to provide any definition for CSAM; (3) 25 have no laws relevant to technology-based CSAM; (4) 38 do not prohibit CSAM possession, regardless of intent to distribute; and (5) 164 do not require ISP reporting of alleged CSAM.

Canada and the U.K. also have comprehensive CSAM laws that extend the protection of children beyond that recognized in the U.S. since the *Ashcroft* decision. For example, Canadian law (Government of Canada, 2020; Criminal Code, R.S.C. 1985, c. C-46, 163.1) does not require an actual child be depicted (e.g., anime) and prohibits both audio and written materials promoting illegal sexual activity with children (Canadian Centre for Child Protection, Inc., 2016). In the U.K., the *Protection of Children Act* (1978)[11] makes it illegal to take or make an indecent photograph or pseudo-photograph of a child or to distribute or show such photographs,[12] or to possess such photographs with a view to their being distributed or shown, or to publish an advertisement conveying that the advertiser distributes or shows such photographs or intends to do so. Criminal Justice Act (Section 160) prohibits possession of an indecent photograph or pseudo-photograph (i.e., computer-generated) of a child, as well as the "taking, making, distributing, and sharing" of it (Protection of Children Act, section 1, 1999). Consistent with *R v Freeman*, there is no requirement for the "child" to be real, as the defendant was found guilty of possessing and

---

[10] Not all of the UN members recognize Palestine (observer state) or the territories of Taiwan (claimed by China) and Kosovo (claimed by Serbia). The U.S. recognizes 194 UN member states plus Kosovo.

[11] See: https://www.legislation.gov.uk/ukpga/1978/37 (10/16/2020).

[12] Consistent with *R v Bowden* and *R v Jayson* (2002), downloading indecent images of children are considered "making" and *R v Fellows and Arnold* ruling covered distribution of CSAM through the internet.

distributing 3000 drawings of children being raped (*Coroners and Justice Act Section 64, 2009*). Border security agents in Canada, Australia, the U.K., and the U.S. discovered child sex dolls being imported, raising the question of whether these could be classified as child sexual abuse material (see **Box 9.2**).

BOX 9.2   ARE CHILD SEX DOLLS CONSIDERED CSAM?

A. In November 2019, Amazon listed an anatomically correct child sex doll for $559.00 that resembled an 8-year-old girl whose picture was shared by her mother on Facebook. The ad stated: *High quality sexy dolly live dolls for men.*
B. In August 2020, Amazon France removed advertisement of Huaduo 3D TPE sex doll for 384,99 Euros: [Features] oral sex, anal sex, vaginal sex; very realistic, like a girl with real flat breasts; USB heating element; clothes (sexy underwear, random).

In the U.S., the *Curbing Realistic Exploitative Pedophilic Robots* (CREEPER) *Act* was introduced and passed by the House in 2018, but it stalled in the Senate. This means no federal laws currently prohibit the advertising, selling, manufacturing, distributing, importing, or possessing of child sex dolls and robots. CSAM laws would apply to Example A because a real child's likeness was used, but not for Example B which portrays a fictious child (Maras & Shapiro, 2017). However, the advertisement violates the obscenity law as it depicts a "child" posed in explicit sexual positions. Of the 50 states, only Florida, Kentucky, and Tennessee have passed state laws prohibiting possessing and selling (or giving away/distributing) of child sex dolls; whereas trafficking and importing of child sex dolls are only prohibited in Kentucky and advertising and displaying childlike sex dolls, mannequins, and robots are only illegal in Florida. Interestingly, although Alabama does not ban child sex dolls, it prohibits the sale of sex toys (i.e., for stimulation of human genital organs)—which is how these "dolls" are advertised (i.e., male sex toys).

Only three countries—Australia, Canada, and Norway—consider child sex dolls (Examples A and B) to be CSAM because they realistically resemble a minor (under age 18) and are anatomically correct for the purpose of simulating sexual intercourse. It should be noted, however, the orifices of the dolls are not in sync with a child's dimensions, but rather are the size that could accommodate an adult male's penis, including an infant doll whose body resembles a 6-month old. Offenders who possess child sex dolls can be prosecuted under Australia's Combatting Child Sexual Exploitation Legislation Amendment Act 2019 for possession (Sections 273 and 273A.1 of Criminal Code Act 1995) and for using a carriage service to obtain CSAM (Section 474.22A). Importing of child sex dolls is also prohibited (Tier 2 goods). The definition of CSAM in Canadian law (Criminal Code, R.S.C. 1985, c. C-46, 163.1) as "visual representation, whether or not it was made by electronic or mechanical means" allows prosecution of offenders who produce, access, possess, and/or distribute child sex dolls. A 2019 Supreme Court (Sundier, 2019) confirmed that child sex dolls are prohibited as three-dimensional representations CSAM and that explicit sexual images of children (advertisement in Example B) are also illegal under Norway's laws (Penal Code, Part II. Criminal Acts; Chapter 26. Sexual offenses: Section 311. *Depiction of sexual abuse of children or depiction which sexualizes children* AND Section 318. *Prohibition of exhibition*).

Although no specific legislation prohibits importing child sex dolls per se in the U.K., current legislation can be applied as Section 42 of the Customs Consolidation Act 1876 prohibits imported goods that are indecent or obscene. However, no laws prohibit possession nor obtaining child sex dolls manufactured in the U.K., yet photographs of the child sex dolls unclothed and posed (Examples A and B) are prohibited as CSAM under the Protection of Children Act 1978.

The Sentencing Advisory Panel scale, first used in *Regina v. Oliver*, is applied to alleged CSAM cases in the U.K. to "grade" the level of indecent images of children (Sentencing Guidelines Council, 2007, p. 109):

1. images depicting nudity or erotic posing with no sexual activity
2. non-penetrative sexual activity between children, or solo masturbation by a child
3. non-penetrative sexual activity between adult(s) and child(ren)

4. penetrative sexual activity between child(ren) and adult(s)
5. sadism or penetration of, or by, an animal (bestiality)

Current cases rely on this category system for judgment and to determine the length of the sentencing for CSAM offenses.

IMPACT OF ONLINE CSAM ON SOCIETY AND VICTIMS

It is important to recognize that online CSAM causes harm to children in three ways: first, through the initial sexual abuse and exploitation by adults who should have protected them; second, violation to their human dignity and privacy through the production of permanent, irretrievable online records of their victimization; and third, through the perpetual viewing and trading of the online CSAM as it circulates in the world wide web forever (Rogers, 2016; U.S. Department of Justice, 2020). Regardless of how they are labeled (contact or non-contact), online CSAM offenders directly injure children through sexual abuse and exploitation to create the image, including associated acts to ensure this occurred (i.e., grooming, soliciting them, paying traffickers), or indirectly harm them either by creating a "demand" for others to sexually abuse and exploit children to satisfy their own sexual desires and by financially gaining from the sale of such images.

Children portrayed in CSAM suffer physically (e.g., genital and anal pain, soreness, bleeding, cuts, sexually transmitted diseases, and disfigurement), socially (e.g., inappropriate sexual behavior; isolation, awkwardness interactions), emotionally (e.g., anxiety, fear, shame), and psychologically (e.g., helplessness, insecurity, worthlessness, humiliation) for months or even years before they are identified by law enforcement or their exploitation stops because they are considered too old to be desirable (Rogers, 2016; Wortley & Smallbone, 2012). Fanetti et al. (2014) reported sex differences in the types of problems experienced by child victims of sexual exploitation—internalizing for girls (e.g., depression, anxiety) and externalizing for boys (aggression, substance abuse). Not surprisingly, most children also displayed academic problems, experienced disciplinary issues at home and in school, exhibited social maladjustment affecting their ability to make and keep friends, and demonstrated inappropriate sexual behavior (Fanetti et al., 2014: Rogers, 2016; Wortley & Smallbone, 2012). Even when these victims become adults, they have difficulty "establishing and maintaining healthy emotional and sexual relationships" (Wortley & Smallbone, 2012, p. 15) and their fears, shame, and distress intensify when they are recognized by others in public and when they are notified that yet another case is being prosecuted in which their image was among those in evidence (Canadian Centre for Child Protection, Inc., 2016; U.S. Department of Justice, 2020).

The FBI has a program, Child Pornography Victim Assistance that functions as a central repository for child sexual abuse material of identified victims and as notification (DOJ Victim Notification System) alerting victims when their images have been seized as part of a case. There are two victim compensation laws (18 U.S.C. § 2259, 18 U.S.C. § 3663A) available for child victims of CSAM. Until recently, however, even when the government was successful in their prosecution of the CSAM offenders, funds were rarely provided directly to victims. As per *Paroline v. United States.* (2014), the Supreme Court placed the burden on the child victim/adult survivor seeking restitution from damages caused by an offender's possession of CSAM with his/her image to prove the portion that individual caused.

In response to the *Paroline* decision (Cassell & Marsh, 2019), the Amy, Vicky, and Andy Child Pornography Victim Assistance Act (AVAA) of 2018 was introduced and became Public Law No. 115–299 (132 STAT. 4383). It requires restitution from convicted *child pornography producers* to cover full amount of victim's losses (i.e., medical service, physical and occupational therapy/rehabilitation, transportation/housing/child care expenses, lost income, reasonable attorney's fees capped at 15%, and other relevant losses) and for each *child pornography trafficking offender* to pay victims a minimum of $3000. Courts now must assess convicted child pornography offenders up to $17,000 for possession; $35,000 for distribution; and $50,000 for production to be placed in the Child Pornography Victims Reserve, capped at 10 million, and is used for a one-time payment of $35,000 to victims of CSAM trafficking. Society still bears the financial burden when it fails to protect children as the process for obtaining funding is long. There are also associated costs for this crime in terms of law enforcement to find and locate the CSAM offenders and child victims; for criminal justice to prosecute offenders and incarcerate them; and for services required by child victims and adult survivors covered/supplemented under public health care.

Society, by failing to protect children online, suffers harm in a myriad of ways. Children who are exposed to CSAM as part of the grooming process are victims, even if they disengaged from contact with the offender before they were sexually exploited. Requests online by offenders for children to send them nude images or images of them performing a sexual act further victimize children by normalizing this behavior as part of the Internet experience and by changing society's standards of what is "obscene," as demonstrated in commercials using sexualized minors to sell products and in minors engaging in sexting (Gottfried et al., 2020;

Maras & Shapiro, 2017). The victims' struggle to cope with their victimization also impacts their families, who are considered secondary victims to this offense (Burke et al., 2002). Society also loses potential benefits, productivity, and contributions that adult survivors may have provided to their community had they not become debilitated by their lifelong trauma from CSAM offenders.

CYBERSECURITY TACTICS

Online CSAM offenders use security protocols, encryption techniques, and anonymous networks on the Darknet to prevent their members and their collections from being detected by law enforcement (U.S. Department of Justice, 2020). Two main cybersecurity tactics for combating CSAM are private-public coordination and technology. InHope (2019) traced the largest distribution of CSAM to servers hosted in three countries—the Netherlands (37%), Russia (20%), and the U.S. (16%)—and another three countries contribute an additional 14%—Norway (5%), Poland (4%), and Luxembourg (3%)—and the rest are on unidentified network servers.

Private-public coordination. Multiple examples confirm that CSAM can be removed from hosted sites when the child protection communities, comprised of private and public entities, work together (Shapiro, 2020). Box 9.3 describes how these entities work together across multiple jurisdictions to find and prosecute CSAM offenders. Specifically, two techniques have been successful in identifying CSAM, victims and perpetrators, and reducing CSAM. First, due to the expansive role of the Internet (Wortley & Smallbone, 2012), cooperation among multiple jurisdictions is needed as the offenders (and victims) in CSAM are likely be in multiple locations (i.e., cities, states, countries and continents). Second, ISPs must be obligated to detect and remove content quickly while preserving evidence for police (i.e., content data, such as the image, and non-content data related to the user, such as IP address) and most importantly, they must be penalized for failing to comply (International Centre for Missing & Exploited Children, 2018). To shield users and maintain codes of conduct, live chat within virtual communities can implement a system called Real-time Message Filter that is able to screen or block inappropriate content completely prior to it getting posted (Cohen-Almagor, 2013). Laws can be devised to narrow the scope and application of the data retained and protect it from unlawful access, with a timeframe for retention of non-content data (International Centre for Missing & Exploited Children, 2018). The burden of this task should not be placed solely on ISPs, instead there should be cooperation among the private and public sectors that will aid compliance.

BOX 9.3   CASE EXAMPLE: EXAMINING
CSAM LAWS IN THREE COUNTRIES

Operation "Unveiled" by the Brazilian Federal Police's Child Exploitation Unit sent officers on September 9, 2020, to arrest an online CSAM offender, age 50, for the production and global distribution of CSAM. INTERPOL received intelligence on CSAM uploaded to their International Child Sexual Exploitation database from Australian officers in 2017 that later matched uploads from Denmark officers. The INTERPOL Victim Identification Task Force was able to identify, locate, and safeguard the two girls (aged 3 and 10, respectively) victimized in the photos and videos posted on several Darknet child sexual abuse forums, which had hundreds of thousands of registered users. During the arrest, the police seized the alleged offender's devices and found newly created CSAM.

Is child sexual abuse prohibited in Brazil? Child sexual abuse is illegal in Brazil, where the crime occurred, under Law No. 8,069 Article 5 (exploitation) and under Sex Crimes (forcing victim to have sex or other libidinous acts; under age 14 to satisfy the lewdness of another).

Do each of the three involved jurisdictions have CSAM legislation? As shown in Table 9.4, all three countries have legislation prohibiting CSAM production (with definitions of CSAM consistent with ages and acts in this case); reproduction through technology; acquisition, storage and possession; and distribution (Council of the European Union, 2017; Federal Register of Legislation, n.d.; Library of Congress, 2020).

Do these countries hold the Internet Service Provider (ISP) accountable for storage/distribution of CSAM? Only Australia has specific legislation (*Subdivision D Section 474.23A, Subdivision E*) that obligates the ISP and Internet content hosts to work with law enforcement to identify and remove alleged CSAM. The *Children and Adolescents' Act* in Brazil could be used to prosecute ISPs if they fail to prevent access (means and service) to alleged CSAM once notified of its existence by law enforcement or upon their own discovery fail to notify authorities (International Centre for Missing & Exploited Children, 2018). Denmark does not have any laws regarding ISP obligations.

Table 9.4 CSAM Laws as Applied in Brazil, Denmark, and Australia

Country	Specific CSAM Laws	CSAM Defined	Technology-Facilitated CSAM	Acquisition, Storage, Possession of CSAM	Distribution of CSAM
Brazil	Law No. 11,829 (Crimes: Child Pornography)	Article 240 Article 241-C, 241-D, 241-E	Article 241-A	Article 241-B	Article 241, Article 241-A
Denmark	Title 3 – Content-related offenses: Article 9 (Offences related to child pornography)	Section 216(2), Section 222, Section 225, Section 232	Section 226	Section 235(2)	Section 226, Section 235(1)
Australia	Criminal Code Act 1995 (Sexual Crimes Against Children)	Section 473.1	Subdivision D—Offenses relating to use of carriage service for child abuse material; Section 474.22	Section 474.23	Section 474.22 Section 474.23

Technology. CSAM offenders are able to escape detection from law enforcement through a variety of sophisticated techniques. Child sexual abuse and exploitation images can be hidden through offenders' adherence to security protocols, use of encryption to contact child victims and for distribution, and storage on anonymous Dark Internet networks (U.S. Department of Justice, 2020). Offenders believe that they can hide by keeping their contact with others to a minimum and by collecting criminal evidence as entrance into their group. They rely on PPN to share files anonymously with little to no oversight because there are no corporate headquarters, central servers, or content moderators (Solan, 2020). CSAM offenders also attain anonymity by using encryption to prevent ISPs from accessing content, while securing it from being viewed or intercepted by law enforcement.

Technology companies have developed three main tools to detect, block, and remove CSAM—*image hashing*, which converts files to images and compares them to known CSAM images; *web crawlers* (aka search bots that systematically review a webpage and its hyperlinks), and *artificial intelligence* (Eneman, 2010; IWF, 2020; Lee et al., 2020; NetClean, 2019). Client-side scanning (CSS) is an application that uses hashing for images and messages being sent or received by users on encrypted sites to determine if content is illegal (Rosenzweig, 2020). The Child Protection System, a forensic tool created by Child Rescue Coalition, scans file-sharing networks (i.e., peer-to-peer/p2p) and chatrooms to locate downloads of previously seized or reported CSAM of victims under 12 (Solan, 2020). This surveillance software tracks child porn offenders through IP addresses when they are connected to the same Wi-Fi network or to individual devices, even when users move attempt to mask their IP addresses by moving or by using virtual private networks. It also keeps track of legal material that may be used to groom children, including stories offenders show victims to normalize sexual exploitation and abuse (Solan, 2020).

Thorn (2020) developed a beta version called *"Safer"* that uses a combination of hashing and machine learning technology to detect CSAM on websites at a 99% success rate. There are multiple advantages for platforms hosting user-generated content to employ Safer technology, including: (1) it can quickly identify and flag an image (or an altered one) in real-time and at the point of upload; (2) companies will be able to remove CSAM content and report it, compliant with its regulatory obligations, without risking user's privacy; and (3) it serves the dual purposes of reducing the amount of unnecessary human moderator viewing of abuse while also protecting the dignity of victims (Thorn, 2020).

Microsoft's *PhotoDNA*, offered free to Cloudflare customers, law enforcement, and the NCMEC, is a CSAM scanning tool that also uses hashing to identify illegal content and alerts website owners—including social media (e.g., Facebook, Twitter)—when CSAM is discovered (European Union Agency for Law Enforcement Cooperation, 2019). As part of their partnership with Internet Watch Foundation, Microsoft modified PhotoDNA (aka *IWF Hash List*) to identify CSAM in videos and it is being used by Google, Microsoft, Yahoo, Facebook, Twitter, Apple, and Amazon.

IWF (2020) also uses a *proactive web-crawler* that is able to review several million webpages daily searching for CSAM, and its effectiveness is improved by pairing it with an artificial intelligence classifier (deep neural networks for image processing) to prioritize content for review. Google's Content Safety API employs *artificial intelligence* (AI) to narrow the focus for CSAM content (NetClean, 2019). Project Arachnid, a web-crawler enhanced with Microsoft's PhotoDNA technology reviews URLs reported on the Cybertip.ca hotline and directly to Arachnid API and has a 98% success rate (The Canadian Centre for Child Protection, 2016). A new tool, CEASE.ai mimics human vision to scan even unknown photos, identify potential CSAM, and prioritize it (Priebe, 2019). The benefit of using efficient technology is in reducing the need for human content reviewers to review large amounts of CSAM as exposure is traumatizing to them.

Guardians/parents can also use *Engine for Relationships Analysis,* a technology that detects online predators' attempts over time to groom children by "monitoring, analysing and assessing online relationships as they develop" in live chat and instant messenger conversations and alerts parents of potential harmful behavior (Cohen-Almagor, 2013, p. 196). Alternatively, the *Engine for Content Analysis* searches messages for the presence of specific language (i.e., sexual, profane) and private personal information (e.g., address, phone number) that may endanger children's safety (Cohen-Almagor, 2013). Two other web content filtering systems that monitor computer activities (e.g., social networks, games, websites) and limit access by age to sexually explicit material are *Net Nanny* and *Surf Watch* (Cohen-Almagor, 2013).

REFERENCES

Adams, W., & Flynn, A. (2017). *Federal Prosecution of Commercial Sexual Exploitation of Children Cases, 2004–2013.* NCJ 250746, U.S. Department of Justice, Office of Justice Programs, Bureau of Justice Statistics, 2017. https://www.bjs.gov/content/pub/pdf/fpcsecc0413.pdf.

American Psychiatric Association. (2013a). *Paraphilic Disorders.* https://www.psychiatry.org/File%20Library/Psychiatrists/Practice/DSM/APA_DSM-5-Paraphilic-Disorders.pdf.

American Psychiatric Association. (2013b). *Diagnostic and Statistical Manual of Mental Disorders* (5th ed). Arlington, VA: American Psychiatric Association.

Astinova, M. (2013). *The Crime of Child Pornography: European Legislative and Police Cooperation Initiatives.* Thesis, Tilburg University. http://arno.uvt.nl/show.cgi?fid=133077.

Beech A.R., Elliott, I.A., Birgden, A., & Findlater, D. (2008). The Internet and child sexual offending: A criminological review. *Aggressive & Violent Behavior, 13,* 216–28.

Burgess, A.W., & Hartman, C.R. (2005). Sexually motivated child abductors: Forensic evaluation. *Journal of Psychosocial Nursing and Mental Health Services, 43,* 22–28.

Burgess, A.W., Mahoney, M., Visk, J., & Morgenbesser, L. (2008). Cyber child sexual exploitation. *Journal of Psychosocial Nursing and Mental Health Services, 46,* 38–45.

Burke, A., Sowerbutts, S., Blundell, B., & Sherry, M. (2002). Child Pornography and the Internet: Policing and Treatment Issues. *Psychiatry, Psychology and Law, 9,* 79–84. Doi: 10.1375/pplt.2002.9.1.79.

Canadian Centre for Child Protection, Inc. (2016). *Child Sexual Abuse Images on the Internet: A Cybertip.ca Analysis.* http://s3.documentcloud.org/docu/ments/2699673/Cybertip-ca-CSAResearchReport-2016-En.pdf.

Cassell, P.G., & Marsh, J.R. (2019). The new Amy, Vicky, and Andy Act: A positive step toward full restitution for child pornography victims. *Federal Sentencing Reporter, 31*(3), 187–194. Doi: 10.1525/fsr.2019.31.3.187.

Clark, R., & Hyland, M. (2007). *The Criminalization of Child Pornography in Irish Law: A Report to the Department of Justice, Equality and Law Reform.* https://papers.ssrn.com/sol3/papers.cfm?abstract_id=1393309.

Cohen-Almagor, R. (2013). Online child sex offenders: Challenges and countermeasures. *The Howard Journal of Criminal Justice, 52*(2), 190–215.

Council of the European Union (2017). *The Practical Implementation and Operation of European Policies on Prevention and Combating Cybercrime: Report on Denmark.* https://data.consilium.europa.eu/doc/document/ST-13204-2016-REV-1-DCL-1/en/pdf.

ECPAT International and INTERPOL (2018). *Towards a Global Indicator on Unidentified Victims in Child Sexual Exploitation Material: Summary Report.* https://www.ecpat.org/wp-content/uploads/2018/03/TOWARDS-A-GLOBAL-INDICATOR-ON-UNIDENTIFIED-VICTIMS-IN-CHILD-SEXUAL-EXPLOITATION-MATERIAL-Summary-Report.pdf.

Eke, A.W., Seto, M.C., & Williams, J. (2011). Examining the criminal history and future offending of child pornography offenders: An extended prospective follow-up study. *Law and Human Behavior, 35,* 466–478.

Elliott, I.A., & Beech, A.R. (2009). Understanding online child pornography use: Applying sexual offense theory to internet offenders. *Aggression & Violent Behavior, 14,* 180–193. Doi: 10.1016/j.avb.2009.03.002.

Eneman, M. (2010). Internet service provider (ISP) filtering of child-abusive material: A critical reflection of its effectiveness. *Journal of Sexual Aggression, 16*(2), 223–235.

European Union Agency for Law Enforcement Cooperation. (2019). *Europol: Internet organized crime Threat Assessment (IOCTA).* Doi: 10.2813/858843. https://www.europol.europa.eu/activities-services/main-reports/internet-organised-crime-threat-assessment-iocta-2019.

Fanetti, M., O'Donohue, W.T, Fondren-Happel, R., & Daly, K.N. (2014). Internet exploitation of children. In *Forensic Child Psychology: Working in the Courts and Clinic* (pp. 125–144). Hoboken, NJ: John Wiley & Sons, Inc.

Federal Register of Legislation. (n.d.). *Criminal Code Act 1995.* https://www.legislation.gov.au/Details/C2020C00245/Html/Volume_2.

Frei, A., Erenay, N., Dittmann, V., & Graf, M. (2005). Paedophilia on the internet – a study of 33 convicted offenders in the Canton of Lucerne. *Swiss Medical Weekly, 135,* 488–494.

Gillespie, A.A. (2018). Child pornography. *Information & Communications Technology Law, 27*(1), 30–54. Doi: 10.1080/13600834.2017.1393932.

Gottfried, E.D., Shier, E.K., & Mulay, A.L. (2020). Child pornography and online sexual solicitation. *Current Psychiatry Reports, 22*(3), 10–17. Doi: 10.1007/s11920-020-1132-y.

Government of Canada. (2020). *Justice Laws Website: Criminal Code R.S.C 1985.* https://laws-lois.justice.gc.ca/eng/acts/c-46/section-163.1.html

Henshaw, M., Ogloff, J., & Clough, J. (2017). Looking beyond the screen: A critical review of the literature on the online child pornography offender. *Sexual Abuse A Journal of Research and Treatment, 29*(5), 416–445. Doi: 10.1177/1079063215603690.

Howitt, D., & Sheldon, K. (2007). The role of cognitive distortions in paedophilic offending: Internet and contact offenders compared. *Psychological Crime Law, 13,* 469–486.

InHope. (2019). *Annual Report 2019.* https://www.inhope.org/media/pages/the-facts/download-our-whitepapers/e09e3a0238-1603115653/2020.10.19_ih_annualreport_digital.pdf.

International Centre for Missing & Exploited Children (2018). *Child Sexual Abuse Material Model Legislation and Global Review* (9th edition). Koons Family Institute on International Law & Policy. https://www.icmec.org/wp-content/uploads/2018/12/CSAM-Model-Law-9th-Ed-FINAL--12-3-18.pdf.

Internet Watch Foundation. (2020). *Case Laws.* https://www.iwf.org.uk/what-we-do/how-we-assess-and-remove-content/case-laws.

Kershner, E. (2020). *How Many Countries Are There in the World?* World Atlas. https://www.worldatlas.com/articles/how-many-countries-are-in-the-world.html.

Kirwan, G., & Power, A. (2012). Internet child pornography: A stepping stone to contact offenses? In *The Psychology of Cyber Crime: Concepts and Principles* (pp. 113–132). Hershey, PA: Information Science Reference.

Kloess, J.A., Woodhams, J., Whittle, H, Grant, T., & Hamilton-Giachritsis, C.E. (2019). The challenges of identifying and classifying child sexual abuse material. *Sexual Abuse, 31*(2), 173–196.

Krone, T. (2004). *A Typology of Online Child Pornography Offending. Trends & Issues in Crime and Criminal Justice, No. 279*. Canberra, Australian Institute of Criminology. https://www.aic.gov.au/sites/default/files/2020-05/tandi279.pdf.

Laulik, S., Allam, J., & Sheridan, L. (2007). In investigation into maladaptive personality functioning in Internet sex offenders. *Psychology, Crime, & Law, 13(5)*, 523–535.

Lanning, K.V. (2010). *Child Molesters: A Behavioral Analysis for Professionals Investigating the Sexual Exploitation of Children* (5th ed.). National Center for Missing & Exploited Children. https://www.missingkids.org/content/dam/missingkids/pdfs/publications/nc70.pdf.

Lee, H-Em Ermakova, T., Ververis, V., & Fabian, B. (2020). Detecting child abuse material: A comprehensive survey. *Forensic Science International: Digital Investigation, 34*, 1–11. Doi: 10.1016/j.fsidi.2020.301022.

Library of Congress. (2020). *Child Protection Law and Policy: Brazil*. https://www.loc.gov/law/help/child-protection-law/brazil.php#_ftn65 (9/30/2020).

Maras, M-H., & Shapiro, L.R. (2017). Child sex dolls and robots: More than just an uncanny valley. *Journal of Internet Law, 21(6)*, 3–21. ISSN: 10942904.

McCarthy, J.A. (2010). Internet sexual activity: A comparison between contact and non-contact child pornography offenders. *Journal of Sexual Aggression, 16(2)*, 181–195.

Merdian, H.L., Curtis, C., Thakker, J., et al. (2013). The three dimensions of online child pornography offending. *Journal of Sex Aggression, 19*, 121–132.

National Center for Missing & Exploited Children (2017). *The Online Enticement of Children: An In-Depth Analysis of CyberTipline Reports*. https://www.missingkids.org/content/dam/missingkids/pdfs/ncmec-analysis/Online%20Enticement%20Pre-Travel1.pdf.

NetClean. (2019). *Using Crawling and Hashing Technologies to Find Child Sexual Abuse Material—The Internet Watch Foundation*. https://www.netclean.com/2019/02/11/using-crawling-and-hashing-technologies-to-find-child-sexual-abuse-material-the-internet-watch-foundation/.

O'Brien, M. D., & Webster, S. D. (2007). The construction and preliminary validation of the /Internet Behaviours and Attitudes Questionnaire (IBAQ). *Sexual Abuse, 19*, 237–256. Doi: 10.1177/107906320701900305).

O'Donnell, I., & Milner, C. (2007). *Child pornography: Crime, computers, and society*. London: Routledge/Taylor & Francis Group.

Pew Research Center. (2016). Marriage laws around the world. https://assets.pewresearch.org/wp-content/uploads/sites/12/2016/09/FT_Marriage_Age_Appendix_2016_09_08.pdf.

Priebe, C. (2019). *Artificial Intelligence Combines with Human Intelligence to Stop Child Sexual Abuse*. http://www.evidencemagazine.com/index.php?option=com_content&task=view&id=2854.

Reijnen, L., Bulten, E., & Nijman, H. (2009). Demographic and personality characteristics of Internet child pornography downloaders in comparison to other offenders. *Journal of Child Sexual Abuse, 18(6)*, 611–622. Doi: 10.1080/10538710903317232

Rogers, A. (2016). The dignitary harm of child pornography—from producers to possessors. In C.B. Hessick (ed.), *Refining Child Pornography Law: Crime, Language, and Social Consequences* (pp. 165–186). Ann Arbor: University of Michigan Press.

Rosenzweig, P. (2020). *The Law and Policy of Client-Side Scanning*. https://www.law-fareblog.com/law-and-policy-client-side-scanning.

Schell, B., Martin, M.V., Hung, P.C.K., & Rueda, L. (2007). Cyber child pornography: A review paper of the social and legal remedies—and a proposed technological solution. *Aggression and Violent Behavior, 12(1)*, 45–63.

Sentencing Guidelines Council. (2007). *Sexual Offences Act 2003: Definitive Guideline.* http://www. sentencing-guidelines.gov.uk/ docs/0000_SexualOffencesAct1. pdf.

Seto, M.C. (2013). Online offender characteristics. In *Internet Sex Offenders* (pp. 137–167). Washington, DC: American Psychological Association.

Seto, M.C., Buckman, C., Dwyer, R.G., & Qualye, E. (2018). *Production and Active Trading of Child Sexual Exploitation Images Depicting Identified Victims.* https://www.missingkids.org/content/dam/missingkids/pdfs/ncmec-analysis/Production%20and%20Active%20Trading%20of%20CSAM_FullReport_FINAL.pdf.

Shapiro, L.R. (2020). Online child sexual abuse material: Prosecuting across jurisdictions. *Journal of Internet Law, 24(3)*, 3–8.

Shelton, J., Eakin, J., Hoffer, T., Muirhead, Y., & Owens, J. (2016). Online child sexual exploitation: An investigative analysis of offender characteristics and offending behavior. *Aggression and Violent Behavior, 30*, 15–23.

Siegfried, K.C., Lovely, R.W., & Rogers, M.K. (2008). Self-reported online child pornography behaviour: A psychological analysis. *International Journal of CyberCriminology, 2*, 286–297.

Solan, O. (2020). *Inside the Surveillance Software Tracking Child Porn Offenders Across the Globe.* https://www.nbcnews.com/tech/internet/inside-surveillance-software-tracking-child-porn-offenders-across-globe-n1234019.

Steinberg, S. (2019). Changing faces: Morphed child pornography images and the first amendment. *Emory Law Journal, 68*, 909–938.

Sundier, S. (2019, September 13). *Norway Court Rules Child-Like Sex Dolls Violate Criminal Law.* https://www.jurist.org/news/2019/09/norway-court-rules-child-like-sex-dolls-violate-criminal-law/.

Tahirih Justice Center. (2020). Analysis of state laws on minimum marriage age and exceptions that permit individuals under age 18 to marry. Appendix A: All states and D.C. https://www.tahirih.org/wp-content/uploads/2020/08/50-state-appendices-with-detailed-scorecards-on-features-of-states%E2%80%99-minimum-marriage-age-laws.pdf.

Terre Des Hommes. (2013). *Webcam Child Sex Tourism.* Netherlands: TerreDes Hommes.https://www.terredeshommes.org/wp-content/uploads/2013/11/Webcam-child-sex-tourism-terre-des-hommes-NL-nov-2013.pdf.

Thorn (2020, August 13). *How Safer's Detection Technology Stops the Spread of CSAM.* https://www.thorn.org/blog/how-safers-detection-technology-stops-the-spread-of-csam/.

Unikowski, J. (2019). Substantive and procedural legislation in the United States of America to combat webcam-related child sexual abuse. In S. van der Hof, I. Georgieva, B. Schermer, & B-J Koops (eds.), *Sweetie 2.0 using Artificial Intelligence to Fight Webcam Child Sex Tourism* (pp. 491–542). The Hague: Asser Press/Springerlink.

United Nations Convention of the Rights of the Child. (1989). https://www.ohchr.org/en/professionalinterest/pages/crc.aspx.

U.S. Department of Justice. (2020). *Citizen's Guide to U.S. Federal Law on Child Pornography.* https://www.justice.gov/criminal-ceos/citizens-guide-us-federal-law-child-pornography.

U.S. Sentencing Commission. (2019). *Quick Facts-Child Pornography Offenders.* https://www.ussc.gov/sites/default/files/pdf/research-and-publications/quick-facts/Child_Pornography_FY19.pdf.

Varrella, A. (2017). Live streaming of child sexual abuse: Background, legislative frameworks and the experience of the Philippines. https://humantraffickingsearch.org/wp-content/uploads/2017/06/Phillippines.pdf.

Webb, L., Craissati, J., & Keen, S. (2007). Characteristics of Internet child pornography offenders: A comparison with child molesters. *Sexual Abuse, 19*, 449–465.

Wells, M., Finkelhor, D., Wolak, J., & Mitchell, K. J. (2007). Defining child pornography: Law enforcement dilemmas in investigations of Internet child pornography Possession. *Police Practice and Research, 8*(3), 269–282.

Wolak, J., Finkelhor, D., & Mitchell, K.J. (2005). *Child-pornography possessors arrested in internet-related crimes: Findings from the National Juvenile Online Victimization study.* https://scholars.unh.edu/cgi/viewcontent.cgi?article=1032&context=ccrc

Wortley, Ri., & Smallbone, St. (2006). Applying situational principles to sexual offenses against children. Situational prevention of child sexual abuse. *Crime Prevention Studies, 19*, 7–35.

Wortley, R., & Smallbone, S. (2012). Child pornography on the internet. *Problem-Oriented Guides for Police: Problem-specific Guides Series. No.* 41. ISBN: 1-932582-65-7. https://popcenter.asu.edu/sites/default/files/child_pornography_on_the_internet.pdf.

ACTS AND LAWS

Child Protection Act (18 U.S.C. §§ 2251, 2252, et seq.).
Child Protection and Obscenity Enforcement Act (amending §§ 2251, 2252).
Child Pornography Protection Act (18 U.S.C. §§ 2252A, 2256(8)).
Child Protector and Sexual Predator Punishment Act (42 U.S.C. §§ 13032).
Sexual Exploitation of Children Act (Pub.L. 95–225, 92 Stat. 7).

CASES

Ashcroft v. FreeSpeech Coalition (2002), 535 U.S. 234

Dodge v. R (2002), A Crim R 435

Miller v. California (1973), 413 U.S. 15, 24–25

New York v. Ferber (1982), 458 U.S. 747, 761

Osborne v. Ohio (1990), 495 U.S. 103, 110–111.

Paroline v. United States (2014), 572 U.S. 434

Regina v. Oliver (2003) 2 Cr App Rep (S) 15.

United States v. Dost (1986), 636 F.Supp. 828, 832 (S.D. Cal.), aff'd sub nom.

United States v. Rayl (2001), 270 F.3d 709

United States v. Wiegand (1987), 812 F.2d 1239, 1244–45 (9th Cir. 1987), cert. denied, 484 U.S. 856.

10

Cyber Sextortionists

DEFINING CYBER SEXTORTION

Cyber sextortion refers to the use of online blackmail, threats, and intimidation to extort sexual acts, sexual content (i.e., sexts, photographs, videos, live-streaming), and/or money from victims in exchange for not exposing

DOI: 10.4324/9781003092292-10

incriminating information or explicit images (Acar, 2016; Department of Justice, 2016; Kopecký, 2017; O'Malley & Holt, 2020; Patchin & Hinduja, 2020; Paquet-Clouston et al., 2019; Veli, 2016; Wittes et al., 2016b; Wolak & Finkelhor, 2016; Wolak et al., 2018). As a technology-based sexual and gender-based violent crime, cyber sextortion is also considered to be a subset of image-based sexual abuse offenses because perpetrators use the threat of nonconsensual online distribution of their victims' sexually explicit images to inflict harm upon them (Liggett, 2019; O'Malley & Holt, 2020; Powell et al., 2019). These images may have been produced voluntarily—consensually exchanged within a relationship that has now ended or stolen from the victim's computer, cloud, or smart phone—or involuntarily—through coercion from a current or past abusive intimate partner or as the result of a sexual crime, including rape, sexual assault, and child sexual abuse (Powell & Henry, 2017; Powell et al., 2018, 2019; Wolak et al., 2018; Wolak & Finkelhor, 2016).

The majority of victims have complied with their cyber sextortionists' demands (62%) hoping the threats would cease, however, in 64% of the cases the threats continued and in 68% of the cases the threats actually increased in frequency (Thorn.org, 2019). For example, 47% of victims reported daily threats; within this group, multiple threats occurred, with half of them being threatened up to 9 times per day, 25% 10–19 times per day, and 25% more than 20 times per day (Thorn.org, 2019). Noncompliance also has consequences—45% of adult victims (ages 18–25) reported their cyber sextortionists enacted their threats and 60% indicated their perpetrators also stalked them (Wolak & Finkelhor, 2016). Cyber sextortionists who knew their victims offline were more likely than those who met them online (38% vs. 20%) to enact their threats (Thorn.org, 2019). Figure 10.1 shows the proportion of victims who reported each type of threat enacted against them (Thorn.org, 2019).

Perpetration of cyber sextortion by non-familiar adults (strangers) has emerged as a major threat to children (Clark, 2016; Department of Justice, 2016), most likely because it is a priority for law enforcement (O'Malley & Holt, 2020). Minors were predominantly coerced into providing additional explicit images (51%–78%), whereas in other incidents they were extorted to provide money (6%–9%) or sexual favors (5%–24%) (National Center for Missing & Exploited Children/NCEMC, 2016; Wolak & Finkelhor, 2016). It is also common for victims of cyber sextortion to indicate that perpetrators were familiar to them, such as former or current romantic partners, friends, family, or acquaintances (Draucker & Martsolf, 2010: Patchin &

Threats enacted

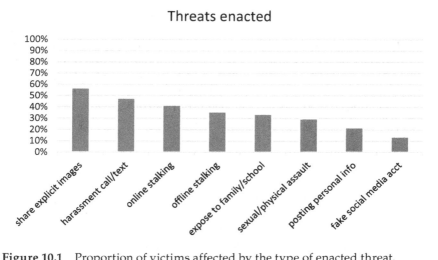

Figure 10.1 Proportion of victims affected by the type of enacted threat.

Hinduja, 2020; Powell et al., 2019; Wolak et al., 2018; Wolak & Finkelhor, 2016). For example, adult victims (59%–71%) reported consensually sexting explicit images to their intimate partners, who then coerced and pressured them (in some cases violently) into online sexual activity and/or to produce additional images (Walker et al., 2019; Wolak & Finkerhor, 2016). In a sample that included minors and young adults (aged 13–25), Thorn. org (2019) reported cyber sextortion victims were almost equally likely to report that they already knew their perpetrators (49%) or met them online (48%). Minors may be more vulnerable than adults to cyber sextortion victimization by strangers because they have higher online exposure from social media sites and/or fewer opportunities to be in serious relationships in which explicit images were exchanged (Thorn.org, 2019; Wurtele & Kenny, 2016).

It is difficult to determine the number of perpetrators or victims because cyber sextortion is not a federal crime (Wittes et al., 2016a). Cyber sextortion of minor victimization was estimated to be 5%–7%, whereas minor perpetration was 3% (Kopecký, 2017; Patchin & Hinduja, 2020). In Reed et al.'s (2016) study of digital dating abuse among college students aged 17–22, the overall prevalence of victimization (perpetration) for partner threats to distribute embarrassing information was 6.8% (2.2%) and sexually explicit images was 1.6% (0.6%). Gámez-Guadix et al. (2015) indicated that overall prevalence for online sexual victimization (OSA) among adults ages 18–60 who reported being threatened and coerced into providing sexual content was 2%. Actual prevalence rates, however, are presumed to be higher given that at least 51% of minors and 46% of adults indicated they never disclosed their victimization to friends or family and only a minority (13% of minors, 16% of adults) reported it to the police (Acar, 2016; Thorn.org, 2019; Wittes et al., 2016b; Wolak et al., 2018). Victims report negative consequences from even short-term exposure to cyber sextortion demands (Thakkar, 2017).

TYPICAL CYBER SEXTORTIONISTS

As indicated in the official statistics, cyber sextortionists are predominantly White, young adult men (aged 18–40), regardless of the age and sex of their victims (O'Malley & Holt, 2020; Wittes et al., 2016b). Perpetrators possessed psychological characteristics of domestic violence abusers, demonstrating malice, cruelty, and the need to control and humiliate their victims (Wolak & Finkelhor, 2016). Male minors were also perpetrators who used cyber sextortion with their face-to-face intimate partners (Wolak & Finkerhor, 2016). Similar to child sexual abuse material offenders described in Chapter 9, the majority of cyber sextortionists who target minors exclusively online (53%, and another 18% who demand physical contact) do so because they are aroused by maturing and mature pre/adolescents, whereas the rest simply find it easier to manipulate youth who cannot legally consent (Liggett, 2019; O'Malley & Holt, 2020; Wurtele & Kenny, 2016). While some offenders prefer only female minors (71%–78%), others prefer only male minors (17%–20%) or simply show no preference (5%–8%) (Liggett, 2019; O'Malley & Holt, 2020). Cyber sextortion offenders (21%) and intimately violent cyber sextortion offenders (13%) prefer adult victims (21%), particularly women (93%); in contrast, transnational cyber sextortion offenders (11%) target male victims they meet online (O'Malley & Holt, 2020).

CYBER SEXTORTIONISTS' MOTIVES AND METHODS

The motives of cyber sextortionists include: financial, personal, and retribution (Kopecký, 2017; NCEMC, 2016; Wolak & Finkelhor, 2016). The goal of receiving money occurs most often when victims can afford to pay, but their images may also be marketable products if the offenders choose to sell them online (Kopecký, 2017; National Crime Agency, 2018; O'Malley & Holt, 2020). Box 10.1 describes two sextortion rings that operated to make money (Duncan, 2019; Kelley, 2019; Parry, 2016). Personal motives include obtaining power and control over victims and/or sexual gratification online and offline, particularly sexually deviant fantasies involving children and adolescents, sadism, and abuse (Acar, 2016; Kopecký, 2017; Liggett, 2019; Wittes et al., 2016b). Retribution by intimately violent cyber sextortion offenders is also a goal for them to manipulate and maintain control over their current or former intimate partners (O'Malley & Holt, 2020). In some cases, the demands are sexual and in other cases they are nonsexual, such as forcing victims to end new romantic relationships, terminate employment, or meet the offender (O'Malley & Holt, 2020).

BOX 10.1   SEXTORTION RINGS OPERATED FOR FINANCIAL MOTIVES

2014 Case: Maria Celilia Caparas-Regalacheulo, with two co-conspirators, ran a cyber sextortion syndicate in the Philippines using both minor and adult "operators" to befriend boys and men on social media websites, ask them to video chat, and convince them to strip and perform sex acts, which were surreptitiously recorded. Demands for varying amounts of money (e.g., £200 to £15,000) from thousands of victims from the U.S., the U.K., Australia, Hong Kong, and Singapore, under threat that they would disseminate the videos on Facebook or to friends and family, totaled an estimated £1.5 million. Her scheme is blamed for the suicide of 17-year-old Daniel Perry from the U.K. and four others.

2018 Case: South Carolina prison sextortion ring, ran by five gang inmates (the Bloods) and 10 outside accomplices, targeted enlisted service members and officers in all four military branches (Air Force, Army, Navy, Marines). Offenders posted fake dating profiles and when military members responded, they were convinced to exchange explicit images. Next, service personnel were contacted by the supposed father, demanding money from the targets under the threat that he would go to the police and/or report them to military authorities for soliciting nudes from an underage girl. The members of the ring made $560,000 and were linked to at least one suicide.

Cyber sextortion involves five stages (Kopecký, 2017; Wittes, 2017). Stage 1 involves locating and contacting the victim. Cyber sextortionists may target strangers or people they already know (Wittes, 2017; Wolak & Finkelhor, 2016). Stage 2 consists of developing the communication relationship by manipulating the target. Stage 3 involves verification of the target to ensure the victim is real and providing authentic photographs. Stage 4 consists of various methods for obtaining explicit images that could be used for leverage. The four strategies are described in Box 10.2. Stage 5 is the sextortion plot in which victims are coerced into complying with the perpetrator's financial (18%), sexual (78%), or behavioral (12%) demands and are monitored to ensure they provide it (Kopecký, 2017; Liggett, 2019). The length of time for victims to interact with the perpetrator to the first image being sent varied (Wolak & Finkelhor, 2016)—a day (11%), up to a week (11%), up to 2 weeks (9%), up to 3 months (24%), and more than 3 months (41%).

Financial threats averaging $500 per adult male victim are common (66%), but cyber sextortionists who are hackers or part of criminal organizations involved in scams were the most likely to extort money from strangers (Liggett, 2019; Thakkar, 2017; Thorn.org, 2019; Wolak &

BOX 10.2   STRATEGIES USED BY CYBER SEXTORTIONISTS TO OBTAIN EXPLICIT IMAGES

Cyber sextortionists may choose from four strategies, depending on their motives, skills, and perpetrator-victim relationship (Liggett, 2019; Wittes, 2017)—grooming (51%); hacking or theft (17%); sexting (20%); or scams (11%).

- *Grooming* is the predominant method for cyber sextortionists to gain control over juvenile victims, make them submissive, and ensure their silence (Acar, 2016; Craven et al., 2006; Kopecký, 2017; Wittes et al., 2016b). Impersonation of a similar-aged peer, even as young as 8 (*United States v. Matthew Chaney Walker*), is often used to lure minors into the initial conversation and flirting and flattery bolstering the youth's feelings of attractiveness and body image (O'Malley & Holt, 2020).
- *Hacking or stealing* to obtain explicit images (Kopecký, 2017; Liggett, 2019; Wittes, 2017; Wittes et al., 2016b) is done by:
  1. gleaning publicly available information and images from target's various social media accounts, which not

    only allows perpetrators to password hack (i.e., guess security question answers, gain access, and change password), but also to apply deep fake technology to convert modest images into sexually explicit ones;

2. installing malware that infects the victims' computers (e.g., Blackshades, DarkComet, Bifrost) and gives perpetrators remote access to control the webcam for photographing and videotaping victims in various state of undress;

3. installing keylogger software that records victims' passwords and allows perpetrators to gain access to their email and social media accounts;

4. installing production software programs (e.g., Bananatag, Toutapp), that allows perpetrators to monitor when the victims read their emails containing the instructions to be performed;

5. hacking into the victims' computer to locate explicit images;

6. spear phishing; and

7. stealing victims' computers or smart phones.

In *United States v. Ryan Vallee*, the perpetrator hacked into female victims' online social media and email accounts by guessing their security answers and locking them out (O'Malley & Holt, 2020).

- *Sexting* is another source as victims consensually share explicit images in their dating or relationship phases with extortionists who are or had been their intimate partners (Liggett, 2019; Wolak & Finkelhor, 2016). For example, in *State of Florida v. James Joseph Krey*, the perpetrator threatened to distribute intimate photographs of his ex-girlfriend unless she quit her job with the police department (O'Malley & Holt, 2020).

- *Scams* involve perpetrators posing as modeling agents requesting explicit images for upcoming jobs; as law enforcement agents threatening to arrest minors for underage sexting to obtain additional explicit images; and as fake online romantic partners requesting and sharing intimate images or requesting webcam sex sessions that are secretly recorded (Liggett, 2019; Nilsson et al., 2019; Thakkar, 2017).

For example, *United States v. Michael Ford*, a state-department employee pretended to be a member of Google's (non-existent) account deletion team to obtain passwords and access computers without authorization, but also posed as a modeling scout; both schemes were successful in his cyber sextortion plot against 800 victims (O'Malley & Holt, 2020).

Finkelhor, 2016). In contrast, cyber sextortionists who made behavioral demands (e.g., talk, stay in relationship, quit job) were often attempting to maintain or regain control over intimate partners (Draucker & Martsolf, 2010; Liggett, 2019; Wolak et al., 2018; Wolak & Finkelhor, 2016). Sexual demands by sextortionists, which occurred more often when victims were strangers than familiar (86% vs. 62%), included creating additional sexually explicit content portraying specific body parts, sexual acts, sadistic acts, bestiality, incest, and/or making victims sexually abuse themselves or other minors (Kopecký, 2017; Liggett, 2019; O'Malley & Holt, 2020; Thorn.org, 2019). For example, male minors in *United States v. Bryan Jacobs* were fooled into providing explicit images believing they were speaking to a female adolescent, whereas a minor victim in *United States v. Joshua James Geer* was coerced into sending explicit images with his nude 11-year-old sister showing his penis in her hand and in her mouth (O'Malley & Holt, 2020).

Figure 10.2 displays the type of demands issued to victims in 2015 and 2017 as reported by Thorn.org (2019). In addition to using fake profiles, many cyber sextortionists are able to avoid detection by hiding their actual IP address using Virtual Private Network (VPN) service, proxy servers, and a dynamic Domain Name System (DNS) service by No-IP.com (Nilsson et al., 2019). When the perpetrator met the victim online, initial contact was often through social media (31%), such as Facebook or Instagram; messaging apps (24%), such as Snapchat and Kik; video chats (12%), such as Skype and Facetime; dating platforms (11%), such as OKCupid or Tinder; or other ways (9%), such as gaming platforms or email (Kopecký, 2017; National Center for Missing and Exploited Children, 2016; Wittes et al., 2016; Wolak & Finkelhor, 2016).

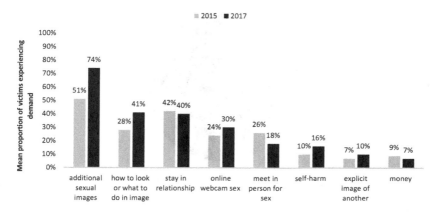

Figure 10.2   Types of cyber sextortion demands in 2015 and 2017.

TYPICAL CYBER SEXTORTION VICTIMS

Many of the prosecuted cases of cyber sextortion involved minors (71%) as this is a prime concern to law enforcement, whereas the rest of the cases involved adult and child victims (18%) or adult only victims (12%) (Wittes et al., 2016b). In minor-focused cyber sextortion by offenders met online, victims were predominantly female (73%–91%), average age of 14–15 years old (range: ages 8–17 for girls and ages 11–17 for boys), and White (79%) (Kopecký, 2017; National Center for Missing and Exploited Children, 2016; O'Malley & Holt, 2020; Thorne.org, 2019; Wittes et al., 2016b; Wolak & Finkelhor, 2016; Wolak et al, 2018). According to Thorn.org (2019), while 25% of cyber sextortion incidents involved minors ages 13 and younger, most of these youth initially met the perpetrator online (60%) and were being coerced to provide explicit imagery (85%). Cyber sextortionists were equally likely to know 14-year-old victims as to meet them online, they were more likely to know victims ages 15–17 offline (57%) than meet online as strangers (Thorn.org, 2019). Research has shown that adult victims were most likely to be female (77%), young adults ages 18–22 (88%), White (78%), with high school degrees (28%–50%) or some college (31%–47%) (Wolak et al., 2018; Wittes et al., 2016b). As shown in Figure 10.3, almost half of the adult respondents (aged 18–25 at data collection) reported that they had been minors when initially threatened by cyber sextortion (Wolak & Finkelhor, 2016).

281

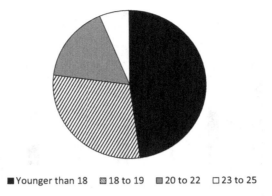

■ Younger than 18   ▨ 18 to 19   ■ 20 to 22   ☐ 23 to 25

Figure 10.3   Age of victim when initially exposed to cyber sextortion threat.

LAWS FOR PROSECUTING CYBER SEXTORTION

As there is no federal statute to address sextortion directly, the number of incidents does not get recorded as part of the FBI uniform crime statistics (Wittes, 2017). Federal prosecution using various offenses will depend upon which elements of the crime matched (e.g., hacking into victim's computer, money is exchanged) and the age of the victim—child vs. adult. Table 10.1 displays the relevant laws for prosecuting cyber sextortion of minors (see Chapter 9 for further descriptions). In contrast, when cyber sextortionists prey on adult targets, few federal sex crime statutes are applicable, particularly if the perpetrator does not issue a threat of force against the victim (Wittes et al., 2016a). Gender-based violence laws (e.g., Violence Against Women Reauthorization Act of 2013/Public Law 113), for example, are not suited for prosecuting sextortion as these require proof of physical force and/or victim non-consent (Thomas Reuters Foundation and International Association of Women Judges, 2015). Additionally, victims have little recourse to prove emotional distress required in criminal or civil prosecution based on offender possession unless there is internet distribution, blackmail payments, or theft from their personal computers (O'Malley & Holt, 2020). Table 10.2 displays possible statutes that may be used, if relevant depending upon the demands made and whether the elements of the statute are met. In their review of cases, Wittes et al. (2016a) reported that 37% of prosecutors used 18 USC § 875, 12% used 18 USC § 2261A, and 15% used 18 USC § 1030.

Table 10.1   Relevant Federal Statutes for Prosecuting Cyber Sextortion Incidents with Minors

- 18 USC § 2251: This statute, which criminalizes the sexual exploitation of children through the production of child sexual abuse material, is most often used for prosecuting cyber sextortionists who coerce minors to self-produce sexual images (55%; Wittes et al., 2016a).
  - 18 USC § 2251(a): This statute can be used to prosecute a cyber sextortionist who has "control" over a minor and forces him/her to be portrayed in sexually explicit conduct.
- 18 USC § 2252: This statute, which criminalizes possession, receipt, and distribution of child sexual abuse and exploitation materials, is also commonly used by prosecutors (36%; Wittes et al., 2016a).
  - 18 USC § 2252A: This statute criminalizes reproduction of child sexual abuse material by means of interstate commerce, including by computer and is sometimes used to prosecute this crime (22%; Wittes et al., 2016a).
- 18 USC § 2422(b): This statute criminalizes coercion and enticement of a minor to engage in any sexual activity, including attempts and is sometimes used to prosecute cyber sextortionists (24%; Wittes et al., 2016a).

As of 2019, 26 states and D.C. criminalized sexual extortion, but general extortion is rarely used as it typically does not include use of technology (Greenberg, 2019). When cyber sextortionists enact their threats of nonconsensual dissemination of intimate images, they can be prosecuted in 46 states and D.C.; however, the charges for this crime varies from misdemeanor to felony offense with corresponding penalties that result in widely disproportionate sentencing (Greenberg, 2019; Wittes et al., 2016b; Wolak et al., 2018). In general, disparity in penalties for cyber sextortion stems from (1) the criminal justice level prosecuting—federal vs. state, former has de facto norm for jurisdiction, presumably as it has greater financial resources available for complex computer forensic investigations than the latter; (2) charges applied; and (3) victim—minor or adult, with the former resulting in harsher sentencing regardless of the number of victims or the degree of cruelty involved in the crime (Wittes et al., 2016a). To encourage guilty pleas, the prosecutor often reduces the number and type of charges. For example, Adam Savader had originally been charged with four counts each of cyberstalking and extortion—which was then reduced to one count each; Richard Finkbiner sextorted hundreds of victims, mostly minors, and his 43 counts of extortion, transmission, child porn possession, and stalking was reduced to 24 counts (Wittes

Table 10.2   Federal Statutes That Potentially May be Used to Prosecute Cyber Sextortion

- 18 USC § 873: This statute criminalizes blackmail involving money.
- 18 USC § 875: This statute criminalizes interstate extortion and is particularly useful when victims are adults.
- 18 USC § 880: This statute criminalizes receiving money or property obtained from extortion.
- 18 USC § 2241: This statute criminalizes aggravated sexual abuse in which a person who is in the special maritime or territorial jurisdiction of the U.S. or in a prison facility is coerced to engage in a sexual act by force or threat that imposes fear of death, serious bodily injury, or kidnapping.
- 18 USC § 2242: This statute criminalizes sexual abuse such that a person is forced to engage in a sexual act because of threat or for fear of death, serious bodily injury, or kidnapping.
- 18 USC § 2246: This statute criminalizes abusive sexual contact, but as per *United States v. Weisinger,* it does not require direct, in-person, physical contact as an element of the crime (Wittes et al., 2016b).
- 18 USC § 2261A: This statute criminalizes cyberstalking and is sometimes used by prosecutors.
- 18 USC § 1030: This statute involves computer fraud and abuse, criminalizes appropriating social media accounts and hacking a victim's computer or network; it is sometimes used by prosecutors either by itself, or with 18 USC § 1028A.
- 18 USC § 1028A: This statute criminalizes identity theft, which may occur when the cyber sextortionist uses a victim's image to lure other victims.

et al., 2016a). A comparison of penalties for sextortion of minor and adult victims at the state level average 7.3 years and at the federal level average 29 years (Wittes et al., 2016a). The average federal sentencing in sextortion cases (Wittes et al., 2016a) is 31 years (ranging from 7 months to 139 years, Median = 24 years) when children are victimized (often charging under child sexual abuse material laws), but is only 3.2 years (ranging from one month to 6.5 years, Median = 3.3 years) when adults are victimized. As shown in Table 10.3, the number and age of victims, as well as the government charging the defendant (federal vs. state) contribute, to the differences in sentencing for cyber sextortion (Wittes et al., 2016a).

It is unlikely that legal gaps will be closed without obtaining prevalence rates of victimization (or at least better estimates), which requires data collection by the government, and educating legislatives on the

Table 10.3 Comparison of Federal and State Cases Involving Sextortion

Federal Cases	Victims	Acts	Charges & Sentencing
United States v. Jared James Abrahams	100s of minor and adult victims	Hacked into 150 computers to control webcams and monitor victims; demanded nudes and to Skype	Computer hacking, Extortion; 18 months
United States v. Adam Savader	15–45 female adults, many of whom he knew from h.s. or college	Hacked their email and social media accounts to access sexual images, then threatened to release photos to family, sorority sisters, Republican National Committee if they did not provide more images; goaded them into responding to his taunts	Interstate Extortion, Cyberstalking' 2.5 years
United States v. David Ackell	1 female minor	Solicited nude images from 16-year-old for two years under threat to disseminate images and rape a 14-year-old girl	Cyberstalking; 33 months
United States v. Mark Robert Reynolds	1 female minor (age 16)	Registered sex offender, sect sexual images of his genitalia and coerced minor victim into sending images of her breasts and genitalia	Enticement of a minor, Receipt of child porn; 6 years (240 months to run concurrently with 180 months, plus 120 months)
United States v. William Koch	20 male minors (youngest age 11)	Previously convicted child molester forced children to send him explicit images	Extortion, Exploitation of a minor, receipt and distribution of child porn; 20 years

(Continued)

285

Table 10.3 (*Continued*) Comparison of Federal and State Cases Involving Sextortion

Federal Cases	Victims	Acts	Charges & Sentencing
United States v. Robert Dion Ables	Unknown# of male adults and female minors	Solicited nudes from female minors (for additional images); Solicited nudes from men posing as 14-year-old (for money)	Receipt Child Porn; Production of Child Porn; 80 years
State Cases			
State of Alaska v. Eric James Adams	1	Blackmailed victim with threat to disseminate explicit images	Coercion: fear of exposure of secret (Class A Misdemeanor); Pled guilty, awaiting sentencing
State of California v. Bryan Asrary	9-year old girl	Impersonated Justin Biber to solicit nudes, then threatened to disseminate if she did not provide more nudes	Using minor to produce child porn; Contacting minor to commit felony; 44 months
State of Rhode Island v. Joseph Simone	Numerous male minors (ages 14 to 17)	Exploited victims through social media by impersonating a girl to solicit nudes and threatening to release them on Facebook if they did not perform more sex acts.	Child pornography, Indecent solicitation of a minor, Extortion, Impersonating police officers; 10 years (1 year at ACI), two years home confinement, remainder suspended with probation
State of Ohio v. Richard D. Schnitker	Multiple girls ages 9–14	Convinced girls to send sexual photos and then threatened to disseminate if they did not provide more images	2 counts: Pandering sexually oriented matters involving a minor; 14 years

(Continued)

Table 10.3 (*Continued*)   Comparison of Federal and State Cases Involving Sextortion

Federal Cases	Victims	Acts	Charges & Sentencing
State of Georgia v. Joshua David Fancher	1 woman	Offenders, a police officer, threatened over 5-month period to kill the woman and her 5- year-old brother and rape her sister if she did not provide images	Making terrorist threats; Not yet prosecuted (faces up to 10 years imprisonment)

impact that cyber sextortion has on victims (Henry & Power, 2016a, 2016b; Liggett, 2019). In particular, a federal law for cyber sextortion is warranted given its "interstate and often international nature" and the seemingly capricious administration of justice currently applied in lieu of legal uniformity (Wittes et al., 2016a, p. 6). The penalties for committing cyber sextortion—an online crime of sexual violence that theoretically parallels sexual assault in the physical world—are out of sync with the degree of harm suffered by victims coerced into performing sexual acts, such as loss of autonomy and dignity, emotional distress, and psychological consequences (Acar, 2016; Clark, 2016; O'Malley & Holt, 2020; Wittes et al., 2016a). As per *United States v. Weisinger*, abusive sexual contact (18 U.S.C. § 2246) does not require direct, in-person, physical contact so forcing someone to masturbate would satisfy this federal criminal statute (Wittes et al., 2016a). According to Wittes et al. (2016a), in-person sexual abusers receive a significantly higher sentencing penalty than cyber sextortionists (median federal sentence of 120 months vs. 40 months, respectively; U.S. Sentencing Commission, 2015), despite the latter typically having multiple victims. For example, multiple victims were found in all of the prolific repeat cyber sextortionist cases Wittes et al. (2016b) reviewed—25 cases each had 10 victims, 13 cases had at least 20 victims each, another 13 cases had more than 100 victims, and 2 cases had from hundreds to thousands of victims (Wittes et al., 2016b). In *United States v. Chansler* (3:10-cr-00100), cyber sextortion of 350 female minors ages 12 to 18 from 26 states, three Canadian Provinces, and the U.K., resulting in 105 years imprisonment (Clark, 2016).

IMPACT OF CYBER SEXTORTION ON SOCIETY AND VICTIMS

Victims and their families experience extreme, long-lasting harm, including development of mental health and physical problems, changing jobs or schools, or being forced to relocate (Kopecký, 2017; Wittes et al., 2016b). Cyber sextortionists took pleasure in tormenting and terrorizing their victims, enjoying when they begged, pleaded, and protested against being forced to submit to the demands—some of these predators (22%) engaged in threats lasting more than 6 months (Wittes et al., 2016b; Wolak & Finkelhor, 2016). Sadist cyber sextortionists forced their victims to record specific acts of self-harm, such as mutilation, sodomy with screwdriver, or incestual molestation (Wittes et al., 2016a). The most common harm experienced by victims included fear that their reputation would be ruined, especially when their images were posted on the internet and/or distributed; helplessness and hopelessness that anything they do will alleviate their pain and suffering or reverse their social situation in terms of loss of respect from everyone in their lives and abandonment of friends; feelings of shame, humiliation, and self-blame for being in the current predicament; and general psychological distress caused by enduring the sextortion, which included panic, fear, and anguish waiting for the perpetrator to make demands and being forced to submit to them (Nilsson et al., 2019). Depending on their social support systems, victims may develop depression, suicidal thoughts and attempts, or perform self-harm (e.g., cutting); abuse substances to induce numbness; experience psychological stress (e.g., trouble concentrating, reduced appetite, inability to trust others); and/or isolate themselves (e.g., not leaving their homes), which induces loneliness (Nilsson et al., 2019; Wittes et al., 2016b; Wolak et al., 2018). According to Wolak et al. (2018), many victims simply do not disclose to family or friends (51% minors, 46% adults), thinking they could handle the situation or were embarrassed by it, but admitted when they did confide in someone that their situations improved (41% for minors, 43% for adults).

CYBERSECURITY TACTICS

Cybersecurity tactics for preventing or mitigating cyber sextortion rely predominantly on educating and training potential and current victims regarding cybersecurity protocols, online scams, and social engineering techniques (see Chapter 12 for a review), but also include cyber solutions for detecting malware and keylogging; implementing secure data management; and installing antivirus software (Thakkar, 2017; Vilks, 2019). Anti-malware software and encryption will help users by detecting harmful programs detected within the computer system, prevent modification, and prevent against data theft, a significant source of sextortion (Thakkar, 2017). Besides computers, smart phones are also vulnerable to mobile cyber threats, including malware attacks; turning on the microphone; monitoring private SMS messages, emails, and voice calls; downloading contacts; and exploitation of GPS data for tracking users' location (Thakkar, 2017). Two examples are FinFisher spyware—which targets both Android phones and iPhones—and SMS Zombie—which targets Android phones (Thakkar, 2017). Thakkar (2017) recommends authentication programs (e.g., Authentication Standards Domain-based Message Authentication, Reporting & Conformance; DomainKeys Identified Mail) to assist in filtering impersonator emails, but these are limited in efficacy when fraudsters use spoofing or DNS services displaying fake routing information. Multi-layered email security approach may also help in prevention, detection, containment, and recovery (Thakkar, 2017).

Law enforcement have access to various apps, like *RADAR*, to monitor texts, social media messages, and phone calls, which can be used as evidence to prosecute child sexual predators (Breslow, 2018). Private corporations that provide social networking services can incorporate specific policies, such as age verification technology, image recognition/photo detection technology (e.g., Microsoft's *PhotoDNA*) using databases and algorithms to identify images that were distributed online without consent (i.e., image-based sexual abuse, sextortion), and block access by violators and remove illegal content (International Centre for Missing & Exploited Children/ICMEC, 2018). It is also recommended that these businesses work with law enforcement to protect users from victimization from solicitation of sexual images and predatory comments, often detected through artificial intelligence and natural language processing (de Jesús Cruz, 2019; ICMEC, 2018). Parents who are actively involved in supervising their children's internet and cell phone use can effectively decrease their vulnerability (Wurtele & Kenny, 2016). They can use mobile apps, such as *My Mobile Watchdog* (Breslow, 2018) to monitor text messages, phone calls, and emails; block user's attempts to access dangerous websites; and monitor users' contact lists. Cyber-safety websites are available to provide users with current digital media safety information consistent with real-world hazards associated with online interactions, such as the risks of Instant Messaging with strangers, joining sketchy or provocative chat rooms, and responding to cyber sexual solicitations by meeting strangers offline (Wurtele & Kenny, 2016). Victims must be encouraged to report sextortion demands and nonconsensual distribution of explicit images to social media platforms, provide information on hotlines, and seek social support services (Veli, 2016; Wolak et al., 2018).

REFERENCES

Acar, K.V. (2016). Sexual extortion of children in cyberspace. *International Journal of Cyber Criminology, 10*(2), 110–126.

Breslow, A. (2018). *The Dangers of the Internet and the Sexual Exploitation of Children.* Ann Arbor, MI: Proquest Dissertations Publishing, 10784925. https://www.proquest.com/openview/23bad1b8be9f410b7a62a690199949b6/1.pdf?pq-origsite=gscholar&cbl=18750

Clark, J. F. (2016). Growing threat: Sextortion. *Cyber Misbehavior, 64,* 41–44. https://www.justice.gov/usao/file/851856/download.

Craven, S., Brown, S. & Gilchrist, E. (2006). Sexual grooming of children: Review of literature and theoretical considerations. *Journal of Sexual Aggression, 12*(3), 287–299. Doi: 10.1080/13552600601069414.

de Jesús Cruz, E.G. (2019). *The Effectiveness of Digital Forensics and Security Strategies in Using AI and Machine Learning to Protect Children Online.* Polytechnic University of Puerto Rico. Ann Arbor, MI: Pro Quest Dissertations Publishing, 13887351. https://www.proquest.com/openview/59cf6b9e181fc4f27c2f74ca762d9084/1?pq-origsite=gscholar&cbl=18750&diss=y

Department of Justice. (2016). *The National Strategy for Child Exploitation Prevention and Interdiction: A report to Congress.* https://www.justice.gov/psc/file/842411/download.

Draucker, C. B., Martsolf, D. S. (2010). The role of electronic communication technology in adolescent dating violence. *Journal of Child and Adolescent Psychiatric Nursing, 23*(3), 133–142. Doi: 10.1111/j.1744-6171.2010.00235.x.

Duncan, C. (2019, Dec. 23). *Gang Members Made $140k Off 'Sextortion' Scam While Behind Bars in SC Prison, Feds Say.* https://www.thestate.com/news/state/south-carolina/article238655293.html.

Gámez-Guadix, M., Almendros, C., Borraj, E., & Calvete, E. (2015). Prevalence and association of sexting and online sexual victimization among Spanish adults. *Sex Research & Social Policy, 12,* 145–154. Doi: 10.1007/s13178-015-0186-9.

Greenberg, P. (2019). Fighting revenge porn and 'sextortion.' *National Conference of State Legislatures, 27*(29). https://www.ncsl.org/research/telecommunications-and-information-technology/fighting-revenge-porn-and-sextortion.aspx.

Henry, N. & Powell, A. (2016a). Sexual violence in the digital age: The scope and limits of criminal law. *Social & Legal Studies, 25*(4), 397–418. Doi. 10.1177/0964663915624273.

Henry, N. & Powell, A. (2016b). Technology-facilitated sexual violence. *Trauma, Violence, & Abuse,* 1–14. Doi: 10.1177/1524838016650189.

International Centre for Missing & Exploited Children (2018). *Studies in Child Protection: Sexual Extortion and Nonconsensual Pornography.* https://www.icmec.org/wp-content/uploads/2018/10/Sexual-Extortion_Nonconsensual-Pornography_final_10-26-18.pdf

Kelley, K. (2019, March 19). *New Data on Sextortion: 124 Additional Public Cases.* https://www.lawfareblog.com/new-data-sextortion-124-additional-public-cases.

Kopecký, K. (2017). Online blackmail of Czech children focused on so-called "sextortion" (analysis of culprit and victim behaviors). *Telematics and Informatics, 34,* 11–19.

Liggett, R. (2019). Exploring online sextortion. *Sexual Assault Report, 22*(4), 58–62.

National Center for Missing and Exploited Children (NCEMC). (2016). *Sextortion.* http://www.missingkids.org/the issues/Sextortion.

National Crime Agency. (2018). *Record Numbers of UK Men Fall Victim to Sextortion Gangs.* http://www.nationalcrimeagency.gov.uk/news/1360-recordnumbers-of-uk-men-fall-victim-to-sextortion-gangs.

Nilsson, M.G., Tzani-Peplasis, C., Ioannou, M., & Lester, D. (2019). Understanding the link between sextortion and suicide. *International Journal of Cyber Criminology, 13*(1), 55–69. Doi: 10.5281/zenado.3402357.

O'Malley, R.L., & Holt, K.M. (2020). Cyber sextortion: An exploratory analysis of different perpetrators engaging in a similar crime. *Journal of Interpersonal Violence,* 1–26. Doi: 10.1177/0886260520909186.

Paquet-Clouston, M., Romiti, M., Haslhofer, B., & Charvat, T. (2019). Spams meet cryptocurrencies: Sextortion in the bitcoin ecosystem. *Association for Computing Machinery 1st Conference on Advances in Financial Technologies,* 76–88. Doi: 10.1145/3318041.3355466.

Parry, S. (2016, December 9). *Inside the Sleazy Filipino Internet Den Where 'Queen of Sextortion' Arrested over British Teen's Suicide 'Made Fortune Duping Men into Stripping for Cybersex and Then Blackmailing Them.'* https://www.dailymail.co.uk/news/article-4000652/Inside-sleazy-Filipino-internet-den-Queen-Sextortion-arrested-British-teen-s-suicide-fortune-duping-men-stripping-cybersex-blackmailing-them.html.

Patchin, J.W., & Hinduja, S. (2020). Sextortion among adolescents: Results from a national survey of U.S. youth. *Sexual Abuse, 32*(1), 30–54.

Powell, A., & Henry, N. (2017). *Sexual Violence in a Digital Age.* Basingstoke, UK: Palgrave Macmillan.

Powell, A., Henry, N., & Flynn, A. (2018). Image-based sexual abuse. In W.S. DeKeseredy, C.M. Rennison, & A.K. Hall-Sanchez (eds.), *The Routledge International Handbook of Violence Studies* (pp. 305–315). New York: Routledge.

Powell, A., Henry, N., Flynn, A., & Scott, A.J. (2019). Image-based sexual abuse: The extent, nature, and predictors of perpetration in a community sample of Australian adults. *Computers in Human Behavior, 92,* 393–402.

Reed, L., Tolman, R.M., & Ward, L.M. (2016). Snooping and sexting: Digital media as a context for dating aggression and abuse among college students. *Violence Against Women, 22*(13), 1556–1576. Doi 10.1177/1077801216630143.

Thakkar, D. (2017). *Preventing digital extortion*. Birmingham: Packt Publishing, Ltd.

Thomas Reuters Foundation and International Association of Women Judges. (2015). *Combatting Sextortion: A Comparative Study of Laws to Prosecute Corruption Involving Sexual Exploitation*. https://www.trust.org/contentAsset/raw-data/588013e6-2f99-4d54-8dd8-9a65ae2e0802/file.

Thorn.org. (2019). *Sextortion*. https://www.thorn.org/wp-content/uploads/2019/12/Sextortion-Infographic-2018-Findings-UpdatedV3.pdf.

U.S. Sentencing Commission. (2015). *2015 Sourcebook of Federal Sentencing Statistics*. http://www.ussc.gov/sites/default/files/pdf/research-and-publications/annual-reports-and- sourcebooks/2015/Table13.pdf.

Veli, K. (2016). Sexual extortion of children in cyberspace. *Journal of Cyber Criminology, 10*(2), 110–126.

Vilks, A. (2019). Cybercrime and sexual exploitation of children in e-environment in the context of strengthening urban and rural security. *SHS Web of Conferences, 69*, 1010–1021.

Walker, K., Sleath, E., Hatcher, R. M., Hine, B., & Crookes, R. L. (2019). Nonconsensual sharing of private sexually explicit media among university students. *Journal of Interpersonal Violence, 13*, 886260519853414. Doi: 10.1177/0886260519853414.

Wittes, B. (2017). Cybersextortion and international justice. *Georgetown Journal of International Law, 48*, 941–947.

Wittes, B.B., Poplin, C., Jurecic, Q., & Spera, C. (2016a). *Closing the Sextortion Sentencing Gap: A Legislative Proposal*. Brookings Institute. https://www.brookings.edu/research/closing-the-sextortion-sentencing-gap-a-legislative-proposal/

Wittes, B., Poplin, C., Jurecic, Q, & Spera, C. (2016b). *Sextortion: Cybersecurity, Teenagers, and Remote Sexual Assault*. https://www.brookings.edu/research/sextortion-cybersecurity-teenagers-and-remote-sexual-assault/

Wolak, J., & Finkelhor, D. (2016). *Sextortion: Findings from a Survey of 1,631 victims*. https://humantraffickingsearch.org/wp-content/uploads/2018/09/Sextortion_Report.pdf.

Wolak, J., Finkelhor, D., Walsh, W., & Treitman, L. (2018). Sextortion of minors: Characteristics and dynamics. *Journal of Adolescent Health, 62*, 72–79.

Wurtele, S.K., & Kenny, M.C. (2016). Technology-related sexual solicitation of adolescents: A review of prevention efforts. *Child Abuse Review, 25*, 332–344. Doi: 10.1002/car.2445.

CASES

State of Alaska v. Eric James Adams (2018), 1PW-18-00018CR

State of California v. Bryan Asrary (2018), Case no. XCNBA456573-01

State of Florida v. James Joseph Krey (2015), Case no. 15003515CF10A (17th Cir)

State of Georgia v. Joshua David Fancher

State of Ohio v. Richard D. Schnitker, 6th Dist. Sandusky No. S-14-039, 2015-Ohio–1685

State of Rhode Island v. Joseph Simone, No. P2-2012-0684A (Providence County Superior Court)

United States v. Robert Dion Ables (2017). No. 17-10796

United States v. Jared James Abrahams (2014), No. 8:13-cr-00199 (C.D. Cal.)

United States v. David Ackell (2017), 15-cr-123-01-JL

United States v. Chansler (2010), 3:10-cr-00100

United States v. Michael Ford (2016), 15 CR 319 (ELR)(N.D.G.A).

United States v. Joshua James Geer (2014). 13 CR36 (N.D.G.A.)

United States v. Bryan Jacobs (2014), 10 CR 801(RMB) (D.N.J.)

United States v. William Koch, No. 13-CR-70 (N.D. Ohio).

United States v. Mark Robert Reynolds, No.14-CR-00547 (D.S.C.).

United States v. Adam Savader, No. 13-CR-20522 (E.D. Mich).

United States v. Ryan Vallee (2017), 15 CR 115 (PB) (D.N.H.)

United States v. Matthew Chaney Walker (2015), 15 CR 119 (M.D.L.A.)

United States v. Weisinger, 586 Fed. Appx. 733 (2d Cir. 2014).

11

Online Image-Based Sexual Abusers

DEFINING ONLINE IMAGE-BASED SEXUAL ABUSE

Image-based sexual abuse (IBSA) refers to the nonconsensual creation, distribution, or threatened distribution of intimate images of a person (i.e., pictures or videos in which the person was fully or partially nude

DOI: 10.4324/9781003092292-11

or was dressing/undressing, bathing/showering, or engaged in sexual activity); these images are disseminated through smart phones, social media platforms, chat rooms, emails, or pornography websites that host any film either of this genre generally or IBSA specifically (Franklin, 2014; Henry et al., 2019a; McGlynn & Rackley, 2017; Walker et al., 2019). Prevalence rates obtained across research studies range from 5% to 20% for production of nonconsensual images, 1%–30% for nonconsensual distribution, and 1%–15% for threats to distribute (Eaton et al., 2018; Fleschler Peskin et al., 2013; Garcia et al., 2016; Lenhart et al., 2016; Henry et al., 2020a; Wood et al., 2015). However, actual incidence is likely higher for all three forms given that many victims do not report this type of crime, either because they do not wish to reveal it occurred due to stigma associated with it, self-blame, or simply being oblivious to their victimization (e.g., some find out years later); yet, even those admitting to perpetrating the crime may be underreporting the number of times they produced, shared, and/or threatened to share intimate images without consent (Office of eSafety Commissioner, 2017; Henry et al., 2019b; Powell et al., 2019; Ruvalcaba & Eaton, 2020).

Sexually suggestive images of a person produced *without consent* include those taken surreptitiously (unbeknownst to the subject) in private and public settings—the latter entails sexual voyeurism such as **"upskirting"** (images beneath a woman's skirt or dress), **"downblousing"** (images of a woman's cleavage), and **"creepshots"** (usually clothed individuals with the image focus on breasts/chest, buttocks, and pubic area)—and those created from AI technology (i.e., Deep Fakes) that splices someone's head/face onto another person's body or artificially removes clothing from the image (Chesney & Citron, 2018; Henry et al., 2020a). According to Patrini et al. (2019, p. 1), of the 14,678 videos posted on the top four Deepfake websites viewed by 134 million users, the most prominently featured were nonconsensual **Deepfake pornography** (96%), particularly of female celebrities. Nonconsensual images may also be produced in conjunction to crimes, such as those produced when victims are under duress (e.g., threats of death or harm, harassment, sextortion, intimate partner violence/coercion) or incapacitated (e.g., intoxicated, unconscious), including during or after sexual assaults and rapes (Henry et al., 2020a; McCann et al., 2018; Powell et al., 2019).[1] Under some of these conditions (see section on *Laws*), both the nonconsensual production and distribution of the images are criminally prohibited. However, even when images are created *with consent* by the subject (self-made/selfies) or by a partner within the context of an intimate relationship, distribution of the images is illegal in most states (often referred to as "revenge porn") when the person portrayed did not authorize to it being shared (Henry et al., 2019a; Nigam, 2018).

In discussing technology-facilitated sexual assault, the term "revenge porn" is not preferred because it: (1) implies the person portrayed consented to image distribution, when in fact this was not true; (2) promotes placement of stigma and blame on the victim rather than on the perpetrator where it belongs (e.g., responses include that the victim created the image and sent it indiscriminately or the victim instigated harm resulting in revenge or humiliation), and (3) minimizes the harm caused by the nonconsensual production and unauthorized distribution of these images, both to the victim and society (Gavin & Scott, 2019; Henry et al., 2020a; McGlynn & Rackley, 2017; Ruvalcaba & Eaton, 2020; Sugiera & Smith, 2020). In contrast, the use of the term "IBSA" to describe technology-facilitated sexual violence, abuse, or exploitation captures the range of criminal activities involved, thereby aiding in the development of legislation without hinderance caused by location (e.g., private vs. public); requirement for partial or complete nudity; expectation of privacy; the need to limit a perpetrator's motives to a few specific ones, such as "sexual gratification;" or agreement by triers of fact that the image is indeed pornographic or obscene (McGlynn & Rackley, 2017; Powell et al, 2019). McGlynn and her colleagues have classified IBSA as a gendered crime of sexual violence—in terms of the perpetrator, victim, and victim-perpetrator relationship—punctuated by online harassment and abuse as regulated by sexual offense laws and policies to signify to society the significant harm it imposes on victim-survivors (Eaton & McGlynn, 2020; McGlynn & Rackley, 2017; McGlynn et al., 2017).

---

[1] Recordings and their distribution of crimes performed by perpetrators themselves or bystanders (Powell et al., 2019), as occurred in 2012 Steubenville, Ohio, when an intoxicated (mainly unconscious) 16-year-old girl's six-hour rape by high school football players at a party was documented by cellphones, distributed by texts, and then posted on YouTube, Instagram, and Facebook, despite it being classified as child sexual abuse material (Oppel, 2013).

TYPICAL ONLINE IMAGE-BASED SEXUAL ABUSERS

Unlike other types of cybersexual predators, demographic information available for the various types of IBSA offenders is hampered by two problems. First, laws criminalizing the different types of IBSA behavior must be in place in order for official statistics regarding offenders to be computed. A few countries, such as Australia and the U.K., have implemented criminal statutes, but the state laws in the U.S. are limited to one or two types of IBSA (e.g., revenge porn; video voyeurism). Thus, sentencing statistics must await guilty pleas or verdicts before demographic information is collected by the Federal Bureau of Investigation's Uniform Crime Reporting Program. Second, it is not always possible to identify who the disseminating culprit is because many platforms allow anonymous uploading of nonconsensual images; the images could be deep fake creations that had been taken surreptitiously or hacked from a computer or cloud storage. Consequently, most of the information known about offenders (and victims) is derived from surveys or from reporting agencies registering complaints (e.g., Office of the eSafety Commissioner, Cyber Civil Rights Initiative).

Consistent with self-report perpetration and victimization, typical IBSA offenders are heterosexual White male adolescents and adults[2] (Eaton & McGlynn, 2020; Eaton et al., 2018; Fleschler Peskin et al., 2013; Franklin, 2014; Garcia et al., 2016; Henry et al., 2019b; Henry et al., 2020b; Ruvalcaba & Eaton, 2020; Wood et al., 2015). Research indicated that adult offenders of nonconsensual pornography were associated with ambivalent sexism (i.e., sexist views entailing positive and negative attitudes toward women) and the Dark Triad traits, that is, Machiavellianism, narcissism, psychopathy (Pina et al., 2017), whereas adolescent offenders' willingness to engage in nonconsensual sharing of sexts was positively correlated with both their pornography use and instrumental sexual attitudes (van Oosten & Vandenbosch, 2020). Table 11.1 summarizes offender demographics and the prevalence rates as reported by victims (and sometimes also by offenders) on nonconsensual production and/or sharing/distribution of

---

[2] The characteristic of being "White" may be an artifact of the data, given that the different projects sampled from various countries contained samples from predominantly White populations.

Table 11.1 Nonconsensual Production and Distribution of Intimate Images Reported by Victims and Offenders in Five Studies

Number of Respondents, Sample Description, and Prevalence Rate	Unauthorized Sharing or Distribution of Intimate Images	Nonconsensual Production of Intimate Images
Wood et al. (2015) $N=4564$ **Sample Description** Ages 14–17 years 48% female, 96% heterosexual 5 countries: Bulgaria, Cyprus, England, Italy, Norway[√]	Victims 20% girls vs. 10% boys had images shared[a] by partner without authorization. Offenders 21% boys vs. 11% girls shared images from partner without authorization.	
Henry et al. (2020b) $N=6109$ **Sample Description** Ages 16–64, 52% female, 89% heterosexual, 74% White, 3 countries: U.K., New Zealand, and Australia. **Prevalence rate**: 37% IBSA ($N=2260$)	Victims 21% reported unauthorized image distribution. 19% threatened with distribution. 14% reported nonconsensual production, threat, and unauthorized distribution of images. Offenders -11% unauthorized distribution. -9% threatened. -8% reported nonconsensual production, threat, and unauthorized distribution of images.	Victims 33% reported nonconsensual production of images Declined with age – ages 16–19 (27%) – ages 20–29 (23%) – ages 30–39 (20%) – ages 40–49 (17%) Offenders 16% reported nonconsensual production of images

(Continued)

Number of Respondents, Sample Description, and Prevalence Rate	Unauthorized Sharing or Distribution of Intimate Images	Nonconsensual Production of Intimate Images
Table 11.1 (*Continued*) Nonconsensual Production and Distribution of Intimate Images Reported by Victims and Offenders in Five Studies		
Powell et al. (2018) $N=4274$ **Sample Description** 16–49 years, 56% female, 88% heterosexual, Australia[√] **Prevalence rate:** 23% IBSA ($N=983$)	Victims 11% unauthorized distribution. 9% threatened.	Victims 20% reported nonconsensual production of images. *Public location*: 5% upskirting; 10% downblousing; *Private location*: 20% nudes/sexual activity.
	Offenders 55% men vs. 32% women were unauthorized distributors. 47% men vs. 36% women threatened to distribute images. More men than women were unauthorized distributors of both female (53% vs. 33%) and male (56% vs. 30%) victim images.	Offenders 59% men vs. 30% women produced nonconsensual images. More men than women produced nonconsensual images of both female (65% vs. 24%) and male (52% vs. 36%) victims.

(Continued)

Number of Respondents, Sample Description, and Prevalence Rate	Unauthorized Sharing or Distribution of Intimate Images	Nonconsensual Production of Intimate Images
Table 11.1 (*Continued*) Nonconsensual Production and Distribution of Intimate Images Reported by Victims and Offenders in Five Studies		
Office of the eSafety Commissioner (2017) N =4122 **Sample Description** Female (79%) Ages 15–46+ Australia√ **Prevalence rate:** – 10% IBSA [Women 15% vs. Men 7%]; – 20% IBSA bystanders (images forwarded to them)	Victims 11% reported unauthorized posting/ sharing. *O/V Relationship*: – 29% friend; – 13% ex-partner; – 12% partner; – 10% family; – 10% acquaintance; – 10% other; – 4% colleague; – 4% stranger; – 9% unknown.	Victims 47% coerced vs. 33% consented to image production. *Nonconsensual image produced of female victim*: – cleavage (20%) – partially clothed/ semi-nude (17%). *Nonconsensual image produced of male victim*: – partially clothed/ semi-nude (30%).
	Offenders (as indicated by victims) 62% unauthorized sharer was same person as producer. 49% Male offenders with female victims *O/V Relationship*: 83% current partner, 86% ex-partner. 35% Female offenders with female victims *O/V Relationship*: 72% friends, 66% family.	Offenders (as indicated by victims) *Nonconsensual image produced of female victim* – semi-nude (21%); – cleavage (14%); – sexual photoshopped (5%); – breast (4%); – nude (4%); – shower/toilet (3%); – consensual sex (3%); – nonconsensual sex (1%); – genitals (1%).

(Continued)

301

Table 11.1 (*Continued*) Nonconsensual Production and Distribution of Intimate Images Reported by Victims and Offenders in Five Studies		
Number of Respondents, Sample Description, and Prevalence Rate	**Unauthorized Sharing or Distribution of Intimate Images**	**Nonconsensual Production of Intimate Images**
Eaton et al. (2018) $N=3044$ **Sample Description** Ages 18–97, 54% female, 82% White, 70% heterosexual, United States. **Prevalence rate:** 13% IBSA distribution or threat of distribution ($N=396$)	Victims 8% *unauthorized sharing of images*[b] [9% female vs. 7% male victims]. 5% *threatened but not shared* [7% female vs. 3% male]. *Unauthorized sharing:* 12% for 26–33-year-olds and 12% for 34–41-year-olds.	
	Offenders: 5% *unauthorized distribution* [7% men vs. 3% women]. Highest for 18–25-year-olds (8%).	

Key: √ Some studies did not report race, but used samples drawn from countries with predominantly White populations.
[a] Sharing included partner/receiver showing image to others on the phone or online.
[b] Shared included distributing, uploading via email, text, social media, app, website, DVD, print; it did not include commercially distributed pornography.

intimate images.[3] The data consistently showed that more offenders were male than female for production, distribution, and threat forms of IBSA. An examination of offender/victim (o/v) relationships indicated different

---

[3] Sharing and distribution are not always differentiated in studies. However, respondents asked about *sharing* usually concerned physically showing or forwarding texts of intimate images to 1 or a few people (i.e., limited circle), whereas *distribution* referred to posting images online and/or forwarded indiscriminately through texts and social media apps, like Snapchat (Henry et al., 2020; Walker et al., 2020). Evidence regarding sexts suggests that prevalence rates reported for sharing were higher than for distribution (e.g., Crofts et al., 2015).

possible combinations, but the data indicates that women were victimized mostly by their male intimate partner or by their female family member or friend (Office of the eSafety Commissioner, 2017).

MOTIVES AND METHODS OF ONLINE IMAGE-BASED SEXUAL ABUSERS

As shown in Table 11.2, four categories of motives explain nonconsensual distribution of images obtained from five acquisition methods (Eaton & McGlynn, 2020; Henry et al., 2019b; Walker et al., 2019).

- The first acquisition method—*relationships*—yields images consensually produced by the portrayed person (selfie/self-produced) and/or by a partner or friend (other-produced) and shared voluntarily as a way to initiate new relationships and/or maintain current relationships (Eaton & McGlynn, 2020; Henry et al., 2019b, 2020a).

The other four methods yield images obtained (i.e., stolen) or produced (i.e., hidden, altered, crime) without consent (Chesney & Citron, 2018; Eaton & McGlynn, 2020; Henry et al., 2019b).

- The *stolen* acquisition method involves stealing images (self/other) produced with consent from the depicted person that was illegally obtained from secured devices (belonging to portrayed, partner, or family) or from the cloud.
- In the *hidden* acquisition method, an image is produced surreptitiously by concealed camera in private spaces that have an expectation of privacy (e.g., home bathroom, store dressing room) and in public spaces with no expectation of privacy (e.g., walking in mall, seated/standing on public transportation). The images range from *completely clothed*, with focus on genitals, buttocks, and breasts (creepshots) to *partially nude*, including areas covered by clothes (upskirting, downblousing) to *naked and/or engaging in personal* (e.g., toileting, showering, changing) *and sexual activities*. The latter may occur when consent for participating in sexual acts was given, however, the recording, sharing, and/or distributing images of the sexual acts are unauthorized.
- The *altered* acquisition method alters an original image through sexualized photoshopping, airbrushing, or AI technology

Table 11.2 Motives for Nonconsensual Sharing/Distribution of Images by Acquisition Method

Motive Category	Consensual Production		Nonconsensual Production		
	Relationship	Stolen	Hidden	Crime	Altered
Sexual					
Arousal		√	√	√	√
Voyeurism		√	√	√	√
Sexual gratification		√	√	√	√
Socio-emotional					
Fun/joke/amusement	√	√	√		√
Boasting	√		√	√	
Showing off/trophies		√	√	√	
Bonding/intimacy	√				
Increase popularity /social status	√	√	√		√
Psychological					
Humiliate	√	√	√	√	√
Threaten	√	√	√	√	√
Distress	√	√	√	√	√
Control	√	√	√	√	√
Harass	√	√	√	√	√
Sextortion	√	√	√	√	√
Revenge	√	√	√	√	√
Financial					
Monetary gain		√	√	√	√

Key: Stolen, illegally obtained from storage on secured device or cloud; Hidden= surreptitious use of camera (e.g., upskirting, downblousing, creepshots, cameras in private spaces or in private areas of public spaces); Crime, obtained as part of crime (e.g., sextortion, rape, sexual assault, IPV coercion); Altered, image was created based on original and then altered using technology (e.g., morphing, disrobing apps); Relationship, obtained within the context of initiating and/or maintaining intimate relationship.

(e.g., morphing face onto a different body that is nude or performing a sex act), aka *synthetic media content* (*DeepFakes*) or use of an AI app (*DeepNude*) that removes clothing worn by the portrayed person.

- The *crime* acquisition method involves a stranger, acquaintance, or intimate partner producing the image by subduing the victim through coercion, incapacitation, force, or preventing escape (e.g., sextortion, intimate partner violence, sex trafficking, harassment, rape, sexual assault).

The motives for nonconsensual distribution of explicit and sexual images, regardless of how these were produced, include all four motive categories (Eaton & McGlynn, 2020; Henry et al., 2019b). For example, they could be shared among a limited number of friends for socio-emotional motives (Eaton & McGlynn, 2020; Henry & Flynn, 2019). Indiscriminate posting, especially on revenge porn websites (e.g., MyEx.com; IsAnyoneUp.com; UGotPosted.com; ShesAHomewrecker.com) and other forms of mass distribution—mobile phone; messaging apps (e.g., Snapchat); email; social media sites (e.g., Facebook); and online sites (e.g., Reddit and Tumblr)— would serve psychological motives for criminals (e.g., rapists, intimate partner abusers) or for ex-partners or ex-friends as justified punishment after a relationship ends because the victims cheated, gave them sexually transmitted disease, stole items or money, or were awarded child custody (Eaton & McGlynn, 2020; Franklin, 2014; Hall & Hearn, 2019; Henry et al., 2019b). Targeted nonconsensual distribution of images that were stolen, taken by hidden cameras, or were altered could be motivated by financial rewards (Henry et al., 2020a; Powell et al., 2019).

TYPICAL IBSA VICTIM

The typical victims of nonconsensual pornography dissemination are female adolescents and young adults aged 15–29 years (Eaton & McGlynn, 2020; Franklin, 2014; Henry et al., 2019b; Lenhart et al., 2016; Powell et al., 2019; Ruvalcaba & Eaton, 2020). Risk factors for IBSA victimization include being a sexual minority and having multiple sext partners, even if production of images was through coercion (Englander & McCoy, 2017; Ruvalcaba & Eaton, 2020).

According to Henry et al. (2019b), unauthorized distribution did not differ much for the three younger age groups (ranging from 12.7% to 14%) and was quite low in the oldest group (5%). The incidence rate of sending an image without the permission of the depicted person to another person ranged from 6% to 10% for adolescents (Crofts et al., 2015, $N = 2243$; Patrick et al., 2015, $N = 2114$), physically showing it to someone was even higher (e.g., 20%, Crofts et al., 2015). About 40% of victims who reported their images had been distributed also indicated it appeared on multiple platforms (Franklin, 2014; Henry et al., 2019b; Neris et al., 2015).

LAWS FOR PROSECUTING IBSA OFFENSES

Despite attempts to close the gap in laws prohibiting the various IBSA forms of cybersexual violence involving nonconsensual image production, distribution, and threat across jurisdictional boundaries inside the U.S., the legal system still today struggles to detect, apprehend, and prosecute these offenders (Cole et al., 2020; Cripps & Stermac, 2018; Eaton & McGlynn, 2020; Henry et al., 2020a; Najdowski, 2017). The development of criminal legislation is hampered by the failure to find a common definition; inconsistency in criminalizing all forms of IBSA—including technology-assisted/produced images without permission, such as surreptitious use in both private or public areas, and for nonauthorized distribution/posting/sharing of intimate images and threat thereof; and limits in evidentiary requirements, such as specific motives for mens rea (Cole et al., 2020; Henry et al., 2019b; Najdowski, 2017).

States differ in what constitutes "consent," in determining that an image is sexual or intimate, and, inconsistent with other crimes, have high threshold requirements for prosecution, such as the victim must be "identifiable" and the offender's motive must be to "cause harm," sometimes asking for "proof" indicative of the legislature's harm minimization attitudes (Cole et al., 2020; Najdowski, 2017; Neris et al., 2015; Powell et al., 2018). Eaton and McGlynn (2020) warned that by excluding self-produced and other-produced images originally taken and shared consensually, laws have a victim-blaming component that negates the crime of "invasion of privacy" entailed in nonconsensual online distribution (p. 194). Notwithstanding the rapid development and pervasive use of digital technology to commit crimes is the difficulty that IBSA victim-survivors and their advocates have in explaining the harms and injuries suffered by individuals, and ultimately society, to the public and legislatures (Inglesh, 2020; Sugiera & Smith, 2020). Finally, states disagree how to categorize IBSA crimes—such as privacy, disorderly conduct, harassment, obscenity, or sexual offenses (McGlynn et al., 2017).

Criminal remedies for production, distribution, and threat to distribute IBSA intimate images entail different principles of culpability. To understand principles associated with different types of IBSA, examples of laws will be presented. Nonconsensual production of intimate images may result from surreptitious surveillance or voyeurism, as a by-product of criminal acts, or from altering images. Currently, there are no laws prohibiting the production of intimate images of adults (at least age 18) using technology to splice together (morph) one person's head onto another person's body, create DeepFakes, or transmit criminal acts, including photographing an unconscious person during rape or sexual assault (e.g., see Footnote 1).

Deep fake pornography distributed online extends beyond any state jurisdiction (Delfino, 2019; Harris, 2019; Inglesh, 2020). Bills have been introduced at the federal and state level to address these two methods of production. The Malicious Deep Fake Prohibition Act of 2018 was rejected for being overly broad in its definition and exemption for the First Amendment speech and its liability on distributors, while being too constricted in its criminal intent and condition requirements for proof (Delfino, 2019; Harris, 2019; Inglesh, 2020). Another bill was introduced in 2019 (H.R. 3230 Deep Fakes Accountability Act § 1041. *Advanced technological false personation record*, 116th Congress). If passed, it would amend Chapter 47 of U.S.C.C. regarding fraud and false statements to establish the criminal offense related to deceptive creation or distribution of artificial-enabled technology media records that appear realistic. Many states do not have a specific law regarding nonauthorized production and/or dissemination of deep fake intimate images, mainly because legislators assume that the image does not depict a "real person" concluding that no dignity harm (from being a sexualized object) occurred (Franks & Waldman, 2019). This reasoning is flawed in multiple ways, but from a legal perspective the current prohibition of computer altered child sexual abuse material in which real children's heads/faces are morphed onto adult bodies could be adopted for IBSA (see *Prosecutorial Remedies and Other Tools to End the Exploitation of Children Today Act*/PROTECT of 2003).

The other type of IBSA production not prohibited is intimate images produced through a criminal act, such as extortion, exploitation, coercion, intimate partner violence abuse, and sexual assault or rape. Like sexual violence offenses, the victim-survivors in these IBSA-type examples are not able to provide consent freely nor have the capacity to do so. An incapacitated person by definition is incapable of consent because s/he is "unable to understand the facts, nature, extent, or implications of the situation due to drugs, alcohol, mental disability, being asleep or unconscious."[4] Many states choose to charge offenders under their current criminal statutes (e.g., extortion, exploitation) rather than constructing separate laws for the image production, typically charging offenders with obscenity rather than with sexual offenses. The Virginia Senate proposed a bill in 2018, the S.B.563—*Unlawful creation of image of another; incapacitated adult*—which would make it unlawful for someone to "knowingly and intentionally create a videographic or still image of a nonconsenting person if such person is totally nude, clad in undergarments, or in a state of undress so as to expose the genitals, pubic area, buttocks, or female breast or if the recording device was positioned directly beneath or between such person's legs." Despite it merely being an extension of §18.2–386.1. *Unlawful creation of image, prohibition to unconscious persons* (Chapter 8. Crimes involving Morals and Decency, Article 5. Obscenity and related offenses), it failed to pass.[5] Most IBSA victim-survivor advocates, however, argue that nonconsensual production (and dissemination) of intimate images should be processed under sexual offenses; to do otherwise demonstrates a lack of understanding regarding the harms caused by this crime to individuals and society (Jacobs, 2016; McGlynn et al., 2017).

Although technology-assisted IBSA in which offenders obtain or create intimate images without the depicted victim's consent or knowledge are prohibited by state and/or federal laws, statutes do not apply to all conditions (Bell et al., 2006; McCann et al., 2018; Najdowski, 2017). Many states had to update their original voyeurism statutes that failed to include the use of electronic means to "peep" into a private space (e.g., retail fitting room) rather than requiring a person to violate property rights by physically intruding (i.e., trespassing) in areas where privacy is expected (e.g., bathroom, bedroom). Video voyeurism laws prohibit the nonconsensual

---

[4] Accessed at: https://stopsexualviolence.iu.edu/policies-terms/consent.html (11/8/2020).
[5] Accessed at: https://www.richmondsunlight.com/bill/2018/sb563/ (11/8/2020).

recording of a person in a state of undress or engaged in sexual activity in places where individuals enjoy a reasonable expectation of privacy. However, these statutes were insufficient to stop technology-assisted surveillance occurring in public areas (e.g., photographs focused up the skirts of women either walking in shopping mall, *State of Washington v. Glas*, 2002 or sitting on a train, *Commonwealth v. Michael Robertson*)[6] where a reasonable expectation of privacy would not apply (McCann et al., 2018). Although these situations were not within the letter of the voyeurism laws, they certainly were within the spirit of the laws. Currently, "upskirting" and "downblousing" video voyeurism in which recording of intimate body parts, even when covered by clothing to protect from public view (i.e., to maintain privacy), are criminalized in only 16 states that do not have privacy requirements;[7] creepshots, in contrast, are not currently prohibited at the state or federal level. Examples of different state and federal laws relevant to the three types of IBSA in their different forms are discussed in the next section, the definitions of "intimate," "private area," and reasonable expectation of privacy differ by state. For the purpose of this discussion, *intimate* refers to images in which the person is engaged in sexual activity and/or appears nude or semi-nude with the focus on private areas (pubic region, genitalia, female breasts), whereas *expectation of privacy* would include being in locations for which the public would not have open access and/or public views of private areas are occluded by clothing.

The wording of the Virginia state law, "created by any means whatsoever" and the definition of "another person" specifies that the image "depict an actual person and who is recognizable as an actual person" suggests that Deep Fakes would be included; but, it is the unauthorized disseminating of intimate images, rather than on the unauthorized production and/or possession of them, that is illegal.

Virginia state law §18.2–386.2:

> A. "Any person who, with the *intent* to coerce, harass, or intimate, maliciously disseminates or sells any videographic or still image created by any means whatsoever that depicts another person who is totally nude, or in a state of undress so as to expose the genitals, pubic area, buttocks, or female breast, where such person *knows* or *has reason to know* that he

---

[6] *State v. Glas*, 54 P.3d 147 (2002); Commonwealth v. Michael Robertson, 467 Mass. 371 (2014).
[7] These include: Alaska, Delaware, Florida, Hawaii, Illinois, Kentucky, Louisiana, Maine, Missouri, New Hampshire, New York, North Carolina, Ohio, Texas, Virginia, and Washington.

is not licensed or authorized to disseminate or sell such videographic or still image. For purposes of this subsection, 'another person' includes a person whose image was used in creating, adapting, or modifying a videographic or still image with the intent to depict an actual person and who is recognizable as an actual person by the person's face, likeness, or other distinguishing characteristic.

B. Venue for a prosecution …may lie in the jurisdiction where the unlawful act occurs or where any videographic or still image created by any means whatsoever is produced, reproduced, found, stored, received or possessed in violation of this section."

The actus reus refers to the acts specified in A (i.e., disseminate/sell intimate images created by any means whatsoever) and the mens rea refers to the *intentions* for the acts plus the *knowledge* that the offender is not licensed/authorized to act, as stated in A. In this law, B allows prosecutors to pursue the case in the jurisdiction where the crime occurred regardless of the offenders' jurisdiction.

New York law uses a broader approach by prohibiting covert nonconsensual production of intimate images in private (see #1, #2, #3, and #5) and public (see #4) settings, as well as the nonconsensual dissemination of such images. However, it does not address the harm from Deep Fakes.

NY Consolidated Laws § 250.45 Unlawful surveillance.[8] A person is guilty when:

1. For his or her own, or another person's amusement, entertainment, or profit, or for the purpose of degrading or abusing a person he or she *intentionally* uses or installs or permits the utilization or installation of an imaging device to surreptitiously view, broadcast or record a person dressing or undressing or the sexual or other intimate parts of such person at a place and time when such person has a reasonable expectation of privacy, *without such person's knowledge or consent*; or
2. For his or her own, or another person's sexual arousal or sexual gratification, he or she *intentionally* uses or installs, or permits the utilization or installation of an imaging device to surreptitiously view, broadcast, or record a person dressing or undressing or the sexual or other intimate parts of such person at a place and time when such person has a reasonable expectation of privacy, *without such person's knowledge or consent*; or

---

[8] Accessed at: https://codes.findlaw.com/ny/penal-law/pen-sect-250-45.html (11/8/2020).

3. a. For no legitimate purpose he or she *intentionally* uses or installs or permits the utilization or installation of an imaging device to surreptitiously view, broadcast or record a person in a bedroom, changing room, fitting room, restroom, toilet, bathroom, washroom, shower or any room assigned to guests or patrons in a motel, hotel or inn, *without such person's knowledge or consent.*

   b. For the purpose of this subdivision, when a person uses or installs, or permits uses or installs or permits the utilization or installation of an imaging device to surreptitiously view, broadcast or record a person in a bedroom, changing room, fitting room, restroom, toilet, bathroom, washroom, shower or any room assigned to guests or patrons in a motel, hotel or inn, there is a rebuttable presumption that such person did so for no legitimate purpose; or

4. *Without the knowledge or consent of a person,* he or she *intentionally* uses or installs, or permits the utilization or installation of an imaging device to surreptitiously view, broadcast or record, under the clothing being worn by such person, the sexual or other intimate parts of such person; or

5. For his or her own, or another person's amusement, entertainment, profit, sexual arousal or gratification, or for the purpose of degrading or abusing a person, the actor intentionally uses or installs, or permits the utilization or installation of an imaging device to surreptitiously view, broadcast, or record such person in an identifiable manner:

   a. engaging in sexual conduct;

   b. in the same image with the sexual or intimate part of any other person; and

   c. at a place and time when such person has a reasonable expectation of privacy, without such person's knowledge or consent."

The actus reus refers to the acts of: (1) uses; (2) installs; (3) permits (a) the utilization or (b) installation (c) of an imaging device; (4) to surreptitiously view; (5) broadcast (6) record a person in an identifiable manner (a) dressing (b) undressing (c) under the clothing (d) the sexual conduct or (e) sexual or other intimate parts of such person; (7) at a place and (8) time when such person has a reasonable expectation of privacy; (9) without such person's knowledge; or (10) consent. The mens rea would include (1) intentionally;

(2) knowingly; and (3) purposefully because the offender performs acts that result in the harms (e.g., degrading, abusing, objectified for entertainment, profit, or sexual gratification) suffered by the victim-survivor.

The federal law relevant for prosecuting nonconsensual production, the Video Voyeurism Prevention Act of 2004 (18 U.S.C. §1801), prohibits creating and disseminating images on federal property (e.g., park, post office, military base) and when multiple jurisdictions are involved.

> Public Law No. 108–495: "prohibits *knowingly* videotaping, photographing, filming, recording by any means, or broadcasting an image of a private area of an individual, without that individual's consent, under circumstances in which that individual has a reasonable expectation of privacy."

The actus reus refers to the acts of (1) videotaping, (2) photographing, (3) filming, (4) recording, (5) broadcasting and image (6) of a private area of individual (7) without consent and (8) when there is a reasonable expectation of privacy. The mens rea of this statute is that the offender did so knowingly.

According to the Cyber Civil Rights Initiative, all but four states (Mississippi, Massachusetts, South Carolina, and Wyoming) have laws prohibiting nonconsensual distribution of intimate images (aka "revenge porn"); however, threats to disseminate in and of themselves without follow-through are not prohibited under these laws, but may be covered as exploitation or extortion, depending how the threats are worded.

Arizona's law (Section 13–1425) makes it unlawful for a person to intentionally disclose an image of another person who is identifiable from the image itself or from information displayed in connection with the image if all of the following apply:

1. "The person in the image is depicted in a state of nudity or is engaged in specific sexual activities;
2. The depicted person has a reasonable expectation of privacy. Evidence that a person has sent an image to another person using an electronic device does not, on its own, remove the person's reasonable expectation of privacy for that image.
3. The image is disclosed with the *intent* to harm, harass, intimate, threaten, or coerce the depicted person."

The actus reus refers to (1) nudity or (2) engaged in specific sexual activities, and (3) has a reasonable expectation of privacy. The mens rea refers to intentions outlined in #3. It is important that the consent to produce or even to share initially an intimate image with another is clearly protected here and cannot be interpreted as consent to distribute (Cole et al., 2020). According to Citron and Franks (2014), "consent to share information in one context does not serve as consent to share this information in another content" (p. 349). They state that privacy laws recognize the contextual nature of consent, particularly when the information being shared in sensitive, such that disclosure to one entity or for one purpose does not preclude sharing with even one other person without authorization.

Consistent with Delfino's (2019) conclusion, "existing criminal laws—both federal and state—were insufficient to punish the creators and distributors and to remedy the harms victims suffered" (p. 918). The lack of consistency in how the statutes are framed, such as breach of privacy or as harassment, and in the level of criminalization assigned (misdemeanor versus felony), renders them insufficient as deterrents and leads to confusion for the victim-survivors and law enforcement alike (Cole et al., 2020; Eaton & McGlynn, 2020; Fay, 2018; Henry et al., 2018; Sugiera & Smith, 2020). For example, many of the criminal laws as written are unable to address people's *invasion of privacy* by nonconsensual use of technology within private and public spaces as a means of committing voyeurism, making a permanent record of the image, and disseminating or threatening to distribute it without consent (Bell et al., 2006; Fay, 2018). Physical intrusion into privacy, already actionable civilly (tort), could also be criminal but only if it is tied to property rights, such as trespass or burglary (Newell, 2017). In New York, criminal trespass requires that the offender knowingly enters or remains unlawfully in a building or upon real property (actus reus). At this time, the priority of law enforcement to investigate IBSA crimes (which are merely misdemeanors in 28 states), or even to consider them to be a form of sexual violence, is low (Bell et al., 2006; Eaton & McGlynn, 2020; Henry et al., 2018; Holt & Liggett, 2020).

As an alternative to criminal redress, IBSA victim-survivors have instead sought civil reparations (e.g., privacy, intentional infliction of emotional distress (IIED), defamation, appropriation). The specific elements of torts depend on state statues, each having definitions for terms that typically are not consistent across states or with the federal statutes. The civil ligation process, however, is not optimal given that it is long, expensive (i.e., filing fees, attorney expenses), and requires the victim-survivors' real name when filing (Citron & Franks, 2014; Henry et al., 2020a). Two examples of litigation using civil torts to prosecute unauthorized distribution of IBSA are described in **Box 11.1**. Further aspects that disincentivize plaintiffs include offenders may be judgment-proof[9] and civil judgments are available as public records, allowing others to learn of their situation (Pollack, 2016). Victim-survivors are advised that it is very difficult to prove fraud claims, even when their intimate images have been shared against their wishes because they would have to prove intent to violate trust at the time of the original transition (Fay, 2018; Franks & Waldman, 2019; Goldman & Jin, 2018). Even more disconcerting is that even when plaintiffs win their lawsuits, it does not guarantee their images will be removed from online sites and social media platforms unless posting of them violates copyright, which is only possible if the plaintiff's images were self- produced (Cole et al., 2020). Moreover, there is also no guarantee that the awarded punitive damages will be paid. For example, in *Del Mastro v. Grimado*, a new suit was filed in 2009 because the judgment from 2005 (affirmed on appeal in 2007), in which Del Mastro was awarded $531,820.47 in damages (based on his financial holdings) due to IIED and invasion of privacy from Grimado's nonauthorized distribution of intimate photographs, had not been paid; in 2013, the Court ruled to vacate the judgment, reinstate her complaint, and remand for new trial due to prejudicial error regarding the defendants' actual holdings, which he attempted to hide fraudulently so as to appear judgment-proof.

BOX 11.1   TWO EXAMPLES OF CIVIL LITIGATION FOR UNAUTHORIZED IBSA DISTRIBUTION

Example 1: *Leser v. Penido*, 62 A.D. 3d 510 (2009), 879 N.Y.S.2d 107 (N.Y. Sup. Ct. 2009)

  Tort: Defamation—Libel

  Timeline: Jean Leser (Plaintiff-Respondent) filed against Christopher and Luz Penido (Defendants-Appellants) in 2007. First decision was July 15, 2008; it was appealed September 28, 2010 and a judgment was entered March 23, 2011. Another appeal was entered January 19, 2012 and then heard, with the final decision provided June 19, 2012, **five years later**.

  Attorney fees: Attorney fees totaled $20,000.

---

[9] *Judgement proof* refers to the inability of a debtor (defendant in civil suit) to provide assets to a creditor (plaintiff) when ordered by Court to do so.

Judgment: Christopher Penido, by his own admission, posted Plaintiff's name and email address along with pornographic materials and remarks on blog and websites that the Court indicated "impugned plaintiff's chastity and therefore were libelous per se." The Plaintiff provided expert evidence that the IP address and phone number linked to the website belonged to the defendant. She stated she suffered harm to her business (EBay Online Store, The Luxury Portal, sells luxury handbags) as the postings implied that she was "sexually lustful and promiscuous." In addition to attorney fees, Lessor was awarded damages based on the "disinterest malevolence on defendant's part, which establishes plaintiff's entitlement to attorneys' fees and supports the Court's award of both compensatory and punitive damages."

Analysis[10]

- **Defamation** is "false statement, published without privilege or authorization" (<u>Dillon v City of New York, 261 AD2d 34, 38, 704 N.Y.S.2d 1 [1st Dept 1999]</u>).
- **Libel** is comprised of "defamatory writing that exposes plaintiff to public hatred, contempt, ridicule or disgrace" (PJI 3:23; see <u>Rinaldi v Holt, Rinehart & Winston, 42 NY2d 369, 379, 366 N.E.2d 1299, 397 N.Y.S.2d 943 [1977]</u>).

    - "Damages are presumed to flow from libelous statements (see <u>Ostrowe v Lee, 256 NY 36, 39, 175 N.E. 505</u> [1931, <u>Cardozo</u>, Ch. J.] ['What gives the sting to the writing is its permanence of form'])."

Example 2: *Taylor v. Franko*, 2011 U.S. Dist. Ct Hawaii (Civ. NO. 09-00002 JMS/RLP)

Tort: Invasion of Privacy (Count I); Public Disclosure of Private Facts (Count II); Negligent and Intentional Infliction of Emotional Distress (Count III); Defamation of Character (Count IV).

---

[10] Accessed at: https://advance-lexis-com.ez.lib.jjay.cuny.edu/document/?pdmfid=1 516831&crid=3b3a6062-0a10-47f1-ae57-814cf3de9ca1&pddocfullpath=%2Fshared% 2Fdocument%2Fcases%2Furn%3AcontentItem%3A57TC-HNB1-F04J-80KS-00000-00&pdcontentcomponentid=9095&pdshepid=urn%3AcontentItem%3A5YHJ-VND1-J9X5-T126-00000-00&pdteaserkey=sr4&pditab=allpods&ecomp=fzx2k&ear g=sr4&prid=a4071a55-b525-4d65-aa59-a8b96756465c (11/15/2020).

Timeline: Taylor filed complaint on January 5, 2009 against Franko and five other defendants (claims were dismissed against four of them in February 2009 for lack of jurisdiction and against the fifth in June 2011). She tried but was denied a temporary restraining order and preliminary injunction. Multiple attempts were made for defendant(s) to come to Court for Pretrial Conferences in 2010, along with continuances, ending with no opposition and motion for Default Judgment in February 2011. There was an evidentiary hearing (non-jury trial) on June 9, 2011 and Proposed Findings of Fact and Conclusions of Law was submitted on June 30, 2011. The final decision was two and one-half years after the initial filing, despite it being unopposed.

Attorney fees: $5000.

Judgment: Leona Taylor (Plaintiff) had been in an intimate relationship with William Franko (defendant) from 2003 to 2004. She permitted him to take pictures of her performing sexual acts; upon dissolution of their relationship (November 2004) and without her knowledge or consent, Franko posted these images on adult Websites with Taylor's contact information (including her home and work numbers), which she learned about in November 2007 through a colleague's instant message. In addition to an erotic amateur photograph website, Taylor found the images posted on a bestiality website alongside a false statement describing her interests—including she wanted people to contact her, website and Craigslist ads stating various (kinky) sexual interests—and the images had been reposted on 23 websites. She felt humiliated by the postings, suffered from shingles, required counseling (diagnosis of Adjustment Disorder with Depression). She received three calls a day almost daily from 2007 to 2008, and still received calls at least monthly until May 2010; strangers who had seen her images online approached her seeking sex. The Court granted Taylor's default judgment in 2011.

Analysis[11]

- **Invasion of Privacy**: Denied, Plaintiff failed to identify which of the four claims she alleges.

---

[11] Accessed at: https://docs.justia.com/cases/federal/district-courts/hawaii/hidce/1:2009cv00002/83758/75 (11/15/2020).

- **Public Disclosure of Private Facts**: Plaintiff adequately alleges all elements
  - Franko publicized information on adult websites available to third-party viewers;
  - Information included nude photographs and personal contact information, neither of which were public concern;
  - Franko's behavior met standard of being highly offensive to a reasonable person.

- **Negligent and Intentional Infliction of Emotional Distress**: Plaintiff adequately alleges all elements for both claims
  - Franko posted nude photographs with personal contact information on at least 11 adult websites, outside the bounds of toleration by decent society;
  - Franko's act caused her extreme emotional psychological distress [e.g., received unwanted phone calls and email requests for sexual encounters, even at work, causing embarrassment].

- **Defamation of Character**: Defendant's publishing of false and defamatory statements (i.e., she is bisexual, has no preference as to age, race, and marital status) alongside intimate photographs, which damaged her reputation in regards to her chastity (50 Am. Jur. 2d Libel & Slander §185, 2011) and sexual orientation (see Restatement (Second) Tort § 574, 1977).

Damages of $425,000 were awarded.

Most states codify their statutes for privacy rights based on some or most of the Restatement (Second) of Torts § 652A, which allows four claims—intrusion, right of publicity, private facts, and false light.

> *Intrusion upon seclusion or solitude* or into private affairs or concerns (based on Restatement (Second) of Torts § 652B)). Intrusion includes physical invasion into a secluded or solitary place by use of perpetrator's senses, with or without mechanical aids, to obtain information about victim's private affairs; use of excessive surveillance, such as binoculars or wiretap; another form of investigation or examination into private concerns

(e.g., opening mail, safe, wallet, bank account). As intrusion on its face has a negative impact on one's dignity, this tort makes the offender liable without an obligation to publish or use photograph or information.

Misappropriation of name or likeness for commercial purposes or *right of publicity* (based on Restatement (Second) of Torts § 652C)). The purpose of this claim is to protect a person against mental distress derived from common invasion by appropriation or use by perpetrator to advertise person's name and image for commercial purpose or for one's own purpose and benefit (Digital Media Law Project, 2020b).

Publication of (embarrassing) *private facts* (based on Restatement (Second) of Torts § 652D)). Communicating or publishing information in public forum (e.g., website, blog) regarding the private life of a person not revealed to the public, not legitimate public concern, and which would be considered offensive to a reasonable person is a violation of privacy (Digital Media Law Project, 2020a, 2020d). An image is only considered a "private fact" if taken in private (making the photographer liable for intrusion), however, images taken in public or semi-public areas when published fall under the liability of "using the likeness of another" (Digital Media Law Project, 2020d). Unauthorized use of an image for an exploitative purpose, such as personal gain, is prohibited in most states (Digital Media Law Project, 2020b, 2020c). The victim's right to sexual privacy is violated when intimate images (not recorded for mass dissemination or entertainment) are made public.

Publicly placing a person in *false light* in the public eye (based on Restatement (Second) of Torts § 652E)). Emphasis on publicity would be highly offensive to a reasonable person and, as long as it is not of legitimate concern to the public, privacy should be maintained (Citron & Franks, 2014).

Table 11.3 (Bell, 2005; Legal Information Institute, n.d.; Mania, 2020; Newell, 2017) provides explanations of civil alternatives through various intentional torts (i.e., tortfeasor intends to bring harm and acts to do so) based on New York statutes. The most common options that plaintiffs can pursue for unauthorized distribution of IBSA content is covered in New York Consolidated Laws by Civil Rights Law – CVR §50. *Right of Privacy* (based on Restatement (Second) of Torts §§ 652A – 652E), in which "a person… <who> uses for…the purposes of trade, the name, portrait, or picture of any living person without having first obtained the written consent of said person…is guilty of a misdemeanor."[12] Victim-survivors may pursue a civil claim against any person who violated their privacy rights,

---

[12] Accessed at: https://codes.findlaw.com/ny/civil-rights-law/cvr-sect-50.html (11/14/2020).

Table 11.3 New York Civil Law Relevant to Unauthorized Distribution of IBSA Content

Intentional Torts	Description of Elements
Privacy *Misappropriation* of name or likeness for commercial purposes or *Right of publicity*	1. Protects full name, portrait and picture (any likeness, not just photographs), and voice; 2. Person must be alive; 3. Identity must be within New York state; 4. Without written consent.
Intentional infliction of emotional distress (IIED)	1. Extreme and outrageous acts; 2. intent to cause or disregard substantial probability acts result in severe emotional distress; 3. causal relationship between act and harm; and 4. severe emotional distress.
Conversion	1. Intent; 2. interference with owner's rights; and 3. possession.
Defamation of character (Libel)[a]	1. Making false statement resulting in public contempt, ridicule, aversion, disgrace; or deprive of social interactions or society forms evil opinions of person;[b] 2. unauthorized publication; 3. fault by negligence standard.

[a] NY Civil Rights Law statute of limitations in New York for suing under the tort of defamation is 1 year after publication.
[b] See *Foster v. Churchill*, 665 N.E.2d 153, 157 (N.Y. 1996) in Mania (2020).

as described in New York Consolidated Laws by Civil Rights Law – CVR §51 (Actions for injunction and for damages), to restrain the use of the image (and name) and/or sue to recover damages for injuries from use of the image (and name).[13]

---

[13] https://codes.findlaw.com/ny/civil-rights-law/cvr-sect-51.html (11/14/2020); Statute of limitations is one year after publication.

Tort claims involving invasion of privacy to produce intimate images require that the victim prove a reasonable expectation of privacy existed, which excludes images self-produced or shared voluntarily with another person and those taken in public, even if done surreptitiously (Fay, 2018). New York does not have common law, per se, for invasion of privacy; instead, the plaintiff would file Right of Publicity (i.e., exclusive right to license the use of their identity) if intimate images were commercially disseminated.[14] The state recognizes the interest of individual in exclusive use of one's own identity. Litigants must show that these images do not fall under these three exceptions—newsworthy events, matters of public concern, or artistic expression.[15]

Litigants may also sue for other types of intentional torts—*Intentional infliction of emotional distress* (based on Restatement (Second) of Torts § 46(1)), *Conversion,* and *Defamation* (Delfino, 2019; Hall & Archer, 2020; Mania, 2020); in contrast, *Sexual harassment* in unlikely to be a viable option for redress as it has not been applied outside of work or educational settings (Citron & Franks, 2014). Lawsuits that claim IIED are hindered by the burden of proving that the defendant's acts were "extreme and outrageous" (Drinnon, 2017; Mania, 2020). The media currently publishes intimate images, therefore, our society by its silence does not deem such acts indecent, appalling, and intolerable (Cyber Civil Rights Initiative, 2020). Another way to regain property is to sue through Conversion by showing that the litigant is the lawful owner and therefore has dominion and exclusion of rights over it (*NY Civil Rights Law § 3.1*).[16] Copyright laws indicate that the producer of the image owns the copyright, thus it would need to be self-produced (Citron & Franks, 2014). Currently Courts are struggling with how to extend this tort from *tangible* property to cover claims of *intangible* property (i.e., including computerized images), with some case law providing exceptions when it is converted into a physical form (Hall & Archer, 2020). Defamation may be appropriate as intimate images are

---

[14] The victim-survivor's consent to the production of said image, or lack thereof, and/or non-consensual altering of the image (Deep Fake) may be considered differently depending on common law or state statutes (Digital Media Law Project, 2020b; Legal Information Institute, n.d.). Some states cover *Right of Publicity* under the *Law of Unfair Competition* to prevent someone presenting a product as "endorsed or produced by the individual" (Legal Information Institute, n.d., para 3).

[15] Litigants may counter defendant claims artistic exemption by showing the image falls under obscenity, which is not protected by the First Amendment (Fay, 2018; Harris, 2019).

[16] *NY Civil Rights Law § 214(3).* The statute of limitations in New York for suing using the tort of conversion (recovery of chattel) is three years.

often published alongside defamatory statements about the victim-survivor. This particular avenue for redress is unlikely to work for suits involving altered images (face of one person transposed onto a body of another person) because it fails to meet the requirement that a real (existing) person is depicted (Delfino, 2019). This makes it difficult for the face victim to sue for exposure of intimate details (publication of private facts) when the body is not hers and the body victim must prove her body is identifiable without her face (Delfino, 2019).

Many of the victim-survivors desperately want to remove the content from the websites. Adding to their humiliation, the *Digital Millennium Copyright Act* of 1998 only allows victim-survivors to request a "takedown" notice to ISPs when they are the legal holder of the image; but, even then, the image may remain online if the victims cannot prove the photograph has been copyrighted—which most understandably are not (Citron & Franks, 2014; Fay, 2018). Civil redress may be the next best method for removing the content. However, third-party posters of IBSA content, including deep fake pornography, do so anonymously, as is allowed on different platforms (e.g., Reddit, Twitter, PornHub), and offenders also use *Tor* to disguise their IP addresses (Delfino, 2019). Internet Service Providers (ISPs) are protected from civil suits through Section 230 of the Communications Decency Act of 1996 (Franklin, 2014). However, as discussed in **Box 11.2**, liability is not applicable when the website administrator fosters the development of harmful content by adding original IBSA material and/or specifically soliciting it (Franklin, 2014, p. 1305).

BOX 11.2   CRIMINAL ACTIONS AGAINST ADMINISTRATORS OF NONCONSENSUAL PORNOGRAPHY WEBSITES

Until the federal and state government legislations prohibit nonconsensual pornography, website administrators can and will post (and profit from) these images with impunity. In the cases outline below (Goldman & Jin, 2018), charges made against administrators were for crimes related to their active role in developing the content and/or involvement in illegal activities, which negated their ISP immunity as "hosts" to third-party content (CDC Section 230).

People v. Bollaert:[17] Kevin Bollaert, the administrator of two websites—UGotPosted.com and ChangeMyReputation.com—was convicted of six counts of extortion (Pen.Code, §520) and 21 counts of unlawful use of personal identifying information (§530.5 subd. (a)), and sentenced to 8 years in prison followed by 10 years of mandatory supervision. The extortion charges stemmed from him requiring victims who requested their images removed from *UGotPosted* to pay him through *ChangeMyReputation* (earning him $30,147.73). In 2016, the Superior Court affirmed his sentence and denied his immunity to liability claim under §530.5 of the Communications Decency Act 47 U.S.C. §230(c)(1) as he designed, maintained, and operated the site and thus was an information content provider; he required users, as a condition of publishing the 10,170 photos on UGotPosted.com, to disclose private facts (invasion of privacy) of the victims and he moderated the comments posted on the website.

United States v. Moore:[18] Hunter Edward Moore, the administrator of *IsAnyoneUp.com*, received a 2.5-year federal prison sentence followed by 3-year supervised release for conspiring with a hacker, Charles Evens, to steal nude photos from hundreds of Google email accounts that were later posted on his website. Moore pled guilty to Count 2 for Unauthorized access to a protected computer to obtain information for private financial gain and Aiding and Abetting the Unauthorized access to a protected computer to obtain information for private financial gain (Title 18 U.S.C. §§ 1030(a)(2)(C), (c)(2)(B)(i), and 2) and to Count 9 for Aggravated Identity Theft (Title 18 U.S.C. § 1028A(a)(2)) of the 15-count indictment.

In re Craig Brittain:[19] Brittain, the administrator of *IsAnybodyDown.com*, made an agreement with FTC to shut down his site, delete all content, and never post intimate photos of people without their consent (McCarthy, 2015). The FTC alleged that Brittain obtained intimate images of victims by using deception (violation of 15 U.S.C. §45), which he posted on his site with their personal information, and made them pay him to remove the photos (McCarthy, 2015).

---

[17] *People of California v. Kevin Christopher Bollaert*, Super. Ct. No. SCD252338.
[18] *United States v. Moore*, 2:13-cr-00917.
[19] *In the Matter of Craig Brittain*, No. C-4564 (F.T.C. January 8, 2016).

Law enforcement agents have not always been successful in identifying the administrators of websites posting IBSA content. Even more disturbing, when law enforcement shut down known sites, they simply reappear elsewhere, like a game of "whack-a-mole" (Kapur, 2020). One such website, *Pink Meth*[20]—hosted on the Darknet—hacked cloud storage of celebrities initially and subsequently expanded to non-celebrities, posting nude photos for anyone to download, and allowed users to post personal information alongside the victims' images (Jacobs, 2016; Kapur, 2020). The FBI, upon discovering its Darkweb connections in selling drugs and firearms, shut it down in 2014, but it reappeared under the brand *Anon-IB* on a Netherlands server (Jacobs, 2016; Kapur, 2020). Anon-IB was then shut down in 2018 by Dutch authorities after arresting the three administrators; however, a nonprofit organization for IBSA victims, *BADASS Army* was able to determine using 4chan and Reddit conversations that Anon-IB had reopened on a Russian domain (Kapur, 2020). As ISPs are pressured to curb IBSA content on their websites and anti-revenge porn legislation is developed, criminals avoid detection by using chatrooms—first Discord and then Slack—which allow users to create workspaces in which to trade IBSA content (Cox, 2018).

IMPACT OF IBSA OFFENSES ON SOCIETY AND VICTIMS

Male and female victims' responses to IBSA may vary due to gender differences in how they process it. For example, Powell et al. (2018) reported that men who learned that intimate images were produced of them were more likely than women to have positive reactions (81% vs. 48%), such as being amused or flattered, rather than negative reactions (73% vs. 81%), such as being humiliated or afraid for their safety. In many cases of IBSA, the unfettered sharing of images co-occurs with doxing (i.e., revealing private, personal information), online harassment, and cyberstalking (Fay, 2018). Office of eSafety Commissioner (2017) reported that alongside the images, 33% of female victims had their names posted and 21% had their social network/profile posted; moreover, 27%–39% of the female victims receive threats and stalking after the images were posted. The long-term

---

[20] *Shelby Conklin v PinkMeth.com aka pinkmethuylnenlz.onion.lt*, 2014, 431 Judicial District Court, Denton County Texas launched a civil suit for invasion of privacy against the revenge porn website with anonymous administrators.

consequences for these victim-survivors consist of different forms of harm, including *physiological* (e.g., stomach-aches, headaches, unable to enjoy sex); *social* (e.g. withdraw from activities, trust issues); *emotional* (e.g., loss in self-esteem, emotional distress, PTSD, anxiety, humiliation and shame, depression, contemplate/engage in suicide); and *educational and professional* impacting current and future financial independence (i.e., they are unable to focus or function in their school or work environment, fired, unable to get/keep employment) that interrupts their lives temporally or permanently (Eaton & McGlynn, 2020; Eaton et al., 2017; Henry et al., 2019b; McGlynn & Rackley, 2017; Walker & Sheath, 2017).

IBSA is also harmful to society in multiple ways (Gavin & Scott, 2019; Henry et al., 2019a; McGlynn & Rackley, 2017; Walker & Sleath, 2017; Wood et al., 2015). First, it induces a culture that tolerates and encourages multiple people within a network sharing nonconsensual images and posting negative comments. This dangerous mentality, often displayed in conjunction with sexual assault and harassment, demonstrates legal and social disregard for sexual boundaries, more specifically the victim's right to consent (Citron & Franks, 2014). Second, it places responsibility on the victim-survivor (instead of on the offender) either for producing such images or not doing enough to ensure the images would not be produced (blame) and/or distributed (shame). Collective harm occurs through systemic humiliation that scaffolds "gendered social subordination, preventing the full civic participation and digital citizenship" of societal members (Flynn et al., 2018, p. 311). Third, it enables perpetrators to continue their coercive behaviors as inadequate criminal or civil legislation signals condoning and/or excusing it as part of the "boys will be boys" phenomenon or "harmless pranks" (McGlynn et al., 2019). A recent survey revealed that more men than women (49% vs. 32%) "minimised the harm, blamed victims, or made excuses for perpetration," reflecting a lack of social control needed to place the onus of responsibility on the perpetrators to reduce criminal enactment (Henry et al., 2019a, p. 14). Fourth, it normalizes the aberrant behaviors comprising this crime, namely the unauthorized production and/or distribution (or threat to distribute) intimate images. Surreptitious photography of women's intimate (albeit partially or fully clothed) body parts while in public areas, such as upskirting, downblousing, and creepyshots, or sexual photoshopped images of a victim's face on a nude body or one engaged in sex (i.e., DeepFakes, especially those of unrequited love interests) combined with nonconsensual posting/

distributing of this content are tolerated forms of sexual violence that perpetuate archaic belief systems in which women exist solely to provide sexual pleasure for men (Flynn & Henry, 2019).

Society's responses to IBSA content, both online and offline, are a reflection of acceptable techno-social beliefs and actions that result in gender inequality and provide a cultural scaffold for learning sexual violence (Flynn et al., 2018). Understandably, when technology develops quickly, there is a gap in people's understanding of the potential abuses and resulting harms, as well as in legislators' ability to create laws to prohibit aforementioned abusive behaviors. The production and distribution of IBSA is an invasion of privacy; when these acts are not met with legal consequences, women (and the men who love them) fear for their safety both in private and in public. Currently, there are thousands of websites dedicated to hosting and distributing IBSA material predominantly of women for heterosexual men, resulting in sexual exploitation and abuse not inconsistent with the "gonzo" element of mainstream pornography, namely that women are subordinate to men and are characterized by physically brutal and verbally degrading sex scenes (DeKeseredy & Schwartz, 2016; Flynn & Henry, 2019).

The Internet has contributed to the growth (and acceptance) of the rape-supportive culture of the online pornography industry, and by default IBSA content, through its ability to provide instant access to millions of people. It "buttresses social patriarchy and helps create an environment that normalizes hurtful sexuality, racism, and even seeking revenge on female ex-partners," whom men conceptualize as being their property (DeKeseredy & Schwartz, 2016, p. 5). Society similarly endorses sexual scripts promoted in online pornography, namely that women are objects deserving of their subjugation to sexual violence in dehumanizing ways, as acceptable forms of behavior by failing to condemn portrayed abuse (van Oosten & Vandenbosch, 2020). Social networks and content sharing platforms often exude the same "toxic masculinity" characteristic of the broader socio-cultural sexism and discrimination apparent in offline environments (Massanari, 2017). For example, online forums discussing the sharing nonconsensual images subdue any viewpoint, particularly those of women, outside the "echo chamber" rhetoric placing blame on the victim and encouraging and legitimating abuse of women within a male peer support system (DeKeseredy & Schwartz, 2016; Yar & Drew, 2019).

CYBERSECURITY TACTICS

Current technology in the 21st century offers users covert ubiquitous mobile surveillance that poses problems for unsuspecting victims, particularly in terms of privacy, and for cybersecurity regulation by legal enforcers (Office of the Privacy Commissioner, 2012). Manufacturers can help combat surreptitious use of digital cameras, as occurs in upskirting and downblousing, by implementing socio-technological solutions (e.g., Privacy by Design). In response to reports that users in Japan and Korea were engaging in hidden photography, Apple modified smartphones sold in this market to prevent the "muting" of the shutter "click" sound when photos are taken (Office of the Privacy Commissioner, 2012). Unfortunately, perpetrators can override this measure by jailbreaking their phones; using a third-party camera app that has a "mute" button; or switching their phones to "iPhone Live Photo," which prevents the shutter sound during filming (Wakephone, 2019).

The most important cybersecurity tactic remains the development of private and public partnership responses. Internet intermediaries (i.e., content hosts), despite being legally immune to third-party prosecution by 47 U.S.C. § 230 (c)(2) protection for "Good Samaritan" blocking and screening of offensive material in the Communication Decency Act, have implemented privacy policies that combat IBSA (Delfino, 2019; Fay, 2018; Franklin, 2014). For example, Reddit, Twitter, and Tumbler have implemented platform terms-of-service policies that prohibit nonconsensual creation and posting of intimate images, including DeepFakes, and vowed to suspend violators' accounts for these transgressions (Delfino, 2019). Microsoft Bing, Yahoo, and Google, in their capacity as server farms and search engines, severed links to revenge porn sites and have de-indexed IBSA intimate images from name searches of victim-survivors (Fay, 2018; Henry et al., 2020a; Office of the Privacy Commissioner, 2012). To be effective against IBSA, however, would require these ISPs to engage in regular self-monitoring to determine when third-party content violates their user terms of agreement (e.g., not sexualizing minors, not actively moderating posts that broke the rule). The enormity of this task makes it almost impossible, as for example, Reddit would need to monitor over 8000 sub-forums. In 2012, Reddit removed their "creepshots" sub-forum (with 12,000 subscribers)[21] after it was exposed on CNN, but this

---

[21] Accessed at: https://www.dailydot.com/irl/reddit-creepshots-candidfashionpolice-photos/ (11/8/2020).

genre of images focused on sexual body parts reappeared shortly afterwards under a differently named sub-forum loosely disguised as fashion evaluations (CandidFashionPolice) with 17,000 subscribers (Jacobs, 2016). Shaming and name doxing is another method that was used effectively to expose anonymous posters of creepshots by compiling their personal information, names, and social media profiles with their contributions and sending the files to their employers and to the police (Baker, 2012).

Additionally, a number of platforms (e.g., Facebook, Twitter, Reddit, Tumblr, PornHub, SnapChat, Instagram, and Flickr) in the U.S., Canada, the U.K., and Australia have partnered with private entities (e.g., Cyber Civil Rights Initiative, National Network to End Domestic Violence, Young Women's Christian Association, Revenge Porn Helpline) to assist IBSA victim-survivors (Henry et al., 2020a). Instagram offers help to its users when intimate images were non-consensually shared on its platform.[22] Someone who believes that images have or will be shared may report this concern using an online form submitted through a secure link; next, the ISP engages hash technology to search, locate, and delete the images on the site; finally, it blocks future attempts to repost the images (Henry et al., 2020a). As of 2015, these social media platforms' privacy policies also specifically state that nonconsensual pornography is prohibited and even PornHub, consistent with the ISP Safe Harbour component of the 1998 Digital Millennium Copyright Act, enacts a *notice-and-takedown* procedure by removing nonconsensual images when requested (Fay, 2018), but this platform in particular has difficulty preventing third-party users from posting new content (Delfino, 2019).

Each of the organizations shown in Table 11.4 lists a variety of toolkits, legal and nonlegal resources, and preventative programs for victim-survivors to improve their online and personal security and restrict access for devices (Henry et al., 2020a). Similarly, the governments around the world also provide support services through websites and advice hotlines for victim-survivors that they monitor or through organizations that they fund. For example, the eSafety Commissioner in Australia (Safety.gov. au) provides general cybercrime information, such as safety guides and education resources for families and schools. It also helps IBSA victims in a number of ways, including how to remove content from platforms; report the crime to eSafety Commissioner and social media/website; deal with sextortion; and get help from police; and obtain legal assistance for

---

[22] What organizations can provide support if someone shares an intimate image of myself or a friend on Instagram without permission? https://help.instagram.com/.

Table 11.4 Nonprofit Agencies Offering help to IBSA Victim-Survivors

Agency/Location/Website	Description of Services
National network to end domestic violence/U.S./ Nnedv.org	*About us* (housing toolkit); *About DV* (description, laws); *Policy center*; *Resource library* (toolkits, get help).
Rape abuse incest national network RAINN/U.S./ www.rainn.org	*Sexual violence* (names and describes types); *safety and prevention* (parents, students); *public policy* (state laws); *materials* (toolkits, handouts); *counseling and training; live chat* (provides advice)
Cyber civil rights initiative/U.S./ www.cybercivilrights.org [also see withoutmyconsent.org]	*What we do* (victim services, outreach and education); *for victims* (crisis hotline, online removal guide, pro bono attorneys, laws, tips); *for legislators* (model laws); see *50 state project* (federal and state criminal and civil laws) on withoutmyconsent.
Battling against demeaning & abusive selfie sharing (Badass)/ U.S./badassarmy.org	*Get Help*—allows victims to sign up for private group and step-by-step process for getting help; *State Laws*—provides revenge porn laws.
YWCA Canada/CA/ Ywcacanada. ca/guide-on-sexual-image-based-abuse	*Get support* provides information on how to get support; websites to help with anxiety; *support for discussing IBSA with others.*
The cyber helpline/U.K./ www. thecyberhelpline.com	*Free help for cybercrime victims,* does include revenge porn (defines it, revenge porn hotline, offers help when ransom is requested, advises on removal from platforms and notify police, provides guide).

civil penalties. The Australian Women Against Violence Alliance/AWAVA (awava.org.au), which provides "leadership and advocacy at the national levels" (e.g., policy development, research, resources), is one of six organizations funded by the government. Of utmost importance to victims, their families, their community, and legislatures is public education to improve awareness of the different forms of IBSA (see Chapter 12 for further information).

REFERENCES

Baker, K.J.M. (2012, October 10). *How to Shut Down Reddit's CreepShots Once and for All: Name Names.* http://jezebel.com/5949379/naming-names-is-this-the-solution-to-combat-reddits-creepshots.

Bell, T. (2005). *Restatement (Second) of Torts.* http://www.tomwbell.com/NetLaw/Ch05/R2ndTorts.html

Bell, V., Hemmens, C., & Steiner, B. (2006). Up skirts and down blouses: A statutory analysis of legislative responses to video voyeurism. *Criminal Justice Studies, 19*(3), 301–314.

Chesney, R., & Citron, D. (2018). *Deep Fakes: A Looming Crisis for National Security, Democracy, and Privacy?* Washington, DC: Lawfare Blog.

Citron, D.K., & Franks, M.A. (2014). Criminalizing revenge porn. *Wake Forest Law Review, 49*, 345–391.

Cole, T., Policastro, C., Crittenden, C., & McGuggee, K. (2020). Freedom to post or invasion of privacy? Analysis of U.S. revenge porn statutes. *Victims and Offenders, 15*, 483–498.

Cox, J. (2018). *Revenge Porn Moves to Slack.* https://www.vice.com/en/article/vbpaj8/revenge-porn-moves-to-slack.

Cripps, J., & Stermac, L. (2018). Cyber-sexual violence and negative emotional states among women in a Canadian university. *International Journal of Cyber Criminology, 12*(1), 171–186. Doi: 10.5281/zenodo.1467891.

Crofts, T., Lee, M., McGovern, A., & Milivojevic, S. (2015). *Sexting and Young People.* Basingstoke: Palgrave Macmillan.

Cyber Civil Rights Initiative. (2020). *Without My Consent: Tools to Fight Online Harassment.* New York: Common Law. https://withoutmyconsent.org/50state/state-guides/new-york/common-law/#intentional-infliction-of-emotional-distress-iied.

DeKeseredy, W.S., & Schwartz, M.D. (2016). Thinking sociologically about image-based sexual abuse: The contribution of male peer support theory. *Sexualization, Media, and Society, 2*, 1–8. Doi: 10.1177/2374623816684692.

Delfino, R.A. (2019). Pornographic deepfakes: The case for federal criminalization of revenge porn's next tragic act. *Fordham Law Review, 88*(3), 887–938. https://ir.lawnet.fordham.edu/flr/vol88/iss3/2.

Digital Media Law Project. (2020a). *State Law: Publication of Private Facts.* https://www.dmlp.org/legal-guide/state-law-publication-private-facts.

Digital Media Law Project. (2020b). *State Law: Right of Publicity.* https://www.dmlp.org/legal-guide/state-law-right-publicity.

Digital Media Law Project. (2020c). *Using the Name or Likeness of Another.* https://www.dmlp.org/legal-guide/using-name-or-likeness-another.

Digital Media Law Project. (2020d). *Publication of Private Facts.* https://www.dmlp.org/legal-guide/publication-private-facts.

Drinnon, C. (2017). When fame takes away the right to privacy in one's body: Revenge port and tort remedies for public figures. *William & Mary Journal of Women and the Law* (Special Issue: Enhancing women's effect on law enforcement in the age of police and protest), *24(1)*, 209–233.

Eaton, A.A., Jacobs, H., & Ruvalcaba, Y. (2017). *Nonconsensual Porn Infographic.* Cyber Civil Rights Initiative. https://www.cybercivilrights.org/wp-content/uploads/2017/06/CCRI-2017-Research-Report.pdf.

Eaton, A.A., & McGlynn, C. (2020). The psychology of nonconsensual porn: Understanding and addressing a growing form of sexual violence. *Policy Insights from the Behavioral and Brain Sciences, 7(2)*, 190–197.

Englander, E., & McCoy, M. (2017). Sexting—Prevalence, age, sex, and outcomes. *Journal of American Medical Association Pediatrics, 172(4)*, 317–318.

Fay, M. (2018). Revenge porn victims at state law and the proposed federal legislation to adequately redress them. *Boston College Law Review, 59(5)*, 1839–1871.

Fleschler Peskin. M., Markham, C.M., Addy, R.C., Shegog, R., Thiel, M., & Tortolero, S.R. (2013). Prevalence and patterns of sexting among ethnic minority urban high school students. *Cyberpsychology, Behavior, and Social Networking, 16*, 454–459. Doi: 10.1089/cyber.2012.0452.

Flynn, A., & Henry, N. (2019). Image-based sexual abuse: An Australian reflection. *Women & Criminal Justice*, 1–14. Doi: 10.1080/08974454.2019.16461.

Franklin, Z. (2014). Justice for revenge porn victims: Legal theories to overcome claims of civil immunity by operators of revenge porn websites. *California Law Review, 102(5)*, 1303–1335.

Franks, M.A., & Waldman, A.E. (2019). Sex, lies, and videotape: Deep fakes and free speech delusions. *Maryland Law Review, 78(4)*, 892–898.

Garcia, J.R., Gesselman, A.N., Siliman, S.A., Perry, B.L., Coe, K., & Fisher, H.E. (2016). Sexting among singles in the USA: Prevalence of sending, receiving, and sharing sexual messages and images. *Sexual Health, 13*, 428–435. Doi: 10.1071/SH15240.

Gavin, J., & Scott, A.J. (2019). Attributions of victim responsibility in revenge pornography. *Journal of Aggression, Conflict and Peace Research, 11(4)*, 263–272. Doi: 10.1108/JACPR-03-2019-0408.

Goldman, E., & Jin, A. (2018). Judicial resolution of nonconsensual pornography dissemination cases. *Journal of Law and Policy for the Information Society, 14(2)*, 286–352.

Hall, T.J., & Archer, J.A. (2020, February 20). The slow expansion of conversion claims to cover intangible property. *New York Law Journal.* https://www.law.com/newyorklawjournal/2020/02/20/the-slow-expansion-of-conversion-claims-to-cover-intangible-property/?slret urn=20201014102345.

Hall, M., & Hearn, J. (2019). Revenge pornography and manhood acts: A discourse analysis of perpetrators' accounts. *Journal of Gender Studies, 28(2)*, 158–70.

Harris, D. (2019). Deepfakes: False pornography is here and the law cannot protect you. *Duke Law and Technology Review, 17*, 99–128.

Henry, N., Flynn, A., & Powell, A. (2018). Policing image-based sexual abuse: Stakeholder perspectives. *Police Practice and Research, 19(6)*, 565–581.

Henry, N., Flynn, A., & Powell, A. (2019b). Image-based sexual abuse: Victims and perpetrators. *Trends & Issues in Crime and Criminal Justice, 572*, 1–19.

Henry, N., Flynn, A., & Powell, A. (2020a). Technology-facilitated domestic and sexual violence: A review. *Violence Against Women, 26(15–16)*, 1828–1854.

Henry, N., Flynn, A., & Renzetti, C.M. (2019a). Image-based sexual abuse: Online distribution channels and illicit communities of support. *Violence Against Women, 25(16)*, 1932–1955.

Henry, N., McGlynn, C., Flynn, A., Johnson, K., Powell, A., & Scott, A. (2020b). *Image-Based Sexual Abuse: A Study on the Causes and Consequences of Non-consensual Nude or Sexual Imagery.* Abingdon: Routledge. ISBN 9780815353836.

Holt, K., & Liggert, R. (2020). Revenge pornography. In Holt, T.J., & Bossler, A.M. (eds.), *The Palgrave Handbook of International Cybercrime and Cyberdeviance* (pp. 1132–1149). Switzerland: Palgrave MacMillan.

Inglesh, A. (2020). *Deepfakes May be in Deep Trouble: How the Law Has and Should Respond to the Rise of the AI-Assisted Technology of Deepfake Videos.* http://cardozoaelj.com/2020/01/19/deepfakes-deep-trouble/

Jacobs, A. (2016). Fighting back against revenge porn: A legislative solution. Northwestern *Journal of Law and Social Policy, 12*, 69–91.

Kapur, B. (2020). *An Army of Women are Waging War on the Web's Most Notorious Revenge Porn Site.* https://melmagazine.com/en-us/story/anon-ib-revenge-porn-badass-army.

Legal Information Institute. (n.d.). *Publicity.* https://www.law.cornell.edu/wex/publicity.

Lenhart, A., Ybarra, M., Zickuhr, K., & Price-Feeney, M. (2016). *Online Harassment, Digital Abuse, and Cyberstalking in America.* Data & Society Research Institute Report 11.21.16. 1–58. https://www.datasociety.net/pubs/oh/Online_Harassment_2016.pdf.

Mania, K. (2020). The legal implications and remedies concerning revenge porn and fake porn: A common perspective. *Sexuality & Culture, 24*, 2079–2097.

Massanari, A. (2017). # Gamergate and the Fappening: How Reddit's algorithm, governance, and culture support toxic technocultures. *New Media & Society, 19(3)*, 329–346.

McCann, W., Pedneault, A., Stohr, M.K., & Hemmens, C. (2018). Upskirting: A statutory analysis of legislative responses to video voyeurism 10 years down the road. *Criminal Justice Review, 43(4)*, 399–418.

McCarthy, K. (2015). *Revenge Porn 'King' Hunter Moore Sent Down for 2.5 Years, Fined $2k.* https://www.theregister.com/2015/12/04/revenge_king_sent_down/.

McGlynn, C., & Rackley, E. (2017). Image-based sexual abuse. *Oxford Journal of Legal Studies, 37(3)*, 534–561. Doi: 10.1093/ojls/gqw033.

McGlynn, C., Rackley, E., & Houghton, R. (2017). Beyond 'revenge porn': The continuum of image-based sexual abuse. *Feminine Legal Studies, 25*, 25–46.

McGlynn, C., Rackley, E., Johnson, K., Henry, N., Flynn, A., Powell, A., Gavey, N., & Scott, A. (2019). Shattering lives and myths: A report on image-based sexual abuse. Project report, Durham University and University of Kent. https://dro.dur.ac.uk/28683/1/28683.pdf?DDD34+DDD19+

Najdowski, C. (2017). Legal responses to nonconsensual pornography: Current policy in the United States and future direction for research. *Psychology, Public Policy and Law, 23*(2), 154–165.

Neris, N., Pacetta Ruiz, J., & Giorgetti Valente, M. (2015). *Fighting the Dissemination of Non- Consensual Intimate Images: A Comparative Analysis*. InternetLab.org. http://www.internetlab.org.br/wp-content/uploads/2018/11/Fighting_the_Dissemination_of_Non.pdf.

Newell, B.C. (2017). *Privacy-Related Crimes in US Law. TILT Law & Technology*, Working Paper Series. http://www.privacyspaces.org/wp-content/uploads/2016/09/Newell_Privacy-related-crimes-in-US-law_wp20170227.pdf#:~:text=US%20criminal%20law%20owes%20its%20origins%20to%20the,generally%20those%20of%20homicide%2C%20assault%2C%20battery%2C%20and%20rape%2C.

Nigam, S. (2018, April 25). *Revenge Porn Laws Across the World. The Centre for Internet and Society*. https://cis-india.org/internet-governance/blog/revenge-porn-laws-across-the-world.

Office of the eSafety Commissioner (OeSC). (2017). *Image-Based Abuse: National Survey: Summary Report*. Office of the eSafety Commissioner. https://www.esafety.gov.au/sites/default/files/2019-07/Image-based-abuse-national-survey-summary-report-2017.pdf.

Office of the Privacy Commissioner. (2012). *Vanishing Surveillance: Why Seeing What is Watching Us Matters*. https://priv.gc.ca/en/opc-actions-and-decisions/research/explore-privacy-research/2011/wood_20112907/.

Oppel, Jr., R.A. (2013, March 17). Ohio teenagers guilty in rape that social media brought to light. *New York Times*. https://www.nytimes.com/2013/03/18/us/teenagers-found-guilty-in-rape-in-steubenville-ohio.html.

Patrick, K., Heywood, W., Pitts, M.K., & Mitchell, A. (2015). Demographic and behavioral correlates of six sexting behaviors among Australian secondary school students. *Sexual Health, 12*(6), 480–487.

Patrini, G., Ajder, H., Cavalli, F., & Cullen, L. (2019). *The State of Deepfakes: Landscape, Threats, and Impact*. DeepTraceLabs. https://sensity.ai/mapping- the-deepfake-landscape/.

Pina, A., Holland, J., & James, M. (2017). The malevolent side of revenge porn proclivity: Dark personality traits and sexist ideology. *International Journal of Technoethics, 8*(1), 30–43.

Pollack, J.M. (2016). Getting even: Empowering victims of revenge porn with a civil cause of action. *Albany Law Review, 80*(1), 353–380.

Powell, A., Henry, N., & Flynn, A. (2018). Image-based sexual abuse. In W.S. DeKeserdy & M. Dragiewicz (eds.), *Handbook of Critical Criminology* (pp. 305–315). New York: Routledge.

Powell, A., Henry, N., Flynn, A., & Scott, A.J. (2019). Image-based sexual abuse: The extension, nature, and predicators for perpetration in a community sample of Australian adults. *Computers in Human Behavior, 92*, 393–402.

Powell, A., Scott, A.J., Flynn, A., & Henry, N. (2020). Image-based sexual abuse: An international study of victims and perpetrators. Summary report. Doi: 10.13140/RG.2.2.35166.59209.

Ruvalcaba, Y., & Eaton, A.A. (2020). Nonconsensual pornography among U.S. Adults: A sexual scripts framework on victimization, perpetration, and health correlates for women and men. *Psychology of Violence, 10*(1), 68–78. Doi:10.1037/vio0000233.

Sugiera, L., & Smith, A. (2020). Victim blaming, responsibilization and resilience in online sexual abuse and harassment. In J. Tapley & P. Davies (eds.), *Victimology: Research, Policy, and Activism* (pp. 45–79). Switzerland: Palgrave Macmillan. Doi: 10.1007/978-3-030-42288-2-3.

van Oosten, J. M. F., & Vandenbosch, L. (2020). Predicting the willingness to engage in non-consensual forwarding of sexts: The role of pornography and instrumental notions of sex. *Archives of Sexual Behavior, 49*(4), 1121–1132.

Wakephone. (2019). *No More Shutter Sound!* https://www.wakephone.com/2019/04/how-do-i-turn-the-camera-shutter-sound-off-on-a-japanese-iphone/.

Walker, K., & Sleath, E. (2017). A systematic review of the current knowledge regarding revenge pornography and non-consensual sharing of sexually explicit media. *Aggression and Violent Behavior, 36*, 9–24.

Walker, K., Sleath, E., Hatcher, R.M., Hine, B., & Crookes, R.L. (2019). Nonconsensual sharing of private sexually explicit media among university students. *Journal of Interpersonal Violence*, 1–31. Doi: 10.1177/0886260519853414.

Wood, M., Barter, C., Stanley, N., Aghtaie, N., & Larkins, C. (2015). Images across Europe: The sending and receiving of sexual images and associations with interpersonal violence in young people's relationships. *Children and Youth Services Review, 59*, 149–160. Doi: 10.1016/j.childyouth.2015.11.005.

Yar, M., & Drew, J. (2019). Image-based abuse, non-consensual pornography, revenge porn: A study of criminalization and crime prevention in Australia and England & Wales. *International Journal of Cyber Criminology, 13*(2), 578–594. Doi: 10.5281/zenodo.3709306.

CASES

Commonwealth v. Michael Robertson (2014), 467 Mass. 371

Del Mastro v. Grimado (2005), WL 20022355 (N.J. Super. Ct Ch. Div.); No. Civ. A. BER-C-388-03E

Foster v. Churchill (1996), 665 N.E.2d 153, 157 (N.Y.)

In the Matter of Craig Brittain (2016), No. C-4564 (F.T.C.)

Leser v. Penido, 62 A.D. 3d 510 (2009), 879 N.Y.S.2d 107 (N.Y. Sup. Ct.)

People of California v. Kevin Christopher Bollaert (2016), D067863 (Super. Ct. No. SCD252338).
State of Washington v. Glas (2002), 54 P.3d 147
Taylor v. Franko (2011), U.S. Dist. Ct Hawaii (Civ. NO. 09-00002 JMS/RLP).
United States v. Moore (2015), 2:13-cr–00917.

12

Combating Cyberpredators through Education

Society was ill prepared for how quickly advancements in technology and the Internet occurred nor their ubiquity in its citizens' daily lives, which severely hampered its ability to protect them from cyberpredators through adequate laws and education (Egresitz, 2020; Witwer et al., 2020).

DOI: 10.4324/9781003092292-12

Digital citizens use information and communication technologies for a variety of reasons, including communication, entertainment, research, and socialization (Wachs et al., 2021). For example, users interact online, access content (e.g., live streaming, webpages), video chat, engage in gaming, and exchange instant messaging (Common Sense Media, 2020). Figure 12.1 compares minors (Rideout & Robb, 2019) and adults (Media, 2018) on three types of online activities. Digital citizens are divided into *natives* and *immigrants* based on how these groups conceptualize information and communication technologies. Digital natives (i.e., born in 2000 or later) have been raised with technology and surfed the Internet regularly from an early age, whereas digital immigrants adopted technology and the Internet later in life (Ribble, 2015). Consequently, these two groups vary in experiences, knowledge, and understanding of the dangers online.

The inherent risks of becoming a victim of cyber predators increase for users who spend long periods of time engaged in online activities. On average, youths use a variety of Internet-accessible devices and 45% of adolescents reported being online almost constantly (Anderson, 2018a). According to Rideout and Robb (2019), tweens aged 8–12 reported an average of four and one-half hours daily use versus adolescents aged 13–18 averaging seven and one-fourth hours daily use for online entertainment media, excluding academic work performed online in or out of school. The majority of adult users in the U.S. (85%) are also online daily—consuming digital media for almost 8 hours, with 31% admitting to going online almost constantly and 48% going online several times (Insider

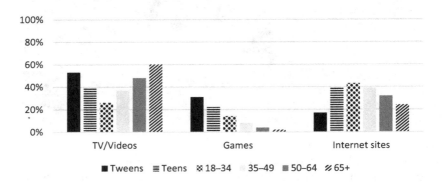

Figure 12.1 Proportion of minors and adults engaging in three types of online activities.

Intelligence, 2021; Perrin & Atske, 2021). Constant online use varied by age (Perrin & Atske, 2021)—with the highest rates reported by those ages 18–29 (48%) and ages 30–49 (42%) as compared to those aged 50–64 (22%) and aged 65+ (8%). To avoid being victimized, users must have the appropriate knowledge and training that will allow them to be safe and treated respectfully when online. Despite their capacity for employing correct terminology related to technology and the Internet or learning how to use a new app, digital natives are not less susceptible to victimization by cyber predators than digital immigrants (Young, 2014).

In the previous chapters, readers were provided with information on cyberpredators and their crimes; the current laws and their adequacy in prosecuting offenders; the negative impact that these crimes have on targets and society; cybersecurity tactics relevant to preventing or reducing prevalence; and the impact of cybercrimes on individuals and society. The current chapter gives recommendations for the types of information that should be included in a cyber curriculum for it to be comprehensive and useful for online users in American society. Specifically, cyber users must **learn and practice essential 21st-century skills** in digital citizenship, digital literacy, digital intelligence, and digital safety; **recognize the challenges** posed by the Internet; and **navigate the Internet safely and civilly** (Bearden, 2016; Hui & Campbell, 2018; Jones & Mitchell, 2016; Willard, 2012; Young, 2014). In particular, cyber users become good *digital citizens* by learning and practicing appropriate, respectful, and healthy interpersonal interactions (e.g., email etiquette, digital footprint, privacy) and performing civil engagement, such as being socially responsible, building the community, and acting to protect public values (Bearden, 2016; Hui & Campbell, 2018; Jones & Mitchell, 2016; Willard, 2012). *Digital literacy* requires that users gain knowledge for locating information and determining its appropriateness, such as researching topics and citing sources appropriately consistent with copyright laws, as well as for operating technology (Sonck & de Haan, 2014). Cyber users will be able to achieve *digital safety* by engaging in practices that keep their personally identifiable information private and secure and by using strategies that allow them to recognize cyber predators, minimize their risk to potentially dangerous situations, and increase their psychological resilience (Genner, 2014; Hui & Campbell, 2018; Jones & Mitchell, 2016; Young, 2014). Cyber users must also learn about risks and understand how the four characteristics of online environment (i.e., toxic disinhibition, de-individuation, anonymity, inculpability) contribute to technology-facilitated abuse. Finally, they must learn different methods for countering the negative effects and ultimately select and rehearse the ones that work best for them.

ROUTINE ACTIVITY THEORY

Routine Activity Theory (Cohen & Felson, 1979) was selected as the framework for preventing and/or mitigating cybercrime. According to this theory, the confluence of three factors in virtual space—a motivated cybercriminal, a suitable target, and lack of capable guardianship—contribute to victimization (Reyns et al., 2011). In the Information Age, it does not make sense to teach minors how to use technology without also giving them the tools for identifying risks, recognizing dangers, and staying safe. This cannot be accomplished simply by having educators endorse strategies that include telling people to avoid specific websites or prohibiting them from using technology as this is no more effective than telling non-swimmers to avoid the deep end of the pool; instead, they must teach resiliency-based strategies that will strengthen users' ability to recognize hazards in cyberspace and feel empowered to address them (Thierer, 2014; Willard, 2012). The user's general and Internet-specific skills are "dynamic, flexible, multifaceted, and/or multilayered" (Choi et al., 2017, p. 111) and as such can be modified through experience and education to reduce their risks from exposure and participation online (Mossberger et al., 2007). Cyber curriculum operating on the maxim that *people only have control over their own behavior* provides users with essential skills and opportunities to practice those skills, thereby reducing their *suitability as targets* through self-regulation and empowerment (Thierer, 2014).

There are two indirect benefits from teaching users how to operate safely online that impact on the level of cyber guardianship. First, it allows guardians who are in charge of minors and young adults to understand the importance and scope of their duties. Educators and parents may be poor protectors because they have limited understanding of the technology and it is not realistic to limit children's access to the Internet. Yet, educators are responsible for ensuring that minors under their care understand the rules and consequences regarding Internet use, which apply both on and off school grounds. Parents are expected to implement strategies (i.e., informal rules and/or formal technical controls) to monitor the social media platforms their children are choosing and determine their appropriateness (i.e., need parent's permission to open an account); supervise them during online activities, especially gaming (e.g., must be in public location at home); and review the private and public content children are posting and exchanging plus check-in periodically to discuss with them potential/actual problems. Additionally, family members themselves need to be careful with content, specifically information; images—especially those with geotags; and messages involving minors that they post and exchange in public forums. Second, educating users about cyberspace not only improves their critical thinking and ethical responsibility online, it also bolsters decisions they make related to being civil, respectful of privacy and property, and attentive to the well-being of themselves and others (Genner, 2014; Thierer, 2014). As they take on the role of guardians, they become cognizant that Internet Service Providers (ISPs) should have an obligation to protect the privacy, security, and safety of its clients and their associated information. A 2017 study indicated that although 49% of American adults indicate ISPs should be responsible for protecting consumers' interests, 59% support net neutrality regulations (CDA Section 230) that prevent ISPs from blocking lawful content and 57% believe ISPs should not be allowed to censor content (CR Consumer Reports, 2017).

DIGITAL DIVIDE

The digital divide in the U.S., rather than shrinking, is growing in a different way than in previous years (van Dijk & van Deursen 2014). Initially the discrepancy was caused by low numbers of users having physical and material access to technology due to the prohibitive cost of devices and/ or Internet Provider service; additionally, inconsistent reliability and quality of the connection also limited internet use, whereas currently it stems from uneven digital skills and daily practice opportunities due to limited access to and location of Internet devices (Khan et al., 2020; van Dijk & van Deursen, 2014). Internet use by income and age group from 2000 to 2021 is shown in Figures 12.2 and 12.3, respectively. The proportion of U.S. adults

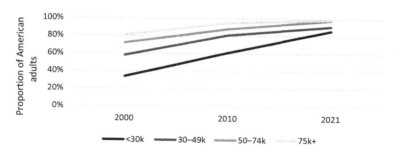

Figure 12.2 Proportion of American adults who use the Internet from 2000 to 2021 by annual household income (Pew Research Center, 2021).

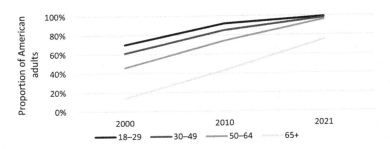

Figure 12.3   Proportion of American adults who used the Internet from 2000 to 2021 by age group (Pew Research Center, 2021).

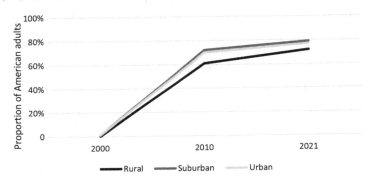

Figure 12.4   Proportion of American adults who had home broadband from 2000 to 2021 by community type (Vogels, 2021a).

who used the Internet varied greatly by annual household income and by age group in 2000, but by 2021 even the oldest Americans and those who had the lowest income were using the Internet. Additionally, of American adults whose household income was less than $30,000—76% owned smartphones, 59% owned desktop/laptop computers, and 41% had tablets vs. 13% who did not have any of these technologies (Vogels, 2021b). Figure 12.4 portrays the proportion of Americans who have/own home broadband by community type from 2000 to 2021. As of 2021, there is little difference in the proportion from the different community types that have/own broadband. Moreover, on average 93% Americans use the Internet, with 90% indicating they connect through home access and 15% who connect solely through their smart phones (Johnson, 2021; Pew Research Center, 2021). On the other hand, rural residents were more likely than urban and suburban residents

(24% vs. 13% vs. 9%) to indicate that they had major problems accessing high-speed Internet (Anderson, 2018b). According to the FCC, rural communities have fewer providers and are less likely to have fast Internet speeds compared to other areas and the infrastructure does not support consistent and reliable broadband (Vogels, 2021a). As a consequence of access difficulty, some rural residents never use the Internet (22%) and rural residents indicated lower daily use of the Internet than their urban and suburban counterparts (Anderson, 2018b).

21ST CENTURY DIGITAL SKILLS

To properly address the digital divide, digital curriculum must include 21st-century digital skills for users to learn and practice. Table 12.1 provides six lists of 21st-century digital skills recommended by experts based on their own assessment of the *information, communication*, and *strategy* requirements for online activities (e.g., Binkley et al., 2012; Ferrari, 2012; Partnership for 21st Century, 2008; Ribble, 2015; van Dijk & van Deursen, 2014; Voogt & Roblin, 2012). It is clear from this table that most of these experts agree on the importance for a subset of skills (e.g., collaboration, communication, responsibility).

The set of 21st-century digital skills that are recommended to be included within a cyber curriculum can be conceptualized as pertaining to one of four categories—digital citizenship, digital literacy, digital intelligence, or digital safety. To acquire *digital citizenship,* users will need skills for interacting with others online similar in many ways to those needed offline (Ribble, 2015; Willard, 2012). Table 12.2 lists and describes ten character and socialization skills that forms the ideal basis for good digital citizenship (Choi et al., 2017; Mossberger et al., 2007; Ribble, 2015; Willard, 2012). According to Ribble and his associates (Ribble, 2015; Ribble & Bailey, 2007; Ribble et al., 2004), the cyber curriculum should focus on the social goal of teaching proper etiquette and legal use of technology for citizens to participate globally online. Binkley et al. (2012) similarly recommends character and socialization skills as part of their "living in the world" as a means of promoting responsibility of citizens who will be using the Internet academically, professionally, and recreationally over their lifetimes.

A second set of skills provide users with *digital literacy* organized under three categories: *instrumental/operational* abilities that include knowing and performing the technical functions, mechanics, and competencies

Table 12.1 List of 21st-Century Digital Skills Recommended by Experts

Experts	Skills
Assessing and teaching of 21st-century skills (ATC21S, Binkley et al., 2012)	Creativity and innovation; critical thinking; problem solving; and decision making; learning to learn; metacognition; communication; collaboration and teamwork; information literacy; information technology; communication literacy; life and career; personal and social responsibility.
Ferrari (2012)	Information management; collaboration; communication and sharing; creation of content and knowledge; ethics; responsibility; evaluation; problem solving, technical operations.
Partnership for 21st century (P21, 2008)	Creativity and innovation; critical thinking; problem solving; communication and collaboration; information, media and ICT literacy; flexibility and adaptability; initiative and self-direction; social and cross-cultural skills; productivity; accountability; leadership; responsibility.
Ribble et al. (2004)	Etiquette; communication; literacy; access; commerce; law; rights and responsibilities; health and wellness; security.
van Dijk and van Deursen (2014)	Operational; formal; information; communication; content creation; strategic.
Voogt and Roblin (2012)	Collaboration; communication; digital literacy; citizenship; problem solving; critical thinking; creativity; productivity.

of related to operating technology; *structural/informational* abilities comprised of locating, selecting, and evaluating information for content, discussion, and work; and *strategic* abilities, which involve personal and professional applications related to using technology and rules for navigating cyberspace (Sonck & de Hann, 2014). Table 12.3 describes digital literacy skills grouped within the three aforementioned categories (Sonck & de Hann, 2014, p. 91; van Deursen & van Dijk, 2009; van Dijk & van Deursen, 2014). Binkley et al. (2012) include literacy skills in information, technology, and communication as part of their "tools for working," whereas Ribble (2015) encompasses them under his goal of being savvy, discussing how users employ tools for working online independently or in groups, communicating within and outside local society, and commercial exchanging of goods. Although digital literacy allows users to operate

Table 12.2 Description of Character and Socialization Skills Needed to Be a Digital Citizen

Skills	Description
Integrity	Act ethically, expressing moral principles consistent with the mutually decided standards of conduct in society.
Law abiding	Uphold the laws of society and expects others to do the same.
Vigilant	Be alert online, ensuring that other users are held accountable for violations of moral principles, as well as competently defending and advocating for anyone wronged by immoral actions.
Courteous	State one's viewpoint in online discussions politely while listening *actively* to other people's views rather than attacking them for not agreeing with your own.
Respectful	Accept that everyone has the right to express a personal opinion—as long as what is said or done does not violate laws or others' rights.
Tolerant	Recognize the need to safeguard people's right to express their opinions, even when these ideas differ from those articulated by others in the group.
Compassionate	Interact with others in ways that acknowledge their feelings while attempting to understand their responses in online activities.
Responsible	Acknowledge that everyone is accountable for his/her behaviors (e.g., harassment, theft), correcting acts or helping to rectify incidents that resulted in harm (intentional or otherwise) of people and/or property, and learning effective ways to handle difficult situations or issues that arise in the course of interacting with others.
Trustworthy	Behave honestly and encourage others to do the same.
Productive	Make a positive contribution to society that results in a better world, whether enhancing good qualities or removing problems.

technology—easily downloading content to read, copy, modify, or share, they must also use their digital citizenship skills to function ethically online (e.g., fair use rule) so as not to violate copyright laws.

A third set of skills involves *digital intelligence,* comprising cognitive abilities that aid users in planning, thinking, enacting ideas, and making appropriate decisions relevant to their academic, occupational, and/

Table 12.3 List of Digital Literacy Skills by Category

Instrumental/ Operational		Structural and Informational		Strategic
Basic skills	Knowledge and use of terms;[a] setting up computer; running applications;[b] adjusting settings on technology; and engaging in cyber-activities[c]	*Formal Internet skills*	Browsing the Internet; navigating websites by operating menus and hyperlinks; developing content; etc.	*Lower Internet skills* — Understanding that technology requires applications
Complex skills	Changing filter settings online; program installation; software updates; partitioning hard drive; etc.	*Infor-mational and evaluation skills*	Performing multiple searches and using keywords; selecting information from results lists; evaluating information; etc.[d]	*Higher Internet skills* — Content-related skills used to obtain information; communicate; and make applications for daily living.[e]

[a] Terms related to hardware, software, servers, operating system, utilities, settings, and applications.

[b] Accessing Microsoft programs from hard drive or Google Drive.

[c] Engaging in online activities for communication (e.g., email, video chat/conferencing, instant message); social networking (e.g., Facebook, Twitter, Dating, Forums); games; etc.

[d] Determining worthiness of information in source by checking the currency, relevance, accuracy, authority, purpose/reliability.

[e] Various activities include commerce selections and purchases based on quality and price of products alone or in conjunction with other needs, such as transportation (e.g., checking timetables).

or personal lives when online, just as they must do when they are offline (Binkley et al., 2012; Griffin et al., 2012; van Laar et al., 2017a, 2017b). Table 12.4 describes skills needed for digital intelligence (Binkley et al., 2012; Partnership for 21st Century Skills, 2008, pp. 10; van Laar et al., 2017a, 2017b). When used in unison, digital citizen, literacy, and intelligence

Table 12.4   Description of Cognitive Skills Needed for Digital Intelligence

Skills	Description
Creativity and initiative	Ability to think unconventionally; question standard approaches; imagine new solutions; produce new content; identify and act on opportunities; create and manage progress on goals; and embrace risk and responsibility.
Critical thinking	Ability to assess the credibility, accuracy and value of information; analyze and evaluate information; and take purposeful action.
Problem solving	Ability to solve complex, multidisciplinary, open-ended problems encountered socially, academically, and occupationally—specifically to identify the problem and generate potential solutions; explore possible benefits and consequences of each solution; determine the best one(s); enact solution and assess its success; and reevaluate as needed.
Decision making	Ability to select the best of increasingly complex options by identifying and evaluating the benefits and consequences for each option—whether for solving problems; developing and enacting plans; or engaging in commerce (e.g., investments, purchases, sales).
Flexibility and adaptability	Ability and willingness to adjust thinking, attitudes, or behavior and recognize the need to make changes when faced with different situations.
Communication and collaboration	Ability to express ideas in ways that everyone can understand; encourage team members to accept and respect different perspectives, particularly those from another culture; consider others' ideas and attempt to incorporate the best ones in the final product; and display willingness to learn from others.
Metacognition	Ability to be aware and understand one's own cognitive skills related to thinking and learning, such as monitoring comprehension, evaluating progress toward task completion, and preferred learning styles.

skills allow citizens to develop personal and sexual relationships (e.g., friendships, intimate partnerships); engage in discussions of worldwide concern (e.g., need for universal definition of child sexual abuse material) by locating and using information from reliable sources as the basis for their decisions; consider different viewpoints thoughtfully and logically; and collaborate on solutions and decide which ones will work for people from various countries and cultures. Users will need direct instruction on determining the characteristics that should be present in healthy intimate and non-intimate relationships (i.e., not exploitative or abusive) and solutions when they are not (Willard, 2012). Combining digital intelligence and digital citizen skills will aid in the development of collaborative problem solving, which requires users to consider other perspectives and be constructive and considerate in their contributions and selection of the best solutions (Griffin et al., 2012).

Users must also learn and practice a fourth set of skills—*digital safety*, which entails understanding the role that technology has on people's mental and physical health and well-being and the need to have protocols to allow users to engage in online activities while minimizing their exposure to harm. Willard (2012) proposes that users develop digital safety skills to allow them to:

1. discern websites with appropriate vs. inappropriate material;[1]
2. develop a healthy balance between online and offline activities rather than an addictive one;
3. protect their personal information by understanding the potential consequences of sharing it, particularly for their safety and reputation;
4. differentiate between private and public communication;
5. learn about cyber predators and how they operate;
6. implement routine computer security by (1) activating and updating anti-virus and anti-spyware software, (2) updating passwords, (3) making regular back-ups of files, and (4) detecting and responding to computer problems, such as malware infections; and
7. seek help when a difficult or dangerous situation is beyond their ability to handle.

---

[1] This is particularly relevant for minors who may "wander" onto sites that are adult-only or when on child-only sites not understand that sometimes adults pose as children to fool them.

Ribble (2015) similarly recommends that to keep safe, users must learn how to interact with others in accordance with *acceptable use* policies (rights and responsibilities); promote their own psychological and physical health and well-being through limited Internet and technology usage (health and wellness); and safeguard their personal information and technology from cyber predators (security).

CHALLENGES OF THE INTERNET

In this section, the four characteristics of the cyber environment—**toxic disinhibition** (lack of concern in response to imposed harm), **de-individuation** (mob mentality encourages deviancy), **anonymity** (hide from others), **inculpability** (fail to accept responsibility for imposed harm)—previously described in Chapter 1 will be discussed. According to Shipley and Bowker (2014), society's dependence on the Internet and technology makes committing online crimes easier to do with fewer risks for being caught in comparison to offline crimes. The anonymity of being online makes people believe that they are invisible while encouraging them to make provoking and inflammatory statements, posts, comments, etc. that are inconsistent with how they would normally act offline. Unfortunately, this means that the same people who in public adhere to the ethics of society may be lured while online into committing cyber-violent criminal acts, such as harassment or bullying, because their inhibitions to do so are not activated (Shipley & Bowker, 2014; Willard, 2012). Additionally, they fail to interpret and acknowledge that their initiating and/or collaborative mob-induced online abusive acts (e.g., bullying, trolling, rumor mongering, stalking) are having a negative or harmful impact on their targets (Campbell et al., 2013).

A list of motivating factors for committing abusive acts online used by people (consistent with Bandura's theory of moral disengagement), descriptions, and examples are provided in Table 12.5 (Willard, 2012, p. 21). The four motivating factors provide a good framework for understanding other abusive behaviors geared toward verbal and behavior harassment (e.g., swatting, trolling, stalking), sexual crimes (sexting, sex trafficking, child sexual abuse material offenses, sextortion, image-based sexual abuse offenses), and financial crimes (e.g., online romance scams). For example, online child sexual abuse material offenders will claim that it is better to look at images than actually engage sexually with children

Table 12.5   The Motivating Factors, Descriptions, and Examples

Motivating Factor	Descriptions	Examples
Reconstructing conduct	Explain behavior as serving a higher goal	"I was joking." "I defended my friend from that troll."
Diffusing responsibility	Assign blame to initiator or no one at all	"Everybody was making comments."
Misrepresenting the injury	Disregard the harm or perceive it as minimal	"It was no big deal." "He really was not angry."
Dehumanizing the victim	Blame the victim for what happened	"She shouldn't have taken a nude picture in the first place, so it really was her fault."

(i.e., reconstructing conduct) or that children enjoy sexual activities (i.e., misrepresenting the injury). In neither claim does the offender acknowledge the fact that children are harmed in the making and existence of these images. The Internet renders the victim less real or identifiable as a person to offenders and, in the absence of cues normally available offline to signal distress, makes it easier for them to ignore the harm they are imposing.

NAVIGATING THE INTERNET SAFELY AND CIVILLY

The four types of digital skills previously recommended serve as the basis for any cyber curriculum teaching users how to navigate online technologies in a safe and civil way. However, digital *skills* differ from digital *understanding* as the latter entails knowing that the risks associated with using the Internet can be managed (Miller et al., 2018). Lessons geared toward staying safe online must build both concepts (Egresitz, 2020). For example, online consumers who seek to purchase a product must have the digital skills to locate and access websites selling these items, but they also must have digital understanding that they should research each product and make comparisons; going online may be subjected to targeted advertisements for specific items—which may or may not be the best ones for them; and many websites used to purchase items collect and store users' personal information with no guarantee it will be protected from hackers

(Miller et al., 2018). To determine the effectiveness of the educational program, instructors must assess the learner's current level of these skills and knowledge as a baseline against which to compare subsequent levels after lessons are learned and practiced (Hui & Campbell, 2018).

There are multiple news stories recounting information and communication technology (ICT) misuse and abuse in all facets of our academic, occupational, and personal lives. Consistent with Ribble (2015), "As members of a digital society, it is our responsibility to provide all users the opportunity to work, interact, and use technology without interference, destruction, or obstruction by the actions of inappropriate users" (p. 15). Specific types of knowledge and behaviors related to technology considered to be appropriate should be codified to empower users to become Internet connoisseurs who are able to be civil, keep themselves safe, recognize difficult situations, seek help when needed, and resolve conflict effectively (Willard, 2012). Risk prevention in Internet use must include specific lessons on how users can protect themselves from victimization and, in some cases, inadvertent criminalization (Kopecký, 2015, 2017; Kopecký & Szotkowski, 2018). For example, adolescents who sext naked images of themselves may be charged with minor sexting or CSAM offenses (depending on their state), whereas those who engage in unauthorized sharing of explicit images of others may be charged with an IBSA offense (Vitis, 2019). The curriculum should acknowledge and discuss various notions of importance to users, such as protected speech, "romance," and sexual image experimentation, explaining that decisions associated with and interpretation of risks in online interactions are affected by one's personal characteristics (e.g., gender, sexuality); encouragement by other users—especially minors—to report online use violations (e.g., sextortion, sharing images of minors); and provision of information on hotlines and other social support sources that could help them to recognize their victimization and receive assistance as needed (Greenhalgh-Spencer, 2019; Kopecký, 2015; Veli, 2016; Wolak et al., 2018).

The Routine Activity Theory provides a framework for creating cybersecurity strategies to educate users in order to make them less suitable targets by helping them to *protect* their **data, identity, reputation, health,** and/or **freedom** plus engage in methods that facilitate early *detection* when any of these aspects have been compromised (Lorenz et al., 2016). Users can reduce the opportunities for offenders to victimize them and protect their privacy by limiting the type and amount of personal data (e.g., passwords, birthdates, addresses, images) they share, even among "friends;"

using two-factor authentication; installing anti-virus and anti-spyware software; following general safety protocols (e.g., do not download attachments from unknown senders); and periodically updating passwords and software programs. Most users who become victims lack the same type of instruction and practice online that they have had in the real world to detect dangerous situations or determine if the intention of another user is to befriend or harm them. Willard (2012, pp. 89–91) emphasizes that one important lesson to learn is that people are not who they seem to be online, in particularly, some people lie about who they are (posers, impersonators, fakes) and some want to cause trouble (trolls) and/or impose harm (creeps, downers). Anyone who has access to someone's online accounts, cloud, and/or hard drive may use the data for nefarious purposes (e.g., reveal secrets, identity theft, extortion and blackmail), therefore limiting a person's exposure is the best and simplest offense.

Both data and identity may be compromised by the user's legitimate online activities. To protect their interests and reduce opportunities for attacks by offenders, users should establish appropriate boundaries that will safeguard their private information from companies (e.g., customized privacy settings, policies, and opt-out third party sharing), especially those that use data mining methods (e.g., social media companies) to obtain and sell their client's data to other companies (e.g., retailers, hotels) who then use targeted advertising to improve profits (Ramirez, 2020). Data can be purchased by cyberpredators as part of their criminal intent, such as establishing a false identity for online romance scams, doxxing targets' information in a swatting campaign, or committing crimes using the user's profile. When users are online for extended periods of time, they subject themselves to various health risks (e.g., addiction, anxiety, stress) and become exposed to cyberpredators who target them for identity theft, fraud, trolling, bullying, harassment, or sexual exploitation and abuse.

To protect both their reputation and health, users must learn the downside of taking and sharing images, especially self-produced ones. The important lesson for users is that *you will lose control over of what happens to any image* once it is (1) sent to intimates, acquaintances, and/or friends, there is no guarantee that these will not be distributed by recipients or viewed by others without authorization from the original owner/sender; (2) posted online or attached to one's profile, particularly on public forums, because offenders can then use these images for their own sexual gratification and voyeurism, for fake profiles to enact online romance scams, or have it sexually photoshopped for a variety of crimes; and (3) stored on personal computer, smartphone, Internet ready device, or cloud because it is now vulnerable to hacks and data breaches, which in turn makes them likely to be shared without permission (Yar & Drew, 2019, p. 580). This point is true even for non-sexually explicit photos posted on social media profiles, such as children attending a birthday party that is geotagged with the birthdate and name of children, as these images offer a treasure trove of personal information to offenders that they may use to commit identity theft; target children for sexual abuse, sex trafficking, sextortion, etc.; create and distribute sexualized photoshopping for CSAM; etc. Unfortunately, the consequences for the victim are often greater than those for the offenders who commit IBSA, CSAM, online romance fraud, hacking, etc.

Users can engage with others globally through social networking, gaming, and discussion forums. The Internet provided a forum for people to state their ideas, as part of their protected speech; however, users must understand that these forums are not policed and therefore pose personal safety problems, such as stalking, trolling, hate speech, and harassment (Greenhalgh-Spencer, 2019). The tech industry hides behind freedom of speech for content while failing to uphold their "terms of use" policies in which users agreed not to engage in harmful actions or behaviors that threaten other member's security or copyright (Willard, 2012). Therefore, users must hold the tech industry accountable, forcing them to take responsibility in protecting them from harm whenever cyberpredators target them in violation of the company's terms of use. If this is not done, then the only voices being silenced will be those of the victims (i.e., violating freedoms) who fear additional attacks. In addition, many social media platforms use their "minimum age" requirement (usually 13 or 16) as a shield for liability, failing to acknowledge research findings that indicate many underage users are members (Odgers & Robb, 2020). Box 12.1 addresses the potential harms of Instagram on children's health as revealed by internal research conducted by Facebook and exposed by whistle blower, Frances Haugen. The overtones of the report seem to be congruent with the "avoid at all costs" prohibition messaging, but realistically the only way to help young users is to understand the dangers and help them navigate safely. For example, knowing that some adolescents are extremely susceptible to the negativity and toxicity of social media, they will need a social support system in place to help them figure out what balance online is right for them. Additionally, informing parents that adolescents are having difficulty with Instagram may help them to understand their own responsibility in guiding their children, such as assessing when they are ready for even limited time on this app. Legislatures must also reevaluate the Section 230 liability immunity, perhaps requiring companies to earn it through concrete steps demonstrating an honest attempt to assess risks and keep users safe.

BOX 12.1   POTENTIAL HARMS OF INSTAGRAM ON CHILDREN

Frances Haugen testified in front of the Senate Commerce Committee, Subcommittee on "Protecting Kids Online: Facebook, Instagram, and mental health harms" hearing that Facebook and Instagram "can be addictive and harmful to children." Instagram fosters the idea that adolescent girls' appearance and boys' financial aptitude are key to their feelings of acceptance, happiness, and love (Wallace, 2021). Facebook, Inc. had collected data using focus groups, online surveys, and diary studies over a 3-year period to examine the effects of its app on young male and female users. According to the findings, one in three adolescent girls experienced worsened body image issues and all groups reported increased rates of anxiety and depression (Wells et al., 2021). In particular, girls were drawn to making social comparisons of images on Instagram with their own (Wells et al., 2021), with 3% of U.S. (2% U.K.) girls concluding that they felt *much worse* about themselves and an additional 18% of U.S. (23% of U.K.) indicating they felt *somewhat worse* about themselves. Instagram also had negative effects on how boys who used Instagram stating that 2% of US (1% of U.K.) felt *much worse* and 12% of U.S. (13% of U.K.) felt *somewhat worse* about themselves (Wells et al., 2021). Another analysis showed that users traced back their need to have a perfect image to Instagram (39% U.S., 51% U.K.), feelings of being unattractive (41% U.S., 43% U.K.), and desire to kill themselves (6% U.S., 13% U.K.) (Wells et al., 2021). Although social comparison is a natural developmental process for adolescents to engage in, youth exposed to consistent negative comparisons are likely to experience social-emotional distress and poor self-esteem.

Facebook's own internal reports indicated that the most prevalent postings, which are promoted and reshared, consists of "misinformation, toxicity, and violent content" (Horowitz, 2021). The Senators crossed bipartisan lines in expressing their concerns for youth lured with a product they considered dangerous, addictive, and intentionally geared to target (against policy) children under age 13 (Allyn, 2021): "Facebook exploited teens using powerful algorithm that amplified their insecurities" (Richard Blumenthal, D-Connecticut) and "It is clear that Facebook prioritizes profit over the well-being of children and all users" (Marsha Blackburn, R-Tennessee). Haugen advised the Senate not to trust Facebook, stating that "Facebook chooses to mislead and misdirect" (Allyn, 2021). Wells et al. (2021) reported that Facebook knew the Project Daisy solution of hiding *like* tallies, which made users feel anxious and negative, did not work, but launched it anyway as senior executives knew the optics would be positive (i.e., Facebook cares). Additionally, in response to the Senate's request to provide Facebook's internal research, which Zuckerberg disclosed he had conducted during the March 2021 Congressional hearing, the company instead sent a letter indicating that the work was proprietary and confidential. During the Senate hearing, Facebook representatives provided evasive answers, and at times failed to answer the question at all (Wells et al., 2021). Moreover, Facebook CEO Zuckerberg and his executives "misstated and omitted key details about what was known about Facebook and Instagram's ability to cause harm" (Allyn, 2021). Clearly, the lack of transparency demonstrated by Facebook should, at the very least, prompt legislatures to consider whether current laws are able to protect U.S. citizens online.

CONCLUSION

There are a variety of education programs that teach 21st-century skills to children (see Willard, 2012, for a good example) that can be modified for adults. It is important for school administrators to choose the right program (or adapt it)—that is, one that is comprehensive—particularly for the age group who will be the learners—and ensure it is inclusive, as administrators, teachers, parents, and others in the community would also benefit. There are a variety of skills that are paramount to making good decisions that contribute to keeping people safe online (and offline).

Basic skills should include learning how to think logically and critically; making judgments based on evidence and research rather than unsupported facts, fears, or opinions; determining whether sources are appropriate and unbiased, which requires diversified sources engendering a variety of viewpoints rather than only those supporting your own; and advocating for oneself and others (Jones & Mitchell, 2016; Wurtele & Kenny, 2016).

Adults also need to learn how to become good citizens online, not only for their own benefit as employees, but also for the sake of their families so they do not expose themselves and others to cyberpredators, whether unwittingly or by failing to prevent it. While endorsing civil and respectful interchanges online, educators must also be cognizant that there will inevitably be one or more users who do not act accordingly. Therefore, instruction in effective problem solving and understanding of risks should also introduce simulated situations in which users can practice prevention by (1) determining the *motivations* of the actors involved, (2) assessing *effectiveness* of various actions taken by the actors, and (3) identifying potential *resolutions* for future situations (Lorenz et al., 2016; Willard, 2012).

Users, particularly the very young and old, will need guidance on (a) how to recognize "online traps" (p. 67) that may lead them to commit criminal acts, unintentionally (e.g., committing mail and wire fraud while believing they are helping someone) or intentionally, sometimes under the belief that anonymous posts cannot be traced back to them, hastily make a permanent and public record of harassment when angry, or engaging in targeted bullying campaign as part of a group; (b) making ethical choices; (c) assisting others in need, whether this entails emotional support or advice for peers; advocating for a peer who it being bullied; and reporting a dangerous situation to an adult (Willard, 2012). In conclusion, an effective cyber curriculum will help users to develop and utilize their 21st-century skills for safe online navigation.

REFERENCES

Allyn, B. (2021). *Here Are 4 Key Points from the Facebook Whistleblower's Testimony on Capitol Hill.* https://www.npr.org/2021/10/05/1043377310/facebook-whistleblower-frances-haugen-congress.

Anderson, M. (2018a). *A Majority of Teens Have Experienced Some Form of Cyberbullying. A Majority of Teens Have Experienced Some Form of Cyberbullying* | Pew Research Center. https://www.pewresearch.org/internet/2018/09/27/a-majority-of-teens-have-experienced-some-form-of-cyberbullying/

Anderson, M. (2018b). *About a Quarter of Rural Americans Say Access to High-Speed Internet is a Major Problem.* https://www.pewresearch.org/fact-tank/2018/09/10/about-a-quarter-of-rural-americans-say-access-to-high-speed-internet-is-a-major-problem/.

Bearden, S.M. (2016). *Digital Citizenship: A Community-Based Approach.* Thousand Oaks, CA: Corwin/SAGE. Doi: 10.4135/9781483392639.

Binkley, M., Erstad, O., Herman, J., Raizen, S., Ripley, M., Miller-Ricci, M., et al. (2012). Defining twenty-first century skills. In P. Griffin, B. McGaw, & E. Care (Eds.), *Assessment and Teaching of 21st Century Skills: Methods and Approach* (pp.17–66). Dordrecht: Springer.

Campbell, M. A., Slee, P. T., Spears, B., Butler, D., & Kift, S. (2013): Do cyberbullies suffer too? Cyberbullies' perceptions of the harm they cause to others and to their own mental health. *School Psychology International, 34*(6), 613–629.

Choi, M., Glassman, M., & Cristol, D. (2017). What it means to be a citizen in the internet age: Development of a reliable and valid digital citizenship scale. *Computers & Education, 107,* 100–112. Doi: 10.1016/j.compedu.2017.01.002.

Cohen, L. E., & Felson, M. (1979). Social change and crime rate trends: A routine activity approach. *American Sociological Review, 44*(4), 588–608. Doi: 10.2307/2094589.

Common Sense Media. (2020). *Children, Executive Functioning and Digital Media: A Review.* https://www.commonsensemedia.org/sites/default/files/uploads/research/children_executive_functioning_and_digital_media_review_1.pdf.

CR Consumer Reports. (2017). *Net Neutrality Survey.* https://digital-lab.consumerreports.org/wp-content/uploads/2020/02/Consumer-Reports-Net-Neutrality-Survey-August-2017-Digital-Lab.pdf.

Egresitz, J. (2020). Teaching digital understanding and citizenship: Modern skills for the classroom and beyond. *Technology and Engineering Teacher, 80*(2), 8–12.

Ferrari, A. (2012). *Digital Competence in Practice: An Analysis of Frameworks.* Seville: Joint Research Centre, Institute for Prospective Technological Studies. Doi: 10.2791/82116.

Genner, S. (2014). Violent video games and cyberbullying: Why education is better than regulation. In S. van der Hof, B. van den Berg, and B. Schermer (eds.), *Minding Minors Wandering the Web: Regulating Online Child Safety* (pp. 229–243). The Hague, Netherlands: Springer.

Greenhalgh-Spencer, H. (2019). Cyber safe curricula and online harassment. *Educational Theory, 69*(1), 73–89.

Griffin, P., Care, E., & McGaw, B. (2012). The Changing Role of Education and Schools. In: Griffin P., McGaw B., Care E. (eds), *Assessment and Teaching of 21st Century Skills.* Dordrecht: Springer. https://doi-org.ez.lib.jjay.cuny.edu/10.1007/978-94-007-2324-5_1.

Horowitz, J. (2021). The Facebook whistleblower, Frances Haugen, says she wants to fix the company, not harm it. *The Wall Street Journal*. https://www.wsj.com/articles/facebook-whistleblower-frances-haugen-says-she-wants-to-fix-the-company-not-harm-it-11633304122

Hui, B., & Campbell, R. (2018). Discrepancy between learning and practicing digital citizenship. *Journal of Academic Ethics, 16*, 117–131. Doi: 10.1007/s10805-018-9302-9.

Insider Intelligence. (2021). *US Adults Added 1 Hour of Digital Time in 2020*. https://www.emarketer.com/content/us-adults-added-1-hour-of-digital-time-2020.

Johnson, J. (2021). *Internet Usage in the United States—Statistics & Facts*. https://www.statista.com/topics/2237/internet-usage-in-the-united-states/.

Jones, L.M., & Mitchell, K.J. (2016). Defining and measuring youth digital citizenship. *New Media & Society, 18*(9), 2063–2079. Doi: 10.1177/1461444815577797.

Khan, M.L., Welser, H.T., Cisneros, C., Manatong, G., & Idris, I.K. (2020). Digital inequality in the Appalachian Ohio: Understanding how demographics, internet access, and skills can shape vital information use (VIU). *Telmatics and Informatics, 50*, 101380. Doi: 10.1016/j.tele.2020.101380.

Kopecký, K. (2015). Sexting among Slovak pubescents and adolescent children. *Procedia Social and Behavioral Sciences, 203*, 244–250.

Kopecký, K. (2017). Online blackmail of Czech children focused on so-called "sextortion" (analysis of culprit and victim behaviors). *Telematics and Informatics, 34*, 11–19.

Kopecký, K., & Szotkowski, R. (2018). Sexting in the population of children and its risks: A quantitative study. *International Journal of Cyber Criminology, 12*(2), 376–391.

Lorenz, B., Kikkas, K., Laanpere, M., & Laugasson, E. (2016). A model to evaluate digital safety concerns in school environment. In P. Zaphiris and A. Ioannou (eds), *Learning and Collaboration Technologies* (pp. 707–721). Lecture Notes in Computer Science, vol 9753. Cham: Springer, Doi: 10.1007/978-3-319-39483-1_64.

Media. (2018). *Time Flies: U.S. Adults Now Spend Nearly Half a Day Interacting with Media*. https://www.nielsen.com/us/en/insights/article/2018/time-flies-us-adults-now-spend-nearly-half-a-day-interacting-with-media/.

Miller, C., Coldicutt, R., & Kitcher, H. (2018). *People, Power and Technology: The 2018 Digital Understanding Report*. London: Doteveryone. http://understanding.doteveryone.org.uk/files/Doteveryone_PeoplePowerTechDigitalUnderstanding2018.pd.

Mossberger, K., Tolbert, C.J., & McNeal, R.S. (2007). *Digital Citizenship: The Internet, Society, and Participation*. Cambridge, MA: MIT Press.

Odgers, C. & Robb, M.B. (2020). *Tweens, Teens, Tech, and Mental Health: Coming of Age in an Increasingly Digital, Uncertain, and Unequal World*. San Francisco, CA: Common Sense Media. https://www.commonsensemedia.org/sites/default/files/uploads/pdfs/tweens-teens-tech-and-mental-health-full-report-final-for-web1.pdf.

Partnership for 21st century skills. (2008). *21st Century Skills, Education & Competitiveness: A Resource and Policy Guide*. Washington, DC. https://files. eric.ed.gov/fulltext/ED519337.pdf.

Perrin, A., & Atske, S (2021). *About Three-in-Ten U.S. Adults Say they Are 'Almost Constantly' Online*. https://www.pewresearch.org/fact-tank/2021/03/26/ about-three-in-ten-u-s-adults-say-they-are-almost-constantly-online/.

Pew Research Center. (2021). *Internet/Broadband Fact Sheet*. https://www.pewresearch.org/internet/fact-sheet/internet-broadband/.

Ramirez, R. (2020). *Social Media Data Mining: Understanding What It Is and How Businesses Can Use It*. https://www.sandiego.edu/blogs/business/detail. php?_focus=76022.

Reyns, B.W., Henson, B., & Fisher, B.S. (2011). Being pursued online: Applying cyberlifestyle —Routine activities theory to cyberstalking victimization. *Criminal Justice and Behavior, 38*(11), 1149–1169.

Ribble, M. (2015). *Digital Citizenship in Schools: Nine Elements All Students Should Know*. Washington, DC: International Society for Technology in Education.

Ribble, M., & Bailey, G. (2007). *Digital Citizenship in Schools*. Washington, DC: International Society for Technology in Education.

Ribble, M. S., Bailey, G. D., & Ross, T. W. (2004). Digital citizenship: Addressing appropriate technology behavior. *Learning & Leading with Technology, 32*(1), 6–12.

Rideout, V., & Robb, M.B. (2019). *The Common Sense Census: Media Use by Tweens and Teens*. San Francisco, CA: Common Sense Media. https://www.commonsensemedia.org/sites/default/files/uploads/research/2019-census-8-to-18-full-report-updated.pdf.

Shipley, T., & Bowker, A. (2014). *Investigating Internet Crimes: An Introduction to Solving Crimes in Cyberspace*. Amsterdam: Elsevier.

Sonck, N., & de Haan, J. (2014). Safety by literacy? Rethinking the role of digital skills in improving online safety. In S. van der Hof, B. van den Berg, and B. Schermer (eds.), *Minding Minors Wandering the Web: Regulating Online Child Safety* (pp. 89–104). The Hague: T.M.C. Asser Press.

Thierer, A. (2014). A framework for responding to online safety risks. In S. van der Hof, B. van den Berg, & B. Schermer (eds.), *Minding Minors Wandering the Web: Regulating Online Child Safety* (pp. 39–66). The Hague, Netherlands: Springer.

van Deursen, A.J.A.M., & van Dijk, J.A.G.M. (2009). Improving digital skills for the use of online public information and services. *Government Information Quarterly, 26*, 333–340.

van Dijk, J.A.G.M., & van Deursen, A.J.A.M. (2014). *Digital Skills: Unlocking the Information Society*. New York: Palgrave MacMillan.

van Laar, E., van Deursen, A.J.A.M., van Dijk, J.A.G.M., & de Haan, J. (2017a). The relation between 21st century skills and digital skills: A systematic literature review. *Computers in Human Behavior, 72*, 577–588.

van Laar, E., van Deursen, A.J.A.M., van Dijk, J.A.G.M., & de Haan, J. (2017b). Determinants of 21st-century skills and 21st-century digital skills for workers: A systematic literature review. *SAGE Open, 10*(1), 1–14. Doi: 10.1177/215824401990176.

Veli, K. (2016). Sexual extortion of children in cyberspace. *Journal of Cyber Criminology, 10*(2), 110–126.

Vitis, L. (2019). Victims, perpetrators and paternalism: Image driven sexting laws in Connecticut. *Female Legal Studies, 27*, 189–209.

Vogels, E.A. (2021a). *Some Digital Divides Persist between Rural, Urban, and Suburban America.* https://www.pewresearch.org/fact-tank/2021/08/19/some-digital-divides-persist-between-rural-urban-and-suburban-america/.

Vogels, E.A. (2021b). *Digital Divide Persists Even as Americans with Lower Incomes Make Gains in Tech Adoption.* https://www.pewresearch.org/fact-tank/2021/06/22/digital-divide-persists-even-as-americans-with-lower-incomes-make-gains-in-tech-adoption/.

Voogt, J., & Roblin, N.P. (2012). A comparative analysis of international frameworks for 21st century competences: Implications for national curriculum policies. *Journal of Curriculum Studies, 44*(3), 299e321. Doi: 10.1080/00220272.2012.668938.

Wachs, S., Costello, M., Wright, M.F., Flora, K., Daskalou, V., Maziridou, E., Kwon, Y., Na, E-Y., Sittichai, R., Biswal, R., Singh, R., Almendros, C., Gámez-Guadix, M., Görzig, A., & Hong, J.S. (2021). DNT LET 'EM H8 U!": Applying the routine activity framework to understand cyberhate victimization among adolescents across eight countries. *Computers and Education, 160*, 1–13.

Wallace, J.B. (2021). Instagram is even worse than we thought for kids. What do we do about it? *The Wall Street Journal.* https://www.washingtonpost.com/lifestyle/2021/09/17/instagram-teens-parent-advice/

Wells, G., Horwitz, J., & Seetharaman, D. (2021). *Facebook Knows Instagram is Toxic for Teen Girls, Company Document Show.* https://www.wsj.com/articles/facebook-knows-instagram-is-toxic-for-teen-girls-company-documents-show-11631620739.

Willard, N. (2012). *Cybersavvy: Embracing Digital Safety and Civility.* Thousand Oaks, CA: Corwin/SAGE. ISBN: 1-4522-6967-X.

Witwer, A.R., Langton, L., Vermeer, M.J.D., Banks, D. (2020). *Countering Technology-Facilitated Abuse: Criminal Justice Strategies for Combatting Nonconsensual Pornography, Sextortion, Doxing, and Swatting.* https://www.rand.org/content/dam/rand/pubs/research_reports/RRA100/RRA108-3/RAND_RRA108-3.pdfc.

Wolak, J., Finkelhor, D., Walsh, W., & Treitman, L. (2018). Sextortion of minors: Characteristics and dynamics. *Journal of Adolescent Health, 62*, 72–79. Doi: 10.1016/j.jadohealth.2017.08.014.

Wurtele, S.K., & Kenny, M.C. (2016). Technology-related sexual solicitation of adolescents: A review of prevention efforts. *Child Abuse Review, 25*, 332–344. Doi: 10.1002/car.

Yar, M., & Drew, J. (2019). Image-based abuse, non-consensual pornography, revenge porn: A study of criminalization and crime prevention in Australia and England & Wales. International *Journal of Cyber Criminology, 13*(2), 578–594. Doi: 10.5281/zenodo.3709306.

Young, D. (2014). A 21st-century model for teaching digital citizenship. *Educational Horizons, 92*(3), 9–12.

INDEX

Note: **Bold** page numbers refer to tables and *italic* page numbers refer to figures.

Printed in the United States
by Baker & Taylor Publisher Services